Challenges for Successful Family Living

CHALLENGES FOR SUCCESSFUL FAMILY LIVING

*A Discussion of Modern Attitudes Toward
Dating, Marriage and the Family*

by

WAYNE J. ANDERSON

*Professor of Family Living,
University of Minnesota, Minneapolis*

Publishers

T. S. DENISON & COMPANY, INC.
Minneapolis

 T. S. DENISON & COMPANY, INC.

301.420973
An2c
96401
Mar 1976

Standard Book Number: 513-01346-6
Library of Congress Card Number: 73-93076
Printed in the United States of America
by The Brings Press

Contents

12

16

Preface

This book is being written at a time when some people feel that society has outgrown the family unit and should delegate all of its functions to other institutions. There is also a notion abroad that conventional marriage is a dull and unexciting institution and that a marriage relationship would fare better if undertaken outside of any legal framework. Such critics of marriage and the family contend that they are doing society a service in that they "are pioneering in a new way of life."

These people must have less than a nodding acquaintance with history. The alternatives they are suggesting to supplant conventional marriage and the family group have all been tried before—and found wanting. Despite these efforts to downgrade it, the family unit still functions in every known society, and its universality demonstrates that all races, ethnic groups and cultures consider the family as the unit that can most satisfactorily serve the needs of the individual and the broader social group.

Of course, successful marriages and happy families do not just happen. They develop as a result of cooperative efforts by their partners and members to meet the challenges they bring. Inasmuch as the author feels that successful family living comes from meeting such challenges, this book is being written in an attempt to point out the challenges and suggest how they might be met in order to experience and enjoy family living. To do this, it discusses the principles, attitudes and practices that help contribute to a satisfying family life.

In preparing the book every effort has been made to draw upon current research, report present-day thinking and trends, and view the family from an historical, sociological and functional standpoint. Consequently, the content is presented within a framework which combines past and up-to-date knowledge. It is hoped that this frame of reference will be helpful to college and university students as they explore and participate in marriage and family living as a way of life.

The book represents concepts that the author has formulated after years of study and efforts made to counsel and help students on all levels—

elementary, secondary, college, and university. A busy schedule has also afforded opportunity for fruitful discussions with many parents.

I am grateful to all of the students, colleagues and parents, as well as my own family group, who have contributed to my understanding of the important role the family plays in life.

Throughout the years, I have also been blessed in my associations with my publisher, Mr. Lawrence M. Brings, a man whose high ideals and dynamic personality have been an inspiration in my life.

Finally, I wish to express my gratitude to my wife and children. My wife, Elise, has been my constant companion, and provided help, encouragement and inspiration in everything I have undertaken. Our daughters, Annette, Cherie Wayne, Julie Gay, and Jill, and our son Jim have been constant sources of joy, and have also given me great satisfaction as I have watched them all meet the challenges that are a part of successful family living.

—Wayne J. Anderson

List of Illustrations

Acknowledgments

Special recognition is given to the following:

The Ortho Pharmaceutical Corporation of Raritan, New Jersey, for their permission to reproduce the illustrations on pages 310, 364, 365, 366, 367 and 371.

The Maternity Center Association of New York for their permission to reproduce from their publication, *The Birth Atlas,* the illustrations used on pages 371, 372, 373 and 374.

The Budlong Press Company of Chicago for their permission to reproduce the illustration used on page 361.

PART I

The Family in Today's World

Chapter I

The American Family System

The family is a basic and remarkable social institution. It is said to exist in all known societies, and throughout the ages has been recognized as the social unit responsible for procreation and the proper rearing of children. If it develops individuals of character and integrity, society benefits. Conversely, if it fails to develop desirable behavioral patterns in its members, society suffers.

The family can also be of great value in meeting individual needs. The right home climate provides each member with a setting in which he can find love, a sense of security, understanding, and acceptance. In addition, parents who are good models not only provide children with continuing emotional support, but also with good examples of how they should behave in society.

There is little doubt that the family is one of man's most valued possessions, and very few persons would be willing to give it up in exchange for fame, fortune, or friends.

Despite these well-known facts, widely different opinions about the family's social value have emerged in contemporary American society. Traditional thinkers still view the family as the basic biological and social unit. On the other hand, there are those who believe that the family has outlived its usefulness, and its functions could be more effectively performed by social agencies. In between these two diametrically opposed schools of thought there are some individuals who feel that the mother and child form the basic human family, with the male necessary chiefly for procreative and economic purposes. Still others see the husband and wife as central in the family unit, and view children as intruders who impose undesirable burdens upon them.

Human nature being what it is, it is quite understandable that such differences of opinion exist. However, what is more difficult to accept is the reasoning of those who feel that society has outgrown the family unit and should delegate all of its functions to other institutions. Such thinking could stem from confusing the reorganization of the family with its disorganization. Family life-styles do change, as changes in the culture are incorporated into family patterns. But, despite these changes, the family as a basic social group continues to endure. It has weathered the vicissitudes of mankind in the past and seems likely to do so in the future.

Another reason this appears probable is because research shows that the nuclear family (the married man and woman with their children) is a universal human social grouping. Murdock reports, "The nuclear family . . . either as the sole prevailing form of the family or as the basic unit from which more complex familial forms are compounded . . . exists as a distinct and strongly functional group in every known society. No exception at least has come to light in the 250 representative cultures surveyed for the present study . . ."[1]

This universality of the family social unit demonstrates, if nothing else, that all races, ethnic groups and cultures have found that the grouping of people into family units has been the most satisfactory way of serving the needs of the individual and the broader social group.

AMERICANS ARE FAMILY-ORIENTED

Controversy Surrounding the American Family

Inasmuch as this book deals primarily with the functions of the American family, a question that should be considered is whether there is general satisfaction with its family system. Reading negative reports about the family in current news media might cause one to conclude that there is widespread dissatisfaction with the family system. Some observers go as far as to say that the American family system, in its present form, is "antiquated" and faced with "imminent extinction." However, an objective look at such reporting reveals that there are no large studies of the family system which substantiate such negative thinking. Thus, the writings that describe the family as a malfunctioning social unit are, in most part, based on the author's personal thinking and have little scientific value. It also must be realized that the press generally devotes more space to the negative aspects of family life than to the positive. This is done primarily because literature which contains shocking and sordid stories usually sells better.

---

[1]Murdock, George, *Social Structures*, New York: The Macmillan Co., 1949, pp. 1-11.

Apparent Strengths of the American Family System

On the positive side, a sound defense of the effectiveness of the present American family system can be made by studying available statistics related to the acceptance of and the effective functioning of the family as a social unit.

Current statistics dealing with the incidence of marriage show that the institution of marriage which is the first step in forming a family unit, is at an all-time high in popularity. Federal statisticians have reported that ". . . national marriage trends over the last 100 years showed that more than two-thirds of all Americans over the age of 14 are married, while in 1890, the first years for which statistics are available, only half the Americans in that age bracket were married. In addition, the latest statistics indicated that marriage is increasing in popularity . . . there were more marriages performed last year (1970) than in any year since the postwar boom in 1946, in part because the population has risen, but also the rate of weddings per capita was the highest in two decades."[2]

Leading sociologists confirm this trend in marriage popularity, and project figures which suggest that in the seventies 97 out of 100 people in the United States will get married.

In addition to the increasing popularity of marriage, there are other factors which indicate that our culture likes its family system.

The rate of home ownership in the nation is high, and there is a sustained consumer demand to meet family needs.

Americans are still child-minded, and a substantial majority of married couples have children and devote much time and energy to their care.

Questionnaire surveys repeatedly indicate that a high percentage of people rate their marriages as happy and their family adjustments as satisfactory.

The most recent survey, released by *Life* magazine on November 12, 1972, was based on 62,000 replies to a questionnaire that appeared in a special section of *Life* (April 28, 1972) devoted to experiments in marriage. Findings revealed "that a large majority — 80 percent — of Americans view their marriages as 'happy' or 'very happy.' The 62,000 readers are a general but not precise cross section of the U. S. Three out

---

[2] "Marriages: Trends and Characteristics," National Center for Health Statistics, Reported by Richard D. Lyons, N.Y. Times Service in the Minneapolis Tribune, Dec. 12, 1971.

of five are presently married. More than 70% have attended college. Forty-five percent, the largest age group, are under 30."[3]

Although the editors of the magazine termed their sample a general rather than a precise cross section, their findings correspond closely with those of the Zimmerman-Cervantes survey of 1960. This was a study in which 60,000 families composed of 250,000 persons living in six large, representative American cities answered a family life questionnaire. At that time 85 percent of the families who responded said they were making successful and happy adjustments.[4]

Alleged Weaknesses of the American Family System

Critics of the functions of today's nuclear family feel that these social units operate in an ineffective manner, and that societal pressures will cause the dissolution of one set family model and the emergence of a number of different family forms. They contend that the family cannot survive in its present form for the following reasons:

The current rate of divorces, separations and desertions is high. For example, about 2,000 divorces per day (well over 700,000 each year) take place in the United States. The divorce-marriage ratio approximates about one to four. It should be mentioned that this ratio is often misinterpreted by concluding that one in four marriages ends in divorce. This is not true. What the statistics mean is that for every four marriage commitments made during the year, one divorce is granted from all existing marriages.

Undesirable divorce procedures also have a negative effect on the family. The resulting emotional problems and high monetary costs which often occur with a divorce action cause some cautious, single individuals to avoid contracting a legal marriage. Instead, they decide to live together and develop a relationship which can be dissolved without divorce action.

A hodgepodge of divorce statutes ranging from stringent in some states to extremely permissive in others cause many couples to take their marriage vows lightly because they know if they can't get along, there is always a place where they can find an easy way out.

Another of the criticisms of the present family system is related to the rising rate of juvenile delinquency in the United States. The delinquent

---

[3]*Life* magazine, Vol. 73, Number 20, pp. 59-62, Chicago: Nov. 17, 1972.
[4]Zimmerman, Carle C. and Cervantes, Lucius, *Successful American Families*, New York, Pageant, 1960.

syndrome is attributed primarily to family malfunctioning and disorganization. Such an observation is simplistic, as studies show that there are a number of contributing factors that produce a delinquent child. This constellation which is made up of at least eight causes includes such things as identification with an adult outside of the family circle who is a faulty model, or association with an undesirable peer group.

A frequent argument used in an attempt to show that the nuclear family is out of step with contemporary society is associated with permissive thinking regarding sexual behavior. Those who advocate such sexual freedom seem to be trying to prove that couples who make a marriage commitment and are true to their vows are letting the joys of life pass them by.

It is also being pointed out that high rates of abortion and illegitimacy add additional evidence that people no longer want to conform to the mores of the traditional nuclear family.

Finally, there is some thinking that human temperament is such that a long-term marriage relationship between two people is foredoomed to boredom. Women's liberationists complain that a married woman is likely to develop the "housewife's syndrome" and stagnate as a person while she loses touch with the outside world. Other critics claim that the average married couple develop the "pass the salt syndrome" and lapse into sheer monotony, only communicating with each other in order to satisfy some mundane need.

Will the Family System Continue in its Present Form?

It is evident that the American family system has both strengths and weaknesses, and predictions regarding its future might vary according to whether emphasis is put on its positive or negative aspects. As such an approach more often than not leads to a stalemate, an attempt will be made in this discussion to take a different approach and try to determine if the family group is structured in the most effective way to meet individual human needs. If such is the case, it should continue to endure in its present form.

THE DEFINITION OF A FAMILY

Before discussing the way the family meets individual needs, the word "family" should be defined. A common definition is, "A family is a social group composed of the married father and mother and their children." However, an investigation of family patterns reveals that other types of groupings are also called families.

The Composition of Families

Some other types of groups that are called families are:

One parent with children, whose partner has died, deserted, separated, or divorced.

The unmarried couple, with or without children.

One unmarried parent with children.

The couple with or without children who have lived together under the common law long enough to be recognized as legally married.

A group of related persons (brothers, sisters, cousins, etc.) living together as one household. Such a group is accepted as a family by the United States Census Bureau.

A group of unrelated persons living together as one household.

A man with several wives, with or without children.

A woman with several husbands, with or without children.

It must be remembered that these different types of family groups were partly structured by the form of marriage the involved couples entered and that there are several forms of marriage existing in today's society. A look at these forms gives some insight into the various ways human needs are met.

FORMS OF MARRIAGE

Monogamy
Polygyny
Polyandry
Group Marriage

1. **Monogamy**—marriage of one man to one woman.

Monogamy is the only form of marriage accepted by all societies and is the single type of marriage that is legally approved in the United States.

Stated Advantages

a. In an area in which the sex ratio approximates 100 males to 100 females each individual is afforded the maximal opportunity to find a mate. Few persons are left out because the supply of the opposite sex is numerically equal to the demand for it.

b. It provides both men and women opportunity for sexual gratification.

c. Intra-familial jealousies and problems are less like to develop if each person has just one spouse.

d. Child-rearing practices should be less complicated because of the possibility of closer identification with parents.

e. The smaller family group can exercise greater flexibility in adapting to the circumstances necessary to provide for its economic needs.

Stated Disadvantages

Opponents claim it does not meet the male's need for a variety of sexual experiences.

2. Polygyny—marriage of one man to two or more women.

Stated Advantages

a. It compensates for a shortage of men in a society by allowing more women the opportunity to marry.

b. It affords the man the possibility of satisfying his desire for a variety of sexual experiences.

c. In an agricultural society, having several wives and many children should be an economic asset.

d. If the polygynous practice is limited to superior males, the quality of the population should be improved.

Stated Disadvantages

(Although Blood[5] reports that eighty-one percent of all societies permit polygyny, many problems have developed when it is practiced.)

a. The sex ratio (male-female balance) in a society may change so there is no serious shortage of marriageable men. Then a polygynous system would permit wealthy and politically powerful males to have several wives while their less fortunate associates would have none.

b. Jealousy and dissension often result between wives who share one man.

c. Although the "first wife" may be accorded superior status within the group of wives, the newest and youngest wife often becomes the husband's darling and displaces the others as the center of attraction. Consequently, bitter rivalries may develop.

---

[5]Blood, Robert O. Jr., *The Family*, New York: The Free Press, 1972.

d. The husband is under constant pressure to avoid discriminating against wives in regard to housing facilities, providing equal opportunities for their children and in the general management of the group's social problems.

3. Polyandry—marriage of one woman to two or more men.

Polyandry as an institutionalized form of marriage is rare. Blood says that it exists in only one percent of all societies and the *World Ethnographic Sample* reports that it is the dominant marriage form in only four societies—the Toda, Marquesas, Nayar, and Tibet.[6]

Michel F. Peissel reported in *McCall's* magazine that it also is practiced among some groups in Siberia and in a few Eskimo communities in Alaska.

Stated Advantages

a. Polyandry performs a practical function in limiting population. The smaller number of family units produces fewer babies, and studies indicate that the woman who practices polyandry becomes less fertile.

b. Peissel reports that his on-the-spot study of polyandrous practices in the Himalayas of Tibet revealed that "most gainful occupations require arduous and time-consuming travel and as a result a man may have to spend many months of the year away from home." He also reports that women are scarce and highly prized and several men will take the same one as a wife in a cooperative effort to maintain a household. Children also seem to benefit as there is always one or more fathers at home to help care for them.

c. It has been considered necessary in other societies where economic conditions were such that it took several male breadwinners to support a household. This was the case in ancient China among the coolies and also in the Toda Society.

d. Ancient Sparta practiced polyandry because their possible supply of wives was kept small by practicing female infanticide. A practice which was engaged in because females were not generally considered as an asset to the nation.

e. Certain Eskimo tribes have practiced it as a form of hospitality to other males.

---

[6]Stephens, William M., *The Family in Cross-Cultural Perspective*, New York: Rinehart and Winston, 1963.

Stated Disadvantages

a. Psychologically speaking, the practice of polyandry runs counter to the presumed male desire for exclusive possession of his woman.

b. Sociological studies show that there are very few societies in which there is a shortage of females.

4. Group Marriage—marriage of two or more women to two or more men.

Group marriage has occurred rarely, and when it has, it has been short-lived. It has been reported as existing in the Indian Toda tribe and the Kain-gang of Brazil.

The most notable example of group marriage in America was the Oneida Community founded by John Humphrey Noyes which existed in central New York state from 1848 to 1879. The community became very successful from an economic standpoint. They found a constant market for their crops, engaged in silk spinning, and manufactured silverware that became so sought after that its production still continues today.

However, the thing that attracted attention to the community was their attitude toward sexual expression. Noyes believed that "the natural man loves the natural woman," and felt that all members of the group should love one another equally. Although sexual relationships were structured in many ways, a man and a woman were allowed to have intercourse if there was mutual desire. But, engaging in the sex act in order to reproduce was another thing. The group practiced a eugenics program called stirpiculture, and reproductive sex was limited to those couples who were considered potential parents of superior children.

As the Oneida Community grew, outside pressures from the public increased, and finally, John Humphrey Noyes left the colony in June, 1879, to live in Canada. Shortly after, the group disbanded.

It is quite evident after reviewing the different types of families and the forms of marriage, that today's controversy centers around the traditional nuclear family. Critics question whether this group composed of the married father and mother and their children will continue in its same form in the future. As was stated before, it should, if its structure provides the most effective way to meet individual human needs.

THE NUCLEAR FAMILY AND INDIVIDUAL NEEDS

The distinguishing characteristics of this primary social group (one in which its members have a face-to-face relationship) have included: a form of marriage or a culturally approved arrangement between two people of both sexes; a socially approved sexual relationship; one or more children, natural or adopted; a common residence; economic cooperation by the group.

Sociologist Reuben Hill says "The family has traditionally performed seven functions: reproduction, protection and care of children, economic production of family goods and services, socialization of children, education of children, recreation, and affection giving."[7]

The question being debated today regarding these seven functions is whether the family group can perform them in such a way as to contribute to the optimum development of each member. To be more specific, will the family, as presently structured, contribute to the development of its members in such a way that each will be motivated to tap and achieve his or her human potential?

It seems that those critics who want to use this criterion and no others to assess the family's performance are ignoring a host of environmental influences which may aid, or on the other hand, run counter to the family's best efforts to guide its members to optimum development. This is so because it is quite evident in contemporary society that some of the seven traditionally performed functions of the family are shared in varying degrees by industry, the school, the church, and the government. For example, the family is no longer a self-sufficient economic producing unit. Very few families build their own homes, grow their own food, or make their own clothes. Today's families look to the school and church to be partners with them in educating their children and providing them with religious guidance. The family also accepts provision for recreational opportunity outside of the home. The development of recreation as a giant leisure-time business has cut into recreation in the home and reduced participation in leisure-time activities as a family group. But, it does not necessarily follow that a negative effect will result from the family sharing these functions with other institutions. It may well be that such functions can be performed more effectively if the family, school, and church share them.

7"The American Family: Future Uncertain," *Time* magazine, Dec. 28, 1970.

Despite the fact that today's family shares the performance of some of its traditional functions such as the economic, educational, and recreational with other institutions, it still holds sway in the areas of reproduction, child care and affection.

Naturally, the reproductive function will stay with the family unless research biologists can prove there is some superior way to have children.

Current studies reaffirm the fact that the family group is peculiarly suited to give proper care and necessary affection to its members.

Consequently, it appears that the family of the future will continue to be the most effective base from which to provide for individual human needs, even though it may share some of the functions with other institutions.

In conclusion, it should again be stated that no society has ever been without some form of marriage and family group. These universal social institutions have been present in all ages and in all cultures. Consequently, mate love and procreation outside of marriage have always been deviations from the norm in the history of mankind.

Why has this happened? Social scientists say that marriage and family life are not instinctual. If this is so, then marriage and family life must be ever-present because men and women in various cultures generally have similar needs and have tended to organize and perpetuate similar institutions such as marriage and the family in order to best meet these common needs.

Suggested Readings

1. Bell, Norman W., and Vogel, Ezra F. (eds.): *A Modern Introduction to the Family,* New York: The Free Press, 1968 (rev.).

2. Blood, Robert O., Jr., *The Family,* New York: The Free Press, 1972.

3. Burgess, Ernest W., Locke, Harvey J., and Thomes, Mary M., *The Family From Traditional to Companionship,* New York: Van Nostrand Reinhold Co., 1972 (4th ed.).

4. Farber, Bernard (ed.), *Kinship and Family Organization,* New York: John Wiley & Sons, 1966.

5. Goode, William J., *The Family,* Englewood Cliffs, N.J.: Prentice-Hall, 1964.

6. Kenkel, William F., *The Family in Perspective*, New York: Appleton-Century-Crofts, 1966 (2nd ed.).

7. Kephart, William F., *The Family, Society and the Individual*, Boston: Houghton Mifflin Co., 1972 (3rd ed.).

8. Klemer, Richard H., *Marriage and Family Relationships*, New York: Harper & Row, 1970.

9. Spiro, Melford E., *Children of the Kibbutz*, Cambridge: Harvard University Press, 1958.

10. Queen, Stuart A., and Habenstein, Robert W., *The Family in Various Cultures*, Philadelphia: J. B. Lippincott Co., 1967 (3rd ed.).

11. Zimmerman, Carle C., and Cervantes, Lucius F., *Successful American Families*, New York: Pageant, 1960.

Chapter II

Current Alternatives to Traditional Marriage

FREE LOVE

Conventional legal marriage seems to have become a dull and unexciting institution to millions of Americans. This boredom with the conjugal relationship has led them to experiment with various marriage forms which at times include sexual practices that used to be considered abnormal. However, even in this sensually-oriented pursuit of happiness, most involved couples seem to feel some sense of commitment to the partner of the moment, and back away from the practice of free love. Of course, the phrase "free love" is a misnomer. What its proponents really mean is sexual freedom. Such writers as Havelock Ellis, Bertrand Russell, and Aldous Huxley have presented the idea that sex desire is a natural urge, and just like hunger and thirst should be satisfied without any imposed restrictions. Those individuals who oppose such a philosophy contend that even though sex desire is natural, it, like other urges, must be controlled, if the individual desires to get along in a social group.

There is a current tendency on the part of some people to cloak the practice of "free love" with a new term called "fun morality." Those who think this way look upon sexual expression as a "fun thing" and attempt to divorce the sex act from any feeling of love for or commitment to the participating partner. Undoubtedly, this might occur when a man buys sexual performance from a prostitute. However, when a girl's participation in the sex act is not put on a pay-as-you-go basis, it is highly unlikely that either sex partner can leave the experience without some feeling of emotional involvement. Such involvement is difficult to prove scientifically, but interviews with hundreds of college students have led the writer to believe that only a small percentage of individuals can engage satisfactorily in "fun morality."

A brief look at some of the current alternatives to traditional marriage reveals that a sense of commitment seems to run through all of the forms.

LIVING TOGETHER

(Trial Marriage—Elsie Parsons, Early 1900s)

Some ritual-resisting couples on today's scene feel that the formality of going through a marriage ceremony is a waste of time and money. They reason that a marriage certificate is just a scrap of paper that has nothing to do with love, so why not just live together? They also feel that their affection for each other should not be straitjacketed with rules and regulations and their relationship will be more meaningful if it is voluntary with no strings attached. Some of their comments shed additional light on their attitudes.

Linda, an attractive, honey-blonde coed, said, "My boyfriend and I have enough trust in each other that we don't need a legal marriage to hold us together. It would take the excitement out of things if we felt we had to stay together and make love just because the law said so."

Pat, an ex-G.I. who has returned to college, commented, "I'm living with Barbara because it is cheaper this way for both of us. We share the cost of our apartment and food. I can't afford to marry a girl and be obligated to provide for her, because I don't know yet what I want out of life. I suppose I love Barbara, but if I felt she were trying to force me into marriage I'd walk out."

Debbie became tense and somewhat hostile when asked if she felt she had any guarantee of future security in living with her boyfriend Bob. Her reply was, "We've lived together for three years and are still happy. I suppose if we had a baby we might get married to give it a legal name. But in the meantime, I wish other people would mind their own business and leave us alone."

When this couple-behavior pattern is discussed, the question is often asked, "When a baby or babies come does the average living-together couple get married?"

The only answer that can be given is that some do and some do not.

The experience of a couple who did was told by a college freshman who said, "Cathie and I lived together for six months and thought we were happy, but when we learned that a baby was coming, we decided to get married. Believe me, going through a marriage ceremony made the difference between night and day for us. Now we feel that we are really a family, and we are proud that our little Tommy has the additional security that playing the game by society's rules provides."

A couple who had a different attitude toward having a child outside of wedlock told their story to *Life* magazine.[1]

In their interview, David and Marjorie said their trust in each other gave them a secure feeling without marriage, and they felt having the baby was like part of nature.

However, these college graduates made an end run around the law to give some legal semblance to their marriage. "When they bought their house, they signed the mortgage as husband and wife, because it was far less complicated that way." And they sidestepped the Massachusetts law to give their daughter, Juliet, David's surname, although their baby as an illegitimate child should have borne her mother's surname.

In reading the article, one gains the idea that this couple would prefer to face one legal complication after another rather than take the simple legal step to marriage.

Other couples who express a favorable opinion about living together without marriage seem to have the idea that they are pioneering in a new way of life and designing a new pattern of male and female relatedness. This is not so. Such relationships have been tried in the past. In fact, Elsie Parsons proposed such a pattern in the early 1900s. She wrote that couples should live together intimately and try each other out before considering the marriage step. To this day, her proposal has never caught on with very many people. Weaknesses which have appeared repeatedly in such relationships are too much emphasis upon sex, unprotected pregnancy and insecure children, and a tendency to exploit one's partner because the living-together-game was played without any clearly defined rules.

MARRIAGE IN TWO STEPS
(Companionate Marriage—Judge Ben Lindsey, 1925)
Individual Marriage—Parental Marriage

Margaret Mead, well-known anthropologist, has her own special

---

[1]"Miss McCann and Mr. Estridge, Unmarried: Have a New Baby Girl," *Life* magazine, Vol. 72, No. 16, April 28, 1972, pp. 63-65.

formula for "investing marriage forms with new meaning." Each of these forms would require its own marriage license and ceremony.

Individual Marriage

The first step would be individual marriage, "a licensed union in which two individuals would be committed to each other as individuals for as long as they wished to remain together, but not as future parents. As the first step in marriage it would not include having children."[2]

In this suggested type of marriage, the responsibility would be ethical, not economic, and either the husband or wife would be the breadwinner. If the union broke up there would be no alimony or support.

Mead's thinking is that such a marriage would afford the couple legally protected intimacy so they can live together and decide if they have the ability to adjust to each other and develop a compatibility that would fit them for parental marriage.

Parental Marriage

This marriage form would always have to be preceded by individual marriage, also this second-step marriage requiring its own license and ceremony would be directed toward having children.

Mead, in writing about this marriage, assumes that the couple having previously passed through an individual marriage would have "eliminated the shattering surprise of discovery" related to undesirable things concerning one's mate. Also that economic stability, emotional maturity and other desirable qualities would be presented.

Margaret Mead admits that her, "Marriage in Two Steps" proposal is not new, and that it in some respects resembles "companionate marriage."

Companionate marriage was proposed by Judge Ben B. Lindsey of the Denver Juvenile Court in about 1925. Lindsey was disturbed by the large number of juvenile delinquents who came from broken homes, and he proposed this marriage form in order to make families more stable. His suggestion was to have married couples use the first few years of marriage as a trial period, and to avoid having children. Then, if they decided they were incompatible, they might divorce by mutual consent.

---

[2]Mead, Margaret, "Marriage in Two Steps," *Redbook* magazine, July 1966, New York: McCall Corporation.

Lindsey's proposal was widely discussed, but not one state legislature adopted it, and it found favor with very few people.

The possible weaknesses in such a marriage form revolve around its negative approach to marriage. A couple who are not sure of the depth of their commitment to each other, and postpone having children may be more likely to experiment, and lack strong motivation to try to adjust. Whereas, having had children might have given them a common goal they lacked, and increased their motivation to work out their differences.

TERM MARRIAGE
(E. D. Cope—about 1900)

Current and past advocates of term marriage look upon the nuptial agreement as a contract that might be renewed or dissolved by mutual consent. It is suggested that the couple marry for about a three-to-five-year term with the option of renewing or abandoning the relationship at the end of the contract period.

This marriage form has been practiced by a few people in some areas of the world, but has never been legalized in America, although it was advocated first in this country in about 1900 by E. D. Cope.

Present proponents of the plan think they have discovered something new, but past history shows us that it has been tried and doesn't work for various reasons.

This approach to marriage fosters experimentation and builds an attitude of impermanence. Such a form leaves wives and children without any legal recourse to receive further help from the estranged husband. Another flaw in such an agreement is that the degree of psychological involvement of the husband and wife in the marriage contract may differ as the period for renewal or abandonment arrives. The husband may have lost interest in his wife because he feels that her physical charms have waned, and the wife may want to discard her husband because his earning power has diminished. Such attitudes may lead one or both partners to seek "greener pastures" rather than attempt to work out an adjustment.

MARRIAGE WITH EXTRAMARITAL SEX
(Remedial Adultery)

A current advocate of extramarital sex is Dr. Albert Ellis, executive director of the Institute for Rational Living in New York City. He says,

"It could appear that in our Judaeo-Christian society, healthy adultery is possible . . . people are not truly monogamous and romantic love is not durable . . . Romantic love tends to last three to five years, especially if the participants are under the same roof."[3]

Dr. Ellis, along with a number of other marriage and family counselors, feels that one way to remedy this alleged disenchantment with marriage is for the partners to engage in extramarital affairs. It is thought that such activity will help rejuvenate the marriage. However, it is doubtful that the therapeutic value of "affairs" could be substantiated statistically.

The writer, throughout two decades of counseling married couples, has found just the opposite to happen. "Affairs" have almost always caused marriage relationships to deteriorate.

Bob and Debbie were an example. Having been discovered in an "affair," Bob insisted that the slate would be wiped clean and their marriage helped if Debbie would also engage in adultery. He felt then, that they could both say that they had enjoyed an extramarital fling, turn their backs on their escapades, and work out a stronger marriage.

After much hesitation, Debbie gave in to Bob's suggestion and had an affair with one of Bob's bachelor friends. Being curious, Bob asked his wife how things had worked out. Debbie replied, "Mr. X was so tender and considerate in his lovemaking that I shall always cherish the experience."

Upon hearing this, Bob became jealous, and their marriage started to fall apart.

The author's concluding comment on "remedial adultery" is that the indulging couple is playing with fire, and the possible effects on their future marriage adjustment are unpredictable.

SERIAL MONOGAMY

Some people feel that marriage is a game of marital chairs. They point to rising divorce statistics and say that the old stigma attached to divorce is gone. Chances of remarriage for divorced persons are greater than in the past. So, why not keep shifting around in marital chairs and only stay in one as long as it feels comfortable?

---

[3]As reported by Brian Knowles in "Wake Up Your Marriage," *Tomorrow's World*, Vol. IV, Number 3, March 1972, pp. 12-18, Pasadena, California: Ambassador College.

Although this practice, which is also called progressive monogamy, seems to be becoming more popular, many questions may be raised concerning its efficacy. For example, which of the several mates will the children develop parent-child identification with? Will weakened family ties result, with accompanying feelings of insecurity? How will a new marriage partner adjust to an established and ongoing family group? Will jealousies and rivalries between present and ex-mates affect intrafamilial relationships adversely?

These and many other problems may affect the much-married person, so that he will eventually feel he is involved with everyone and belongs to no one.

GROUP SEX
("Swinging")

Several years ago, a professional colleague, during a casual conversation, said, "This week-end our mate-swapping club meets. We get together in a member's home, throw our house keys down in the middle of the room, and then leave for a night of lovemaking with the person who picks up our key."

Subsequent discussions revealed that this mate-swapper was cynical about marriage, and life in general. In fact, the activity seemed to give him no deep satisfaction, and talking about it appeared to be the employment of an adjustive mechanism engaged in to compensate for unmet needs.

Group sex, mate-swapping, or "swinging," as it is popularly called, is a practice which sounds intriguing to couples who are bored with their marriage. The definition of this practice signifies a husband's and wife's willingness to swap sexual partners with friends or strangers. As Bartell says, the word "swinging" is preferred by participants because, "It means a free, easy, venturesome, 'with it' style life. And this reinforces the sexual swinger's own ego image."[4]

What type of persons "swing"?

Bartell found those in his study to be middle class, with a higher level of education than the general population. Their median age was around thirty. They tended to be conservative in their sexual outlook, and placed great importance upon looking young.

---

[4]Bartell, Gilbert D., *Group Sex*, New York: Peter H. Wyden, Inc., 1971.

The men's average height was about five-feet-ten and they tended toward paunchiness. Forty percent of them were salesmen. Seventy-eight percent of the women remained in the home as housewives. Their average height was five-feet-four, and they were either overweight or overendowed to the extent that their figures suffered.

How do "swingers" make initial contacts?

Usually by advertising in "swinger" magazines or underground newspapers. After contact is made, telephone conversations are held, and personal visits of a social nature follow. The stage is usually set for group sex at the second meeting, and the scene is structured to stimulate erotic arousal. Soft lights, romantic music, and drinking precede the magic hour, and when it finally arrives, the participants decide to swing "open" (the two couples remain together, possibly in a king-sized bed) or swing "closed" (the swapped partners go to different bedrooms for lovemaking).

How are the "swingers" affected? Does the activity revitalize their marriages?

Several studies suggest that many "swingers" are paranoid. They do not develop meaningful relationships with other people and they don't want their children to behave in the same manner as they do.

Bartell in his study concludes that they put too much emphasis on sex. He also says that, "Swinging will not cause a breakdown in the family . . . it will lead to sexual variety for those who desire it . . . but it need not destroy close emotional involvements between two (married) people. Such relationships are not easily cast aside; the mechanical-physical involvements of contemporary swingers can be, and are.

"We feel that the individuals we interviewed are not benefiting from swinging . . .

"Swingers may be acting out their dreams and receive psychological and physical support from their activities. However, their human relationships outside the dyad (couple) are not good . . . reflect mechanical interaction . . . and the impersonalization of human relationships in our own culture."

POLYGYNY AFTER SIXTY

Victor Kassel, a psychotherapist engaged in the private practice of geriatrics, feels that the greatest frustrations for individuals over sixty come from unfilled social necessities. He says such unmet needs are caused by the loss of the marriage partner, lack of money, retirement, loss of status and the inability to find satisfying activities.

He then suggests that allowing the practice of polygyny after sixty would help eliminate many of these frustrations.[5]

He thinks some of the advantages of allowing this practice would include the following:

More older women would have the chance to marry or remarry. Studies show that wives in America outlive their husbands from five to fifteen years, so after age sixty there are several women for every man. Consequently, polygyny would offer excess, unattached women the opportunity to have a husband.

Women and men would benefit by reestablishing a meaningful family group. This would eliminate the feeling that they were intruders in or operating on the fringe of their children's family constellations. It wouldn't sever contacts between parents and their children and grandchildren, but would ease the burden for both groups.

Studies indicate that proper nutrition is neglected when individuals live alone. On the other hand, the social atmosphere that comes from a group of people living together stimulates interest in cooking and preparing varied menus.

Living conditions would be improved, as several wives and one husband could pool their financial resources so all would benefit from improved surroundings.

Good health could be more readily maintained because members of the group could share the responsibility of nursing the sick.

Houses could be kept more attractive if several people shared cleaning and maintenance tasks.

Depression and loneliness would be reduced. This would occur if the married partners developed a family unity and had similar interests. It would result in more social activities among family members and increased confidence in participating in activities outside of the home.

Kassel admits that the sex life of the group would present a sensitive adjustment area. He covers this by saying that older men and women need and enjoy sex.

However, such a statement leaves many questions unanswered. Would the husband have favorite sexual partners? Would jealousy re-

[5]Kassel, Victor, "Polygyny After Sixty," *Geriatrics*, Vol. 21, April 1966, Lancet Publications.

sult? Would the older man's sex drive be strong enough to satisfy the needs of several wives? Studies show that the male's sex drive gradually diminishes with age. Whereas the female's drive after reaching a peak in the late twenties stays on a plateau stage and usually increases slightly when she reaches the menopause.

Kassel, and others who agree with his thinking, claim that impotency in the elderly male usually results from boredom and lack of an attractive, interested partner. Such an explanation is too simple. This controversial area of the male behavior is not clearly understood. Some studies suggest that older males are impotent even when attempting to make love to much younger, and sexually provocative women. Perhaps when researchers learn more about glandular changes in the older male, his potential capacity for sexual expression will be more fully comprehended.

Although polygyny after sixty seems in some ways to be a sensible idea, religious doctrine and social philosophy in America would have to undergo considerable change before it could be put into effect. Even then it is doubtful that the older man who wanted to practice polygyny could find several women in the same age group who were flexible enough and had interests similar enough in nature to allow them to live in the same household as wives to one man.

FAMILY COMMUNES

Care must be exercised in listing and describing a family commune as a current alternative to traditional marriage, inasmuch as sometimes it is and sometimes it isn't.

A commune is defined as "a residential situation where three or more individuals represent two or more family units, share a residential facility and a significant portion of living activity."[6]

Proponents of the family commune feel that it offers the individual opportunity to seek his identity through cooperation rather than competition. Some participants reject the "establishment" which they say is a way of life that puts too much emphasis on the value of material symbols and identity objects. They feel if they get away from the imposed rules, hypocrisy, and competition for material success of the establishment, that they can exercise more individual creativity and develop a clearer view of what life is all about.

---

[6]Ouradnik, Robert, "Center Seeks to Spur Growth of Communes," University of Minnesota Daily, April 12, 1972.

Some communes have a religious orientation, others a social, and many an economic.

Naturally, a commune is not considered a current alternative to marriage unless couples or single members of the group work out an arrangement in which there is group sex or some relationship different from the married sexual pairing of couples. The writer has not made a systematic study of such communal groups, but reports from other observers suggest that they are short-lived.

It might be of interest for those who contemplate joining a communal farm as a way of getting away from the establishment's rules to read the report of Debbie L., a college student who joined a communal farm. She submitted an outline of the commune's structure and activities as a term report in one of the author's classes, with the accompanying statement.

"I thought when I joined a communal farm, I would get away from a lot of rules. Man, was I wrong! I soon found out that the only way a commune could survive was by its members sticking to set rules. I have titled my report, 'What Do You Think a Communal Farm Is?' "

I. Background
A. Information
   1. I lived on a farm for four months.
   2. Frank lived on the same farm. (Frank is my fiance).
B. Ownership
   1. The original payment was made by a married couple.
   2. The farm is legally in their name, although it is being transferred to a church.
   3. For all practical purposes, the farm is owned and operated by the people who lived there.
C. The size of the farm is about 130-odd acres.
D. Long range plans: Members working together to maintain the farm as a community.
   1. Development of the land for organic farming.
   2. Becoming financially stable within the farm itself.
   3. To develop a unity among all its members.
      a. Find people who are willing to work for the group.
      b. To make this function, the members must have self-imposed laws.

    1. Getting up in the morning.
    2. Doing work without being asked.
    3. Taking the responsibility to see that the work gets done.
    4. Judging the amount of work you put in.

E. Changing of policy usually comes about by an event.
  1. The farm was busted for growing marijuana.
    a. The wife and mother of two is on two years' probation, and if she does anything wrong she will go to jail and her kids will be taken away.
    b. The farm now does not allow dope on it.
    c. The members are now oriented toward organic farming.

II. Structure

A. Basic structure
  1. Membership—varied from 10 to 30.
    a. Anyone who wants to live on the farm may.
      1. You find people who use the farm for their own needs.
        a. Using the farm as a place to meditate.
        b. Using the farm as a place to talk about ideals.
        c. People use the farm as a free vacation.
    b. Members are determined by the group.
      1. The way we eliminated people was by group pressure.
      2. We joined because a letter was sent requesting help.

B. Work Distribution
  1. The way work is divided up by skill, interest, and need.
    a. Goats milked and herded.
      1. Herding goats gave you an opportunity to see the land.
      2. If you got tired of milking the goats, you could find someone and teach them how, easily.
    b. Different people took it upon themselves to make sure part of the garden was taken care of, by
      1. Doing the work themselves.
      2. Finding people to help them.
    c. We had vehicles that needed repairs. One of our members did the work.
    d. Meals
      1. We had a sign-up sheet for days to work in the kitchen.

    2. Two people usually cooked about once every two weeks.

    3. When a person cooked there was not time for anything else. Other people would do their work. We used a wood stove, and water was heated on the stove.

C. Meetings

  1. One day a week was set aside to plan for the next week's activities such as:

    a. Pea picking before breakfast.

    b. Strawberry picking for a day.

  2. Future Plans

    a. Buy a walk-in freezer.

    b. Discuss need for membership control.

D. Social activities

  1. Recreation

    a. Cherry stomping became a group party.

    b. Weddings.

      1. All friends would get together.

      2. A good friend would read something.

      3. The couple would say something.

      4. All would huddle around the couple and sing.

      5. Feast.

  2. Man versus woman.

    a. Ideally all were equal and expected to do the same work.

      1. Both sexes did roofing.

      2. Both sexes took care of the garden.

      3. Both sexes did housework and cooking.

    b. Reasons why this didn't work.

      1. Women aren't as physically strong as men.

      2. Some men and women wanted to retain their separate sex roles.

  3. Interaction between men and women.

    a. Monogamous sex.

    b. Couples have close friends of either sex and they will always be there for social and emotional support.

    c. If you feel the need to be away from your partner there are lots of places to go on the farm.

      d. Both persons can develop their own interests and still have a common goal.

E. Housing
1. Individual dwellings.
   a. Cabins around the farm.
   b. Tents or camp sites.
   c. The barn which was partitioned off.
   d. Some lived in the main house with their own rooms.
2. Main house contained:
   a. Library.
   b. Sewing room.
   c. Dining room and kitchen.
   d. Social lounge.

III. Sex and Nudity
A. Nudity
1. Nudity was only engaged in for practical reasons.
   a. On a hot summer day it was more comfortable to work in the nude.
   b. Taking a sauna would be difficult with clothes on.
   c. It was too much bother to get a swimsuit before swimming, so that was always done in the nude.
2. Attitude toward nudity.
   a. Generally accepted as no big deal.
   b. Wasn't indicative of promiscuity.
   c. No one flaunted their nudity.
   d. Almost taboo if someone sat in the house nude.

B. Sex
1. No public lovemaking.
2. No exploitative hustling.
3. No sex orgies.
4. The only sex was between couples, and a very private thing.
5. Sex rarely mentioned.
6. There were a few single women passing through that were free with their sexual favors.
7. We were like a small community of monogamous people.

IV. Finances
  A. Total amount needed per year was about $2500.
    1. Twenty-one hundred for the payment on the house and farm.
    2. The rest for staples, vehicles, etc.
  B. Received money by:
    1. Donations.
    2. Cash crops. We are a truck farm.
    3. We went apple picking for the farm payment.
  C. We get much of our building materials by tearing down old buildings for other people.

* * *

At the present time there is not much evidence to suggest that the family commune with group sex will find wide acceptance as an alternate form of marriage. It does seem likely, however, that some traditional nuclear families may structure their lives differently in an effort to improve their circumstances. Forms of family living that are finding favor include the collective, a cooperative economic venture participated in by families that do not necessarily live together; the family cluster, an organization of two or more family units that share resources, skills and services, but retain separate residential arrangements; the suggested intimate network of families, described as, "a circle of three or four families who meet together regularly and frequently, share in reciprocal fashion any of their intimate secrets, offer one another a variety of services and do not hesitate to influence one another in terms of values and attitudes."[7]

This intimate network concept of family life emerged from the development of the family workshop, and its possibilities are being explored by contemporary sociologists.

THE FUTURE OF TRADITIONAL MARRIAGE AND THE NUCLEAR FAMILY

Although many predictions regarding the future of marriage and the family are being made, there are no studies that are large enough and conclusive enough to state with authority what the future might be. It is doubtful that the family is "near the point of complete extinction" as Ferdinand Lundberg, author of *The Coming World Transformation,* says. Neither is there widespread evidence that it is "slowly disintegrating."

[7]Stoller, Frederick H., "The Intimate Network of Families as a New Structure," Ch. 13, *The Family in Search of a Future*, Editor, Otto, Herbert A., New York: Meredith Corporation, 1970.

On the positive side, it can be said that the family has withstood the test of time, and should continue to do so. Dr. Irwin M. Greenberg, Professor of Psychiatry at the Albert Einstein College of Medicine, says, "People will marry for stable structure." His viewpoint which is espoused by many in the family life field is that as society becomes more complex and the pressures of change increase, the family will continue to play a vital role as a solid center from which the individual can meet and evaluate the forces of change. Furthermore, if the family group as it exists today undergoes future changes in structure, they will be the result of changes in the quality of the family experience as related to the fulfillment of family members' needs.

Suggested Readings

1. Cavan, Ruth S. (ed.), *Marriage and Family in the Modern World,* New York: Thomas Y. Crowell Co., 1969 (3rd ed.).
2. Cox, Frank, *American Marriage: A Changing Scene?,* Dubuque: William C. Brown Co., 1971.
3. Delora, Joann S. and Jack R., *Intimate Life Styles, Marriage and its Alternatives,* Pacific Palisades: Goodyear Publishing Co., 1972.
4. Gordon, Michael, *The Nuclear Family in Crisis: The Search for an Alternative,* New York: Harper & Row Publ., 1972.
5. King, R. J. R. (ed.), *Family Relations: Concepts and Theories,* Berkeley: The Glendessary Press, 1969.
6. Lopata, Helena Z. (ed.), *Marriages and Families,* New York: D. Van Nostrand Co., 1973.
7. Otto, Herbert A. (ed.), *The Family In Search of a Future, Alternate Models for Moderns,* New York: Appleton-Century-Crofts, 1970.
8. Reiss, Ira L., *The Family System in America,* New York: Holt, Rinehart, & Winston, Inc., 1971.
9. Schulz, Mildred W., *The Changing Family: Its Function and Future,* Englewood Cliffs, N.J.: Prentice-Hall, Inc., 1972.
10. Skolnick, Arlene S. and Jerome H., *Family in Transition,* Boston: Little, Brown & Co., 1971.
11. Winch, Robert F., *The Modern Family,* New York: Holt, Rinehart and Winston, Co., 1971, (3rd ed.).

PART II

Prologue to Adulthood

Chapter III

How We Prepare for Marriage

THE PERSONALITY WE BRING TO MARRIAGE

What are the most important things we bring to marriage?

One male student said, "Money in the bank." He went a step further and added, "Until I have ten thousand dollars in a savings account, I won't even consider getting married."

Granted, money is a tangible asset that should contribute to marital happiness, but so are other things such as a new car, a complete setting of expensive silverware, a lavish wardrobe, and a lucrative job. However, as important as these things may seem, there is something else that will have much greater impact on our marital adjustment. It is the attitude we have toward ourselves and others. If we have attitudes which enable us to accept ourselves and understand and accept others, there is a good chance that our marriage will work out well. Because if we possess personalities that include these attributes we will be sensitive to the needs of our mates, willing to try to adjust to new and changing situations, and have the desire to accept the responsibilities of our new partnership.

Such sensibilities are easy to discuss but difficult to develop. They do not appear magically at the time one decides to take the marriage step, but begin to develop or not develop as the individual personality is shaped during the experiences of infancy, childhood, and adolescence. Thus, the reasons for marital adjustment difficulties can often be traced back to the husband's or wife's areas of maladjustment during childhood. Studies of marital adjustment affirm this as they show that an individual who has a happy childhood has a greater chance for happy marriage than one whose childhood is unhappy.

The knowledge that personality traits that affect marriage adjustments begin to develop long before the individual reaches the marriageable age makes the study of personality formation an important part of the family life field. Consequently, the discussion which follows deals with the definition of personality, how it develops, and the stages of socialization a person must pass through to reach the level that is necessary to get along satisfactorily with another individual in a marriage relationship.

Personality Defined

Contrary to popular opinion, everyone has personality, and not just those individuals who seem to possess the charisma necessary to lead out or hold the center of the stage in a crowd. Furthermore, no one is born with a pleasing or displeasing personality, but the kind of personality one has is the result of many contributing factors. Before discussing some of them, it is necessary to state what is meant by personality. A definition widely accepted by psychologists is one by Gordon Allport who stated that personality is "the dynamic organization within the individual of those psychophysical systems that determine his unique adjustment to his environment." To make this definition a bit simpler, it might be said that personality is the sum total of one's physical, mental and moral characteristics. In other words it is the individual's total self.

Genetic Factors That Shape Personality

Now, just how did we become what we are? Many things determined this, and it is enlightening to look at a few of them.

To begin, it is interesting to note that each individual at the time of conception is endowed with certain physical characteristics that come from his family line. These traits are transmitted through the genes which are tiny, complex molecules (deoxyribonucleic acid—DNA for short) which are located on the chromosomes that are contained in the nucleus of each body cell.

Inasmuch as this pool of genes is passed on from one generation to the next, grandparents or even great grandparents may contribute traits to the newly formed individual. Consequently, each one of us is born with a distinctive family trademark. For example, the shape of a person's nose, the color of his eyes and his general body structure are all the result of the genes transmitted through his family line. Therefore, we must accept the fact that our physical characteristics do not all come from the same mold and that we may inherit a dainty nose or a prominent one and be tall or short, and so forth. Our role is to make the most of what we have.

Prenatal Influences on Health and Personality

It used to be thought that there was nothing that could influence the shaping of the newly conceived individual's personality while he was growing in the uterus. Recent research suggests otherwise. For example, Ashley Montagu, the distinguished anthropologist, says the individual's personality can be affected. He states, "It is through the neurohumoral system, the system comprising the interrelated nervous and endocrine systems acting through the fluid medium of the blood (and its oxygen and carbon-dioxide contents), that nervous changes in the mother may affect the fetus. The common endocrine pool of the mother and fetus forms a neurohumoral bond between them. The endocrine systems of mother and fetus complement each other."[1]

Very simply put, what Montagu and other researchers are saying is that the emotional states and psychological reactions of the expectant mother affect her body chemistry, and these chemical changes are in turn transmitted to the fetus and affect it in certain ways.

Sonntag, who has done considerable work in this area, reports that some infants whose mothers have undergone severe emotional stress during pregnancy are from the beginning of life, hyperactive and irritable children. He states further that such a child "is to all intents and purposes a neurotic infant when he is born . . . the result of an unsatisfactory fetal environment. In this instance, he has not had to wait until childhood for a bad home situation or other causes to make him neurotic. It has been done for him, before he has ever seen the light of day."[2]

Other studies also suggest that the fetus may become predisposed to anxiety by traumatic stimuli that are not connected with the mother's emotional state. Such research indicates that stimuli such as sudden sounds, strong vibrations, and similar factors may contribute toward producing a neurotic infant.[3]

Examples of such sounds or vibrations that have startled a fetus and produced a convulsive response or increased fetal activity are:

A doorbell buzzer held opposite its head (thirtieth week).

---

[1]Montagu, Ashley, "Constitutional and Prenatal Factors in Infant and Child Health," Haimowitz and Haimowitz, *Human Development, Selected Readings,* 2nd Edition, ch. 19, New York: Thomas Y. Crowell Co., 1966.

[2]Sonntag, Lester, "War and the Fetal-Maternal Relationship" *Marriage and Family Living,* 6, 1944.

[3]Greenacre, P., "The Biological Economy of Birth," *The Psychoanalytic Study of the Child,* ed. O. Fenichel, et al. New York: International Universities Press, 1945.

Tapping upon the side of a bathtub in which the mother was lying (thirty-one days before birth).

Vibrations from an orchestra, piano or washing machine.[4]

Some Other Influences on the Fetus

There is now general consensus that the pregnant woman's nutritional pattern affects the fetus. Babies born of mothers whose nutritional needs have not been met often suffer from basic organic deficiencies.

Pregnant mothers who use drugs are increasing the possibilities of congenital defects in their babies. Taking quinine for malaria during pregnancy has produced cases of congenital deafness. Mothers who are addicted to morphine have borne infants suffering from morphinism. There is evidence that babies born to mothers who have taken LSD and other similar drugs have experienced alterations in the number of their chromosomes (either missing some or having extra chromosomes or parts of chromosomes) which have caused congenital malformations. Of course, there is considerable documented evidence that thalidomide is responsible for congenital malformations.

There has been a division of opinion as to whether an expectant mother who smokes will harm the fetus, but now, studies dating from 1960 and on indicate that expected babies of smoking mothers have a lower birth rate and a higher rate of prematurity than babies of those mothers who do not smoke. Studies also show that "Alcohol used in excess, may have a depressant effect unfavorable to the fetus's normal functioning after birth."[5]

An extremely cautious, yet logical position toward the use of drugs by the pregnant mother is taken by Mendelsohn who says, "The effects of most drugs on the developing fetus are still largely unknown. Therefore, prudence dictates the avoidance of tranquilizers, weight reduction pills, and possibly even aspirin."[6]

Additional things that may have an adverse effect upon the fetus are:

Massive doses of X rays during the first two months of pregnancy.

---

[4]Bernard J., and Sonntag, L. W., "Fetal Reactivity to Fetal Stimulation: A Preliminary Report," J. Genet. *Psychol*, 70, 205-210, 1947.
[5]Bowman, Henry, *Marriage for Moderns*, 6th Edition, p. 468. New York: McGraw Hill, 1970.
[6]Mendelsohn, Robert I., M.D., "Child Development: Physical Growth" Part Four: The Child in the Family, *Successful Marriage*, ed. Fishbein and Fishbein. Third revised edition. Garden City, New York: Doubleday and Co., 1971.

Umbilical entanglements.

Difficulties during the process of birth.

Viral infections.

Childhood Behavioral Patterns Which Affect Later Marital Adjustment

From the moment a baby arrives in this world, influences begin to play upon it that will in some way affect its future adjustments as a marriage partner. Levy and Monroe say, ". . . marriage starts in infancy. The child prepares for marriage during every minute of his waking hours."[7]

Although babies display different personalities at birth, they all have to learn certain fundamentals of good behavior if they are to grow up to be understanding marriage partners.

The first step a baby should take in this developmental process is to learn to love his parents. This is not an easy task, because an infant is a selfish creature and is primarily concerned with the satisfaction of his own needs. He expects to be fed when hungry, cuddled when lonely, and be changed when he is uncomfortable. If these needs are not met, he sets up a fuss. Despite this preoccupation with his own needs, the infant must gradually learn to love and be considerate of others. Later, in adulthood, this learned behavior will affect his marital adjustment.

Just how does a baby start learning to love and be considerate of others? Erikson states that, ". . . the component of the healthy personality (one that is capable of loving others) that is first to develop is a sense of trust."[8] This sense of trust develops in the following manner: If the parents take care of the baby's needs in appropriate and consistent ways he will begin to trust them. As he becomes older and aware of himself as an individual, he will feel that his world is a dependable place as he knows about what to expect in his relationships with others. Conversely, if his parents are not sensitive to his feelings during this early period and approach him too quickly or speak too sharply, he loses his sense of trust and has a feeling of uneasiness. However, if the parents strive to keep their associations with their baby filled with understanding and tenderness, the infant will gradually feel accepted as a person and develop a sense of trust. This newly developed sense of trust, combined with a feeling of

---

[7]Levy, John, and Monroe, Ruth, *The Happy Family*, New York: Alfred A. Knopf, Inc., 1950. p. 18, 19.

[8]Erikson, E. H., *Childhood and Society*, New York: Norton, 2nd Edition, 1963.

acceptance, enables the baby to become less preoccupied with his own needs and to learn to return love to those who give him pleasure.

If the baby does feel unloved and insecure, it is possible that he will grow up with a feeling of distrust for the human race. This is often the case with "psychopathic personalities." These individuals see no reason to trust their fellow men and consequently have no sense of responsibility toward them.

Erik H. Erikson, who is a widely quoted psychologist and training psychoanalyst and has engaged in a considerable number of anthropological and child development studies, also states that at each stage of development a child has a central problem to solve. If it is solved temporarily at least or sufficiently to make an adjustment, the child proceeds more confidently to the next stage and subsequently develops a healthy personality. He calls these the eight ages of man.

Eight Ages of Man

1. Basic Trust vs. Basic Mistrust
2. Autonomy vs. Shame and Doubt
3. Initiative vs Guilt
4. Industry vs. Inferiority
5. Identity vs. Role Confusion
6. Intimacy vs. Isolation
7. Generativity vs. Stagnation
8. Ego Integrity vs. Despair[9]

The following discussion of the development of a healthy personality uses Erikson's "Eight Ages of Man" as a frame of reference.

THE DEVELOPMENT OF A HEALTHY PERSONALITY

1. The Need to Develop a Sense of Trust.

This basic need has already been briefly touched on. But to reinforce what has been said, consideration will be given to Harlow's findings in his studies of the relationships of monkey mothers to their offspring. He states that baby monkeys also follow this trust-love pattern and need "contact comfort" which is received by clinging to and nursing from their mothers. "The monkey mother both gives and receives contact comfort,

---

[9]*Ibid.*, p. 8.

and it may be assumed that contact is an important mechanism in eliciting maternal love from the mother."[10]

Another interesting finding of Harlow's is that "during the infant monkey's first week of life maternal love is indiscriminate, and during this period a monkey mother will respond with equal intensity to her own or to a strange infant of similar age." However, after this period of time has elapsed, the monkey mother "develops feelings specific to her own infant," and will not be satisfied with interaction with any other baby monkey.

Harlow points out that a similiar process takes place between the human mother and her baby, at least with her first child. "Until the infant is four to six weeks old the mother perceives it as an anonymous asocial object and reports only impersonal feelings of affection." When the infant is in its "second month of life," the mother's "maternal feelings intensify" and after three months, the mother becomes so attached to her baby that separation from it becomes intolerable. The development of such an attitude on the part of the mother is contributed to when the infant in its second month of life begins to exhibit visual fixation which leads "to smiling responses and eye contacts." These behavioral patterns combined with the infant's unique characteristics cause the mother to recognize it as a person with its own identity and she believes that the baby recognizes her.

Much more could be said about the individual's need to develop a sense of trust as a beginning step toward developing the capacity to love one's self and others. But to summarize briefly, it may be stated that this need continues throughout life. Each individual needs to feel a trusting relationship with others, so that realizing others care about him, he can value (love) himself. This self-acceptance will enable him to move away from preoccupation with his own needs and direct his energies outwardly toward loving others.

2. The Need to Develop a Sense of Autonomy.

All of us need to feel capable of doing something on our own, and Erikson says this is the child's central problem from the age of about one to three years. During this period of time, he likes to explore new things and is constantly reaching out to touch and grasp new objects. Such activities as throwing and dropping things and climbing out of bed at night

---

[10]Harlow, Harry F., *Learning to Love*, San Francisco: Albion Publishing Co., 1971, pp. 8, 9.

to wander around all give him a sense of "feeling his oats," and the realization that he can do things and make choices concerning what he does.

Such a spirit of independence is a necessary component of a healthy personality providing it includes the awareness that individual independence must be combined with self-control and respect for others. It is the adult's job to help the child develop self-control without loss of self-esteem. If this is not done, the child's resulting loss of self-confidence may cause him to have a continuing sense of doubt in others, feel inadequate and withdraw from society, or compensate for his inner feelings of inadequacy by becoming overly aggressive or hostile toward others.

The child's development of a sense of autonomy at this stage is complicated by a basic physiological problem. This is a period of muscle-system maturation and the consequent need to learn how to coordinate several conflicting action patterns. The child has to learn how to hold and to let go; to seize and to drop; when to withhold and when to expel body wastes; to walk or remain immobile; to talk or remain silent. Attempting to master such activities can lead to moments of frustration, even without considering the social implications of each specific act.

A typical problem of this period is that of toilet training.

Toilet Training

Toilet training can result in emotional problems if the parent has a compulsion to establish a schedule before the child's bodily musculature is ready for such an effort.

Parents often become tense and irritable when they have difficulty with the child's toilet training. This happens because they expect "too much, too soon." In order to accomplish proper training they may scold and shame the child so he begins to feel that the parts of the body which deal with elimination are not nice. And inasmuch as the sex organs are so close to those of elimination, he may develop an attitude of disgust toward that entire area of his body. It also is possible that he may carry this attitude into his adult life and consequently, view sexual relations in marriage with negative feelings.

To avoid such negative conditioning, parents must realize when they start toilet training that children's timetables of development differ, and that successful toilet training is dependent upon a certain amount of development in the child's nervous system. Thus, the child who has a slow timetable of development cannot be forced into earlier performance. Because of these differences in children it is difficult to generalize at what age successful toilet training should take place, but pediatricians say that the average child may begin to develop bowel control in his second year and bladder control in his third.

Another important practice is to make the child's toilet training as pleasant as possible. Providing a comfortable training chair or equipment and the displaying of a calm and understanding attitude by the training parent are both beneficial.

Sometimes, children will want to handle the waste products of the body. This may happen out of curiosity or because of the pleasure they derive from touching the substances. They may also engage in such activity to shock their parents or get even with their elders for having punished them previously. Rather than displaying horror when this occurs, it would be wiser for parents to investigate the reasons for such behavior, provide substitute materials such as sand or clay for their children to play with, and also impress upon them the hygienic reasons for not allowing such activity.

Before leaving this period of development, it must be stressed that although the child's sense of autonomy usually comes into being at this time, threats to its maintenance may occur throughout life. Adults, as well as children, are affected by such factors. Consequently, it is extremely important in all interpersonal relations that each interacting individual is treated in a manner that affirms his or her personal dignity.

3. The Need for Individual Initiative.

Everyone likes to do things. However, individuals soon learn that carrying out one's desires and transferring the products of one's imagination into overt activity may possibly bring about disaster if the resulting acts violate the culture's social codes. In this respect children are no different from adults. When the child reaches the age of about four, he wants to find out what particular kinds of things he can do. A boy's imagination or social conditioning may cause him to play at adult activities such as being a truck driver, a policeman or a doctor. Similarly, the girl may enjoy play-acting as a mother, nurse, shopper, and so forth. Inasmuch as the child's conscience has come into being at this time, his activities will be regulated to some extent by the voice within him as well as by the admonitions of his parents.

The favorable outcome of this central problem of exercising initiative would be for him or her to learn to engage in creative and constructive activity without being burdened by a sense of guilt. Failure to do this might cause the child to be overrestricted by the naggings of a guilty conscience.

How does this happen? Why should an individual who exercises creativity feel guilty? He should not, if his behavior does not violate the moral codes of his society. Nevertheless, his harmless imaginings and sense of initiative can be stifled by feelings of guilt when his parents openly discourage perfectly proper acts and make him feel they are undesirable.

Later on, when the child enters school, his sense of initiative will continue to get weaker if his teacher requires him to conform to activities that allow no room for imagination or originality. Such pressures by parents, teachers, and other adults may so discourage a creative individual that he may lose interest in learning, and often may, in his resentment, compensate by engaging in undesirable activities.

On the other hand, if an individual's imaginings and sense of initiative are continually encouraged and subtly guided into acceptable channels, the concerned person and society both benefit. America would not be an economic power in the world today, if many persons had not dreamed dreams and then translated their ideas into action.

The first three stages in the development of a healthy personality which have been discussed, if passed through properly, form a sound foundation on which the total healthy personality can be built. If the child develops a sense of trust, a sense of autonomy, and expresses his imaginings and sense of initiative in a controlled and acceptable manner, he will likely progress through Erikson's other "Ages of Man" without much trouble. Such an observation is in accord with the psychological theory that the so-called formative years from birth to about age six determine about how the individual's personality will be set. However, it must be pointed out that some children become psychologically healthy adults despite a bad start, and others who show great promise in childhood have problems later in life. Therefore, the above observation is subject to many possible modifications. Be that as it may, the rest of the developmental stages will be touched on very briefly.

4. The Need for a Sense of Responsibility and Accomplishment.

Erikson calls this age the one of a "sense of industry." It begins at about age six and extends to about twelve.

At this stage of development, the child discovers that he can gain recognition by producing things. He has already learned the rudimentary skills of walking, talking, and the acceptable ways of regulating bodily functions, so now he can direct his energies to given skills and tasks. With careful direction he can become an integral part of a productive situation, learn to accept responsibility for his assigned task, and derive satisfaction from completing his assignment well.

Adults can help children develop this responsible behavior by encouraging them to take pride in positive accomplishment. However, care must be taken that an individual's accomplishments are not compared unfavorably with the achievements of others. The challenge for the adult is to help each child to work toward the potential that is related to his individual capacity and stage of emotional development.

5. The Need for a Sense of Identity.

With the onset of adolescence the individual becomes deeply concerned with the development of a sense of identity. Rapid physical growth and concern with self-image, plus the tangible adult tasks that lie ahead cause the adolescent to seek the answers to an avalanche of questions. Typical ones are:

Am I a child or an adult?

Why am I unpopular?

What kind of job should I prepare for?

Should I get married or remain single?

How can I get people to like me?

As the adolescent finds satisfactory answers to these and other questions, he gradually becomes aware of the role that is his to play and the life-style he should follow.

Developing this sense of identity is often made more difficult by the culture in which he lives. If his society has no clear-cut ideas as to when adulthood begins, the teen-ager may vacillate between childlike and adult behavior and never feel quite comfortable in either role. More will be said about this stage of development in a later chapter. But in summary, it should be stated here that adults who associate with adolescents should avoid superficial evaluation of their behavior and never label them as ne'er-do-wells. What young people need and appreciate is guidance from individuals who understand adolescent psychology and are aware of the cultural problems which the adolescent faces in the world of today.

6. The Sense of Intimacy.

One of the distressing problems in current society is that of loneliness. Because it is so widespread, many encounter groups have been developed in which lonely persons can open up emotionally and develop a sense of closeness with others by sharing common problems. One of the techniques suggested for use in these groups is physical touching of each other's bodies. Such procedures might offer some help, but developing a sense of intimacy requires much more than mutual touching of bodies.

A sense of intimacy is more fully fostered when the individual can accept himself, see and accept the other person's viewpoint, and respect his and the other individual's personhood. If he wants to fuse his identity with others, he should be ready for the responsibilities of intimacy, which entail "the capacity to commit himself to concrete affiliations and partnerships and to develop the ethical strength to abide by such commitments even though they may call for significant sacrifices and compromises."[11]

A person who fails to develop this kind of a sense of intimacy may remain psychologically isolated and incapable of having warm and spontaneous relations with other people.

7. The Parental Sense.

The parental sense is most clearly demonstrated by individuals who want to produce and care for children of their own. However, in some cases childless adults may have this sense more fully developed than those who have produced several offspring.

The essential element of the parental sense is the desire to nourish and nurture children, coupled with the attitude that the children are a sacred part of the community.

Parents who regard their children as extensions of their own personality, or beings they have to put up with, never achieve the parental sense.

8. The Need for a Sense of Integrity.

The core of the healthy personality is the development of a sense of integrity. It includes such characteristics as faith, courage, honor, duty,

---

[11]Erikson, Erik H., *Childhood and Society*, New York: Norton, Second Edit., 1963.

fairness, self-discipline, and so forth. In Erikson's words, the individual "becomes able to accept his individual life cycle and the people who have become significant to it as meaningful within the segment of history in which he lives."

This results in a sense of comradeship and respect for men and women of other cultures, past and present, and appreciation of their efforts to preserve human dignity and demonstrate love. This sense of integrity also enables an individual to love his parents without criticism, accept the responsibility for his own actions, and fulfill the purpose of his existence with a sense of dignity.

The person who has met and solved the central problem of these eight ages of personality should reach adulthood with a healthy personality. Nevertheless, before leaving the discussion of personality as related to mature adulthood, it should be helpful to look at some of the specific areas of interpersonal relationships that also have bearing on healthy personality and future marital adjustments.

Suggested Readings

1. Adler, Manfred, *A Parents Manual: Answers to Questions on Child Development and Rearing,* Springfield, Ill.: Charles C. Thomas Co., 1971.

2. Alderfer, Helen and Edwin, *Helping Your Child to Grow,* Scottdale, Pa.: Herald Press, 1968.

3. Brown, Daniel G., "Masculinity-Femininity Development in Children," *Journal of Consulting Psychology,* 21:3 (1957), 197-202.

4. Freiburg, Selma, *The Magic Years,* New York: Charles Scribner's Sons, 1964.

5. Hadfield, J. A., *Childhood and Adolescence,* Baltimore, Md.: Penguin Books, 1962.

6. Haimowitz, Morris L. and Natalie R., *Human Development, selected readings,* New York: Thomas Y. Crowell Co., 1973, (3rd ed.).

7. Harlow, Harry F., *Learning to Love,* San Francisco: Albion Publishing Co., 1971.

8. Kawin, Ethel, "Parenthood in a Free Nation," Volume I, *Basic Concepts for Parents;* Volume II, *Early and Middle Childhood;* Volume III, *Later Childhood and Adolescence,* New York: The Macmillan Co., 1963.

9. Stone, Joseph L. and Church, Joseph, *Childhood and Adolescence,* A Psychology of the Growing Person, New York: Random House 1973, (3rd ed.).

Chapter IV

Maintaining a Positive Self-Image

PARENT-CHILD INTERACTION

The average individual's home provides a small social unit in which practice can be gained in getting along with other people. Although this interaction with others takes place in many ways, there are specific areas which tend to have a definite correlation with future marital adjustment. A brief exploration of these should indicate the extent of their importance.

Childhood Discipline

Inasmuch as we will discuss discipline in a later chapter, only a passing comment will be given here.

Beginning with the infant's first day in life, he experiences conflict—that which arises from his efforts to develop a satisfactory behavior pattern which will allow him to express his desires and still conform to the pressures of his social group. In order to learn group standards he is expected to internalize (take into his thought processes) the thinking of his parents concerning what is good and what is undesirable behavior. If the parents force their concepts of right and wrong, or what is good, down the baby's throat, or make him feel that he is in a cultural straitjacket, he may possibly develop a feeling of hostility toward them as symbols of authority. Conversely, if the growing child is allowed to question his parents and discuss with them why they think certain things are good or bad, he will be less likely to keep this hostility bottled up inside, ready to explode at some future date.

Dorothy Baruch in her book, *New Ways in Discipline,* stresses the importance of the parents seeing, accepting, and reflecting how the child feels toward their discipline. She counsels parents to help the child "get out the poison," and to help him "steer his actions."

A man who comes to marriage with the feeling that "My parents never saw my side of things," may have considerable difficulty in accept-

67

ing any suggestions from his mate, and might even view her as a parent image who is a symbol of authority.

There are so many ways that individuals can react to harsh and unfeeling discipline, that it is not wise to make generalizations. However, marriage counselors often meet some clients who bristle with hostility toward symbols of authority and others who meekly say, "Let people dominate me. After all, I don't really count for much as a person."

Understanding discipline in the home enables a child to grow up in a climate which helps prepare him for future marriage adjustments.

Leading pediatricians report that there is a relationship between marital adjustment and the kind of discipline that a child experiences at home.

Sex Attitudes in the Home

How fortunate, and how rare is the individual who has grown up in a home in which sex has been accepted and discussed as a wholesome part of life! If his parents talk to him naturally and with sound attitudes about the place of sex in life, they are taking a big step in preparing him to understand one of the important adjustments in marriage. Right in his own home he can learn to understand sexual self-discipline and his sexual feelings, and realize that in marriage, intimate sexual contact is an expression of love between husband and wife. And that this sexual expression of their love is tied up with their responsible interest in each other's welfare.

If this attitude toward sex is not taught in the family circle, a person may piece together fragmentary bits of knowledge of misinformation from many sources and eventually arrive at the marriageable age with feelings that can make marriage adjustment difficult. He may think, as many adults do, that sexual intimacy in marriage is an unpleasant obligation to be fulfilled, or that marital sexual expression is necessary to satisfy biologic drives and has no connection with a sense of responsibility and a feeling of love in marriage.

The Child's Interaction in the Family

The way the child interacts with parents and siblings may also have some influence upon his ability to make future marital adjustments.

Relationships With Parents

The images of the parents which develop in the child's mind will often affect his selection of a marriage partner. If the girl admires her father, she may consciously or unconsciously seek a husband who resembles him (a father image). Conversely, if she dislikes her father, she will be more likely to select a husband who is as different from him as possible. The boy also reacts in the same manner, according to his relationships with his mother.

If a parent is overprotective or overaffectionate, a child may develop such a strong attachment for the mother or father that no one else can take his or her place. If this attachment involves sexual feelings it is possible that an Oedipus complex may develop. According to psychoanalytic thinking, this is, "A conscious or unconscious erotic attachment for the parent of the opposite sex, together with a jealous attitude toward the other parent. Normally, it occurs at about age five, and then infant sexuality begins to be repressed and the child emulates the parent of the same sex (from six to about fourteen).[1]

If the child does not get over this erotic attachment to the parent of the opposite sex, this fixation may influence his thinking throughout life. An example of how the Oedipus complex can adversely affect marital adjustment is the case of the newly married husband who paid a visit to his mother the morning after his wedding. The purpose of the visit was to tell his mother all about the first night with his wife, so she would not be jealous.

Children who develop overattachments to their parents may never give their future marriage partners the feeling that they are as important to their lives as are their parents. A marriage counselor encounters this situation quite frequently in the course of therapy. Often an attractive young wife will begin to sob during a counseling session and blurt out between tears, "I am only the number two woman in my husband's life. I will never be number one as long as his mother is alive. He compares everything I do with what his mother does. All I hear is, 'Why can't you cook like my mother?' or 'Mother always had the house tidy when Dad came home from work. I wish you had a little of her ambition.'

"Sometimes I think he would be happier if I would move out so his mother could come and live with him."

We must not assume that parent-child relationships produce nothing but harmful attitudes toward future marriage adjustments. If the father

[1] Eidelberg, Ludwig, Ed. *Encyclopedia of Psychoanalysis*, New York: The Free Press, 1968.

and mother live together in love and understanding within the family group, their good relationship should have a positive influence upon their children's future marriages. If it does not, at least the parents will feel that they have tried to be good models to their children and have attempted to demonstrate how a husband and wife can make good marriage adjustments.

Sibling Relationships

The manner in which the child reacts to his ordinal position in the family which determines whether he is the oldest, the youngest, or an "in-between" sibling, may have some affect upon his future marriageability.

Older children often have a tendency to be jealous of their younger brothers and sisters for a number of reasons. Two of the most common reasons for this jealousy are resentment in sharing the spotlight with these newcomers to the family, and also the feeling that the parents are more lenient with their siblings than they were with them at the same age.

The youngest children may feel that because they are the "babies" of the family, they should be overindulged.

"In-between" children may get the impression that they are treated unfairly. A girl may think, "I don't count. Why, I never have anything to call my very own. Why do I have to wear Mary's dresses just because they are too tight for her?" Or an "in-between" boy may say to himself, "I wish I could pick out a bike of my own instead of having to use the one that is now too small for my brother Bill."

Parents should always be sensitive to their children's individual differences and treat each child with respect and love if they want to avoid the development of sibling jealousies. They should never compare one child's achievements with another's, but should encourage each individual to discover and develop his own latent potentialities.

Community Influences That Affect the Individual's Attitude Toward Adulthood and Marriage

In today's world, schoolteachers, church leaders, athletic coaches, and civic workers all exercise an important influence upon the growing individual. If he possesses wise and understanding parents they can guide him during his contacts with these various people so that his experiences with them will develop increased capacity to adjust to his future marriage.

PREPARATION FOR MARRIAGE DURING ADOLESCENCE

When a person reaches adolescence, which we commonly refer to as the teen-age period, he experiences a great awakening and suddenly persons of the opposite sex become interesting and even attractive to him. (This stage is technically called the heterosexual level of development.) We discuss teen-age experiences in a later chapter, so just a brief summary of how this period helps in preparation for marriage will now be given.

First, the teen-ager is concerned with becoming popular. If parents have taught and guided well during the periods of infancy and childhood, the teen-ager should realize that popularity will usually come if he has a natural manner, develops his talents, and is considerate of others.

During this period of life, development of social skills is important to the adolescent, and understanding adults, including parents, can help him develop these skills.

If the teen-ager has the self-confidence that comes from feeling "accepted" and having acquired a workable set of social skills, he usually has the poise that is necessary to engage in the activity which is extremely important to the future selection of a mate and marriage adjustment—getting acquainted with different kinds of personalities. The more different people he meets and learns to understand, the more practice he will get that will aid him in developing a good relationship with a future partner in marriage.

As far as preparing for marriage is concerned, the most important thing a teen-ager can do is to learn to understand himself and others. If he accomplishes this, he will be more capable of deciding whether his dating partner will be a suitable marriage companion.

As the child has the opportunity at home, and later in the school and community to learn to get along with others, he should develop the emotional sensitivity necessary to understand other people's moods, needs, and reactions. The development of such sensitivity should aid him in making the transition from egocentric to group-oriented behavior. Thus, his subsequent relations with other members of his group will be good if he combines this sensitivity with the ability to communicate and interact with them within a framework of mutual understanding. This sensitivity or socializing process does not happen all at once. It is also difficult for the individual to go through, because to achieve a favorable outcome from his efforts he must develop interpersonal relationships in which he exercises self-control and gets along with others without loss of his own self-esteem. To achieve this dual goal of learning to get along with others and still feel he is a respected individual, each person usually progresses through five stages of socialization. The highest stage is called that of creative cooperation, one in which the individual is able to make his own selfish needs secondary to the needs of the group. Obviously, some people never reach this highest level.

STAGES OF SOCIALIZATION

1. Receiving—Babies are constantly thinking about their own needs and if such are not met, they put up a fuss. They want what they want, when they want it. Explosive outbursts occur if they are hungry and not fed, or uncomfortable and not tended to.

Parents put up with this self-centered "gimme" attitude in babies because they know if their needs are not met, they will not survive.

But what about adults who remain on this babyhood level of behavior? Those who have not progressed from this receiving level are difficult to live with. Their expressions are a constant round of: "Give me this." "I want that." "You don't love me or you would do it." Such an attitude often leads to a behavioral pattern called narcissism, a self-love characterized by excessive interest in one's own appearance, comfort, importance, and so forth. Such a person is extremely difficult to live with in marriage.

Narcissism in marriage was demonstrated by one of the author's counseling clients who said she could not understand why her sexual adjustment in marriage was so unsatisfactory. Then she proceeded to answer her own question by saying that she felt she had been blessed with such a beautiful body that her husband should not expect to have frequent sexual contact with her.

If you or your intended marriage partner are still operating on this level, watch out! Fireworks are in the offing.

2. Manipulation—Babies soon learn that there is a relationship between what they do and what happens. Observe an infant coo when it is fondled or cry when it wants attention. It is learning to react in such a way that it gets what it wants in each particular situation. As it gets older, it may discover that it can get what it wants by teasing, coaxing, bribing, or resorting to temper tantrums.

It is important that parents offer firm resistance to such attempted manipulations. Otherwise the child might continue to practice them with disastrous results in adult life. Obvious attempts by adults to manipulate others often cause their actions to become suspect, and when they resort to tantrums to get their way, other persons who are involved with them have difficulty according them respect.

Typical adult manipulators whom the author has encountered were:

The professional man who lay on his stomach and beat his fists on the floor when his wife didn't go along with his desires.

The attractive young wife who sobbed, "You don't love me," when her husband said he couldn't afford to buy her a new fur coat.

The husky, young newlywed who got angry, doubled up his fists and dented their living room wall with savage blows, when his wife said she thought it would be extravagant for him to buy a new rifle.

3. Compromise—Children display encouraging social growth when they cease to operate on the levels of receiving and manipulation and learn how to compromise with others. This means that they have learned to recognize the rights, values and interests of others.

Have you ever watched two children at play in a sandpile? A typical situation is one in which Kathy is playing with Jack's blocks because he has agreed to let her, in return for using her pail and shovel.

Compromise is a common practice in adult society, and a skilled mediator who can persuade disagreeing factions such as labor and capital to compromise on a controversial issue commands a high fee for his services. During the early history of our nation, Henry Clay, a distinguished statesman, became known as "The Great Compromiser" because of his efforts to preserve the Union. He is best known as the author of the "Missouri Compromise" which restricted slavery in the territory that made up the Louisiana Purchase to the region lying south of 36° 30′ north latitude, except in the new state of Missouri.

Although learning to compromise is a positive step toward becoming a socialized person, it is by no means the most desirable way to interact with others. Husbands and wives who get along because they have learned to compromise still haven't developed an understanding and cooperative partnership.

4. Sharing—Someone has rightly said that when two people share, each individual possesses more than before. This pooling of resources can have beneficial effects on all levels of life. Children who learn to share their toys have more toys to play with, and if they continue their sharing ways as they grow older, they receive many advantages. For example, two teen-age sisters who share their blouses, slacks, and so forth, both have a more varied and attractive wardrobe.

Brothers also find it less expensive in the long run if they share their sports equipment.

Of course, husbands and wives who learn to share each other's interests and also feel that the material possessions of each may often profitably be used by both are on the road to building a satisfying marriage partnership.

5. Creative Cooperation—The rewards of this highest stage of socialization exceed those of any other stage.

If both married partners have reached this stage which enables them to view the needs of their partnership as more important than their individual needs they will have much smoother sailing in their marriage. Husbands and wives who function on the level of creative cooperation usually think and speak as follows:

> Young wife, "Of course I would like a new coat, but right now it is much more important that we use our money for Bill's college tuition so he can make progress toward getting a degree."

> Husband (to hunting pals), "I would like to go hunting with you fellows, but our little boy has outgrown his crib and we are spending our extra money to buy him a youth bed."

Do you catch the vision of having achieved the top level of socialization—that of creative cooperation? Family members who operate on this level always put the needs of the group first. This is done without any individual resentment or feeling of persecution, but simply because it seems the right thing to do.

One cannot assume that having reached the highest level of socialization, he will always operate on that level. Neither can it be taken for granted that a healthy personality indefinitely stays that way after it is once developed. Such functions and facets of personality are dynamic things which are constantly subject to change for better or worse. A basic factor which has much to do with continued and effective social functioning and maintaining a healthy personality is one's self-concept, more popularly called one's self-image.

MAINTAINING A POSITIVE SELF-IMAGE

A person who has a healthy personality will usually have a positive self-image. Yet it is important to realize that adverse conditions may often cause one's positive self-image to change to negative. The difficulties implicit in maintaining a positive self-image may be compared with the struggles a butterfly has as it attempts to fly to its goal against adverse wind currents. It may be happily winging its way, and then have a sudden downdraft push it below its course. It may then struggle valiantly to attain its previous flight level, and having regained it have the same blowing off course happen over again.

Humans also have similar difficulties in maintaining a positive self-image. An individual may feel pleased with himself and think he is playing his role in life well, when an adverse criticism or disheartening experience occurs and pushes him down off his course, weakens his self-confidence and makes him struggle to be optimistic about his future. And as with the butterfly these experiences may occur time and again and make it difficult for him to stay on his course.

The Importance of Self-Acceptance

Accepting one's self as a person of worth who has a definite role to play in life is an important factor in maintaining a positive self-image.

Religious writers have pointed out one possible way to do this, and have made a significant contribution to the principles of mental health with their stress on the worth of each individual person. Their point of view is that a person should not reject any part of himself, but instead that as a child of an all-wise and all-loving God he should accept himself in totality as one who has a definite role to play in God's plan.

No matter what the motivation, religious or otherwise, self-acceptance requires the following:

1. *Acceptance of the kind of body one has.*

People come in all sizes and shapes. The healthy personality accepts this fact, and makes the most of what he has. The male doesn't feel inferior because he is short, nor the female, self-conscious because she is tall, but both accept their basic bodily structure as a desirable part of themselves.

2. *Acceptance of one's sex.*

Babies come in two sexes—male and female. Unless the growing individual suffers from a hormone imbalance, or a physical anomaly that pushes him toward the role of the opposite sex, or has had a traumatic experience or conditioning that has made him feel the other sexual role would be more satisfying, he usually enjoys the sexual role to which he is born. Rejecting one's role of male or female and going through life being envious of the lot of the opposite sex does not enhance one's self-image. Some people cross over and play the role of the opposite sex in an effort to improve their self-concept. Regardless of these different behavioral patterns, the general statement may be used that the way one feels about his sex role is an important part of self-image.

3. *Acceptance of one's ethnic group or race.*

The healthy personality takes pride in being a member of a certain ethnic group or race. It is highly probable that most individuals at some time may be subjected to discrimination because of nationality or race. However, the well-adjusted individual does not let this diminish his pride in his heritage.

Emotional Stability and Self-Image

The individual's positive self-image may be shattered by emotional instability. Consequently, there are many contributing factors that should be understood if one is striving to keep his emotions on an even keel (in a state of equilibrium). There are many hypotheses concerning how this might best be done. Space will be given to a summary of a few basic things here.

Satisfaction of Human Needs

Physical Needs

Very few people can think positively when they are starving, nor can they live very long without taking liquids into their body. Neither can they function effectively if they don't have proper rest, shelter and exercise.

When the needs for food, liquids and other things that affect physiological functioning are met, the individual is said to be in a state of homeostasis. In other words, every part of his body is functioning in balance and he is free of aches and pains. There are seven basic needs, which if satisfied, help promote this state, yet they are often overlooked.

They are: air, liquid, food, elimination, rest, shelter, and exercise.

The individual who is deprived of air, liquid, and food, and is unable to eliminate waste from the body soon dies. Although the effects may not be so obvious or harm the physical self so soon, lack of rest, shelter and exercise can lead to general deterioration and eventual death. Therefore, it is logical that physical needs must be met if one would maintain a positive self-image.

Emotional Needs

If physical needs are met and emotional needs are left unsatisfied, a positive self-image is not likely to be maintained.

A few basic emotional needs are:

The need to feel secure against physical threats and dangers.

The need to receive attention or love.

The need to belong and possess status in a group in which one is accepted, valued, and appreciated.

The need for "self-actualization." Maslow suggests "self-actualization" as a need that comes directly from what he called the basic psychological needs for safety, love, and "self-actualization" and he defines it as "the need to fulfill the best that is in you."[2]

Even though one's needs are met, there is a constant challenge to defend one's self-image.

DEFENDING ONE'S SELF-IMAGE

Freud's Contribution to Understanding Self-Image

People are constantly required to defend their self-images, and each individual reacts differently to insults or to deprivation of emotional needs that present a threat to a positive self-image. To protect themselves against these threats, individuals have unconscious or semiconscious patterns of behavior which they learn in childhood and continue to use throughout life. Such patterns of adjusting to insults, conflict or frustration may be neither logical nor problem-solving, but they enable the person to maintain emotional balance.

---

[2]Maslow, Abraham H., *Motivation and Personality*, New York: Harper and Row, 1954.

Before discussing these patterns of adjustment, which are called defense mechanisms, something should be said about the phrase "unconscious patterns" which is used with a Freudian connotation.

Sigmund Freud was a Viennese neurologist, a specialist in diseases of the organic nervous system, who lived from 1856 to 1939. He is considered the father of the psychoanalytic approach to emotional problems. Today, he has become a controversial figure, and some accept his thinking while others reject it. Nevertheless, it is essential to have a simple grasp of his theory of personality in order to understand the psychological usage of the word "unconscious."

Freud postulated that the individual's total personality is made up of three major systems which he called the id, the ego, and the superego. He said that in the mentally healthy person these systems work together in harmony and enable the individual to have satisfactory transactions with his environment in which his basic needs and desires are fulfilled.

How does this happen?

Freud says that the id is found in the unconscious, the substructure of the personality which constitutes nine-tenths of the individual's psychic make-up. The unconscious also acts as a repository for all of the individual's experiences. When a baby is born, the id, which is an animalistic, unbridled drive, seeks expression in order to fulfill the initial principle of life, the pleasure principle, the aim of which is to reduce or rid the person of tension. Contained in the id is also the libido, the sex drive. The id has no morals, cannot tolerate tension, and wants immediate gratification, so it is demanding, irrational, and antisocial. Parents realize that their child cannot get along in society if it does not control the id, so they teach it what is considered acceptable and unacceptable behavior. The child incorporates these teachings (internalizes them) into its thinking and gradually builds a superego or moral code which acts as the internal policeman to the id. The superego is composed of the ego-ideal and the conscience. "The ego-ideal corresponds to the child's conceptions of what his parents consider to be morally good. The parents convey their standards of virtue to the child by rewarding him for conduct which is in line with their standards. For example, if he is consistently rewarded for being neat and tidy, then neatness is apt to become one of his ideals. Conscience, on the other hand, corresponds to the child's conceptions of what his parents feel is morally bad, and these are established through experiences of punishment. If he has been frequently punished for getting dirty, then dirtiness is considered to be something bad. Ego-ideal and conscience are opposite sides of the same moral coin."[3]

The superego, after it is established, attempts to regulate and control expressions from the id, namely, sexual and aggressive impulses which would endanger society.

The superego, which comes into being because of the pressures and demands of the external world, is in nearly constant conflict with the id. Therefore, it is necessary to have an executive in the personality to mediate between the superego and the id and so control them that the total personality can adjust harmoniously to its environment in the external world. This executive is the ego (self) which is the conscious, perceiving, organizing part of the personality. The ego continuously acts as an intermediary between the external world and the id and is governed by the reality principle, being conscious of the need to adjust to conditions as they exist.

Now, to return to the discussion of defending one's self-image. The foregoing brief discussion should make it clear, if Freudian thinking is accepted, that when unconscious patterns of behavior are used as defense mechanisms that a complex organization of psychological processes is put into action, much of which is not in the realm of our awareness.

When one's self-image is threatened, the anxiety resulting from the threat could be combatted by fighting back (direct aggression) or running away (complete withdrawal). However, very few people resort to either of these devices, instead according to Freud they react in unconscious ways to conflicts and frustrations. These defense mechanisms are employed in the everyday behavior of normal people. Most people probably could not continue to feel positive about themselves without using them. On the other hand, they can be used so frequently that they interfere with adequate functioning and impair emotional health.

DEFENSE MECHANISMS

The following adjustive or defense mechanisms are generally employed by the individual to defend his sense of personal worth. This helps him keep his emotional self in a state of equilibrium.

---

[3]Hall, Calvin S., *A Primer of Freudian Psychology*, New York: Mentor Books, 1955, p. 31.

Behavior Mechanisms

One of the reasons why we are not more conscious of the situations and occurrences of our everyday lives which are potential producers of anxiety is that we have developed techniques of ignoring or misinterpreting them and thus avoiding the anxiety we would experience if we saw them in their true proportions. Furthermore, when our anxiety is aroused we continue to use the same techniques so that we shall not feel its full force. It's important to note that these methods of dealing with anxiety operate unconsciously or almost entirely so. In other words, when we employ a behavior mechanism, we are not only unaware of the anxiety we are avoiding, but we are even unaware that we are using a device to avoid or disguise it.

Some behavior mechanisms are described below:

Rationalization: The practice of giving explanations for behavior which are quite reasonable, but which do not reveal the more basic and fundamental reasons for the behavior. Example: The person who blames the bus for his being late, when he really overslept.

Projection: Appears in situations in which individuals ascribe their own motives or feelings to the acts or statements of others. Projection also occurs when individuals misinterpret or distort their perceptions of persons, situations, or events. Example: The person who sings off key and says, "I was the only one who kept in tune."

Compensation: A device we use to bolster our feeling of adequacy as a way of avoiding the anxiety that would be incurred in facing or admitting some real or fancied weakness. Example: The individual who would prefer to shout rather than admit he is wrong.

Reaction Formation: A special form of compensation. Persons who employ this maneuver develop actions or attitudes which are at opposite extremes from impulses which they fear and which would produce much anxiety if expressed. Example: The person who would like to drink, but does not, and compensates by condemning those that do.

Introjection: The adoption of attitudes and ideas from parents, friends, teachers, etc., which make a person the same as the rest of the group. Example: The person who says, "I am a Republican because my family is."

Identification: The automatic imitation of the behavior or mannerisms of another person. This works hand in hand with introjection, and usually takes place when there are strong emotional ties with another. Example: The girl who says, "I just love this dress; it's exactly like Jackie's."

Sublimation: The means by which persons convert their drives, such as sex, hunger, hostility, etc., into patterns that are acceptable to family, friends, and other social groups. Example: The husband who arrives home ravenously hungry, but waits until dinnertime to eat so that his wife won't be upset.

Idealization: The unrealistic rating of someone or something as being perfect rather than as is actually the case. Example: The woman who has remarried and tells her second husband that he is not "half the man" her first husband was, or the teen-ager who thinks that going to another school would be perfect.

Displacement: The transfer of an emotion produced in one situation to another unrelated situation. Example: The man who goes home and shouts at his wife in place of talking back to his boss.

Conversion: The shifting of an emotional upset into a physical upset. Example: The teen-ager who is so worried about the final examination that he gets a headache.

Fantasy: The act of daydreaming or engaging in reverie. Example: The individual who withdraws from reality.

Negativism: The tendency to do the opposite of what is expected or ordered. Example: The person who always disagrees with others' ideas.

Suppression: The act of consciously inhibiting an impulse, emotion or idea, as in the deliberate attempt to forget something and think no more about it. Example: The person who displays the Scarlet O'Hara tendency to say, "I'll think about the problem tomorrow."

Repression: The unconscious tendency to exclude from consciousness unpleasant or painful ideas. Example: The individual who has been hurt in an accident and can't remember what happened.

Regression: Retreating to a childish or less mature behavior pattern in order to escape frustrations in the present situation. Example: The person who has a tantrum when the situation becomes difficult.

Fixation: Abnormal attachment of the libido (sex drive) to some person, object, or level of psychic development. Example: The individual who behaves on the babyhood level of self-love.

Suggested Readings

1. Aller, Florence D., "Self-Concept in Student Marital Adjustment," *Family Life Coordinator,* 11 (April, 1962), 43-45.

2. Bennett, E. M., and Cohen, L. R., "Men and Women: Personality Patterns and Contrasts," *Genetic Psychology Monographs,* 59 (1959), 101-155.

3. Berne, Eric, *Games People Play, The Psychology of Human Relationships,* New York: Grove Press, Inc., 1964.

4. Bossard, James H. S., and Boll, Eleanor, *The Sociology of Child Development,* New York: Harper & Row Co., 1966.

5. Duvall, Evelyn M., "Adolescent Love as a Reflection of Teenager's Search for Identity," *Journal of Marriage and the Family,* 26 (May 1964), 226-229.

6. Fast, Julius, *Body Language,* New York: M. Evans & Co., 1970.

7. Frankl, Viktor E., *Man's Search for Meaning,* Boston: Beacon Press, 1962 (Revis. ed.).

8. Harris, Thomas A., *I'm OK—You're OK,* New York: Harper & Row, 1969.

9. Langer, Ellen J. and Dweck, Carol S., *Personal Politics, The Psychology of Making It,* Englewood Cliffs, N.J.: Prentice-Hall, Inc., 1973.

10. Moss, Joel and Gingles, Ruby, "The Relationship of Personality to the Incidence of Early Marriage," *Marriage and Family Living,* 21 (Nov. 1959) 373-377.

11. Powell, John, *Why Am I Afraid to Tell You Who I Am?,* Chicago: Argus Communications Co., 1969.

12. Van Dyke, Vonda Kay, *That Girl in Your Mirror,* Westwood, N.J.: Fleming H. Revell Co., 1966.

Chapter V

American Dating Patterns and Personal Growth

THE AMERICAN DATING SYSTEM

The American dating system that allows free individual mate selection has been widely criticized for its permissive structuring of dating practices. Nevertheless, this system is being adopted in many other parts of the world as young people are beginning to demand the right to choose their own mates. Some characteristics of the dating patterns in our culture in addition to free individual choice of a mate are:

Early Dating

Studies show that the median age for starting to date is fourteen, although interestingly enough, some individuals start before eleven.

Dating With Very Little or No Chaperonage

The present age of affluence in the United States has made it possible for many teen-agers to have access to automobiles for dating purposes. The resulting increased mobility has placed the responsibility for controlling sexual behavior in dating relationships squarely upon the dating partners. Often, teen-agers are unable to handle the freedom, and to some a car becomes a mobile bedroom which leads to unfortunate consequences.

Breaking Down of Class Barriers in Selecting Dating Partners

The growth of an urban industrial culture and a highly mobile population has enabled young people to have contact with, and consequently, date more individuals of different ethnic and racial origins and religious backgrounds. The American frontier early banished caste lines, but today increased mobility has promoted greater mingling with persons of different origins and background.

Affectional Expression in Dating

Until the last few years, American girls have been considered promiscuous by European women who have frowned upon the American practice of necking and petting on casual dates. The traditional European approach has been to withhold affectional favors until dating partners have made a commitment to each other. Current reports from Europe now suggest that girls are moving toward American practices.

An interesting European attitude toward expressing affection on dates was brought vividly to the writer's attention when he was doing research on European dating patterns on a recent trip abroad.

For example, in one area in Switzerland, it was learned that couples shook hands at the beginning and end of a date and avoided any bodily contact during the period of the date.

EARLY MARRIAGE AS A RESULT OF SEXUAL INVOLVEMENT

Current statistics released by the Population Reference Bureau reveal that forty percent of today's brides in the United States are between fifteen and eighteen years of age, and forty percent of these marriages took place when the girl was pregnant.

Although premarital pregnancy rates appear to be staying about the same, there does seem to be a slight tendency toward later marriage, which may be accounted for to some extent by some college students who are questioning marriage as an institution and living together for some time before undergoing any legal ceremony.

TYPES OF DATING

A date is a spoken agreement between individuals to meet and associate with each other for some specific purpose. Usually the individual goes through the following types of dating as he or she progresses toward finding a marriage partner.

Group Dating

Casual Single Dating

Dating Steadily

Going Steady

Engaged to be Engaged

Engaged

Before discussing these types of dating, it must be stated that some persons do not follow these dating patterns, and may develop a going-steady relationship with the first dating partner they meet. However, a brief analysis of the results of going through the different types of dating in chronological sequence indicates that certain advantages result.

Group Dating

Group dating offers a setting in which a teen-ager can learn about the life-styles and attitudes of his community's adolescent world. It's no secret that today's adolescents have fashioned a culture of their own. Their manner of dress, ways of communicating, and patterns of behavior differ sharply from those of the adult world. Inasmuch as a date is an agreement to meet with another person for some specific purpose, it is of great help to the inexperienced person if he or she can fulfill this agreement in a group setting without feeling the threat of not knowing how to behave in a one-to-one or single dating relationship. This gives the shy boy the opportunity to observe how the other fellows talk to and treat girls. And the girl who is lacking in self-confidence can mingle with the group during parties, dances and other programmed activities, without feeling the need to be a constantly entertaining conversational companion to her partner. She can also watch, listen, and learn how the most popular girls talk and act around boys.

Such group experiences also enable individuals of both sexes to learn what types of personalities they enjoy, and help them build personal friendships in the group that may later become a basis for single dating and possible mate selection. Another often overlooked advantage of group dating is that individuals who start dating as a group experience and later go steady have established friends to turn to who can help ease the shock of a broken going-steady relationship. It is much easier for girls or fellows to get back into circulation socially after breaking up such a relationship if friends from their former dating group know and appreciate them as personalities.

Church and school groups and community activities which have some adult sponsorship and are also subject to some adult supervision usually provide the most desirable group settings for boy-girl social activities. Unsophisticated teen-agers who join questionable social groups devoid of adult supervision may unwittingly begin engaging in undesirable social behavior in an attempt to be popular.

Casual Single Dating

Casual dating involves the random selection of a dating partner. A fellow may be attracted by a girl's smile, or notice that she is a good dancer and want to take her out. On the other hand, a girl may be interested in having a date with a fellow because he is an athletic hero or popular on the campus. This playing the field of potential dating partners usually involves fleeting relationships with little sense of commitment. They may be quite impersonal, with slight involvement beyond the particular date.

Such casual dating affords an opportunity to get acquainted with different personalities, keep busy with interesting social activities, and gain practice in developing social skills. However, it cannot be a substitute for getting thoroughly acquainted with several persons.

Dating Steadily
(The noncommitment steady date.)

Dating one person repeatedly with no sense of commitment has the advantage of giving one more insight into different types of personalities. In contrast to casual dating, in which contacts are fleeting, dating steadily enables both partners to learn more about basic differences in people. Such a practice also offers the advantages of gaining new depths of understanding in a companionship relationship along with the opportunity of dating other partners during the same period of time. Consequently, the persons involved have the opportunity to make more precise comparisons of the individual differences in their various dating partners.

One disadvantage to the girl who dates casually or steadily is that she is subject to the initiation of action by the male. In other words, she doesn't usually take the initiative and ask for a date, and in most cases is asked to go to some event that her male partner had in mind. Many of today's girls, especially those who are pushing for women's liberation, think this is nonsense. Nevertheless, most dating partners are still influenced by the patriarchal structure in our society which casts the male in the role of the aggressor in relationships between the sexes.

Going Steady

The interpretation of going steady varies in different communities and with different persons. To some, it means dating twice a week for at least three months. To others, it implies a commitment to one's partner to consider future marriage. Still others, take the practice of going steady lightly and have the attitude of one coed who said, "I'm going steady with Terry and I save all of my weekends for him. But of course, whomever else I date during the week is none of his business."

So, going steady may be thought of as a temporary and mutually convenient arrangement between the couple or as indicating a serious interest in marriage.

Advantages

Some of the reasons given by students for going steady are:

Prestige—You rate with the group.

In some communities, going steady is a status symbol, and insecure people engage in it to build their self-confidence.

It is less expensive—Both persons are satisfied to find entertainment at home with simple pleasures. A fellow doesn't have to spend money to keep his girlfriend interested, and she in turn learns to value his true qualities more than the money he spends on her.

Social security—Steady dating insures a satisfying social life. You always have a date for important events. It also provides instant dating, so the girl doesn't have to be miserable wanting to date and hoping the phone will ring, and the fellow doesn't have to go through the embarrassment of being turned down for a date.

Understanding companionship—The couple gets to know and confide in each other. They have opportunities to learn to share and not take advantage of each other. Feelings of loneliness and rejection can be avoided because you always know there is someone who cares and is concerned about your future.

Preparation for marriage—Steady dating gives you practice in preparing for marriage because you have made a commitment to each other.

Two-way initiation of action—An advantage to the girl and a practice that probably helps the relationship is the fact that the male is no longer the sole initiator of the action. The fact that both persons have made a commitment to each other makes it possible for the girl to feel freer in suggesting dating appointments and activities to engage in. She should be able to do this without being accused of pursuing her boyfriend inasmuch as he has shown his preference for being with her.

Disadvantages

Some reasons given by students for avoiding steady dating are:

Steady dating is too limiting—You get out of circulation. It cuts down the number of your dating partners, and you are deprived of the wider experience of casual or close dating relationships with other interesting persons.

You can become bored with each other—One or the other may lose interest.

The partners' difference in degree of involvement in the going-steady relationship can cause trouble. If the couple breaks up, the person who has taken the relationship more seriously may suffer an emotional hurt that leads to loss of self-confidence or a state of depression.

It is easy to become emotionally and sexually involved—Emotional involvement may cause feelings of frustration and a negative attitude toward school and friends. Sexual involvement may lead to pregnancy and undesirable marriage.

The type of emotional involvement which may lead to an undesirable marriage is illustrated by the following story. It was told by Kate, an attractive seventeen-year-old coed, who came to the writer's office for counseling.

She said: "I came to you for help because I do not know where else to turn. I'm supposed to get married the week after next, and everyone in our small town is looking forward to my wedding as the social event of the season. The trouble is, I don't love my fiance, but I am afraid to break our engagement. We started going steady when I was fifteen. After going together for a year, I realized that I didn't love Jack and I tried to break up. He refused, got drunk, and drove his car off the road in an attempt to kill himself. He was in the hospital for two weeks and I felt it was my fault and that he must have a great love for me, so we started going together again. Now, I feel the same way as I did before, that we are not suited to each other, but Jack tells me if I ever withdraw my love from him again that he will do a better job than he did last time in attempting to commit suicide. Please help me. I'm afraid and do not know what to do."

After discussing Kate's situation, it was decided that she should postpone her wedding, and tell Jack it was necessary because she had to leave town immediately and take care of her elder married sister who had moved to another state, and was expecting her first baby within a few days. It was hoped then that all of the town interest in the wedding would subside and Kate could subsequently, quietly and gracefully avoid the marriage.

But the plan did not work out. Kate lacked the courage to tell Jack of her intended change in plans, and the following week she married him, on schedule, a man she did not love.

Engaged to Be Engaged
(Pinning)

A practice that developed after World War II is a quasi-engagement arrangement known as pinning or chaining. This is nothing more than a trial period of tentative commitment in which the couple explores their feelings about becoming formally engaged. The same advantages and disadvantages of going steady are present in this arrangement. However, there is a new dimension added to the relationship, in that it is oriented to the future and possible marriage.

Why don't these couples just become engaged?

There could be a number of reasons. It is less expensive for the fellow to give his girlfriend his school ring or fraternity pin, or for the two of them to put their fraternity pins together on a chain. It may be a campus practice that meets with peer-group acceptance and accords the couple certain social status. And finally, it's not considered as firm a commitment to possible future marriage. Thus those partners who have secret reservations about continuing on to marriage would have fewer guilt feelings related to breaking off the relationship.

Engaged

When a couple becomes formally engaged, they make it known to the public that they are getting ready for marriage. Such a relationship is highly personalized, monogamous, intimate and filled with emotional involvement. It is a definite planning period which is oriented to the future. Because it is a relationship that is definitely correlated with future marital happiness, it will be discussed in detail in a subsequent chapter.

INDIVIDUAL GROWTH IN DATING
Consideration for Others

When individuals begin dating, much more than recreation is involved. Although motives for dating may not consciously be tied in with future marriage, dating participants will be better prepared for married life if they learn to understand the opposite sex and develop skills in interpersonal relationships. They are more likely to succeed in this if they consider their family as a group who can offer helpful suggestions to them as they encounter different experiences in the dating world.

Some teen-agers fail to do this. In fact, they try to burn their family bridges behind them and want "to do their own thing" with no restraints. This should not happen. Young people who date should be reminded that they are still part of the family group, and they should conduct themselves as considerate members. They should bring their partners into their home and introduce them to the family. They should also tell their parents where they are going and what time they intend to return home. If the time for return seems unreasonable to parents, all concerned should discuss the planned activities, and then a mutual decision as to a reasonable time to get back home should be made. This practice will do much to avoid ill feelings and family tensions.

Sometimes college students feel they should have complete freedom in their dating practices. This is not desirable if they are living at home with their families. This point of view was given by one student:

"I feel that my parents are completely stupid and old-fashioned fogies. They blew their tops last week-end, and I have about decided to leave home. This is what happened. Dad let my boyfriend and me take the family car and we went to a movie. After the show was over, it was such a beautiful night that we decided to go for a drive, and before we knew it we were in Duluth (180 miles away). We were both so tired that we didn't feel like driving back home, so we went to a hotel and spent the night in separate rooms. We awoke at noon the next day and I phoned my folks and told them where we were. They were furious and said I was extremely inconsiderate. I think they are narrow-minded. After all, I'm a college student and a mature woman, and if I want to stay out all night with my boyfriend, it is none of their business."

It took a joint counseling session with the coed and her parents before she finally realized that her parents had a right to be angry.

If there is a climate of understanding in the home, and family members can talk to one another easily and freely, those who date can gain reassurance from parents and their brothers and sisters when they meet with dating problems which are difficult to handle.

Anne demonstrated this when she said, "My mother is just like a big sister to me. A lot of the fun I have in dating comes from telling her where I went and what I did. She's helped me through many rough times."

Judy, who felt differently about her family relationships, said: "Where I go and what I do is my own business. If I told my parents what happens on my dates, they'd probably kick me out of the house."

Subsequent counseling sessions with Judy brought out the fact that her parents had unwittingly contributed to her hostile attitude toward them. They had never listened to her in an objective way, or tried to see her viewpoint. They had always treated her with distrust, and when she left for a date would say, "Try to get back at a decent time. You're going to get into trouble if you don't change your ways."

During one counseling session Judy looked sad as she said, "You know, my parents act like I have no moral standards. They seem to think that I go to bed with every guy I date. I've never gone all the way with my date, but perhaps I should, as long as they think I do."

It is quite apparent that teen-agers won't get much help from their families during their dating days unless parents and other family members treat them as respected individuals, listen to them with understanding, try to see their viewpoint, and work with them to find mutually satisfying solutions to problems and differences of opinion.

PREFERRED QUALITIES IN DATING PARTNERS

Many teen-agers who are engaged in random dating are preoccupied with the question, "How do I rate as a date?" If you have the same concern, studies show that being natural and cultivating desired personality characteristics will help boost your rating.

But what are the most highly desired qualities?

Many studies have been made and long lists have been compiled to answer this question. The author studied a cross-section of University of Minnesota students and compared the findings with those of representative studies of other college and high school students (1973). An interesting finding resulted.

Dating participants indicated that the qualities desired in a dating companion and a marriage partner are about the same.

The following basic qualities appeared near the top of both types of surveys.

1. Pleasant disposition.
2. Considerate.
3. Sociable and natural.
4. Sense of humor.
5. Same interests and standards.
6. Neat in appearance.
7. Stable and dependable.

Such a list is reassuring because it indicates that one does not have to be a superstar in order to rate high as a date or as a possible marriage partner.

DEVELOPMENT OF INTERPERSONAL SKILLS

In today's society, individuals who are skilled in interpersonal relations are in demand in the business, civic, and social worlds. This is so, because they have learned how to get along with people and communicate effectively with them.

The development of such skills is equally important in dating relationships, and dating provides opportunities to develop skills that are not only useful in marriage, but also contribute to success in the world outside of the home.

The Art of Communication

Much misunderstanding exists in the world today because people do not know how to communicate. How often have you had a friend say, "I don't understand your viewpoint," or "Why don't you listen to me"?

Effective communication depends upon three basic things, nonverbal expression, verbal expression and empathy. Lack of understanding in using these contributing factors can cause dating problems and marriage difficulties to develop. Many a dating relationship never got off the ground, or has deteriorated because the involved partners couldn't communicate.

A typical example of inability to communicate on a date was given by Sybil. She said:

"The first time I saw Tad in class, he impressed me as a sharp guy and I secretly hoped he would date me. Finally, the big moment arrived, he asked me to the school dance. You know when we got out on the dance floor, I froze. I was so afraid I'd say the wrong thing that my lips were paralyzed. I don't know what he was thinking, but he didn't say anything either. Finally, after we had danced about an hour, he looked at me and asked, 'Do you think using Ever-brite toothpaste, like the ads say, really gets your teeth whiter?'

"I couldn't understand why he was talking about teeth. Maybe mine looked dingy. Anyway, I managed to stammer, 'Golly, I don't know, I've never tried it.'

"Can you believe it? That's all we said to each other during the entire dance. Tad hasn't dated me since and I suppose he thinks I'm stupid, but what could I do? I didn't know what to say?"

If you have difficulty communicating and want to avoid an experience similar to Sybil's, you should get busy and work at expressing yourself.

Non-verbal Communication

First, let's look at nonverbal communication. Fast[1] suggests some techniques that should be helpful.

Some of his ideas are:

Don't wear a face mask. Rigid features don't let your real feelings come through. Let your emotions, such as smiling or sadness, come from within. People will understand you better.

Talk with your eyes. Eyes that show interest sometimes speak more eloquently than words.

Body posture can telegraph your thoughts. The way you use your arms and hands, move your eyes, set your mouth, sit, stand or walk can reveal what's going on inside your mind.

Fast suggests that you play the game of body language consciously and it will help your associations with others.

Verbal Communication

Effective verbal communication consists of having something to talk about, and then knowing when and how to talk and when and how to listen.

With the flood of reading material that is available nowadays and the information that is projected via television, radio, and movies, a person who says he has nothing to talk about would have to be turned off

---

[1]Fast, Julius, *Body Language*, New York: M. Evans and Company, 1970.

from life. Girls who date are quite sure of getting an interesting conversation started if they can talk to their boyfriend about sports. Fellows can usually evoke interested response from their female companions if they know something about women's clothing styles.

Proper timing is important in deciding when to talk. Nonstop talkers are not the most sought after companions. One must develop conversational sensitivity when talking with others. For example, knowing when to ask your companion what he or she is thinking is extremely important. Sensing when to remain silent and avoid any comment also can make dialogue take place more smoothly.

The art of being a good listener is sadly neglected. There are times to listen with animation and make such comments as: "Well, how about that!" "How delightful!" "I appreciate how you feel." And there are times to remain silent and respond with an understanding look. However, in all cases, the listener should give the speaker his full attention. There is nothing more ego deflating to one who is talking than to have a listener show half-hearted attention or indifference to what is being said.

Empathy

Communication can never be completely effective without empathy, which is the ability to project one's own consciousness into another being. In other words, it is knowing how to perceive your partner's feelings and attitudes. The ability to use empathy can only come with practice, and dating provides abundant opportunities for the same. To become a skillful empathizer, one must learn to sense a dating partner's needs and wishes, be aware of his changing moods, and be sensitive to the areas of discussion that should be entered into diplomatically. To do this, it is necessary to listen carefully in order to interpret the partner's voice tone properly and know what he or she is trying to convey with the use of certain words and expressions.

It is also extremely important to be sensitive to nonverbal clues and interpret facial expressions, body posture and movements.

It should be made clear that empathy and sympathy are not the same thing. Sympathy involves agreement or fellow-feeling with one's date. Empathy is a skill that enables one to perceive his attitudes and feelings. A more detailed discussion of communication will be given later in the chapter "Communication and Married Love."

Making Satisfying Mutual Decisions

Dating partners gain needed practice for settling problems after marriage, if they learn to decide what to do when both have different preferences. If the fellow wants to go to a ballgame and his girlfriend would prefer to hear a concert, learning how to make a choice satisfying to both partners fosters personal growth.

Developing the Ability to Make a Commitment

Individuals who are critical of the institution of marriage say that couples who take marriage vows are unrealistic, because a male and a female who are biologically and psychologically different and are the products of different environments are not capable of making commitments to each other.

This would undoubtedly be true if each person grew up in isolation on his or her own island and had no interaction with other humans until getting married. But with rare exceptions, people have opportunities for learning how to make commitments with others from their childhood on.

During dating days many opportunities are afforded to make tentative commitments on a partnership basis. And as the individual meets and assesses personality types and gradually sorts out the kind of person he wants for a marriage companion, his desire and ability to make a lasting commitment should grow. Ordinarily, by the time marriage is scheduled to take place both partners should be eager to and capable of making a commitment. If such is not the case, problems of individual personal adjustment may be interfering.

Other Indications of Personal Growth and Readiness for Marriage

It would be unrealistic to try to give an exhaustive list of indications of the average individual's personal growth during the dating period. So just a few other things will be mentioned in summary.

Understanding and learning to care for one's physical self.

An individual is better prepared for marriage if he or she has developed good habits as related to adequate rest, proper diet, and sufficient exercise so his or her body will function at peak efficiency.

Learning to define and work toward goals.

Major objectives usually include educational growth, choice of a vocation, and successful marriage. These and other goals should be clearly defined and plans made and followed in order to achieve them.

Developing a sound attitude toward sex.

This means understanding sex as a natural part of life. Also learning how sex may be utilized in making satisfying adjustments in life and marriage.

Developing the insight and maturity needed to make personal adjustments that become necessary at different age levels. Surely an individual about to marry should behave in a more socialized manner than a young teen-ager.

Deciding upon standards and ideals that one wants to follow in life. Life standards and ideals do not suddenly develop after the wedding. There is a much better chance for marital happiness if both partners understand and accept each other's ideals before marriage.

Developing a satisfying philosophy of life.

Finding answers to the age-old questions of, Who am I? Where did I come from? Where am I going? will help each individual and each couple to operate in a life's framework of greater understanding and more security.

Suggested Readings

1. Blood, Robert O., Jr., *Marriage,* New York: The Free Press, 1969, (2nd ed.), Chapter 1, "Dating: Practice for Marriage."

2. Burchinal, Lee G., "The Premarital Dyad and Love Involvement," in Christensen, Harold T. (ed.), *Handbook of Marriage and the Family,* Chicago: 1964, Chapter 16.

3. Duvall, Evelyn M., *The Art of Dating,* New York: Association Press, 1967.

4. McGinnis, Tom, *A Girl's Guide to Dating and Going Steady,* Garden City, N.Y.: Doubleday and Co., 1968.

5. Saltman, Jules (ed.), *Teen Love, Teen Marriage,* New York: Grosset and Dunlap, 1966.

6. Turner, E. S., *A History of Courting,* New York: E. P. Dutton & Co., Inc., 1955.

Chapter VI

Premarital Sex Standards and Practices

PREPARATION FOR DATING

Sexual desire may or may not be the starting point of courtship, or the reason for dating. Nevertheless, whenever it is present, it may cause dating partners to give it too much stress and interfere with their developing a fully personal relationship in which they might learn about all of the interests that they share. The individual's sex drive is the moving force behind the impulse to physical intimacy. Consequently, in order to handle it properly, dating partners should know something about it, and they should realize that its need for expression results from normal physiological processes—the secretion of hormones into the bloodstream and the accumulation of semen in the male sex glands. They should also understand that the drive can be restrained by conditioning and that the human mind triggers its overt expression.

Dr. Joseph B. Trainer and his associates performed studies at the University of Oregon which revealed how the impulse toward sex arises. He reported the following findings in a paper given before the Illinois State Medical Society:

"Man, unlike other animals, is impelled toward sex almost continually.

"Sex is usually thought of as an activity which can be turned on and off at will. But our studies have shown that it is an automatic, unconscious, repetitive activity."

The impulse toward sex arises from the erotic nerve endings in the skin of the face and other parts of the body, Dr. Trainer said.

Once started, the impulses travel uninhibited up through the nervous system to the brain, which activates the hormonal and genital systems.

Fortunately, the higher centers of the brain constantly step in and abort the relentless process. Otherwise, males would be involved in sexual activity almost constantly, in contrast to all other animals, in which the activity is only periodic.

"From a physiological point of view, man has a conscious sex drive that peaks every 20 to 40 hours." In females, the sex hunger occurs only every 320 hours, he said.[1]

Parents can play an important role in disseminating such information, and before their sons and daughters begin dating they should also tell them how their bodies react to sexual stimulation.

This knowledge should be given to them by their parents in adequate detail and within a framework of sound values. A considerable number of parents fail miserably in discharging this responsibility, and as a result, many of their children engage in permissive sexual activity, doing so in complete ignorance of the possible consequences.

This lack of knowledge may cause a girl to stop dating a fellow simply because she misinterprets his difficulty in controlling his sexual feelings and labels him in her mind as an animal whose only interest in her is sexual.

The boy may become frustrated and "drop" a girl he really likes, because her lack of physical warmth leads him to think that she has no serious interest in him.

Many of these unhappy incidents would not occur if the couple's parents had helped them to understand each other's sexual natures.

The following excerpt from a college student's paper graphically portrays the feelings of the girl whose parents told her nothing about sex:

> The item which has most greatly affected my life is lack of sex education in our home. As a child I must have been pretty "dense," because I don't ever recall asking either of my parents any questions pertaining to sex. I don't know if my mother thought I knew all the answers or what the deal was, but she never made any effort to explain the facts of life to me. If my best girlfriend hadn't answered many of my questions I still wouldn't know anything about sex. This may seem hard to believe, but not until fall quarter of this year did I know how a couple had intercourse. After learning some of the facts from my girlfriend, I began reading books and magazine articles on the subject.
>
> This lack of information has so greatly affected my life that I can hardly believe it. One example of this took place last summer when the boy I was going with came up from Miles City, where he lives, to visit me. He had just graduated from college. Thus he was four

---

[1]Snider, Arthur J., *Chicago Daily News*, June 10, 1971.

years older than myself. One night he was trying to make love to me, and I just couldn't understand why a boy would want to unbutton my blouse and when I didn't let him he was rather disturbed. I only wish I would have known the facts of life, then I would have been able to understand his feelings and desires. In his mind, because I didn't show any affection toward him, I didn't like him, so that ended that romance. Now I blame my mother because if she would have given me the proper sex education I might not have lost him.

I have found out that girls who have had early sex education are more at ease in mixed situations, and in many cases are more successful socially, because they are sure of themselves.

The lack of sex education has made my morals extremely high because I am afraid of it. I just cannot accept the idea that sex is a natural part of life and that it isn't a dirty, vulgar thing.

This account needs no comment. Perhaps the only statement to make is that it represents the thinking of many girls who receive no sex education at home.

What about fellows? Do they also feel a need to receive information pertaining to sex from their parents?

Listen to this student's viewpoint:

I was never the kind of person who wanted to confide in my parents with problems I have or had. It's not that they won't understand or something like that, but around our house you just don't talk about such matters which are personal to you. If something bothers me to a point where I must tell someone, I will usually tell my girlfriend. I trust her and she always provides comfort. I don't want you to get me wrong, my parents are very good to me, but as I stated before, in some houses the parents talk freely with the children about sex and personal problems, but at our house this subject is avoided almost completely. I will say, that my family, when I am married, will speak more freely on sex. I actually gained more from this course than I ever knew before.

Let us consider the information parents can give their sons and daughters in order to improve their dating relationships. The young man and young woman both should know that the male is usually more easily aroused sexually than the female. This is partly due to the fact that his sexual feelings are more localized in the genital area. The female is quite different from the male in that her sexual feelings tend to be more diffused throughout her entire body. She likes to be petted and caressed, but usually experiences no urgent need for actual intercourse.

The male's sexual sensitivity and response are much more spontaneous than the female's. He is extremely interested in seeing and exploring the female body. The teen-age girl on the other hand, usually has less interest in such activities. She is more likely to "give herself" to her boyfriend as part of their love, rather than because she seeks sexual gratification.

Of course, the male and female should know much more about sex differences than the few things mentioned above. A general summary is presented below.

In presenting the following chart of differences between the sexual natures of men and women, it must be understood that the descriptions are generalizations. There are individuals of each sex whose patterns will deviate from the norms which are presented. Also, no attempt has been made to indicate whether the differences are biologically determined or have been brought about by environmental influences.

Differences in the Sexual Natures of Men and Women

Men

1. Considerable interest in sex and the discussion of sexual activities.

2. Early development of sexual responsiveness which reaches its peak in the late teens and early twenties and subsequently gradually declines into old age. (Disclosed by Kinsey's research.)

3. "Sexual capacity is determined by the ability of the nervous and muscular systems to respond to sexual stimuli by orgasm and to recuperate from that experience to the point where orgasm can again be experienced. This capacity varies from person to person and probably represents the actual physical sex difference between individuals."[2]

4. Accumulation of seminal fluid may constitute an internal stimulus for sex outlet. Recent research tends to negate this thinking as it relates to sexual desire, but even so, the same process does not occur in the female.

Women

1. Less interest in sex and the discussion of sexual activities per se. Tend to think of sex more in the context of love and affection.

2. Later development of sexual responsiveness which reaches its peak in the late twenties and then maintains about the same level throughout life.

3. It is thought that the sexual capacity of the female is determined by the same factors as those which determine the capacity of the male.

4. There is nothing equivalent to the accumulation of seminal fluids within the female body.

[2]Kirkendall, Lester A., "Sex Drive." Ellis, Albert and Abarbanel, Albert, *The Encyclopedia of Sexual Behavior*, New York: Hawthorn Books, Inc., 1961, Vol. 2, p. 944.

5. Nocturnal emissions experienced by most males, and they are usually accompanied by sexual dreams.

6. A greater tendency to masturbate. Could be partly due to the fact that the male genitals are more readily available and easily viewed than those of the female.

7. Experience orgasm plus ejaculation, but cannot achieve orgasm as frequently as the female within a limited span of time.

8. Experience nothing equivalent to menstruation.

9. Sensory arousal.
   a. Interested in tactile sensations. Like to touch and be touched by the opposite sex.
   b. Sexual impulse more localized in the genital organs.
   c. Sexually stimulated by seeing the female body, nude pictures, burlesque shows, and so forth. Thinking about or dancing with desirable women may also be sources of erotic stimulation.

10. Have a greater tendency to dissociate sex from tenderness, love, and an over-all pattern of affection and companionship.

5. A high percentage of women may also have sexual dreams which sometimes lead to orgasm, but they experience nothing which is equivalent to nocturnal emissions.

6. Masturbation engaged in by fewer females and probably during briefer periods of life.

7. Experience orgasm which is accompanied by internal throbbing, but have nothing comparable to the male ejaculation.

8. Menstruate.

9. Sensory arousal.
   a. Less interest in tactile sensations. May enjoy being caressed, but not extremely interested in touchin the male body.
   b. Sexual impulse more diffused throughout the body.
   c. Have no intense interest in seeing the male body or having the other sensory experiences which stimulate men.

10. Tend to see sex more in the context of love, companionship, and togetherness, rather than in terms of an isolated physical drive which needs orgastic release.[3]

A knowledge of these differences between the sexes should make it easier for one to develop more satisfactory relations with a member of the opposite sex. Naturally, when it comes to choosing a mate, the experiences and characteristics of the two concerned persons should be recognized and understood. It may well be that each of the partners deviates somewhat from the normative sex differences between male and female which have been presented here. Nevertheless, unintentional offense to the other person will be less likely to be committed if both persons are aware of the typical differences between the sexes as related to their sexual natures.

SEXUAL INVOLVEMENT IN DATING

Even though dating participants have adequate information about their own sexual drives and understand the differences in the sexual

---

[3]Anderson, Wayne J., *How to Understand Sex—Guidelines for Students*, Minneapolis: T. S. Denison & Co., 1966, pp. 119-120. Reprinted by permission.

natures of men and women, they still may have problems of affectional control in the actual dating situation. The fellow may feel that if he lets his sexual impulses go, he may be rebuffed and spoil what could have otherwise been a pleasant relationship. The girl, on the other hand, is faced with the dilemma of deciding whether she is giving too much affection or acting too reserved. She realizes that either choice might make her a loser. Being openly affectionate, may lessen her desirability in the boy's mind and also result in a general lowering of her reputation. Whereas choosing to be reserved, may discourage her current partner or others from asking her for future dates. Because dating partners seem unable to discuss their sexual feelings frankly with each other and they receive conflicting advice on controlling them if they seek information from either their peers or adults, they often resort to playing games on their dates. Of course, this hinders their progress in developing full and satisfying interpersonal relationships.

TYPES OF SEXUAL EXPRESSION USED BY DATING PARTNERS
The Kiss—Its Meaning

Kissing used to have a different meaning. Not so many years ago, dating partners used to consider the kiss as one way to show that they felt affection for each other, or to signify that they were developing a sense of commitment to each other, based on love. Today, kisses are often bestowed lightly, and many mean no more than that the couple enjoys each other's company. Some individuals consider the kiss of no greater significance than a friendly handshake. Despite these modern interpretations, a kiss still indicates, as in the past, that a line has been crossed in the dating relationship, and that there has been a subtle change in the partners' personal attitudes that may lead to petting and intercourse or the development of love for each other as personalities. Today's kisses vary in type from a light, friendly greeting or a goodnight kiss to "French kissing," which to students means deep and exploratory contacts with each other's lips, tongues, and the caverns of the mouth. Such deep kissing is erotically stimulating and is likely to lead to more intimate forms of sexual experiences.

Usually, individuals who want to avoid subsequent sexual intimacies will avoid deep kissing and will also learn to signify with any kisses they give what their attitude toward the dating relationship is.

It is highly possible that a girl who wants to can show warmth of affection for her boyfriend and keep him interested without resorting to kissing or other forms of physical affection, if she uses all the facets of her personality in order to be an exciting companion.

Petting

Today's society offers opportunities for more freedom of physical contact between the sexes than existed during past generations. However, no one knows precisely how these opportunities for freedom are being used. Individuals in defending their point of view regarding today's sexual behavior often make generalizations on what is being done based upon their own limited experience and observations of their associates' practices. Obviously, such pronouncements are of little scientific value as they are based upon the sexual behavior of an infinitesimal segment of today's population. There are some studies of current sexual behavior, but they do not provide conclusive data; first, because they are too small to be representative of the nation's sexual practices, and second, because they are based upon how individuals say they behave, rather than upon their almost impossible to determine actual behavioral patterns. Some research specialists contend that such fragmentary studies suggest behavioral trends. Even if such thinking were accepted, the reported behavioral standards would offer the young person who is dating no sound guidance because there would be no accompanying evidence that adopting such behavior would produce desirable consequences for him. In other words, if one hundred people in a group of one hundred and fifty behave in a certain way, this does not prove that such behavior is desirable. What this all adds up to is that choosing one's premarital sexual standards is a personal moral choice, and no studies or suggested trends can prove scientifically that an individual ought to choose one particular standard. Group and cultural pressures may make one's choice more difficult, but it still remains his to make.

Many of today's young persons are of the opinion that the term "petting" is obsolete, and say, "Why discuss it, it's just part of a date." Even if petting is casually accepted and called by other terms such as "making out" or "playing around," its implications need discussion, because engaging in it creates the problem of deciding whether it helps or harms the dating relationship. The couple must decide whether such physical intimacy is beneficial or emotionally damaging to them.

Does Petting Harm or Help the Couple's Relationship?

Definitions of Petting

Although petting is defined in various ways, a simple definition is, "Petting is the act of caressing each other's bodies in order to receive pleasure."

Petting may vary in intensity from exchanging mild caresses to employing fondling activities which cause maximum sexual arousal and produce orgasm but stop short of intercourse. Although petting is a term which most students use when referring to mutual acts of affection, their attitudes toward engaging in it vary widely.

Student Attitudes Toward Petting

The author made a survey of student attitudes regarding petting, in his Marriage and Family Life classes, and discovered that college students hold a wide variety of opinions regarding the practice of petting on dates. The responses were given anonymously, and although the sampling is too small to be of significance statistically, it does show the diverse opinions which students hold toward engaging in petting. A few of the more interesting comments appear below.

Students Who Engage in Petting

Female—"To me petting is an act that is not immoral nor one that is very bad . . . I feel it should be done if the couple are mature enough to control their emotions and not let it lead to other things which could be disastrous to both of them."

Female—"Petting has always seemed like a natural thing to me. . . . It is one way of expressing your feelings for someone you like very much."

Male—"I believe that petting is a part of growing up. I mean it is almost a cinch that most people will do it. . . . They must be able to stop short of intercourse before marriage though."

Male—"There is nothing wrong with petting if the girl is someone you really care for."

Students Who Avoid Petting

Female—"I definitely don't believe in petting. I've never been touched by a boy and don't intend to be until after I'm married. To me, my body is sacred and belongs to me until I'm married."

Female—"I'm against petting. . . . It should be reserved for married people. . . . I think it is really wonderful for a married couple to look at each other and know that the affection and love they have for one another was shared with no one else."

Male—"Petting should be avoided like the plague. It is too easy to be carried away by emotions, and the results can be heartbreak or hardship for the couple involved."

Male—"I feel that if you pet, you will commit yourself to a good deal more than you bargained for. You may wind up supporting a wife you don't love and a child you didn't want."

Reasons Why Controlling Petting Is Difficult

1. Differences in male and female sex drives. This has been discussed in detail in a previous chapter, but in applying these differences to the dating relationships it would be well to remember a few basic things. Women are generally more contrectative than men (contrectation—the impulse to touch, snuggle up close, rest their heads on manly shoulders, etc.). Men seem to react in the same way as women in that they enjoy light touching when they are in their early teens, but as they approach the late teens they change, and light touches and kisses stir them to a desire for intimate sexual contact.

But the average girl stays on the level of enjoying mild caresses and feels satisfied with this type of affection. Thus it is difficult for her to understand the desire for more intimate sexual contact that her male partner has developed. Because of this lack of awareness she may caress him with no thought of more intimate contact. But these caresses may arouse her partner sexually and he may want to have intercourse. The girl who does not understand this may be dumfounded when her lover appears to want more intimate contact. She may even become angry and call him an "animal" because his sexual desires have been aroused.

A fellow who has become so aroused will often rationalize his inability to control his sexual desires with the statement, "I can't help myself. I'm a man." Even though research suggests that the male does become sexually aroused more easily, studies also show that the male sex drive can be sublimated. If this were not so, and the average man gave way to all of his sexual impulses, very few attractive women would be able to venture out in public.

There is some disagreement among authorities as to whether this different overt behavior exhibited by male and female is due to differences in sex drive. Dr. Kinsey suggests that males and females do not differ in sex drive. He feels that women have natural sex desire equal to that of men, but that it has been overlaid with inhibitions developed because of cultural pressures. Dr. Robert Blood is of the opinion that hormonal chemistry, greater genital awareness, and seminal pressures combine to make the male more aware of and put greater emphasis upon sex.[4]

Regardless of what causes different sexual behavior in the male and female, it is necessary that dating partners be sensitive to these differences and interact in such a manner that they can help each other control their sexual desires.

2. A certain girl may have difficulty controlling her desire to pet because she has been deprived of needed affection in childhood. Consequently, when she begins dating she wants to give affection to and receive it from someone whom she feels is the first person to love and understand her.

3. A girl who feels inadequate as a person may deliberately attempt to trap a man by petting and thus reassure herself that she is desirable. She may also be so lacking in self-esteem that she feels she must pay her boyfriend for the dating evening by granting him sexual favors.

4. The fellow may be seeking reassurance that he is desirable and have a greater feeling of self-esteem when his date pets with him.

5. Another type of fellow may be seeking conquests and use a petting relationship to build his feelings of masculinity. He also may pet with girls and then leave them in an effort to deliberately hurt them because of cynicism toward women in general.

6. Petting is also difficult to control because when the erogenous zones of the body are caressed, the couple is taking the first biological step in preparing themselves for sexual intercourse.

Reviewing just a few of the biological and psychological factors which enter into controlling petting makes it easy to perceive the couple's problem, namely that of deciding upon the degree of sexual contact which will exert either positive or negative influence on their relationship. The decision is made more difficult because the dating partners feel the pressures of their concepts of what is right or wrong which are opposing those of their sexual desires.

---

[4]Blood, Robert O., Jr., *Marriage.* New York: The Free Press of Glencoe, 1962, pp. 120, 121.

The Possible Consequences of Petting

Needless to say, one cannot generalize on the possible consequences of petting. This is so, because each dating couple is unique and the consequences of their petting will be shaped by their backgrounds, home training, religious beliefs, and adopted moral standards. Other factors that will affect their reactions and the results are their temperaments, the extent, frequency, and intensity of the petting practice and how they associate it with a sense of commitment to each other.

Some individuals look upon petting as a way of sublimating the drive for sexual intercourse and also a way of getting acquainted with different personalities and determining the type which would make a suitable marriage partner. These viewpoints are expressed by Harper and Klemer:

Harper states, "Petting offers the opportunity for young people to learn particular lovemaking techniques and responses to various types of persons of the other sex.

"A fairly expansive premarital sexual experience would appear to provide background against which young people can make sounder marital choices."[5]

Klemer says, ". . . there is considerable evidence that sometimes—perhaps most times—petting is a sublimal release; it substitutes for intercourse rather than precedes it."[6]

Possible Arguments Against Petting

It should be pointed out that the following negative consequences apply to the unmarried, not a husband and wife, and are simply given as possibilities:

Time spent together before marriage must be scheduled, and is subject to limitations. Thus, if attention is directed toward petting, adequate opportunities may not be afforded to get acquainted with each other's personality characteristics.

The involved dating partners' thinking may become body-centered rather than person-centered and thus cheapen their meaning of affection.

---

[5]Harper, Robert A., Chapter 17—"Pros and Cons of Petting," *Sex in the Adolescent Years*, Edit., Rubin, Isadore and Kirkendall, Lester A., New York: Association Press, 1968, p. 103.
[6]Klemer, Richard H., *Marriage and Family Relationships*, New York: Harper and Row, 1970, p. 167.

A girl who pets may be considered an interesting sexual partner, but not a desirable future marriage companion.

A couple may mistake their sexual desire for each other as love and consequently, go on to an unhappy marriage.

Frequent petting may produce undesirable physiological effects such as headaches and backaches. It may also cause emotional strain that prevents the development of a mutually satisfying relationship that may lead to marriage.

Petting may result in loss of emotional control, leading to sexual intercourse, pregnancy, and a marriage entered into out of a sense of obligation.

Suggestions for Controlling Petting

Those who feel the need for some help in controlling their desire to pet, might consider some of the following suggestions.

1. Face the petting problem squarely. A frank discussion of how you both feel about petting and the effects it may have on your relationship should do much to clear the air. If you do not want to pet, explain why in such a manner that you do not belittle your partner. Once you have stated your position, adhere to it.

2. Seek to understand each other's personalities and work at developing mutual interests so you can keep interestingly engaged in activities while together and not resort to petting because of boredom.

3. Develop little symbols or signals which you can use to halt the sexual stimulation of each other when you feel it necessary. The couple who said they keep a hand fire extinguisher in the fellow's car and take turns pointing it at each other to interrupt awakened sexual desires with laughter illustrate what can be done.

4. Avoid getting into situations or parking in places where it is easy to pet. Naturally, you cannot plan or prepackage romantic moments, but you can be sensitive to times and places when and where control will be more difficult to maintain.

5. Keep in mind that you have a greater possibility of developing lasting bonds if you build a good total relationship and do not put undue emphasis on your physical desires.

Suggested Readings

1. Bell, Robert R., *Premarital Sex in a Changing Society,* Englewood Cliffs, N.J.: Prentice-Hall Inc., 1966.

2. Bernard, Jessie S., "The Fourth Revolution," *Journal of Social Issues,* 22 (April, 1966), 76-87.

3. Bowman, Henry A., *Marriage for Moderns,* New York: McGraw-Hill, 1970, (6th ed.), Chapter 4, "Dating Practices, Standards, and Values."

4. Christensen, Harold T., "Cultural Relativism and Premarital Sex Norms," *American Sociological Review,* 25 (Feb., 1960), 31-39.

5. Cox, Frank D., *Youth, Marriage and the Seductive Society,* Dubuque, Ia.: William C. Brown Co., 1968 (rev.).

6. Duvall, Evelyn M., *Why Wait Till Marriage?,* New York: Association Press, 1965.

7. Ehrmann, Winston, "Marital and Non-marital Sexual Behavior," in Christensen, Harold T. (ed.), *Handbook of Marriage and the Family,* Chicago: Rand McNally, 1964, pp. 585-662.

8. Reiss, Ira L., *The Social Context of Premarital Sexual Permissiveness,* New York: Holt, Rinehart and Winston, 1967.

Chapter VII

Attitudes Toward Premarital Sexual Intercourse

Today, many people talk "knowingly" about the extent of premarital intercourse and go so far as to say, "Everyone who is normal engages in it."

Such thinking was recently echoed by a male college student in one of the writer's family life classes who said, "It is completely unrealistic in today's society to expect a fellow to abstain from sexual intercourse before marriage. Everyone does it."

Individuals who think this way have undoubtedly had their thoughts shaped by irresponsible writers who write volumes about the so-called "New morality" which they interpret as a rapid and complete cultural change from controlled to permissive behavior on the part of the majority of the population. Such authors have contributed to the general confusion surrounding the extent and consequences of premarital intercourse. Such confused thinking is present on a public scale and is prevalent among parents, and those who are dating. Although these three areas of confusion are closely interrelated, looking at them separately might clarify the problems which exist today.

PUBLIC CONFUSION

Few people have the time or the necessary skills to engage in direct research on a broad enough scale to really learn what is going on in the world today. Consequently, they rely on the writings, lectures, and teachings of people whom they consider experts in the specific area with which they are concerned.

Currently, in the area of sexual behavior, the experts who tend to get the most publicity are those who titillate the mind and present permissive concepts that appeal to the average person's adventurous nature. As a result, many writings which contain a more objective appraisal of what is happening are overlooked. What is the result? Again, the obvious fact that although nobody knows precisely the extent of today's premarital sexual behavior and what forms it takes, the average parent thinks he does because of his exposure to permissive writings that are not adequately documented. Thus, when a student or anyone else, says, "Everyone engages in sexual intercourse before marriage," that individual simply does not know what he is talking about.

Dr. Paul H. Gebhard, Director of the Institute for Sex Research in Bloomington, Indiana, who joined the late Alfred C. Kinsey at the institute in 1946, recently made an interesting appraisal of the present situation.[1] He said: "For a while we'll go through this chaos, this obsessive interest in sex, flooded with pornography. Then I think we'll get a little bit fed up with it and settle down and things will probably be healthier in the long run.

"There hasn't been a revolution in terms of behavior, because in my mind the term revolution means something rapid, rough. Really, what's happening is there's been a continuation of pre-existing trends, things that we can see beginning at the start of this century.

"However, in terms of the mass media the changes have been abrupt enough to call it a revolution. When you stop to think that we still have things locked up in our cabinets that you can now buy at the local drugstore, that's a revolution.

"Over 25 years we have become by and large healthier. All of these things that we used to try to sweep under the carpet are now out in the open and we're confronted with realities. I can't think how the individual or society can come to any satisfactory solution of their problems if they're struggling in an atmosphere of ignorance.

"We'd better learn what's going on if we're going to get the answers."

Dr. Gebhard's statement, "We'd better learn what's going on if we're going to get the answers," implies that at present we don't know. A brief look at existing research reveals this to be the case.

RESEARCH EVIDENCE REGARDING THE EXTENT
OF PREMARITAL INTERCOURSE

Ira L. Reiss, Director of the Family Studies Center at the University

---

[1]United Press Information Service release by David Smothers. As reported in the Minneapolis *Star*, Jan. 5., 1973.

of Minnesota gave a summary in 1967 regarding our knowledge of premarital sexual behavior in America.[2]

"However, despite the sampling limitations of many studies, there are some basic facts that seem to persist and that have been assumed to be accurate for America. For example, there is widespread agreement that premarital coitus is more common for males than for females and for Negroes than for whites. There is also widespread agreement that affection is a more important factor in motivating the female to perform sexually than it is in motivating the male. Further, it is generally assumed that different social and cultural factors produce different sexual behavior and attitudes, although the literature is not unanimous as to just what these factors are and how they work. Several researchers have found that those relations wherein the male has higher social class than the female are much more likely to involve premarital coitus than those relations wherein the female has higher status than the male. Religiousness in several studies was found to be an inhibiting influence on sexual permissiveness; that is, religious persons are less likely to engage in sexual intimacies. There is also evidence that the consequences of coitus vary according to the standards an individual holds. Many studies support the contention that an increase in sexual behavior of several types occurred during the 1920s."

It should be noted that Reiss avoided giving any statistics regarding the incidence of premarital intercourse and also said, ". . . there are some basic facts that *seem* to persist and that have been *assumed* to be accurate for America."

Before looking at some representative studies of the extent of premarital intercourse in America it should be noted that all of them give percentages of frequency in terms of "cumulative incidence," namely, the lifetime figures of the respondents in the sample who had *ever* had premarital intercourse. The "active incidence," namely the percentage of the reported sample who are currently having premarital intercourse is not reported.

Consequently, a study reporting the cumulative incidence of premarital intercourse would give a higher figure than the present frequency because it would also include past behavior. It would be similar to a state health department reporting 1000 cases of influenza existing in the region,

[2]Reiss, Ira L., *The Social Context of Premarital Sexual Permissiveness*, Holt, Rinehart and Winston, New York: 1967, pp. 7, 8.

a figure arrived at by counting all the cases that had occurred in the past twenty years, whereas the actual present count might only be one hundred.

It should also be stated that, at the present writing, there is no one study in existence that does not have some type of shortcoming such as an inadequate sample, errors in methodology, or a time-lag that negates its present validity. All of the studies have the weakness of disclosing reported behavior which may or may not reflect actual behavior nor be representative of the group being studied.

The first large study of sex behavior, the Kinsey Study (1948) of the adult male reported that of 5,300 males interviewed, 92 percent was the overall rate and 51 percent the rate of college men who had had intercourse by the time they were twenty-one.[3]

The same group's study (1953) of 5,940 adult females disclosed that about one-half of the total sample reported having had premarital intercourse, and about 27 percent of those who ever went to college.[4]

Burgess and Wallin (1953) who interviewed 666 married couples reported that 68 percent of 580 men and 47 percent of 604 women stated they had engaged in premarital intercourse.[5]

Ehrmann (1959) learned in a sampling of 841 students at the University of Florida that 65 percent of the males and 13 percent of the females had engaged in premarital intercourse.[6]

Two later studies published in 1968 revealed that there had been no drastic change from the general conclusion made in 1967 by Reiss.

Landis and Landis (1968) gathered data from 3,189 students in 18 colleges, and found that among those who had not ever had a serious love relationship, over 60 percent of the men and over 90 percent of the women had never had premarital intercourse.[7]

Packard (1968) from a sample of 1,393 students (665 males, 728 females) gathered from 21 American colleges and universities reported that 57 percent of the males and 43 percent of the females said they had

[3]Kinsey, Alfred C., Pomeroy, W. B. and Martin C. E., *Sexual Behavior in the Human Male*, Philadelphia: Saunders, 1948, pp. 335-337.

[4]Kinsey, Alfred C. et al, *Sexual Behavior in the Human Female*, Philadelphia: Saunders, 1953, p. 296.

[5]Burgess, Ernest W. and Wallin, Paul, *Engagement and Marriage*, Philadelphia: Lippincott, 1953.

[6]Ehrmann, Winston, *Premarital Dating Behavior*, New York: Holt, Rinehart and Winston, 1959.

[7]Landis, Judson T. and Landis, Mary G., *Building A Successful Marriage*, 5th ed. Englewood Cliffs, N.J., Prentice-Hall, 1968, p. 167.

engaged in premarital intercourse by the age of 21. These findings showed an increase of 6 percentage points in the number of college males saying that they had had intercourse by age 21 when compared with the Kinsey findings of college-educated males in 1948.

Packard's study also showed an increase of 16 percentage points in the number of college females who said they had had premarital intercourse when compared with Kinsey's college-educated female sample of 1953.[8]

Bell and Chaskes (1970) in a comparison study of college coeds made at the same college in 1958 and 1968 reported an increase in premarital coitus from a rate of 31 to 39 percent among girls during the engagement period. However, as the study was limited to females, on one college campus (Temple University, Philadelphia, Pennsylvania) its conclusions would have to be considered suggestive, rather than indicative of any national trend.[9]

Zelnik and Kantner (1972) reported from interviews of 4,611 girls living at home or in dormitories in 1971, that 46 percent had experienced premarital intercourse by age 19. These researchers reported that most teen-agers do not have sex frequently, and that only 13 percent (average of whites and blacks) tended toward promiscuity (four or more partners).[10]

In summary, it should be stated that although existing studies of the extent of premarital intercourse do not give conclusive information, they should not be dismissed as having little significance. Their findings are the results of serious study and much effort, and they do provide insights from which we can make generalizations.

However, they furnish no firm evidence that there is a recent national trend toward more frequent premarital intercourse. It should also be pointed out that more open attitudes toward discussing sexual behavior have likely contributed to some of the changes in reported statistics. This has undoubtedly happened because more of today's people feel free to admit their sexual experiences.

[8]Packard, Vance, *The Sexual Wilderness*, New York: McKay, 1968, pp. 161-162.

[9]Bell, Robert R. and Chaskes, J. B., 1970, "Premarital Sexual Experience Among Coeds 1958 and 1968." Journal of Marriage and the Family 32, Minneapolis: The National Council on Family Relations, Feb., pp. 81-84.

[10]Zelnik, Melvin and Kantner, John, as reported to the Commission on Population Growth and the American Future, *Time Magazine*, May 22, 1972.

GENERAL ATTITUDES TOWARD PREMARITAL INTERCOURSE

There are four general philosophies regarding premarital intercourse that exist in the United States today.

Reiss summarizes them as follows:

1. Abstinence—Premarital intercourse is wrong for both men and women, regardless of circumstances.

2. Permissiveness with Affection—Premarital intercourse is right for both men and women under certain conditions when a stable relationship with engagement, love, or strong affection is present.

3. Permissiveness without Affection—premarital intercourse is right for both men and women regardless of the amount of affection or stability present, providing there is physical attraction.

4. Double Standard—Premarital intercourse is acceptable for men, but it is wrong and unacceptable for women.[11]

These four philosophies are reflected in the writings of leaders in the family life field.

Professor Henry Bowman, of the University of Texas, whose book, *Marriage for Moderns* enjoys wide usage, makes a strong case for abstinence with his thinking. Bowman gives a number of points to show that abstinence from intercourse before marriage contributes to the partners' ability to achieve a oneness in marriage that is based upon respect, mutuality, sharing and sexual exclusiveness.

Poffenberger also affirms the value of premarital abstinence.

He writes: "The present preoccupation with sex in the culture needs to be replaced by other values. First, the survival of our highly technical society is dependent on inculcating in young people a drive for educational and intellectual achievement as well as occupational and professional productivity. Second, the stability of our democratic society depends on the effective functioning of the family unit. To facilitate these objectives, it seems necessary for the society to take the position that young people must hold chastity as a value at least until they have reached relative economic, social, and emotional maturity."[12]

---

[11]Reiss, Ira L., *Premarital Sexual Standards in America*, Glencoe, Illinois: The Free Press, 1960, pp. 83, 84.

[12]Poffenberger, Thomas, "Individual Choices in Adolescent Premarital Sexual Behavior," Marriage and Family Living 22, Minneapolis: National Council on Family Relations, Nov. 1960, p. 330.

Professor Lester Kirkendall of Oregon State University believes that "permissiveness with affection" serves as a criterion in determining proper sexual behavior. He reasons that dating partners who exercise discretion in controlling their sex drives and feel a sense of commitment to each other should be able to work out a satisfactory sexual relationship. In other words, the decision to engage in premarital intercourse or not would be decided on the basis of whether the couple felt it would improve their relationship.

The author has suggested Kirkendall's thinking to large numbers of students, and the general reaction has been that the majority of dating partners do not have a deep enough sense of commitment to each other to restrain their sexual drives and orient them toward positive mutual goals.

The Reverend Joseph Fletcher, professor at the Episcopal Theological School in Cambridge, Massachusetts, presents his "situation ethics" view of engaging in premarital sex. His proposal embraces two general ideas:

1. Premarital sex is immoral if engaged in without some care and commitment.

2. In every situation each individual should ask himself, "How, here, and now, can I act with the most concern for the happiness and welfare of those involved—myself and others?"[13]

Unwed mothers whom the author has counseled, when asked to react to Fletcher's suggestions, have in the majority of cases replied,

I had intercourse with my boyfriend because I loved him and thought he loved me. I didn't even bother to use contraceptives, let alone think of our future welfare. People don't behave that way in real life.

Permissive without affection is endorsed by Albert Ellis, New York City consulting psychologist. His thinking is that most educated and informed individuals no longer view premarital sexual relations as morally wrong. They should be enjoyed, and those who abstain from them for long periods of time will most like suffer:

Impairment of physical health.

Impairment of psychological health.

Impairment of sexual adequacy.

Impairment of sound values.[14]

[13]Fletcher, Joseph, *The New Morality*, Philadelphia: The Westminister Press, 1966.
[14]Ellis, Albert, *Sex and the Single Man*, New York: Lyle Stuart, Inc. 1963, pp. 12-18.

Although contemporary writers tend to avoid endorsing the double standard, two well-known authors have made interesting comments on its continued existence. Bell says: "The traditional belief in the double standard continues to be accepted by many Americans of both sexes. . . . Historically, the double standard has often been applied to the male and the abstinence standard applied to the female."[15]

Reiss writes: ". . . there are two main types of double standard . . . the orthodox . . . the adherents abide fully by the double standard and allow few if any exceptions." ". . . the transitional. This has become increasingly popular in the last century. . . . In this case, exceptions are made, and the woman who engages in premarital coitus because she is in love or engaged is not condemned. This is still the double standard, for men are allowed to engage in coitus for any reason . . ."[16-17]

PARENTAL CONFUSION

Inasmuch as most parents rarely read books that discuss contemporary sex standards in an objective manner, and get a vast amount of information from popular magazines, they have some difficulty in deciding how to influence their sons' and daughters' sexual behavior. If parents are going to offer any constructive help to their children, they must first have some sound convictions of their own. Then they must know how to communicate them. If this is done effectively, it will help their sons and daughters to develop the confidence to behave according to their learned standards in their associations with their peers. To accomplish this, parents should try to envision what they want the future to hold for their children. Surely, those who care want to protect their children from exploitation, help them build a positive self-image, and guide them to adjusting satisfactorily to life.

What about holding to their convictions? Parents must first realize that change is not a value in itself. They should compare their traditional beliefs and standards with proposed new ones, and after an objective appraisal, decide which would be more beneficial. One advantage of hold-

[15]Bell, Robert, *Premarital Sex in a Changing Society*, Prentice Hall, Englewood Cliffs. New Jersey: 1966, p. 65.

[16]Reiss, Ira L., *Premarital Sexual Standards in America*, Glencoe, Ill.; The Free Press, 1960, p. 97.

[17]Reiss, Ira L., *The Social Context of Premarital Sexual Permissiveness*, New York: 1967, Holt, Rinehart and Winston, p. 19.

ing to traditional values, as contained in Judaeo-Christian teachings, is that they have been tested by time and been proven helpful.

Those individuals who say that such teachings are outdated and unrealistic have often been influenced negatively by misinterpretations of the Judaic-Christian sex ethic. Many parents who are afraid of being called old-fashioned hesitate to teach any values at all. And although young people are reluctant to admit it, they feel more secure when their parents suggest guidelines and set limits on sexual behavior. Some of the most insecure students the author has counseled are those whose parents "left them on their own" in their decision-making.

The kind of communication that takes place between parents and children determines whether the sexual values which are taught become meaningful. To communicate effectively, parents must know the facts regarding human reproduction, the differences between the sexes, how the emotions enter into self-control, and so forth. Then, they should try to present them in a framework of attitudes that makes sex natural, meaningful, and associated with a love relationship. If this information is presented, and the attitudes are taught in a setting in which there is a free and easy interchange of ideas, the child will be more likely to accept his sexual personality and learn how to express his sexuality with discipline and self-confidence.

The self-confident individual who has adopted a set of values which make sense to him and knows he can discuss his dating experiences in a nonjudgmental setting with his parents will be much less likely to bow to group pressures and engage in sexual activities which exploit his personhood or cause him to become cynical toward traditional and tested values.

In essence, parents who care try to help their children understand and value themselves, so they can in turn learn to understand and value others.

CONFUSION AMONG THOSE WHO DATE
Individual Attitudes Toward Premarital Sexual Intercourse

Before discussing individual attitudes toward premarital sexual intercourse, two points should be made. First, unmarried individuals of both sexes do not follow any general pattern in their attitudes toward sexual behavior. Consequently, those who stereotype young, single men as sex-demanding individuals who play games to get all the sexual favors they can from their female companions are drawing conclusions that reflect their own thinking, rather than any actual knowledge of what is going on in today's society. All men are not cast from the same mold, and many value their girlfriends too highly to exploit them sexually. It is also unrealistic to stereotype all young, unmarried girls as virginal maidens who fight their male companions off in order to protect their chastity. There are single girls who are eager to experience intercourse, and they often encourage their male partner's sexual advances.

Second, the current idea that some people entertain that virginity is no longer important to either the boy or girl is not founded on sound evidence.

This kind of thinking often comes from reading such published surveys as a recent Gallup Poll (1970) in which 1,114 college students from 55 campuses were interviewed. The question asked was:

> There's a lot of discussion about the way morals and sex are changing in this country. Here is a question that is often discussed in women's magazines. What is your view on this: Would it be important to you that the person you marry be a virgin or not so important?
> Response:

All students   Important 23%
                Not Important 73%
                  No Opinion   4%

Such evidence as the above suggests that virginity is not viewed in the absolute sense that it once was, but there is no conclusive information presented by the study to show that most girls take the loss of virginity lightly. The same thing is also true of many boys.

Typical comments written on anonymous questionnaires from a sampling made in the writer's class in Marriage and Family Living show varied attitudes among both sexes relating to virginity.

Female Students' Comments:

No. 1: "Yes, it would be nice to marry a virgin. But are there any guys who are virgins left today?"

No. 2: "I would not like to marry a male virgin. When I get married, I would not know what was going on, and someone should."

Male Students' Comments:

No. 1. "Generally, I would like to marry a virgin. However, if a girl has made an unfortunate mistake there is no need to condemn her, you should not be in love with an ideal, but rather with the individual."

No. 2: "It makes no difference. I would not marry a girl who is a tramp, but sometimes during a girl's life, she thinks she is in love and will have intercourse. I think if a girl is still a virgin by the age of 21, there's something wrong with her."

Students' Comments on Premarital Intercourse

The writer has had abundant opportunity to learn of young, unmarried peoples' views toward premarital intercourse from sources such as individual interviews, class discussions, and submitted term papers. The general findings have been that such views vary widely.

Among those who look upon premarital intercourse with disfavor are individuals who wish to abstain from intercourse until marriage because they want to abide by parental and religious teachings regarding chastity.

On the other hand, among those individuals who are permissive, are some who try to make a case for the merits of their sexual experiences.

It provides insights for both groups to openly discuss their individual attitudes so they can see how widely students' attitudes differ.

Given below are students' statements regarding premarital intercourse which illustrate the variety of prevailing attitudes. They represent the thinking students have expressed verbally or in written form.

Engaged Coed:

There are several reasons why premarital satisfaction in intercourse may not result in good postmarital sex adjustment. Sex desires may have been satisfied through novelty and new experience and they both may have responded favorably. How true! I'm sure many people just feel elated to know that they have conquered that first step. They are sexually compatible! This wouldn't prove anything to me if I were the one testing it. They can sexually arouse each other when they get the chance to, when the parents aren't home, or in the car if no one's around nearby. Each time they get this chance, they both function together. So they say they're compatible.

Male Student:

I feel premarital intercourse is wrong. I think that if you can't come to understand the person whom you intend to marry, socially, emotionally, and spiritually, by just plain being together and talking, you have lost a great deal of life's meaning. I feel too much emphasis is put on sex. Sex is not the whole component to marriage. There are also the problems of religion, raising the children, if the wife should work, and money matters in general.

I have always felt that having premarital intercourse just proved you could not master mind and will over the body. I also feel a certain amount of respect is lost whether it is ever admitted or not.

Female Student:

If marriage is impossible at present for two people who have a relationship in which both give all the satisfaction that life can offer . . . mutual understanding, mutual striving for goals, and mutual love that includes mental stimulation, emotional tranquility and spiritual inspiration, and through this their total communication adds sexual satisfaction, I feel under these circumstances that premarital sexual intercourse cannot be wrong.

Engaged Coed:

I have been engaged for four years, and during the last three years I have engaged in premarital sex. I have found it the most wonderful, rewarding expression two people in love can share. I have never felt regret, embarrassment or guilt.

Male Student:

The prove-you-love-me approach is, in my estimation, ridiculous. There are many more things to a relationship besides sex, and if the partners can't sense the feeling of love without copulation, there is something lacking in their rather shallow relationship.

Male Student:

I believe that the vast majority of persons in the 18 to 19 age group are perfectly capable of stopping love play at any point, and if they do have coitus it is with the permission of both parties. I feel that a sexual relationship between people in their late teens can be as physically, mentally, and morally healthy as the same relationship within marriage. Why should there be any strings attached? Cut out pregnancies with effective contraceptives and venereal diseases with proper medicines and what harm can free sex relations cause? Teenagers can develop a meaningful sexual relationship before they have met the rigorous preparation which society demands in order to get married and raise a family.[18]

ARGUMENTS FOR AND AGAINST PREMARITAL INTERCOURSE

1. *The first argument which proponents of premarital sexual intercourse use is that abstaining from sexual intercourse is unhealthy physically and disturbing psychologically.* Those who feel this way believe that continence has adverse physiological effects because man has a biological need for sexual release. They point out that males reach the peak of their sexual drive in their late teens and must have the sexual outlet which intercourse provides. They also state that girls, with some exceptions, do not reach their peak of sexual need until some years later than boys, thus their problem is not so great.

The answer that opponents of premarital intercourse give to this argument is that there is no medical evidence or competent biological opinion which indicates that abstinence from sexual intercourse results in physiological harm.

In regard to psychological disturbance of the individual, the writers who contend that controlling sexual drives can cause individual psychological problems point to the increasing number of sexually stimulating influences which are present in contemporary society and say that it is hazardous under such circumstances to condition individuals to inhibit themselves sexually. They feel that the sex drive cannot be sublimated and channeled in other directions for gratification.

Those who oppose this viewpoint say that its advocates have become entangled in the confusion of moral relativism with which they rationalize permissive behavior by saying, "It's all a matter of cultural conditioning."

Beach states the case against this permissive thinking in the following manner:

"This assumption about sexual rights is assisted by popular Freudian folklore and passwords describing the dangers of sexual repression, the need for libidinal self-expression, and the foolishness of guilt feelings as only the hangovers from a Puritan culture. No aspersions are cast here on the whole Freudian development in psychology which has been of

---

[18]The above cases are taken from, Anderson, Wayne J., *How to Discuss Sex With Teenagers*, Minneapolis: T. S. Denison & Co., 1969, pp. 116-121, reprinted by permission.

such tremendous value in contemporary man's self-understanding. The only point to be noted here is that campus Freudianism is little more than a useful kit of terms to rationalize dubious activity or to cover moral uncertainty."[19]

It is possible that those individuals who see dangers in conditioning a person against permissive behavior have lost sight of the basic fact that the average person has enough intelligence to make value judgments which will have some influence on how erotic stimuli will affect him. Consequently, the set of values which the person has will determine in great measure whether controlling sexual desires will affect him negatively. His value system will also aid him in sublimating his drives.

2. *A second argument which is advanced in favor of premarital sexual intercourse is the testing argument.* A student often says, "I wouldn't think of buying a pair of shoes without trying them on first, so I think it is only common sense to try each other out sexually to see if you are suited to each other before you marry."

Individuals who make this and similar statements seem to have a fear of getting married and then learning after the wedding that they are sexually incompatible. One must give them credit for thinking clearly when they say that a couple should try to find out if they are sexually compatible before marriage. However, their thinking becomes confused when they believe that engaging in premarital sexual intercourse and achieving mutual satisfaction assures them that they will make a good sexual adjustment in marriage.

There are several reasons why premarital sexual satisfaction may not result in good postmarital sexual adjustment. For example, their premarital sexual satisfaction may have resulted from one of the following reasons: It could have been that the novelty and new experience of the sex act caused them both to respond favorably sexually. Perhaps the spirit of adventure had so stirred them that they, at the moment, felt that they had really become one in body and spirit. And it might even have been the case that the fellow or the girl had knowledge of and used some of the mechanical techniques that might be employed to excite the other. Inasmuch as they have been so satisfied, are they justified in concluding that they will be sexually compatible in marriage because of this experience or a dozen more like it?

---

[19]Beach, Waldo, *Conscience on Campus.* New York: Association Press, 1958, pp. 88, 89.

Let us turn the situation around and consider the couple who engage in premarital intercourse to test their sexual compatibility and have a disappointing experience. The girl does not respond and the fellow feels that the mutual spark necessary to sexual satisfaction is simply not there. So they try having intercourse again and again and still have disappointing results. Should they then decide that they are sexually incompatible? Not necessarily. Perhaps the response has not been satisfactory because the relationship has been entered into furtively. Perhaps the setting was undesirable for good sexual adjustment because the sex act took place in the back seat of a car or in a cheap motel. It could be that guilt feelings or fear of pregnancy have blocked sexual response.

Again let us repeat the question. Are these sex partners who have not had a satisfactory premarital sexual experience justified, in the light of their experience, in concluding that they will be sexually incompatible in marriage?

In reviewing the cases of these couples it becomes evident that neither set of partners has learned through premarital intercourse whether they will or will not be sexually compatible in marriage. This is true because good marital sexual adjustment usually develops as a result of living and learning together over an extended period of time and a satisfactory sexual adjustment between a married couple sometimes may take years to achieve and is very rarely worked out in a matter of days, weeks, or months.

If we examine the "trying on a pair of shoes" analogy, it becomes apparent that a student who has this sexual attitude toward his girlfriend will gradually realize that there is a vast difference between footwear and a lovely young girl. Shoes are inanimate objects and they have no emotions, while a girl is a *person* who has a background of attitudes, a future of hopes and aspirations, and a personality that will respond in different ways to various kinds of treatment.

We must conclude that a couple cannot test their sexual compatibility before marriage. All that they can do is learn whether they are physically capable of having intercourse.

If you and your partner have any doubts about your ability to have sexual intercourse after you get married, a gynecologist can determine if there are any genital differences and can also advise you how to adjust to any great variations in physical size.

3. Another argument advanced by those who favor premarital sexual intercourse is that postmarital orgasm (reaching a climax sexually) is more likely to be achieved by wives who have had premarital sexual experience. There is no conclusive evidence that this is true. The Kinsey, Terman, and Burgess and Wallin studies all suggested that this might be the case, but subsequent analyses of these studies, such as the one of the Kinsey Study by Hamblin and Blood, show no correlation between premarital coitus (sexual intercourse) and the subsequent sexual adjustment of the wife in marriage.[20]

The reason this relationship is so difficult to prove statistically is because each dating twosome or set of marriage partners will react in their own way to sexual intimacy, and the variables in each instance are so great that no two sets of partners will react in identical fashion. Also, even if this could be worked out statistically, the researcher would still be left without the knowledge of whether a wife was more responsive sexually in marriage because of premarital experience or because she was a more sexually responsive person. There is also no evidence that the woman who has the greatest orgastic capacity in marriage is the happiest.

Other arguments that proponents of premarital intercourse advance are the Sex-Is-Fun-Why-Not-Enjoy-It-Now? argument (the hedonistic approach) and the argument that other societies allow premarital intercourse with no ill effects, so why shouldn't we?

STUDIES REPORTING THE EFFECTS OF PREMARITAL INTERCOURSE ON MARITAL ADJUSTMENT

Some of the studies which have inquired into the effects of premarital intercourse on marital adjustment show that such activity produces undesirable results. Burgess and Wallin, in their study of engaged couples, discovered that almost twice as many engagements were broken by couples who had intercourse when compared with those couples who had not (18.2 percent as compared with 10.9 percent).[21]

Locke gave evidence that premarital intercourse had been engaged in more by divorced men and women than by happily married couples.[22]

---

[20]Hamblin, Robert, and Blood, Robert, "Premarital Experience and the Wife's Sexual Adjustment," *Social Problems,* October 1957, pp. 122-130.

[21]Burgess, E. W., and Wallin, Paul, *Engagement and Marriage.* New York: J. B. Lippincott Co., 1953.

[22]Locke, Harvey J., *Predicting Adjustment in Marriage.* New York: Holt and Co., 1951.

Kirkendall, in his study of two hundred college men, evaluated the impact of premarital intercourse on the relationships of the couple. His general conclusion is that as their emotional involvement is intensified, the couple tends to put more emphasis on their total relationship and the use of sex to exploit or gain certain ends diminishes.[23]

The "Chesser Report," an English study of 6000 cases, states that wives who had premarital sexual experience seemed to enjoy sexual relationships more than virgins in early marriage, but with a longer period of marriage, the virgins seemed to have the greater enjoyment.[24]

Kanin and Howard found that wives who engaged in premarital intercourse seemed to have greater sexual satisfaction on their honeymoon and during the first two weeks of marriage.[25]

You undoubtedly have observed that nearly all of the studies quoted here are those indicating the negative results of premarital intercourse. Consequently, the author, in all fairness, must remind you that these research findings are far from conclusive and that general statements cannot be made that apply to all marriages.

So, in the final analysis, your decision regarding engaging in premarital intercourse cannot be made by reading existing research, but it will be based on your religious attitudes and your ideological values.

POSSIBLE NEGATIVE CONSEQUENCES OF ENGAGING IN PREMARITAL INTERCOURSE

No prediction can be made regarding how each of the involved participants will react to engaging in premarital sexual intercourse. Consequently, it is also almost impossible to know how such activity will affect their future relationships.

A few of the possible consequences are:

If the dating relationship is terminated, either partner may develop a cynical attitude toward the other sex. The girl may feel like Cheryl who said, "I've been loved and left too often, so my relationship to men is abnormal—friendships, but aversion to sexual encounter. I think men are monsters. They prefer their sex comforts to exploring new relationships. I honestly think they are all narcissists."

[23]Kirkendall, L. A., *Premarital Intercourse and Interpersonal Relationships.* New York: Julian Press, 1961.
[24]Chesser, Eustace, *Women.* London: Jarrolds Publishers, Ltd., 1958, pp. 95-97.
[25]Kanin, Eugene J., and Howard, David H., "Postmarital Consequences of Premarital Sex Adjustments," *American Sociological Review,* 23: pp. 556-652.

Or the fellow may feel like Bill who said, "Mary told me she enjoyed me sexually, but she married Harry because he could buy her the things she always wanted. Women! Are they all golddiggers?"

Sometimes a girl feels that she will always belong to the man with whom she first had intercourse. A typical example was Marcia who wept as she said, "Clyde told me he loved me, so I gave myself to him. Now, he has lost interest and doesn't want to marry me. Now, that I'm no longer a virgin, I don't feel worthy of any other man's love."

The future husband or wife may resent the fact that their mate had premarital sexual intercourse with someone else. John displayed this attitude. He bitterly remarked, "I found out last week that my wife was sexually intimate with another guy before she met me. Now, when I start to make love, I can't stand to look at her. How much does it cost to get a divorce?"

Sexual desire may cause a couple to make a premature commitment to each other, which may be difficult to keep after they become more fully acquainted. Mark felt this way when he said, "I don't know what I saw in Linda. She's good looking and fun in bed, but boy I've found out now that she's selfish and as lazy as they come."

Using premarital intercourse as a testing device related to future marital adjustment, may give the partners a false picture of what their married future might be. Joe illustrated this in the following way. He said, "I wanted to marry Jackie, so I talked her into premarital intercourse as a final test of whether we could adjust sexually in marriage. She responded like a dead fish, so I dropped her."

Joe realized later that Jackie might have been an exciting sex partner in marriage if he had been willing to wait until then for intercourse.

Premarital intercourse may result in a pregnancy and subsequent pressure to enter an undesirable marriage. Joy's story illustrated this. She said, "I felt I must marry Earl because I was expecting his child. What a mistake I made. He's never supported us and is out most of the time running around with his gang."

STUDENTS' REPORTED EXPERIENCES
WITH PREMARITAL INTERCOURSE
Excerpts Taken From College Students' Papers

One of the assignments in the writer's classes in Marriage and Family Living is to write a self-analysis in which the student discusses some of the areas in which he is having adjustment difficulties. Although, they are not required to, many students write about premarital sex. The following excerpts from student papers show some of their attitudes and problems. Naturally, none of the writings extols what some people would consider the pleasures of premarital sex because the focus of the papers is on adjustment difficulties. All names and places have been changed.

I

Tom, a college freshman, reported how premarital intercourse had affected him emotionally. He said: "I was kind of the shy type. I had moved downtown close to the hospital so I wouldn't have far to go to work. It wasn't much of a place but it had a bed. I had moved in with my other sister's boyfriend.

"We had two girls living downstairs from us. I went down one night to borrow a pot or maybe just to meet them. One of the girls, Kay, answered the door. From the first time I saw her I knew that there was something there.

"I started asking her out. We'd go out and have a good time and everything seemed fine. Then I found out she had a fellow in Viet Nam whom she intended marrying. Our sexual relationship hadn't gone any farther than kissing so she had no reason to mention him. I didn't know what I wanted to do. I decided to try and win her away from him. I respected her very much and I was very much in love with her. We would what you might call make out and do maybe light petting, but no further. I knew that she was a virgin and I wanted to keep it that way.

"Then she started going out with this other guy. She asked me if I minded the first time. I told her I did, but she should do what she wanted. About two months later she was pregnant. She was in love with this other guy. So she married him. She told me he said, 'I don't want to marry you because I love you, but because I want to live with you.' But she was in love with him, so they got married. I was in a deep case of depression.

"I was still working at the hospital. I liked my work quite a bit, and I was going out regularly. I liked all the girls I dated but somehow I kept thinking of Kay. I compared each girl with Kay. I wasn't quite as shy at this time as I was when I started dating.

"I met this girl named Judy. I went and lived with her for three months. We had intercourse quite frequently. Judy wasn't the first girl

I had intercourse with and she wasn't the last. But she was the girl I had the strongest feeling for since Kay. There was security living with her. She had two kids that I liked very much. We did everything I ever wanted to do. I had everything I had ever wanted, but at night when I would lie there beside her I would think of Kay, the first girl I loved.

"Sometimes Judy would lie there and cry. I would ask her what was wrong and she would ask me what I felt for her. I felt like I was the devil himself. I couldn't say I loved her because I didn't. Once you say you love somebody you can't take it back. I haven't to this day said to any girl that I loved them.

"So to get away from this situation I went to camp again. Slowly our relationship dwindled. Since that time I have been very careful what I do and what I say to any girl."

II

Michele asked for help after relating her experiences. She said: "The third person I went with was Steve. I met him up here at the dorm. He is very nice. I went with Steve for about four and a half months. He broke up with me because he said he wasn't getting much studying done and that he didn't want to hang on to just one girl (does anyone?). I really liked Steve—and I guess I still do. I liked him for many reasons: he was very well-mannered, a good conversationalist, didn't date to park, respectful, and other reasons. He was never aggressive, sexually I mean. This is one of the main reasons I liked him. Most guys try to get as much out of a girl as they can. If they can't, they shove the girl off. I went out with a guy up here three times. The fourth night, he asked me to go to bed with him and I told him 'no.' He told me 'good-bye' and that he never wanted to see me again. Why is it that boys *always* have sex on their minds? I'll never know!

"I still wonder why Steve *really* broke up with me. Oh God, I wish we could get back together again. I really miss him!!! The *least* he could do is ask me out once in awhile. Somebody, please help . . ."

III

Rosalie described her disillusionment as follows: "When I was a teen-ager, I had very little social life. I had few clothes and a skin condition. I would babysit all the time and use my earnings to pay for a skin specialist. Finally, when I was sixteen, my family sent me to California to live with my older brother and his wife. Because of my constant depression, my parents felt they could no longer handle me. They had never really made me feel I was part of the family.

"I stayed with my brother and his wife until I was nineteen. I met a fellow during the time I was staying there. We dated, and after a while started going steady. Perhaps I was turning to him because I had known only misery and loneliness with my family. After we had dated for three months, my boyfriend became insistent on having sexual relations. I had always been very religious and had resisted his advances up until then. Now he threatened to take back his ring and, up until now, we had been discussing marriage. I finally gave in to his wishes as I could not bear another separation and the ensuing loneliness. I became pregnant. After learning this, my boyfriend enlisted in the Army. I wrote to him for two years, still hoping that we would get married. Fortunately, this never occurred.

"While I was pregnant, I lived in a wage home. After my daughter was born, I went to work at University Hospital. I was happy to have my daughter, as now I had someone who wouldn't leave me. I vowed to work and support her and never go on welfare. I felt that going on welfare would be just what my relatives expected of me.

IV

Keith gave the following feelings about his premarital and postmarital sexual adjustment: "The-Prove-You-Love-Me approach to me is just a way for a dude to get a chick to have sexual intercourse with him, if she falls for the line. There are far too many other ways of proving one's love for the other.

"One argument which proponents of premarital sexual intercourse use is that abstaining from sexual intercourse is unhealthy physically and disturbing psychologically. Personally, I adhere to what the opponents answer, that there is no medical evidence or competent biological opinion which indicates that abstinence from sexual intercourse results in physiological or psychological harm.

"Another argument advanced by those who favor premarital intercourse is that postmarital orgasm is more likely to be achieved by wives who have had premarital sexual experience. I believe this to be a fallacy because I have yet to hear of a woman who has reached a climax the first time or even the first several times. Sexual intercourse gets better over a period of time, so consequently premarital sexual intercourse has nothing whatsoever to do with postmarital orgasm."

V

Mary explained why she wanted to save herself for her future husband: "I'm 'gung-ho' about saving myself for my husband. Some guys have stopped dating me because I wouldn't go to bed with them, and I couldn't help but feel hurt because I liked them. However, I can now look back and feel glad that I didn't have premarital sex because these guys did not love me, they just wanted to satisfy their sexual desires, and knew that they couldn't accomplish that with me. Each time this happens, I'm glad my virginity is still intact and that I can give this to my husband, whether he thinks it's important or not."

THOUGHTS FOR THE INDIVIDUAL WHO HAS HAD PREMARITAL INTERCOURSE

It would be grossly unfair to make the generalization that all unmarried individuals who have premarital intercourse will suffer from negative consequences. Consideration of the following points should show that this does not have to happen. Examples of actual cases will not be given, as such situations are ongoing.

The couple's sense of commitment to each other and their willingness to work at adjusting to each other can result in future marital happiness.

Living in the present is important. The past cannot be changed. So individuals with positive attitudes live in the present and work out their problems as they meet them.

Just because an individual regrets an act does not mean he should be burdened with guilt that interferes with future adjustment.

Maintaining one's self-confidence is an aid to living with integrity in the present. One can be sorry for past mistakes and then redirect his future behavior to more desirable activities.

Keeping involved in interesting and constructive things can be an antidote to guilt feelings from the past. Counseling or religion may be sources of help here.

Couples who look upon premarital sexual intercourse as a natural part of their relationship may feel no negative pressures from the church or society.

Suggested Readings

1. Bell, Robert R., "Parent-Child Conflict in Sexual Values," *Journal of Social Issues,* 22 (April 1966), 34-44.

2. Blood, Robert O., Jr., *Marriage,* Glencoe: The Free Press, 1969 (2nd ed.), Chapter 5, "The Sexual Expression of Love."

3. Cannon, Kenneth L. and Lang, Richard, "Premarital Sexual Behavior in the Sixties," *Journal of Marriage and the Family,* 33:1 (February 1971), 36.

4. Elias, James, "Current Research—Sex Practices and Attitudes on Campus," in Taylor, Donald R., *Human Sexual Development, Perspectives in Sex Education,* Philadelphia: F. A. Davis Co., 1970, Chapter 15.

5. Glassberg, B. Y., "Sexual Behavior Patterns in Contemporary Youth Culture: Implications for Later Marriage," *Journal of Marriage and the Family,* 27 (May, 1965), 190-192.

6. Kardiner, Abram, *Sex and Morality,* New York: Charter Books, 1962.

7. Kirkendall, Lester A., *Premarital Intercourse and Interpersonal Relations,* New York: The Julian Press, 1961.

8. Klemer, Richard H., "Student Attitudes Toward Guidance in Sexual Morality," *Marriage and Family Living,* 24 (August 1962), 260-264.

9. Poffenberger, Thomas, "Individual Choice in Adolescent Premarital Sex Behavior," *Marriage and Family Living,* 22:4 (November 1960), 324-330.

10. Robinson, Ira E.; King, Karl; Balswick, Jack O., "The Premarital Sexual Revolution Among College Females," *The Family Coordinator,* 21:2 (April 1972), 183-188.

Chapter VIII

Choosing a Marriage Partner

SOCIAL FACTORS THAT AFFECT MATE SELECTION

When an individual who is about to marry is asked why he or she has selected a particular person as a future partner, answers often given are, "I feel comfortable with him." Or, "She is just what I want in a wife."

What the respondent really means, but doesn't say, is that a person has been found who seems to meet his or her need expectations, appears ready to accept the responsibilities of marriage, and apparently has the competence necessary to help contribute to the material needs of the marriage and family structure.

This development of the awareness of when and whom to marry doesn't just happen; it is not a matter of chance. In fact, it is one of the most intriguing and complicated studies in the field of family life.

A brief exploration of the social and psychological factors which play a part in one's choice of a mate reveals to some extent who marries whom and why. It also shows that American freedom of choice in choosing a mate usually operates within a general framework of societal expectations.

Propinquity

Despite the fact that many fellows look upon the girl next door as a sister rather than a potential wife, studies show that they usually marry girls who live in the same area, and the chances are better than 50-50 that their future bride will live within walking distance. This is due to the influence of propinquity which is defined as a state of being near, and in mate selection would specifically mean geographical nearness. Couples have to meet before they can marry, although one does hear occasional accounts of some who have made marriage commitments to each other on the basis of a letter-writing rather than a face-to-face relationship. Such courtships are the exception and subsequent marriage is fraught with hazards.

The effects of propinquity on mate selection, some writers call it the ecological theory (the study of the relationship between organisms and their environment), has been demonstrated by several studies. Bossard took data from 5000 marriage licenses in Philadelphia in 1931 and discovered that one-sixth of the applicant couples lived within a block of each other, one-third lived within five blocks, and more than half lived within twenty blocks of one another.[1]

Numerous studies have been made since and they all substantiate Bossard's original findings.

Typical of more recent studies in which the investigators found that couples who applied for marriage licenses lived within a short distance of each other were those made by Koller[2] in Columbus, Ohio in 1938 and 1946, and Catlon and Smircich[3] in Seattle in 1964.

The argument has been presented that because of greater travel opportunities and the rising rate of college attendance, propinquity is currently of lesser importance because people now meet others from wider geographical boundaries. However, regarding greater travel opportunities, Katz and Hill (1958) with their "interaction-time-cost theory" suggested that people are more likely to spend more time with others where related travel time and cost are minimal, so the increased time and money needed to meet with others who lived at a greater distance would discourage all those but the wealthy.[4]

College attendance figures show that most students attend institutions not far from home, and of course, if both partners live on the same campus, propinquity still has influence in their selecting each other as marriage partners.

How can the individual benefit from understanding the influence of propinquity?

If you, as a reader, want to marry, and feel that your home area does not offer suitable potential marriage partners, the obvious thing to

---

[1]Bossard, James H., *Marriage and Family*, Philadelphia: University of Pennsylvania Press, 1940, pp. 39-92; also "Residential Propinquity as a Factor in Mate Selection," *American Journal of Sociology*, September, 1932, pp. 219-224.

[2]Koller, Marvin R., "Residential and Occupational Propinquity," *American Sociological Review*, 1948, pp. 13, 613-616.

[3]Catlon, William and Smircich, R. J., "A Comparison of Mathematical Models for the Effect of Residential Propinquity on Mate Selection, *American Sociological Review*, August 1964, pp. 522-529.

[4]Katz, Alvin M. and Hill, Reuben, "Residential Selection: A Review of Theory, Method, and Fact," *Marriage and Family Living*, 1958, pp. 20, 27-35.

do is move to a place where there is an opportunity to meet desirable members of the opposite sex. For example, data show that a single woman would find a number of eligible men in large cities which are the center for or near graduate schools.

Exogamy

Exogamy is another social factor that limits mate selection. It is an ancient, culturally imposed custom, and requires the individual to marry outside of his kinship group or clan. It is still practiced in some parts of the world.

Some reasons commonly given for the practice of exogamy have been:

Looking upon incest (sexual intercourse between close blood relatives) with horror.

The mistaken notion that inbreeding would always produce defective children.

Greater sexual attraction for people outside of one's group.

Female infanticide which caused a scarcity of marriageable women in the group.

A man was considered more valorous if he captured and wed a woman from another tribe.

Baber, who did extensive research into exogamous practices, thinks the validity of the above reasons is debatable and says ". . . we are still left groping among the mysteries of exogamy . . . the origin remains hidden."[5]

Exogamy still exists in the United States in the form of laws against incest and the marriage of close blood relatives (consanguinity). Also, those related by marriage are not allowed to marry (affinity).

Endogamy

Your choice of a marriage partner is also affected by whether your family or social group practices endogamy which is a custom that requires one to marry within one's tribe, town, race, religion, or socioeconomic class. At present in the United States, group pressures and group values cause many people to practice endogamy in relationship to race, religion, nationality, and socioeconomic status.

---

[5]Baber, Ray E., *Marriage and the Family*, New York: McGraw Hill, 1939, First Edition, pp. 23-30.

Racial Endogamy

Despite increasing mobility in our culture and the resulting greater opportunities people have to mingle with other races, there is still strong sentiment against interracial marriage in the United States. Until 1967 seventeen states had laws prohibiting interracial marriage. Then in that same year, the Supreme Court made a decision nullifying all laws banning interracial marriage. It was expected that such marriages would show a sharp rate of increase, especially in the states that had previously banned them. But a survey made a year later by the Associated Press (1968) revealed that fewer than one hundred interracial marriages had taken place in those same seventeen states.

Students who are planning interracial marriages often express the following thinking in the writer's family life classes: "If we love each other, what difference does it make if we belong to different races?"

Two answers can be given to that. First, their love for each other must be strong enough to withstand the possible cultural pressures that the couple may be required to bear. Second, growing up with different racial backgrounds might also cause two people to bring different attitudes and ways of doing things to the marriage relationship. If both partners are flexible enough to adjust to these pressures and differences, things probably should work out all right; otherwise, there will be conflict.

The most common problems that seem to appear regarding adjustments in interracial marriage are caused by (1) pressures exerted by disapproving relatives or peer groups, (2) possible limiting of occupational opportunities, (3) difficulty in finding a compatible social group, and (4) the possibility that the couple's children might be discriminated against and not be accepted by their peers of either racial group.

It is difficult to determine if the rate of interracial marriages is increasing in the United States, first, because national figures on interracial marriage have never been available, and second, because there is a time lag between studies reporting rates of marriages and what is currently happening. Another problem is that studies made in certain areas of the nation may not reflect what is happening throughout the country. For example, Burma reported that in Los Angeles, interracial marriages had nearly tripled between 1948 and 1959. But the fact that Los Angeles has a greater variety of racial and ethnic groups than the majority of other cities makes this report unrepresentative of the nation.[6]

Also, the percentage of interracial marriages was small, amounting to only 1.5 percent of all marriages.

Studies by Monahan in other states—Pennsylvania (1956-1966), Iowa (1937-1967), and New York (1916-1964) all showed increases in Negro-white marriages, but like the Los Angeles findings, it is questionable whether they are representative of the nation as a whole.[7]

A special United States Census Bureau report on marriage released on February 15, 1973, showed a 63 percent increase during the 1960s in marriages between whites and members of minority groups. However, they are still only a tiny portion of the nation's marriages, as those recorded in 1970 rose from 0.44 percent of the total to 0.70.

The question is often asked regarding what type of personality is most likely to enter an interracial marriage. Although no definite studies cast light on this question, Klemer[8] has made some generalizations adapted from Barnett's[9] review of the available studies on interracial marriage.

Among Klemer's generalizations are the following:

Whites appear to be more willing to engage in interracial marriage with Orientals than with Negroes.

Religiously less devout persons more often marry interracially than the religiously more devout.

Persons who have experienced disorganized and stressful parental families are more likely to marry interracially than those who were raised in cohesive and stable families.

American males and females marrying out of their racial group are generally older than average at the time of marriage.

There are no up-to-date large studies which indicate how successful interracial marriages are. An old study (1937) by Baber indicated that

[6]Burma, John H., "Interethnic Marriages in Los Angeles, 1948-1959," *Social Forces*, December, 1963 pp. 156-165.

[7]Monahan, Thomas, "Interracial Marriages: Data for Philadelphia and Pennsylvania, *Demography*, August, 1970, pp. 287-299. "Are Interracial Marriages Really Less Stable?" *Social Forces*, June, 1970, pp. 461-473. "Interracial Marriages in the United States: Some Data on Upstate New York," *International Journal of Sociology of the Family*, March, 1971.

[8]Klemer, Richard H., *Marriage and Family Relationships*, New York: Harper & Row, 1970, p. 90.

[9]Barnett, Larry D., "Research on International and Interracial Marriages," *Marriage and Family Living*, February, 1963, pp. 105-107.

their average happiness rating was lower than those of mixed nationality or mixed religion.[10]

More recent studies, such as the Seattle Urban League Report, suggest that Negro-white marriages have more problems of adjustment than Oriental-white marriages and many partners in interracial marriages have adjustment difficulties.[11]

SOCIAL CLASS AND MARRIAGE

Evidence suggests that young people in America tend to marry someone from the same socioeconomic level. Even on the college campus where individuals are considered more liberal in their thinking, studies by Reiss[12] suggest that (1) students tend to date others from the same class stratum, and (2) stay with the class system adopted by their parents.

For years, sociologists have suggested that the *mating gradient* operates when individuals from different social classes marry, which means that women tend to marry up socially, and men to marry down. There have been heated discussions as to whether this happens because women are "golddiggers" or they are seeking a mate whose ambitions match theirs. As more women work outside of the home, it may be that more such marriage partnerships may result from working on the same occupational level.

A social status problem related to marriage occasionally occurs when a college student desires to marry someone from a different social level, and parents object.

Natalie's story illustrates such a situation. She and her boyfriend burst into the writer's office one morning with the exclamation, "We wanted you to be the first to know," as she proudly flashed a diamond on her third finger, left hand. She and Tom were bubbling over with excitement as they discussed their marriage plans. However, their joy was short-lived. Two weeks later, Natalie came back in tears, and between sobs said, "My parents won't let me marry Tom."

---

[10]Baber, Ray E., "A study of 325 Mixed Marriages,'" *American Sociological Review*, October, 1937, p. 715.
[11]"People Who Intermarry: Pioneers or Protesters?" Seattle Urban League Special Report, Seattle, Washington, April, 1967.
[12]Reiss, Ira L., "Social Class and Campus Dating," in Hadden, Jeffrey and Borgatta, Marie (eds) *Marriage and the Family*, Itasca, Illinois: F. E. Peacock Publishers, 1969, pp. 234-244.

When asked why, her reply was, "My family is very wealthy and they insist that I, as their only child, marry someone within our social circle. They like Tom, but feel he is not good enough for me because he comes from a large middle-class family and is required to work his way through school."

An effort was made to reassure Natalie and Tom that if after an objective appraisal of all the circumstances was made, they still wanted to marry, their decision should be honored. But things did not work out that way. Natalie's parents shipped her off to an exclusive girls' college on the eastern coast, and subsequently pressured her to break her engagement with Tom.

Two years later she again came to the writer's office for help. She had married a man approved by her parents and due to extreme incompatibility was considering divorcing him.

She was seen again, three years later, as a divorcee who had remarried, marrying a man from a middle-class family. She beamed with happiness as she said, "Life is just great now. Dick is going to school, working part time and we are expecting a baby."

Natalie's experience illustrates a problem that often occurs when an individual who is not endogamous as to social class is pressured by family or friends to marry on his or her socioeconomic level. If the person who comes from a wealthy family has a temperament that causes him to enjoy a middle-class life style, he may be happier marrying outside of his social group. It also may be that he is rightfully putting more emphasis on his future mate's achieved status, that which she has earned on her own, rather than her ascribed status which has been more or less handed to her by her family.

Homogamy—Like Marries Like

Although some people feel that opposites attract, past studies of those who have married have suggested that this has not been true.

A recent study was made by Bernard I. Murstein, a professor of psychology at Connecticut College. After ten years of research on American mating habits, his findings show, as did those in the past, that individuals still marry those with personalities similar to their own.[13]

---

[13]Murstein, Bernard I., "Birds of Feather Best Mates," Universal Science News, Inc. report of study sponsored by National Institute of Mental Health, Minneapolis Tribune, October 18, 1970, pp. 1 and 6.

Murstein says: "Persons with the same personality traits, physical attractiveness, sense of values, level of neuroticism or mental stability and sex drive tend to court and marry more often than opposites.

"Looking at the process of mate selection from the bargaining standpoint, like attracts like because of a mutual benefit.

"Take a contrary case as an example. Say a man who is physically unattractive desires a beautiful woman. Assuming that his nonphysical qualities are no more rewarding than hers, she has less to gain than he does from the relationship. Thus his suit is likely to be rejected.

"Because rejection is a cost to him in terms of lowered self-esteem, he may decide to avoid attempting to court women whom he perceives as much above him in attractiveness."

Murstein's findings reinforce what family life analysts have been saying for years that in the initial stages of courtship, similar physical attractiveness, and such things as manner of dress and personal grooming draw persons to each other. However, dating participants who hold similar values and attitudes will be more likely to develop stronger positive feelings for each other as they advance into more serious dating relationships.

Murstein also pointed out why opposites do occasionally marry. He said, "Studies indicate that opposites are attracted to an ideal image, as perceived in their mate. If an individual is satisfied with himself or herself, there is a high correlation between the actual self and the ideal self. It follows that such people will attempt to marry someone similar. However, individuals highly dissatisfied with themselves seek to marry someone close to their ideal self."

Age

May-September marriages (one partner very young — the other considerably older) receive much publicity, and it is often said that if the couples really love each other, wide differences in age do not matter. But if such theories are put aside, and one looks at the actual facts, most people tend to marry someone within their own age group. Figures released by the United States Census Bureau in 1970 show that the median age at which men marry is 23.2 years. Girls enter their first marriage nearly three years earlier, the median age being 20.8 years. A report released by the Census Bureau on February 15, 1973 disclosed that most women marry between the ages of 17 and 23, while most men marry between 19 and 26. The median marriage age for male college students is 26 and for coeds, 24.

Age at marriage has been shown to have a significant relationship to future marital adjustments. Early marriages, those in which brides are under 20 and grooms are under 21, account for about 60 percent of the nation's divorces. However, when one looks at the wide age differences in marriage, aside from the risks that occur from marrying at an early age, there are no consistent findings to show that chronological age differences between the husband and wife affect the marriage adversely. Successful marital adjustment seems to hinge more upon role expectations and general attitudes. A young husband may enjoy having his older wife nurture and fuss over him, and a young bride may feel more secure if her husband is an older, fatherly type. In addition, couples who differ a number of years in age may be drawn to each other because they have similiar values, agree on life plans, and feel a deep sense of commitment to each other.

Despite holding similar values and having a sense of commitment to each other, couples with wide age differences may be required to face certain special problems. Social pressures often come from in-laws who find it difficult to accept the age difference, especially if their new daughter-in-law or son-in-law is younger than their own children. Or, if their daughter marries a man even older than they are and they must play the roles of parents to him. The couple may also find it difficult to have a circle of common friends. For instance, if the wife is much younger than her husband, the husband's peers may look upon her as a naive, inexperienced person or a threat to the older women in the group! On the other hand, the older husband may find it difficult to keep up with the vigorous recreational activities of his wife's youthful friends.

Problems that may occur between the two of them might include less flexibility on the part of the older partner to adjust to new clothing fashions, modern entertainment, or different methods of child rearing. Differences in physical vigor and sexual capacity may bring frustration to both partners. To meet these and other possible adjustment difficulties, a couple should become informed of, understand, and be willing to adjust to physical life changes such as the menopause in the older wife and the declining sexual drive in the older husband. Such can be done if they both retain a deep sense of commitment to each other as total personalities.

Education and Marital Status

Studies reveal that Americans also tend to marry someone from about the same educational level. They also usually marry someone with a similar marital status: divorcees marry divorcees, widows marry widowers, and those who are single usually find a partner among their single friends.

After considering the foregoing facts, it can be concluded that Americans generally marry people similar and not of opposite culture and background.

Udry suggests three basic reasons for this phenomenon.

First, he says there is more interaction between those who come from the same type of social group. Second, he feels that similar social values encourage people from similar social categories to marry. Third, he believes that people from similar social groups interact more easily because they have about the same attitudes and mannerisms and employ about the same type of vocabulary.[14]

RELIGION AND MARRIAGE

Evidence suggests that the rates of interfaith marriages are increasing and the ecumenical movement to bring about worldwide Christian cooperation is growing. But despite these current movements toward social integration and ecumenicity, the majority of people still marry someone from their own religious faith.

Liberal thinking college students often become impatient when they experience conflict because of religious differences between themselves and their future marriage partners, or in-laws, and then tend to blame the *different religious* denominations for their personal adjustment problems. "Why don't you different religious leaders get together and form one church, so we can get married without having to worry about religious differences?" is a question they often ask a panel composed of Catholic and Protestant clergymen and a Jewish rabbi who periodically visit the writer's classes.

When the religious leaders patiently answer that they as persons are good friends and have high respect for one another's beliefs but their theological doctrines are too far apart to bridge, the questioning students often become cynical toward religion in general and say they will shut

---

[14]Udry, Richard J., *The Social Context of Marriage*, New York: J. P. Lippincott Co., 1966, pp. 343-344.

it out of their marriage entirely or that their great love for each other will compensate for their religious differences. A better course for the students to follow would be to study the religious beliefs of the two which they both hold, get their feelings toward them out in the open, and see if they can live with them as married partners.

It would be an impossible task to describe the basic attitudes toward marriage of all the religious groups existing in the United States today. There are nearly 300 Christian denominations, plus several varieties of Jewish groups, as well as other groups of believers and nonbelievers. However, there are two types of interfaith marriages which occur with continued frequency in which differences in attitudes toward marriage are often overlooked. The Catholic-Protestant marriage and the Jewish-non-Jewish marriage.

Catholic-Non-Catholic Marriages

The official clerical viewpoint of the Roman Catholic Church is to discourage interfaith marriage, based upon their traditional position that such marriages are detrimental to the welfare of the church. As a result, a number of restrictions have been developed that pose problems of adjustment to the mixed marriage partners. These teachings or requirements regarding interfaith marriage are formulated by the top level authorities, the Pope and the College of Bishops. It must be stated that some of the clergy do not agree with the bishops on everything, and lay Catholics may behave in different ways related to church pronouncements. But despite some lattitude, individuals who wish to continue as Catholics must accept certain basic standards.

Due to recent changes, the non-Catholic no longer is required to sign three pledges: (1) to respect or not interfere with the Catholic spouse's free exercise of his religion; (2) to allow the children to be baptized as Catholics; and (3) to educate the children as Catholics. Rulings made by the Vatican in 1966 and 1970 may be summarized as follows:

A civil marriage ceremony is not recognized as valid.

The ceremony must take place in the Catholic church.

"For serious reasons" a non-Catholic clergyman may be granted permission to perform the ceremony.

The Catholic partner may make written or oral promise to bring up the children as Catholics. However, the Catholic is no longer subject to excommunication if the children are brought up in another faith.

The non-Catholic partner is no longer required to make any commitment regarding the religious upbringing of the children.

The Catholic church is opposed to abortion.

The rhythm method is the only type of birth control sanctioned by the church.

Despite these changes, and additional ones may have been made since this writing, the Roman Catholic Church still officially frowns on interfaith marriages.

Jewish-Non-Jewish Marriages

It is difficult to present official Jewish attitudes toward interfaith marriage because there is no central hierarchy which formulates general policies. The Jews are organized into three main divisions: the Orthodox group who adhere to traditional Hebrew beliefs and customs such as rigid dietary laws; the Conservative group who are not so rigid in belief and observance; and the Reform group who ignore ancient ritual, and freely reinterpret Hebrew religious writings.

The Jewish faith is not missionary-minded and does not seek to convert other people to Judaism. Some Jewish groups prohibit Jewish-non-Jewish marriages and some Rabbis refuse to officiate at a wedding unless the non-Jewish partner has converted to Judaism.

Jewish people have a lower rate of mixed marriages than Protestants and Catholics. One of the reasons for this may be the fact that there is often a two-way prejudice between Jews and non-Jews. The involved couple may also find it difficult to make common friends, and often the children of such a mixed marriage are not readily accepted by the in-laws of the other faith.

Other things that may pose difficulties in marital adjustment are different family rituals and dietary differences. Jews and Christians observe different religious holidays, and important Christian festivals such as Christmas and Easter may have little meaning to the Jewish partner. The non-Jewish partner may have difficulty observing the Jews' important holidays of which the most solemn are:

Jewish New Year

Yom Kippur (Day of Atonement, observed with fasting)

Passover (Festival commemorating liberation from Egyptian bondage)

Hanukkah (an 8-day holiday beginning on the 25th of Kislev (the 3rd month of the civil year or the 9th month of the ecclesiastical year in the Jewish calendar) and commemorating the rededication of the Temple of Jerusalem after its defilement by Antiochus of Syria.)

The Success of Interfaith Marriages

Although few people who are about to enter an interfaith marriage will bother to consult statistics, studies do show that such unions tend to be more fragile than others. So the concerned individual who will consider such studies, does have some indication of the prospects for failure or satisfactory marital adjustment.

Three large studies have been made in order to compare divorce rates of interfaith marriages with those of couples who marry in the same faith: Judson T. Landis presents an analysis of data from 4,108 mixed and nonmixed marriages among the parents of college students in Michigan.[15] Where both parents were Catholic the divorce rate was 4.4 percent; if both were Protestant 6.0 percent of marriages ended in divorce. Jewish parents showed a divorce rate of 5.2 percent. If neither parent claimed any religious faith 17.9 percent of the marriages ended in divorce. The highest divorce rate occurred in marriages in which the husband was Catholic and the wife Protestant. In these marriages the rate soared to 20.6 percent.

Another study was made by Ashley Weeks who analyzed the divorce rate of 6,548 parents of public and parochial school children in Spokane, Washington.[16] In this research he found data quite similar to those presented in the Landis study. When the parents were both Catholics the divorce rate was 3.8 percent, both Protestants 10.0 percent, 17.4 percent in mixed marriages and 23.9 percent if neither had a religious belief.

[15]Landis, Judson T., "Marriages of Mixed and Non-mixed Religious Faith," *American Sociological Review*, 14:3 (June 1949) 401-407.

[16]Weeks, H. Ashley, "Differential Divorce Roles by Occupation," *Social Forces*, 21:3 (March 1943) 336.

The third large study was made by Howard M. Bell in Maryland.[17] Bell studied the marital status of 13,528 couples. He found a divorce rate of 6.4 percent among Catholics, 4.6 percent among Jews, 6.8 percent among Protestants, 15.2 percent in mixed marriages and 16.7 percent among couples who had no religious belief.

These three studies seem to give weight to the thinking of church leaders that those who enter interfaith marriages will have more problems of adjustment. However, in all fairness to inquiring young people we must state that these surveys all dealt with couples who have children. At the present writing, there are not sufficient existing data to indicate that the divorce rate is higher in mixed marriages when there are no children. Dorothy T. Dyer and Eleanor Luckey in a study of college students at the University of Minnesota[18] and Burgess and Cottrell in their Illinois Study[19] found no significant difference between the happiness of couples in mixed and nonmixed religious marriages. These studies, however, were of couples in the early years of marriage. They had not yet met the problems of religious versus public education of their children, etc.

More recent studies continue to show a higher rate of divorce or separation for interfaith marriage. Zimmerman and Cervantes (1960) studied 40,000 urban families throughout the nation and concluded that divorce rates were almost three times higher in Protestant-Catholic marriages than in unmixed marriages.[20] Burchinal and Chancellor (1962) in a study of Iowa interfaith marriages licensed during the 1950s found they did not last as long as those of the same faith.[21]

Whether one puts much weight on these cited studies or not, it seems likely that most people would agree that those entering interfaith marriages should be aware of the possible additional adjustments to be made. Such an awareness can be developed by asking the following questions.

[17]Bell, Howard M., "Youth Tell Their Story," Washington, D. C. American Council of Education, 1938, p. 21.

[18]Dyer, Dorothy T. and Luckey, Eleanor, "Religious Affiliation and Selected Personality Scores as They Relate to Marital Happiness of a Minnesota College Sample," *Marriage and Family Living*, 23, Feb. 1961, pp. 46, 47, Minneapolis: The National Council of Family Relations, 1961.

[19]Burgess, E. W. and Cottrell, L. S., "Predicting Success or Failure in Marriage," Englewood Cliffs, N. J.: Prentice-Hall, Inc., 1938.

[20]Zimmerman, Carle C. and Cervantes, Lucius F., *Successful American Families*, New York: Pageant, 1960, p. 76.

[21]Burchinal, Lee G. and Chancellor, Loren, "Survival Rates Among Religiously Homogamous and Inter-religious Marriages," Research Bulletin No. 512758. Ames, Iowa: Agriculture & Home Economics Experiment Station, Iowa State University, December, 1962.

Questions to Answer Before Entering an Interfaith Marriage

1. What does my religion mean to me? Does my church activity stem from meeting with a social group I like, or do I believe in God and am I active religiously because of deep convictions? Do I feel that my church is the only true church? If so, will I condemn a marriage partner who cannot believe as I do?

2. If I marry outside of my faith, will my associations with my family and friends become strained? Is it possible that they might even reject me? Can I isolate myself from them and still be happy?

3. Do my future mate and I have other interests that will compensate for lack of religious unity?

4. How do we plan to bring up our children? What church will they attend? Will they go to a church or public school?

5. Can we both join a new and different religious group which will more effectively meet our needs as a couple?

If those about to marry will ask themselves these and other related questions, they will usually recognize that they cannot separate the religious element in their lives from their total relationship. They will also realize that if they do have a "great love" for each other it must be nurtured in a climate of understanding and of meeting each other's needs.

Suggested Readings

1. Berman, Louis A., *Jews and Intermarriage,* Cranbury, N.J.: 1968.

2. Besancency, Paul H., S. J., *Interfaith Marriages: Who and Why,* New Haven, Ct.: 1970.

3. Burchinal, Lee G., and Chancellor, Loren E., "Social Status, Religious Affiliation and Ages at Marriage," *Marriage and Family Living,* 25 (May 1963), 219-221.

4. Coombs, Robert H., "A Value Theory of Mate Selection," *Family Life Coordinator,* 10 (July, 1961), 51-54.

5. Gardner, LeRoy, *The Truth About Interracial Marriage,* St. Paul, Mn.: Gardner, 1965.

6. Gordon, Albert I., *Intermarriage: Interfaith, Interracial, Interethnic,* Boston: Beacon Press, 1964.

7. Hathorn, Raban, Genne, W. H., and Brill, Mordecai (eds.), *Marriage: An Interfaith Guide for All Couples,* New York: Association Press, 1970.

8. Pike, James A., *If You Marry Outside of Your Faith,* Chicago: Harper, 1954.

9. Rodman, Hyman, "Mate Selection: Incest Taboos, Homogamy, and Mixed Marriages," in Rodman, Hyman, (ed.), *Marriage, Family and Society:* A Reader, New York: Random House, 1965.

Chapter IX

Interpersonal Factors in Mate Selection

Although the choice of a marriage partner may be circumscribed by the social factors previously discussed, young Americans still have great freedom in selecting a mate. In exercising this freedom, many couples find that they feel drawn toward each other and cannot explain why. So it might be interesting to review some of the theories that have been proposed in an attempt to explain why this mutual attraction takes place.

SOME THEORIES OF MATE SELECTION

Finding One's Soul-mate

It is difficult to summarize this approach to mate selection as it is usually derived from religious thinking and brings into play the spiritual dimension of life that rests upon a faith and individual belief that can be tested only by the concerned person. Consequently, if an individual feels that he or she had a mate who was known in a previous existence who is predestined to become a marriage partner here, such thinking should be respected by others as a religious belief.

People often recount different ways that certain circumstances have brought them to their soul-mate. One interesting account is given by Michael.[1] Very briefly his thoughts are: "All of us carry around within us an image of our ideal counterpart; a male or female in human form who is a great source of attraction to our hearts and minds." (p. 47)

Soul-mates meet in dreams during their regular sleeping hours for a period of time before they meet physically. Their physical meeting can be speeded up by regular prayer, at the same time each day, with implicit faith that the meeting will soon occur. Once your inner contact is made, your soul-mate will be drawn to your geographical vicinity. You will be attracted to each other and have an enduring relationship if you have the same soul rays and personality rays (Ch. 7).

---

[1]Michael, Russ, *Finding Your Soul-Mate*, Lakemont, Georgia, CSA Press, 1971.

Complementary Needs

Robert Winch in his theory of complementary needs defines love and presents a principle of mate selection in the following terms:

"Love is the positive emotion experienced by one person (the person loving, or the lover) in an interpersonal relationship in which the second person (the person loved, or love object) either (1) meets certain important needs of the first or (2) manifests or appears (to the first) to manifest personal attributes (e.g., beauty, skills, or status) highly prized by the first, or both.

"In mate-selection each individual seeks within his or her field of eligibles for that person who gives the greatest promise of providing him or her maximum need gratification."[2]

In working out this hypothesis, Winch decided that there were two types of complementary-need satisfactions that lead to mate selection. One, both partners have the same basic need with a difference in intensity. For example, a man with a high dominance need would select a woman with a low dominance need for his wife. Two, both partners have complementary needs. For example, a woman with a high need to give sympathy and aid to a weak person (nurturance need) would get satisfaction from a husband who liked to be nursed and fussed over (succorance need).

Among the other specific need-complements which Winch assumes exist are recognition-deference, hostility-abasement, achievement-vicariousness and others.

Winch also states that the complementary need pattern is not always entered into on the conscious level by partners.

Proponents of the homogamous method of mate selection have questioned Winch's findings, and several studies by others have been divided in results. Some have failed to confirm his theory and others have upheld it. It should be said that these studies did not contain the in-depth type of interview that Winch used in formulating his theory.

In summary, the generalization may be made regarding Winch's theory that some partners do marry because of complementary needs, and others because of like needs. So, despite this theory, each set of partners must, in the final analysis, determine which kind of needs will help them build a satisfying and enduring relationship.

---

[2]Winch, Robert F., *Mate Selection, A Study of Complementary Needs*. New York: Harper & Brothers, 1958, pp. 88, 89.

Other Theories

Other theories of mate selection that have been presented include: *The Kerckhoff-Davis filter theory* which describes mate selection as a multi-stage process. Briefly stated it assumes that potential partners proceed as follows: Choose from those with like social, physical and religious characteristics—agree on values—feel they complement each other's needs —result—marry and help each other maintain a positive self-image.[3]

The Kerckhoff-Davis theory supports endogamy, homogamy, and heterogamy, and states that these "filtering factors" operate at different stages of courtship, and may either block or facilitate the selection of a mate.

Murstein's Stimulus-Value-Role (SVR) theory.[4] His thinking is that in a culture where couples are allowed freedom of choice in mate selection, they go through three stages before marrying.

One. Stimulus stage—Couples are attracted to each other by physical, social, and mental qualities; roles played in society, personal aspirations, and background.

Two. Value comparison—After mutual attraction has brought the couple together, they begin to compare each other's values. Through verbal interaction they explore such things as their attitudes toward religion, politics, purpose of life, sex, male and female roles. In learning whether they have similar values, they also have greater opportunity to appraise each other's physical attributes and temperaments. If they find they hold similar values, and each is pleased with the other's temperament and physical attributes they continue to the role stage.

Three. Role stage—If on this stage, the couple finds they are compatible regarding roles and goals, they go on to marriage. In some cases, marriage may take place because of strong attraction or similarly held values. However, people usually function better in marriage if they also have compatible roles and goals.

THINGS FOR THE INDIVIDUAL TO CONSIDER IN CHOOSING A MARRIAGE PARTNER

It is highly possible that one could be well-informed in the theories of mate selection and still be beset by anxiety and confusion when about

[3]Kerckhoff, Alan C. and Davis, Keith E., "Value Consensus and Need Complementarity in Mate Selection," *American Sociological Review*, June, 1962. pp. 295-303.
[4]Murstein, Bernard, "Stimulus-Value-Role: A Theory of Marital Choice," Journal of Marriage and the Family, August, 1970, pp. 465-481.

to take the final step into marriage. Some writers attempt to offer help at this time by stating, "If you can answer 'yes' to these twenty questions you will be certain to have a happy marriage." Of course such thinking is simplistic, and is about as valid as saying, "If you possess these twenty physical characteristics you can become an Olympic gold medal winner," or "Answering these twenty questions with 'yes' will assure your future as a Hollywood star."

If you are about to marry, you know such tests will be of little help to you. Neither will it guarantee you a successful marriage if you check out your potential mate as possessing the twenty traits you desire in a marriage partner. Nevertheless, there are some things that might be helpful for you to consider, and carefully pondering the following things may give you some of the insights you need.

Are You Ready for Marriage?

Your Reasons for Marrying at This Time

Knowing when to marry can often be as important as knowing whom to marry. If two people marry at the right time, that is at the stage in their lives when they have the highest motivation to adjust to each other and the aptitude and competency necessary to meet the needs of their newly established family unit, they are more likely to succeed. There are a number of reasons that cause some people to marry at a certain time which might work counter to good marriage adjustment.

Marrying to Escape Something

Getting married is often looked upon as a remedy for all ills or difficulties, consequently, some individuals marry to escape a difficult situation. Others marry to get away from their homes and parents. They say they are misunderstood and cannot be happy at home. Still others are bored with school and do not want to exercise the self-discipline needed to fulfill study assignments. Marriage seems to offer a way out of their unpleasant situation. Getting married to avoid the burden of earning one's living also causes some to go to the marriage altar.

There are at least two reasons why marrying to escape something may result in an unsatisfactory marriage. First, the desire to escape an unpleasant situation may be weighted more heavily than the future relationship with the potential marriage partner, which would put the marriage on a shaky foundation from the start. Second, the person who wants to escape unpleasantness may feel the present situation is undesirable because he has not learned to adjust to other people. So chances are that the same inability to adjust to others will pose difficulties in adjusting to the marriage partner.

Marrying Hurriedly Because of Pregnancy or Other Factors

It frequently happens that dating partners are sexually intimate, after short acquaintance, and if pregnancy results, feel it is their duty to hurry and get married. One has to respect such individuals for their sense of commitment to each other, but the trouble is that they may marry as complete strangers from a personality standpoint. If the husband feels he was compelled to marry because of social pressures or his own guilt feelings, he may never value his wife as a marriage partner. The wife may harbor deep feelings of resentment toward her husband, and the circumstances that caused them to get married may produce a vulnerable area in their relationships that may persist for years.

A typical counseling case illustrates these problems.

Jennifer came for counseling because she felt she must marry her boyfriend. She said, "I have given myself to Ralph, and am carrying his baby, but now he doesn't want to marry me. He simply must, because I could never sleep with another man, and if he doesn't become my husband I'll go through life feeling like a fallen woman."

The interview took place late in the evening, and Jennifer had insisted that Ralph come with her. He did, but remained outside and refused to enter the writer's office. Consequently, his opinion about getting married was solicited outside in the cold night air.

"I just don't know what to do," he responded, when questioned about getting married. "I thought I loved Jen, but when she told me she was pregnant, something came over me, and I wondered if she had slept with some other guys. After all if she did with me, why shouldn't she? I don't think I love her enough to take on the responsibility of marriage and a baby."

Ralph eventually bowed to the pressures brought by his parents, Jennifer's family, and the group's minister and went through with the marriage. But it has never been a happy one. The circumstances surrounding their marriage have combined to develop a sensitive area in their relationships which they have never been able to overcome.

MARRIAGE AND MILITARY SERVICE

Marriages have often been entered into hurriedly, because the male partner faced a period of military service. It is impossible to generalize and say such a marriage should be avoided, but there are certain factors to be considered that might affect the decision to marry.

Fear of Separation

If a couple marries sooner than they intended because military service or something else might separate them, they are on shaky ground because they may be entering a marriage they may not be ready for. On the other hand, if they have planned to marry at a certain time, and the prospect of service appears and they accept it as fitting into their long-range plans, there is much greater likelihood of their marriage succeeding.

Getting married before the male partner goes into the service does not guarantee that the couple will be able to continue living together, as much depends upon the branch of the service the husband enters, and the rank he holds. If living together cannot be arranged, the stability of the marriage often rests upon how long the couple was married before being separated, so their marriage could develop roots, and how deep their commitment is to each other. Those couples most likely to succeed think of their marriage in terms of long-range goals, rather than immediate satisfactions. Sometimes one of the partners has the long-range view and the others does not. Take for instance, Tim's experience. He said:

"Joy and I married shortly before I was sent overseas. And you know the big thing that kept me going while I was away was the fact that I had a beautiful, loving wife waiting for me after the war ended. When peace was declared and we headed home, my mind was filled with all kinds of dreams about what Joy and I could do in the future. She was waiting at the railroad station, and she looked so beautiful that I hugged her with happiness. But my dreams for the future were soon shattered. As we drove home, she gave me a strange look, and then turning away from me said, 'Tim, I want you to know how much I respect you, but you were away so long, and I got so lonesome, that I just couldn't—well, I just couldn't take it. I started dating and I love someone else. I want a divorce.'

"You can't imagine what that did to me—the bottom just dropped out of everything. I tried to talk her out of separating, but couldn't do it.

Now, I'm back in school working toward a degree, but believe me divorce has been a more rugged thing to go through than my combat experience overseas."

Being Together

Even if the couple can arrange to live together after the husband enters the service, things do not always work out. One of the partners may enjoy adventure, change, and new experiences, the other may not. Many war brides have told the author that they finally got tired of trying to adjust to army life, left their husbands and went back to their home towns. Typical of these was Colleen whose husband, Jack, was a major. She said:

"I thought it would be a lark to live with my husband on military bases and meet all of the interesting wives of the other officers. For awhile it did seem glamorous, but you know we'd barely get acquainted in one place and then be transferred somewhere else. The ways of the army are hard to understand. After crisscrossing the continent several times and making one set of chintz curtains after another to put up in all of our different apartments, I gave up and went home to mother. Jack didn't see things the way I did. He loves change, and decided to make the army his career, so we separated."

Your Plans

As this is being written, there is some indication that military service will operate from now on and into the future on a voluntary basis. If this happens, many couples will not be faced with the foregoing problems. However, no matter what the circumstances are that surround your coming marriage, your partnership will be on more solid ground if you can assimilate possible separations into your long-range plans and not let them stampede you into premature marriage.

SOME SPECIAL PROBLEMS OF CAMPUS MARRIAGES

Marrying while still in college also is associated with proper timing. Is this a good time to marry? Apparently many students think it is.

About three decades ago, very few college students who married remained in school. This situation has changed. Bowman states, "In 1966, there were 6,085,000 students enrolled in institutions of higher learning in this country. Of these, 1,256,000 (20.6 percent) were married and living with their spouses. These figures do not, therefore, include students who were married but whose spouses were absent, for example, in military service. More male students (24.4 percent) than female students (14.5 percent) were married (U. S. Bureau of the Census, 1967).[5]

From these statistics you can be reassured that if you want to marry before completing college, you are not alone, there are many others like you. However, the fact that others are entering marriages while on the campus does not give one any license to enter a hasty, unrealistic, or a "cloak-for-sex-desire" marriage. In fact, if you intend to marry before completing college, you have all of the things to consider which any couple planning marriage does, plus a few more. And it is these additional problems of adjustment which often cause the college marriage to fail. Let us look at a few of these special problems.

Special Problems of College Marriage

1. Establishing a satisfactory financial structure.

It costs money to maintain a marriage and it costs more to live as a family group and attend college. Just how do you plan to meet these costs?

a. Getting financial help from parents.

Will your parents subsidize your marriage? If so, how will the relationship be worked out? Will they lend you the money at a low rate of interest (or no interest) and have you repay it when you graduate and become established in your job? Do they plan to hand you the money as a gift with the attitude that it is a privilege to assist you financially as you pursue your goals?

In either case, whether you sign a promissory note to get the money or receive it as a gift, how will this financial aid affect your relationships with your parents? Will it cause you to feel unduly obligated to them, to resent their help, or to more fully appreciate them as not only your parents, but your friends? What will the parental reaction be to giving financial assistance? Will they remain completely objective or tend to exercise undue influence on your future plans?

b. Making your own way financially.

Suppose you make it "on your own" financially. Will both work or just one? If so, which one? How will this affect your attitudes toward

---

[5]Bowman, Henry A., *Marriage for Moderns*, New York: McGraw-Hill, 6th Edition, 1970, p. 343.

each other? For example, if your wife works and you attend school, will she be resentful?

Can you struggle through with scholarships and other loans to be repaid after graduation?

Many more things could be considered about your financial plans, but the few mentioned here should enable you to get the problems out into the open and consider them objectively.

The key for answering these questions is that you, as partners, are in complete agreement on the course you decide to follow.

2. What will you do if a baby arrives?

Despite the fact that many college couples plan to postpone having babies until after graduation, it does happen that children arrive ahead of the proposed time schedule. How will having an unplanned baby affect you? Will you take any of the following steps? Quit school? Go part-time? Stay in school and get an additional job? Cause tension in your marriage by blaming the other for carelessness in the use of contraceptives? Accept the baby as a blessing and continue with your schooling? Arrange for the baby's care so you both can stay in school?

3. Academic pressures versus your social life.

If you, as the husband, attend college and your wife works, will she be irritated by your study schedule? When she wants social contacts and recreation will she see your studies as an unfair rival for your attention? Will your preoccupation with your studies cause her to feel you have lost interest in her?

Let us assume that your wife is also attending school. Will you have a tendency to depreciate the importance of her education?

4. Growing together intellectually.

In some cases when the husband attends college and the wife works to help him through, the husband begins to sense an intellectual gap developing between himself and his mate. Is it possible for the two of you, no matter what the work-study combination, to remain stimulating intellectual companions?

5. Your future goals.

Do you both have sufficient motivation, and abiding faith in each other, and a sound love relationship which will enable you as partners to achieve your mutual goals? If these goals should be altered because of new insights or unforeseen circumstances, will you be able to accept and understand these changes as good for your partnership?

Finally, can you both live, grow, and be happy with all of the special "pressure points" (Bowman) which college marriage entails?

These special problems have not been presented in order to discourage you from marrying while in college, but to make you aware of the adjustments which must be made.

The consensus of married students in the writer's classes is that these special adjustments related to college marriage are a bit easier to make if the couple waits to marry until the husband or the wife is past the halfway mark toward graduation. Their thinking is that the couple would then be closer to their mutual goal and would also have tested the study habits of each or both, and thus have learned more about their academic possibilities.

Insights into these special problems of adjustment can often be gained by learning from couples who have had successful college marriages. A typical experience is given below. The couple wrote their case history at the author's request, knowing that it would be used to present to other students.

CASE HISTORY—"I BELIEVE IT IS POSSIBLE TO HAVE A SUCCESSFUL COLLEGE MARRIAGE"

"A recent occurrence in my life gives me the assurance that I can present a brief discussion regarding marriage among students. I believe students can be married while both of them attend college. I am certain of this for I was married four months ago and my husband and I are presently both university students.

"It is necessary that a few assumptions be presented before discussing the merits of the situation. The primary assumption would be that the couple have enough money to finance the period of their education remaining. This could be in the form of savings, scholarship awards, or GI compensation to the husband. We are fortunate to have all three sources helping us. Now this does not mean that we're on easy street, it means that we worked previously to save our money and to get the scholarships so our finances could be in this shape. If students have only little or no aid in any of the above forms, it would be necessary for one or both of them to work. If this complication became too intense, more problems could arise to hinder success in their marriage. I know of cases in which couples combine employment and college; there appears to be success in the combination for them.

"The other important assumption is that one of the pair has two years or less of college remaining. If both have more than two years, financial assurance in advance would be necessary. Also, after a few years of marriage, the couple may desire children and would have conflicts about whether to finish school or have them. This could lead to a strain on the relationship. It was because we both had two years left that we waited until the following year to be married; now we each have one year left.

"Now that we are married, the apparent good points appear. First and foremost, since marriage we have a more stable emotional attitude. Before I was married, I would not keep my mind on studying very long. My thoughts kept darting off on concerns, such as: 'Wonder if I'll get a date for Saturday night?'; 'That guy next to me in psych class sure is a doll'; 'Wonder if Bill will phone tonight like he said he would.' These thoughts are representative of what most single girls experience. As a married woman, my main interest, my husband, is always with me. While I'm trying to study now, if I think of him all I have to do is look up and he's right there with me. In social situations or classes, I am not constantly striving to impress other men; therefore, I am more relaxed socially and more intent during classes. Consequently, it is quite obvious that my entire emotional make-up has improved. I might add that this is not only true for me; we have discussed this change in our lives occasionally and my husband has noticed the same improvement in himself. So, the move was for the better for both of us, I might say.

"When considering marriage, I had thought that the time it would take me to clean the house and prepare the meals would be an awful lot; it would detract from my study time and so forth. Apparently, most girls think the same thing, for nearly everyone asks me that question now. The answer is very simple. I want to do my work, keep our apartment clean, and it is a great pride to me. Also, and perhaps most important, I see now that the time it takes me to prepare our meals is less than the time I formerly spent talking with the girls. While living in a house or dormitory for three years, I found that we girls always gabbed for at least an hour in the evening; it was usually more like an hour before and an hour after dinner. It now takes me an hour and a half, at the most, to make dinner, eat it, and clean up afterward.

"In regard to cleaning time, the same thing holds true. I find if I do a bit of cleaning every minute or two I have free, it never piles up and becomes a real chore. Of course, this always involves ironing from 7:30 in the morning until the first hour class, doing a little hand-dusting instead of reading a magazine in the evening, floor-scrubbing instead of sleeping on Saturday morning, and that sort of thing. This may sound ghastly to the single girls. But to me it is really no chore at all because I'm happy doing it. When I consider all the time I formerly wasted, I see now it can be utilized more wisely.

"Not only do we find it easy to get work done, we find we have even more free time. When we were going together, the only way to talk was for an hour on the telephone when we couldn't see each other. If we wanted to be together, he had to drive over, after which I had to be in on university-enforced dating hours. Now we are always around and can talk for as long as we want to, can talk as we do household chores together, and of course, never have to be in at certain hours. All these factors combine to produce more time for one another.

"If I may ask pardon for sounding practical, there is also the financial advantage of marriage over singularity. In our present situation, our costs are less than what it cost us to live apart. The sum of dormitory bills we each paid far exceeds the cost of food, rent, and utilities now. These economic advantages are all fine and dandy and, I might add, we had them figured out over a year before we were married. However, that is not the reason we got married; it just helps a lot.

"Now to the people who profess that a girl should finish her college education before she considers marriage, I have one answer. I am happier married than I was single; therefore, why should I put off marriage when we figured out that it was actually possible beforehand? It is our feeling that we could put off the children for one year until I finished. Even if I never use my career for ten or twenty years, while we have a family, it is still there ready for me to use. As my husband says, it is the best insurance I can have.

"I believe that covers all the advantages I would like to cite about college marriages. To get off the subject somewhat, I simply must add this anecdote. When I came to college I was not eager to find a man, as I know many girls are. Therefore, I just acted naturally with all the fellows, not trying to nab every one I went out with. Then when my man came along it was much to my surprise and a great delight to discover that here I was in love and considering marriage."

OTHER REASONS FOR POOR CHOICE OF A MARRIAGE PARTNER

Possible success in marriage may be affected negatively by some of these other reasons for marriage:

Thinking marriage will reform your future partner. People's basic personalities are not changed much by marriage; so it is better to accept your future mate as he or she is.

Marrying at too early an age. An individual who appeals to you when you are seventeen, may be of little interest to you when you reach your twenties. This may happen because your attitudes and tastes are not fully developed at the earlier age.

Marrying because the rest of your crowd is. One basic principle of human development is that each individual has his own timetable of growth, consequently, you cannot base your readiness for marriage on the fact that others your age are taking their marriage vows.

Marrying for money, out of pity, or to please others also may hinder good marriage adjustment.

One common mistake which impels some to marry is confusing infatuation with love. If you feel that you might be caught in such confusion, answering the following questions may help clarify your thinking.

BACKGROUND AND PREMARITAL FACTORS THAT MIGHT AFFECT MARRIAGE ADJUSTMENT

Do factors from the individual's background have any effect on his marriage adjustment? A number of studies indicate that they do. Kirkpatrick has listed those most highly associated with good marital adjustment:

Factors in the Choice of a Mate Which Are Related to Happiness in Marriage

1. Happiness of the parents' marriage.
2. Adequate sex information in childhood.
3. Personal happiness in childhood.
4. Harmonious affection with parents during childhood.
5. Adequate length of acquaintance, courtship and engagement.

6. Approval of the marriage by parents and others.
7. Engagement adjustments and normal motivation toward marriage.
8. Ethnic and religious similarity.
9. High social and educational status.
10. Mature and similar chronological age.[6]

It must be remembered that these factors are used in *predicting* possible marital success; they are not infallible. For example, an individual who had quarreling parents and an unhappy life as a child in the home may be highly motivated to avoid such mistakes in his marriage and work hard at making his wife and children happy. Nevertheless, these predictive factors merit careful consideration if for no other reason than the fact that learning about them helps one to get better acquainted with and more fully understand his or her marriage partner.

PERSONALITY TRAITS OF FUTURE MATE

To help in the choice of a mate, many books offer long lists of traits to check in the possible marital partner, before a decision should be made. This will not be done here. If you want such a list, you can make it yourself. If you make the list too long, and check it too closely, you might find yourself in the same situation as Diogenes, the Greek cynic, who roamed the streets at midday with a lighted lantern vainly seeking an honest man. If you did, by some miraculous chance, find a person who measured up to every characteristic on your check list, you would probably become bored with him—or her, anyway. It is more realistic to accept the fact that no one is perfect.

Three simple questions that might be asked to guide one in choosing a life's partner are:

Are we attracted to each other physically?
Are we mentally stimulating to each other?
Are we spiritually in harmony?

Are We Attracted to Each Other Physically?

There is nothing wrong with physical attraction between a couple

---

[6]Kirkpatrick, Clifford, *The Family as Process and Institution*. New York: Ronald Press, 1963, pp. 375-405. (As reported by Moss, Joel J., "What Is a Good Marriage?" Provo, Utah: *Family Perspective*, Spring 1966, Vol. 1, No. 1, pp. 24, 25. Published by the College of Family Living, Brigham Young University.)

who plan to marry. Some people say they intend to marry, but that their life together will be a platonic relationship (a spiritual comradeship or love between persons of the opposite sex, in which there is assumed to be no element of sexual desire). This type of relationship makes marriage incomplete. A complete marriage includes a sound sexual relationship; therefore, it is important that two people who plan to marry are physically attracted to each other.

You couples who are contemplating marriage should realize that physical attractiveness is not necessarily produced by certain bodily dimensions. Undoubtedly, many of you girls dream about marrying a man who is at least six feet two inches in height and possesses a muscular build, while you fellows think about your future married life with a girl with a perfect figure.

You will find after you have married that you will not be disappointed when you take a "good look" and realize that your mate does not fit the physical image of your former dreams. But despite these discrepancies between your former dreams and present realities, both of you will still be happy and physically attracted to your mates.

We might give you the answer to this strange phenomenon by using such cliches as "handsome is as handsome does," or you found out that "beneath his torn coat is a heart of gold," and so forth. But what has really happened is that you as marriage partners have finally realized that your mate's physical attractiveness is the result of a personality that is compatible with your own.

So the final test of your marriage partner's physical attractiveness is found in your answer to the two questions:

Is he handsome to you?

Is she beautiful to you?

In connection with being physically attractive to each other, some individuals who are about to marry may ask, "What about ill health or a physical disability? Should these things disqualify a person as a marriage partner?"

The answer to these questions is an emphatic "No!" The only decision to be made in this respect is to determine how *you* feel about the physical condition of your future partner. If you accept this condition as part of the total personality which you love, this is all that matters.

Are We Mentally Stimulating to Each Other?

Many couples marry before they discover whether they are mentally stimulating to each other. If they marry and learn later that there is no interesting interplay between their minds, their marriage is likely to become as flat as food without spices.

It is important to learn before you marry if you are interesting mental companions. Much can be learned about this by engaging in frank discussions centered on world affairs, religion, politics, one's philosophy of life, and so forth. Another help is to find out what mutual interests you have in music, art, literature, sports, dancing, and all of the other interesting activities of contemporary society.

The amount of formal schooling that each person has acquired should also be considered. Although a difference in the degree of formal education can cause some problems, it is much less likely to if both persons have the same attitude toward learning new things and expanding their knowledge and appreciation of life.

As is true with physical attractiveness, the mentality of your partner is an important part of the total personality which you love.

Are We Spiritually in Harmony?

The only way your possibilities of spiritual harmony can be ascertained is for you as a couple to express openly, *how* you think and feel about the spiritual things of life such as your concept of God, your attitude toward church-going, and what you believe is the purpose of life. Engaging in mutual religious activity will help you both to be more perceptive of the other's reaction to spiritual matters.

Your partner's spiritual nature is of equal importance, if not of greater importance than his physical and mental characteristics in being an integral part of the personality which you love.

CAN AN AGENCY HELP YOU CHOOSE A MATE?

Recently, there has been widespread growth of agencies designed to help one find a marriage partner. Typical of these are lonely hearts clubs, matrimonial agencies, and computerized services to assist in dating and mating. Although such agencies speak in glowing terms of their successes, no solid figures have been published to back up their claims.

Some observations should be made about the functions of these services. If they have a cross-section of eligible marriage partners in their files, and if the data they have about their clients is relevant to marriage adjustment, they can render helpful service. However, one problem is that many people who go to such services for help, do so because they do not feel confident or attractive enough to find a mate in their general social interaction. Thus agencies may be overstocked with those who would be difficult to adjust to in marriage.

Finally, although such services may provide two eligible individuals with the opportunity to meet, no amount of data that is fed into a computer can predetermine whether they will be physically attracted to each other. Thus, they are on their own to decide whether the spark necessary for a happy marriage is present. Inasmuch as most young Americans seem to feel that dating and romantic love are part of selecting a mate, the artificiality of having an agency find a mate for them may cause them to forego such help.

Suggested Readings

1. Bossard, James H. S., and Boll, Eleanor S., *One Marriage, Two Faiths,* New York: Ronald Press, 1957.

2. Coombs, Robert H., "Sex Differences in Dating Aspirations and Satisfaction With Computer Selected Partners," *Journal of Marriage and the Family,* 28 (February, 1966), 62-66.

3. Hunt, Morton M., *The World of the Formerly Married,* New York: McGraw-Hill, 1966.

4. Murstein, Bernard I. (ed.), *Theories of Attraction and Love,* New York: Springer Publishing Co., 1972.

5. Shedd, Charlie W., *Letters to Karen: On Keeping Love in Marriage,* Nashville, Tn: Abingdon, 1965.

6. ———, *Letters to Phillip: On How to Treat a Woman,* Garden City, N.Y.: Doubleday, 1960.

7. Terman, Lewis M., et al; *Psychological Factors in Marital Happiness,* New York: McGraw-Hill, 1938.

8. Udry, J. Richard, "Complementarity in Mate Selection: A Perceptual Approach," *Marriage and Family Living,* 25 (August, 1963), 281-289.

9. Winch, Robert F., *Mate Selection: A Study of Complementary Needs,* New York: Harper & Row, 1958.

Chapter X

Engagement—The Prelude to Marriage

Strephon kissed me in the spring,
Robin in the fall,
But Colin only looked at me
And never kissed at all.
Strephon's kiss was lost in jest,
Robin's lost in play,
But the kiss in Colin's eyes
Haunts me night and day![1]

The above poem points out the fact that each individual person has to decide whether he or she loves another. Thus, when it comes to choosing a marriage partner, statistics and theories regarding future marital adjustment have little meaning when compared with how two people really feel about each other. One of the best ways for a girl to find out what the look in her boyfriend's eyes ("the kiss in Colin's eyes") really means is to become engaged so she and her possible marriage partner can have a period of time to explore each other's qualities and find out if they are compatible. Doing this before they make a marriage commitment should cut down their risk of failing in marriage.

Beginning with primitive societies, great emphasis has usually been put on the betrothal or engagement as one of the rites marking the transition to marriage. Eichler[2] states that among certain tribes and cultures such as those in Afghan and Greece, it has been the custom to prohibit the man from speaking to his betrothed until they are married. Naturally, such a practice would hinder rather than help an engaged couple to get better acquainted. Eichler says, "It would appear that customs such as these grew out of the fear of the bride's parents or people of being cheated

---

[1]Teasdale, Sara, "The Look." in Marjorie Barrows, ed; *The Quintessence of Beauty and Romance*, Chicago: 1955, p. 151.
[2]Eichler, Lillian, *The Customs of Mankind*, Garden City, New York: Doubleday, Page and Co., 1924, pp. 196-197.

of the bride-price if she decided to elope with her betrothed before the day set for the wedding, although in many instances it was necessary to pay the bride-price even before the wedding day was set."

Engagement rites with varying degrees of ceremony are still practiced throughout the world with couples in the United States providing no exception. However, in contemporary American culture, engagement is looked upon in different ways by different people. Some adhere to formal rites; others prefer an informal casual arrangement; and a few consider the engagement period unnecessary. Nevertheless, many couples still see it as an important testing period preceding marriage. This is born out by statistics contained in a recent *Seventeen* magazine survey. They showed that in the United States 800,000 adolescent girls became engaged each year; the median age being 16.9 and at any one time there are about one million teen-age girls who are engaged.

SIGNIFICANCE OF THE ENGAGEMENT

When two people become engaged, several changes take place in their relationships with each other and also with their social groups. *First,* their formal engagement announces to their friends and relatives that they intend to marry. In most cases, a ring is worn by the girl as outward evidence that she and her partner have made a commitment to seriously consider getting married. In times past, a diamond was considered the only gem that could symbolize the betrothal. "This thinking came from an old superstition that the sparkle of the diamond is supposed to have originated in the fires of love. Therefore, the diamond engagement ring is considered by superstitious persons to be the only true engagement ring, portending love and happiness throughout life."[3]

Today's couples are either less superstitious or more practical regarding their betrothal, and the diamond is no longer the automatic synonym for the engagement ring. Other settings that have become popular are opals, rubies, tourmalines, and pearls. Some girls say they feel just as engaged when wearing a plain band or their boyfriend's school ring.

Second, the announced engagement is a notice to former dating partners that the engaged pair are out of the mating market and intend to confine their dating activities to each other.

_____

[3]*Ibid.*

Third, the engagement allows both persons to be on display to potential in-laws and friends, and in the process, also learn whether relationships with them in the future will tend to help or hinder their marriage.

Fourth, the engagement provides a period in which a couple should learn, through frank and relaxed discussion, the attitudes each has toward the married relationship, and marriage goals. Developing such a climate of understanding should help each partner feel more secure in that neither can be accused of "jumping the gun" if either one introduces a discussion regarding the number of children desired or feelings about renting or buying a house.

LEGAL ASPECTS

American courts have traditionally held that the engagement is a form of contract, and if either of the engaged persons refuses to go through with the marriage without a justifiable cause, a breach of contract is in evidence and a breach-of-promise suit may be initiated. A typical court case that transpired in Minnesota illustrates these legal implications of becoming engaged. A prominent professional woman became engaged to a man who resided in a distant state. After the couple had set their marriage date, public announcements were made of their coming wedding, and the career woman gave her employer notice that she was resigning her position in 60 days. Her friends gave her a series of parties and showers, and she and her fiancé happily made arrangements for a gala wedding reception. Two days before the scheduled marriage date, and after she had terminated her employment, she made a long distance telephone call to her fiancé to get his opinion on a certain detail regarding the final wedding arrangements. To her surprise, a woman answered the phone. Subsequent events revealed that her husband-to-be was already married and had apparently planned to commit bigamy and enjoy the favors of two wives who lived a thousand miles apart. The bride-to-be was humiliated, and after recovering from the shock, eventually became so enraged that she had her attorney bring a breach-of-promise suit before the court. Her complaint was that she had suffered irreparable financial loss in resigning her job, and in addition had been publicly humiliated and would need at least $55,000 to compensate for the damages she suffered. Her claim was upheld by the court because of the obvious fraudulent behavior of her fiancé.

Breach-of-promise suits came into being during the colonial period, and for a time, beautiful and ofttimes conniving women burdened the courts with suits seeking damages to compensate for being jilted by their lovers. Theoretically, jilted men have the same rights, but the courts generally have not considered their claims seriously.

In recent years, a number of states have outlawed breach-of-promise suits and there has been a tendency to look upon the engagement as a time for testing compatibility rather than a contractual agreement. Despite these trends, breach-of-promise suits which are popularly called "heart-balm" cases still take place in some states. However, these same states do protect the man against breach-of-promise action if he can show justifiable reasons for jilting his fiancée. Valid reasons include cases where the woman is sterile, sexually promiscuous, has a venereal disease, or has deliberately misrepresented herself and her life-style.

LENGTH OF ENGAGEMENT

Couples often ask, "Does a short or long engagement give us a better chance for happy marriage?"

Such a question can be given no set answer, inasmuch as the circumstances surrounding each couple's engagement differ. Much depends upon their temperaments, how long they have known each other before becoming engaged, and how well they have become acquainted during their pre-engagement days. If they have seriously tried to understand each other's personalities, had the opportunity to observe each other in a variety of everyday activities, and set a pattern for solving problems arising from their interaction, a short engagement period may be all that is necessary.

An engagement can also be too long if the partners begin to feel that they are "neither fish nor fowl," neither enjoying the freedoms of single life nor the privileges of marriage. This can produce a sense of frustration with the accompanying feeling that their marriage might never take place. The resulting discontent may lead them to substitute living together for marriage, or to plunge into marriage with the hope that taking the nuptial vows will cause all of their problems to vanish.

Because of these different factors, the only realistic way a couple can determine how long their engagement should be is by objectively examining their personal interaction, and future marriage goals.

Three widely quoted studies give some indication that there is a positive relationship between length of engagement and happiness in marriage. The Burgess-Cottrell[4] study revealed that only 11 percent of married couples who had been engaged two years or longer showed poor marital adjustment. Terman's[5] findings showed a happiness peak among couples who had been engaged five years or longer. Locke's[6] sample revealed that divorced couples had shorter engagements than happily married couples, the length for men being 3.5 and women 5.4 months. Whereas the average length for the happily married was men 9.5 months and women 11.1.

One weakness in these studies is that they were made with married couples rather than those contemplating marriage, so that a study of couples not yet married might produce different results. In summary, it can be suggested that regardless of length, the engagement does offer a couple the opportunity to get acquainted in a special setting that is oriented toward future marriage.

SHOULD THOSE WHO ARE ENGAGED DATE OTHER PERSONS?

Once a couple in our culture becomes engaged, it is assumed that they will have no further desire to date others. If they do, the engagement loses its meaning because it should signify that each person has made the final or at least the tentative choice of a marriage partner. If either feels the need to "step out" with others, it could be that the individual who has the desire to stray entered the engagement without sufficient forethought or enough experience in dating a variety of individuals to know what he or she really wants in a marriage partner. However, if an engaged couple is separated geographically for a long period of time due to military service or the need to work or attend colleges in widely separated towns, the exclusive dating pattern may need some modification. If either of the partners feels socially deprived, or the strain of separation precipitates feelings of despondency, then dating others might be helpful therapy. Such dating should be approved and understood by the other partner. The dating should also

[4]Burgess, E. W., and Cottrell, L. S., *Predicting Success or Failure in Marriage*, New York: Prentice Hall, 1939.
[5]Terman, Lewis M., et al. *Psychological Factors in Marital Happiness*, New York: McGraw-Hill, 1938.
[6]Locke, Harvey, *Predicting Adjustment in Marriage: A Comparison of a Divorced and a Happily Married Group*, New York: Holt, Rinehart and Winston, 1951.

be considered purely a social experience without thoughts of involvement or affection. Naturally, the concerned individual should avoid dating one person exclusively. Such dating often produces unpredictable results such as those experienced by Harry. He said:

"My tour in the military service separated me from Carol for a long time, and I could tell from her letters that she was becoming lonely. So, when my best buddy, Don, was released ahead of me, I asked him if he would watch out for Carol and help her to avoid loneliness until I returned. Man, he really did a good job for me, so good that he and Carol fell in love with each other. Now, I'm the lonely one—it's a tough break."

An attempt was made to show Harry that perhaps Carol was not the right girl for him as her love couldn't stand the test of time and space —but it did little to erase the hurt look in his eyes.

Bowman comments in the following manner on engaged couples dating others when separated, "It is also a good test of the couple's devotion, for if their love and trust cannot withstand a simple test like this they are not ready to marry and their engagement is insubstantial."[7]

Despite Bowman's comments, engaged couples who date others during periods of separation should remember that they are human and despite the best of intentions either or both may become enamored of another person. As the old saying goes "Absence often makes the heart grow fonder—for someone else."

TESTING FOR COMPATIBILITY

The engagement period is the time when the couple should learn as much as they can about each other as personalities, so they can decide whether they will likely be compatible in marriage. Things that might be done which would help in making this decision would include the following:

1. Making opportunities to see each other in everyday clothes and everyday life experiences.

2. Taking time to talk freely about spending and saving habits and developing a plan for handling the financial part of marriage.

3. Learning about each other's attitudes toward sexual expression in marriage. This will enable couples to determine whether either partner

---

[7]Bowman, Henry A., *Marriage for Moderns*, New York: McGraw-Hill, 6th Edition, 1970, p. 201.

is beset with fears about sex or lacks proper information that might cause frigidity or insensitivity to the other's needs that might result in marital sexual adjustment difficulties. Such problems can be sensed without engaging in premarital intercourse.

4. Discussing attitudes toward having children, ideas about child care and discipline, and developing an understanding of how each feels about the wife working.

5. Determining the marriage roles each expects to play in relationship to family authority, household maintenance, social and religious activities.

6. Getting acquainted with, and learning what kind of relationships will take place with future in-laws.

If the couple takes advantage of these and other opportunities for testing compatibility, they should have a general preview of sensitive adjustment areas in their future marriage.

Couples with whom the author has discussed the above suggestions usually agree that they have merit, but point out that the most difficult activity for them to initiate is that of getting better acquainted with future in-laws. A common complaint is that they don't know what to do or say when in their presence. The following suggestions regarding in-laws are adapted from a recent issue of *Varsity,* a magazine that is oriented toward college students:

A Few Suggestions for Winning the Approval of In-laws

   a. Be natural and do not "put on airs" around them.

   b. Talk in terms of their interests. For example: If you know the father likes to play golf, talk about golf and listen with enthusiasm to his experiences.

   c. Avoid controversial subjects. You may never be able to get your in-laws to see the "light," religiously or politically, so at least put off trying to convert them to your way of thinking until you are better acquainted.

   d. If you are invited over for an evening, always leave a little earlier than they expect you to. This will make a good impression and not wear out your welcome.

   e. Be considerate. Don't stay up too late on dates, and phone your families if something unexpectedly delays the time you planned to return to either home.

f. Show appreciation. Remembering birthdays with thoughtful gifts and expressing thanks for a well-cooked meal will strengthen your relations.

g. If invited over to a party or dinner, offer to help clean up afterwards. This offer may not always be accepted, but to make it is much better than to hurry off and leave these chores to the tired hosts.

REVEALING THE PAST

There is a tendency on the part of many engaged couples to want to reveal their past lives to each other. Each will say, "I want to belong to you completely, therefore, you should know everything that has ever happened to me."

Such revelations are not always wise. If either has guilt feelings related to past indiscretions, it might be better to discuss them with a minister or a marriage counselor. Telling one's "intended" about past mistakes may sow seeds of doubt in his or her mind that can lead to breaking the engagement or have an effect upon future marital happiness. It is probably true that every person makes a few mistakes in the process of growing up that are best forgotten.

One engaged man's happiness over his approaching marriage turned to gloom when his bride-to-be gave back her ring and called off the wedding. The reason? Because as the final step to marriage he insisted on knowing whether his fiancée was a virgin.

Naturally, past experiences that will affect future marriage adjustment should not be concealed. Such things as a previous marriage, existing financial obligations, hereditary or other defects, serious diseases, previous mental problems, and prison records should be discussed with frankness.

HOW INTIMATE SHOULD AN ENGAGED COUPLE BE?

Controlling physical intimacy and determining what degree of sexual expression should take place are problems that never cease to perplex engaged couples. Certain types of couples seek answers by playing games with each other. The girl decides that she will be just intimate enough to keep her fiancé eager for the future joys of marriage, but avoid granting physical favors that would make her partner satisfied with the present situation and thus reduce his motivation to marry. On the other hand, the fellow is caught in a dilemma. Should he press for further sexual intimacy and risk his fiancée's possible accusations that his only interest is in her body, or struggle to control his desires and perhaps be accused of lacking warmth of affection?

The only way out of such a situation is for the couple to have a frank talk and explain to each other how they feel and why they feel the way they do about premarital intimacies.

Burgess and Wallin, who made a study of one thousand engaged couples, presented three general attitudes that were revealed regarding sexual intercourse.[8]

1. One group of couples had standards and ideals that enabled them to abstain from intercourse without experiencing tension.

2. The second group looked upon intercourse as a private affair, and engaged in the sex act without feeling that they were violating their moral standards.

3. The third group, which had a numerical majority, experienced conflict between physical desires and moral standards.

This study and others suggest that the strongest reason couples give that deters them from having intercourse before marriage is that it is not right, an attitude which usually stems from their family training and religious beliefs.

So how does the individual couple decide how much intimacy to allow, regardless of what group they might belong to? The first step, as stated before, is to have a frank discussion about their religious beliefs and moral standards, and then decide what kind of behavior will enable each of them to maintain a positive self-image. The second, is to be aware of the possible consequences of premarital intercourse. Things to be considered are:

Will sexual feelings be awakened to the extent that it will be difficult to reestablish control, and their frequency obscure other important things the couple should be considering?

One engaged coed commented:

Since we started having intercourse, it's hard to get our minds on other things. Every time we are alone, we both want to go to bed. Man, it's great but the trouble is we're not learning anything else about each

[8]Burgess, Ernest W., and Wallin, Paul, *Engagement and Marriage*, New York: J. P. Lippincott and Co., 1953, pp. 387-390.

other. We've decided we're going to quit having sex until we get married. But it's one of the hardest things we've ever tried to do. Ray agrees about abstaining until marriage, but he seems under such strain that I wonder sometimes if we're doing the right thing.

Will an intimate sexual relationship cause the girl's drive toward marriage to increase while her fiancé's begins to slow down?

A frequent complaint registered by engaged coeds is the one presented by Sally. She said: "My boyfriend keeps putting off our marriage, and when I try to set a date, he says 'What's your hurry?' I almost believe that he considers me as a body rather than a person and as long as he gets all the sex he wants, nothing else matters."

Does a couple need to have premarital intercourse to learn how their sexual adjustment in marriage will be?

The testing argument that an engaged pair should try each other out sexually before marriage to see if they are suitable sex partners can mislead couples. If they have anxieties as to whether either person is physically incapable of intercourse, a physical examination can dispel or confirm their fears. Otherwise, it is extremely difficult to isolate any factor such as premarital intercourse from the others which contribute to marital sex adjustment and determine whether it will be equally satisfying before and after marriage. This is so, because different circumstances may heighten or diminish erotic arousal, primarily because it is the mind which triggers or dulls sex desire. Consequently, performing the sex act before marriage may be exciting to the couple due to the novelty of the relationship, or because of an adventurous attitude. Whereas, later in marriage when the novelty wears off, and sex ceases to be a daring adventure, and the total personalities of each partner have greater influence on their physical desire for each other, sexual intercourse can become disappointing.

A more reliable premarital test of probable postmarital sexual adjustment would be for the couple to consider the natural warmth of response, the ability to communicate, and the consideration they have for each other. If these things are present during the engagement period, the chances are good that the pair will work out a good sexual adjustment in marriage without feeling the need to test each other in intercourse before.

Finally, it should be stated that happily married couples report that good sex adjustment is usually a by-product of learning how to meet each other's physical and emotional needs over an extended period of time.

LIVING TOGETHER

Another approach that some couples use in testing for compatibility is to decide to live together. They reason that a couple should learn as much as possible about each other before marriage; and the only way this can be found out is by living together. Consequently, they shun engagement and set up housekeeping in an apparent effort to learn how they would get along if they were married. Their approach is different from that of the couples mentioned in Chapter Two, in that they see living together as a test of possible marriage compatibility.

Blood makes an incisive comment to explain why he thinks the couple would not get a realistic picture of marriage this way. He states:

> One trouble is that marriage requires a crucial element that would be missing—commitment. The purpose of compatibility testing is to provide a basis for deciding whether to make that commitment. To live together without commitment is to confuse the test program with the action program. It is to blur the distinction between being married and not being married. It is to drift into marriage so imperceptibly that marriage loses its meaning.
>
> At some point, testing needs to end and commitment begin. That turning point is at engagement. To get engaged to be married means to replace the possibility of test failure with an affirmation that the tests have been passed and that soon the partners will irrevocably commit themselves to living together.[9]

It may be that a greater number of unmarried couples in today's society are living together without any sense of commitment because Americans currently seem generally more tolerant and attach less stigma to it than in the past, at least this is what a recent survey published by *Life* magazine suggests. "Sixty-two thousand replies to a questionnaire showed that 22 percent approved of the status of the unmarried couples, with 50 percent saying it was up to the couples themselves. Only 22 percent of those responding registered disapproval.

"The survey revealed, however, that the stigma of illegitimacy is still alive, with the respondents rejecting, 48 to 38 percent, having and rearing children outside of marriage."[10]

[9]Blood, Robert, O. Jr., *Marriage*, 2nd Ed., The Free Press, New York: 1969, p. 58.
[10]UPI press release, New York, N.Y., as reported in the Minneapolis *Star*, Nov. 13, 1972.

This lessened social pressure may be one of the factors which misleads couples into thinking that living together is a realistic test of future marital adjustments.

Class discussions with students have shown that some individuals think a sense of commitment is unnecessary. Male students openly stated that they were living with their girlfriends without any feeling of commitment.

Just one or two brief examples will be given which focus on testing for compatibility inasmuch as several case studies regarding attitudes toward living together have already been given in Chapter Two.

Clyde, an ex-GI in his late twenties, said, "I've been living with my woman for four years to see if we want to get married. I've given her all the sex she needs, so once in a while I buy her something to show her I really love her. We feel we are compatible, but don't know whether we want to get married. So, we've agreed that if either of us meets someone we like better it will be all right to move out. This keeps us on our toes to please each other."

Joe, a mod dresser in his mid-twenties, expressed some before and after living-together comments. While living with his girlfriend he said, "It's really great. I've moved in with her and her parents. They're swell, and treat me like a son. The only thing they have insisted on is that I don't leave my clothes lying around in the living room, so when relatives visit they won't learn what's going on."

Later, he came in for counseling and appeared to be deeply depressed, saying, "I've moved out. My girlfriend began to bore me, and you know it finally dawned on me that I wasn't living with her to see if I loved her, but for sexual satisfaction. Now, she phones me at least three times a day, begging me to come back. What can I do? I don't love her, but I feel guilty."

One of the best illustrations of testing for compatibility with a lack of commitment was submitted to the author by a female student to fulfill a term paper assignment. Excerpts appear below. As in all cases, names and places are changed to protect confidentiality.

"I am 26 years old. I have been married and divorced and I have three children. Their ages are seven, five, and three. The two oldest boys are from my first marriage.

"At present I am not married, but I have been living with a man for the past five years (Steve), to be sure we love each other before I get married again. Steve is 29 years old. He has never been married. He works as an electrician. My youngest son is his. I am very moody and therefore need a man who is both patient and understanding. Steve has all of these qualities. Not that we don't have our ups and downs, because we do. Sometimes we take a vacation away from each other for a couple of days. We have found that this works quite well.

"Steve and I feel that we are compatible and plan to marry someday, but neither of us feels that there is a great urgency to rush into it. We both have problems to work out and adjustments to make before we get married. Somehow, marriage seems so much more of a binding relationship. It places many more responsibilities on him. I don't think that he is ready to handle them any more than I am ready to marry again. But maybe we won't get married, I just don't know."

Although the practice of living together is being highly publicized by popular magazines, it is difficult to determine what percentage of the marriageable population is following this pattern and what type of person enters such an arrangement. Such studies are emerging, but at present, the samplings are too small to be definitive. Two typical surveys have been made by Ald and Karlen.

Ald makes the following statements after 136 interviews with students from fourteen college campuses.[11]

"Such couples were largely representative of the general student population loosely defined as—average. They were concerned with the opinions of their parents, the society at large, and could be held in check by the threat of punitive action, possibly expulsion by the university administration." The reasons given to Ald in support of the cohabitive relationship seemed to be more oriented toward present adjustments, than long-term commitments. Typical were (pp. 17, 18)

"I know it is a much better setup for study. . . ."

"You can't beat it for economy."

"I think that, really, it is a thing everybody is doing so you just fall in with it. . . ."

Ald states further, that many reasons given are quite indefensible. He adds, "Nor does the student gloss over the conflicts, the often deep-

---

[11]Ald, Roy, *Sex Off Campus*, New York: Grosset & Dunlap, 1969.

hidden guilt, in some instances, the superficiality and the tawdriness of the relationship. Advertently or not, in the course of lengthy and intimate discussions, 'facts will out,' often saddening, sometimes tragic."

Karlen found a much smaller percentage of living-together relationships than he had been led to believe existed, and also reported couples he interviewed usually belonged to the dissident youth subculture.[12] His study as summarized reported that "Several psychiatrists he interviewed in connection with the study felt that involved men are generally dependent and passive and the women they cohabit with are the mothering type." Karlen suggests that these youth desperately need a sense of family but lack a basic trust of families.

In conclusion, it can be said that present studies by others, and numerous interviews conducted by the author with students who are living together as a test of compatibility for marriage indicate that it is not the most realistic way to determine if future marital adjustment will be satisfactory.

BREAKING AN ENGAGEMENT

It frequently happens that couples who have become engaged break their relationships with resulting disappointment, disillusionment—or relief to one or both partners.

Studies show that broken engagements are not uncommon. Burgess and Wallin in a study of 1,000 engaged couples found that a third of the men and about half the women had broken one or more engagements.[13]

Bowman in a study of over 8,000 women who had been married, found that "More than one-fourth, (26.8 percent) had been engaged at least once before becoming engaged to the men they married."[14]

Some of the causes given for breaking engagements include:

Changing interests. One partner may grow more intellectually and socially because of continued education, and subsequently, both may feel that common interests no longer hold them together.

[12]Karlen, Arno, "The Unmarrieds on Campus," New York: *The New York Times Magazine*, Jan. 26, 1969, 28.

[13]Burgess, E. W., and Wallin, Paul, *Engagement and Marriage*, Philadelphia: J. B. Lippencott Company, 1953.

[14]Bowman, Henry A., *Marriage for Moderns*, New York: McGraw-Hill, 1970, Sixth Edition, p. 205.

Geographical separation. If work or school separates the couple for a period of time, they may discover that physical intimacies have been over-stressed in feeling they were meant for each other.

Religious, ethnic, and cultural differences. Some couples find that their affection for each other cannot surmount pressures brought by peers and parents who disapprove of their intended mixed-marriage. They also learn that religious, ethnic, and cultural differences present problems of adjustment that they are unable to make.

Personality problems. During the engagement period, emotional immaturities and disagreeable personal qualities may surface that were hitherto unrevealed. Thus the revelation that both partners are subject to human frailties may cause disillusionment and lead to a parting of the ways.

One of the problems accompanying breaking engagements is that both parties may feel different degrees of involvement to each other. Consequently, the one who feels the lesser involvement may be happy with the break-up, while the one who feels the heavier sense of involvement may suffer. This may even result in the sufferer threatening himself or his partner with destruction if the engagement is broken off. What can the lesser-involved person do? Obviously, an individual who makes threats is not a good marriage bet, as the same pattern of behavior will undoubtedly reoccur if a crisis develops in marriage. The safest procedure is to arrange for professional counseling in order to help the emotionally upset person develop the insight needed to accept the changing situation.

Once either partner, after careful deliberation, has decided that wedding plans should be called off, the other person should be told and the situation discussed as calmly as possible. In the long run, such a procedure works to the advantage of both people. If the engagement break is postponed, the emotional hurt in the partner who wants to continue may build up, and the person who has lost interest may feel like a hypocrite because his or her true feelings are not being revealed to the other.

Despite the fact that some persons say the bottom will drop out of their world if the engagement is broken, studies show that most people recover quickly. A typical study reported by Landis and Landis showed that 50 percent of the males and 49 percent of the females got over the emotional involvement of the engagement within a period of eight weeks or less. Two thirds of the total group had recovered emotionally within six months, and *only* 12 percent took two years or more to recover from the trauma.[15]

Suggested Readings

1. Amstutz, H. Clair, *So You're Going to Be Married,* Scottdale, Pa.: Herald Press, 1971.

2. Berger, Miriam E., "Trial Marriage: Harnessing the Trend Constructively," *The Family Coordinator,* 20:1 (January, 1971), 38.

3. Boll, E. S., *The Man That You Marry,* Philadelphia, Pa: Macrae-Smith, 1963.

4. Bossard, J. H. S. and Boll, E. S., *The Girl That You Marry,* Philadelphia, Pa.: Macrae-Smith, 1960.

5. Burgess, Ernest W., and Wallin, Paul, *Engagement and Marriage,* Philadelphia, Pa.: J. B. Lippincott, 1954.

6. Burgess, Ernest W., Wallin, and Schultz, *Courtship, Engagement and Marriage,* Philadelphia, Pa.: J. B. Lippincott, 1954.

7. Duvall, Sylvanus M., *Before You Marry,* New York: Association Press, 1959.

8. Landis, Judson T., and Landis, Mary G., (eds.), *Readings in Marriage and the Family,* Part V, Reading 1, "Marriage Adjustment and Engagement Adjustment," Englewood Cliffs, N.J.: Prentice-Hall, Inc., 1952.

---

[15]Landis, Judson T., and Mary G., *Building a Successful Marriage,* Englewood Cliffs, New Jersey: Prentice Hall, 1968, 5th Edition, Chapter 14.

Chapter XI

Getting Married

LEGAL ASPECTS

Why can't couples just live together without getting married? After all, the marriage certificate is just a piece of paper and has nothing to do with their love for each other. Love is a private affair between two people and is no one else's business.

The above complaint is brought up frequently by students when the class discussion centers on the legal aspects of marriage.

It is true that for many years marriage was considered a private affair, not between two individuals, but between families of the participants who both arranged and regulated it and, in some cultures these rites still prevail. However, as social groups have grown more complex, it has become increasingly evident that society as a whole must regulate marriage. In America, each state or territory has been granted jurisdiction in regard to marriage and family law, and in their efforts to maintain a stable society, the states have found it necessary to set minimum standards for marriage and make guaranteed privileges and assumed obligations parts of the marriage contract. This has been done to give children legal status, provide them with, if at all possible, a stable home in which to grow, and grant them rights of inheritance. In addition, the laws are designed to protect women, and prevent both husband and wife from being exploited. Such regulations are also in the best interests of the states, because unstable and disorganized families produce individuals who add to the community's economic burdens.

Other things that have been considered necessary to keep the marital system functioning properly are the prevention of bigamy and incest, prohibiting marriages between children, providing for specific licensing procedures, and setting up conditions under which annulments and divorces may be granted.

Marriage as a Contract

Although there has been some debate as to whether marriage is a contract or a status relationship, it is probably better to combine the two and say that marriage is a contract that commits the involved partners to a new status. The fundamental and binding part of the marriage contract is the consent of the two parties to the agreement. However, such consent is not valid unless the bride and groom, in taking their marriage vows, say *I do* with the following conditions present:

Both parties must be free to marry. For example, neither one may have a prior divorce that is invalid.

Each must be competent to enter marriage. (Mentally capable of understanding what is taking place).

Both must willingly enter the contract. (Not be forced into marriage).

The prescribed procedure must be followed regarding licensing of the marriage as dictated by the state in which the marriage takes place. (The exception to this would be the common-law marriage).

This might include such things as:

1. Being of the legal age for marriage.

2. Passing a premarital examination to show absence of venereal disease or having such a test waived for good cause. For example, if the groom is in the armed forces, and time and distance make such a test impractical. Some states don't require a premarital test for venereal disease. On the other hand, a few states have even more stringent premarital health requirements, and in addition to the venereal disease tests, prohibit the marriage of those with a communicable disease, mental defectives, epileptics, psychotics, and even alcoholics.

3. Abiding by the state's waiting period which would ordinarily require a time of one to five days to elapse between obtaining the license and undergoing the marriage ceremony.

4. Being married by an authorized official which would include clergymen, judges, mayors, recorders, magistrates, justices of the peace, and even notary publics.

Consanguinity

All states prohibit marriages between close blood relatives. However, they vary in the degree of restriction. Although there is universality in denying members of the immediate family the right to wed (father and daughter, mother and son, brother and sister, grandfather and granddaughter, grandmother and grandson, uncle and niece, aunt and nephew) states differ in granting marriage rights to other relatives. More than half prohibit first cousin marriages, and a few extend the prohibition to second cousins and marriage to a grandnephew or grandniece.

These restrictive laws developed from the incest taboo (sexual intercourse between close blood relatives) and the biological finding that close blood relatives are more likely to have the same hereditary defects and pass them on to their children. It is true that relatives who have superior traits are also more likely to transmit them to their children, but the possibilities of defects appearing in the offspring have caused the prohibitory laws to be enacted. Some states are even stricter and prohibit marriage between those who have become related through marriage (affinity) father and daughter-in-law, mother and son-in-law, stepparents and stepchildren, and so forth. There is no logical biological reason for such prohibitions, but there is some thinking that they help prevent intrafamilial problems such as the jealousy which might result if the stepdaughter attracts and marries her older male stepparent.

Void and Voidable Marriages

In addition to the laws restricting and regulating marriages, there are statutes which protect the individual if his or her marriage partner has engaged in deceit at the time the ceremony transpires. For example, a marriage has never taken place in the eyes of the law if either of the parties has a prior divorce that is invalid. In such a case the marriage is void from the beginning, and the couple may go their separate ways at any time without court permission.

Voidable marriages, those that might be annulled, require court action to invalidate them. This means, in other terms, that there is an existing marriage, but there is a defect or impediment in it. Thus, a complaint alleging that a defect or impediment exists must be presented to the court, and if the judge finds such to be true, he annuls the marriage. This court action frees both parties to marry again, and the woman resumes using her maiden name.

The most common categories for annulment are:

Fraud or duress. Fraud may occur when a pregnant woman gets a man to marry her by falsely stating that her unborn child is his. A typical case of duress is the "shotgun marriage" which takes place when the man succumbs to the threat of "you marry her or else!"

Being underage or lacking parental consent. Such marriages may usually be annulled unless the judge feels that one of the parties has deceived the other. This could occur if one of the partners is honest in complying with marriage licensing procedures and the other is not. For example, the fellow falsely states he is of legal age for marriage and the girl truthfully says she is. Later, if the husband tires of his wife and wants the marriage annulled on the ground of his having been underage when the marriage took place, the judge might reject his plea.

The lack of mental capacity to understand the requirements of marriage or the physical inability to perform sexually. Mental capacity may play a role in annulment when one party has the minimal capacity to understand the marriage ceremony, but not enough intelligence to play the role of a marriage partner. From a sexual standpoint, in the eyes of the law, the capacity to have sexual intercourse is a prerequisite for marriage, and if either party, before the marriage takes place, conceals inability to perform the sex act, the other may later seek and get an annulment.

TYPES OF MARRIAGES

Common-Law Marriage

It seems strange after discussing the numerous laws states have to regulate marriage, to report that sixteen states and territories waive most of these restrictions when they recognize marriages of couples who ignore the law. Such commitments are called common-law marriages which occur when two married people take each other as husband and wife without obtaining a marriage license or undergoing any wedding ceremony. If both members of the partnership are of legal age and are not within the prohibited degrees of blood or relative relationships, the marriage will be upheld.

Some states that allow common-law marriages require the couple to let their community know that they are living together as man and wife before the marriage will be validated, but the basic requisite is still mutual consent of the partners.

Common-law marriages are still allowed in the following states and
territories:

Alabama	Oklahoma
Colorado	Pennsylvania
Georgia	Rhode Island
Idaho	South Carolina
Kansas	Texas
Montana	Washington, D.C.
Ohio	Virgin Islands

A number of additional states also recognize common-law marriages
that took place in their jurisdiction before a certain date, and those states
which prohibit such marriages, usually accept them as valid if they take
place in a state where they are allowed to be contracted.

Reasons Why Common-Law Marriages Came Into Being

Common-law marriages were recognized among ancient peoples such
as the Hebrews and Romans because marriage was then considered a
private affair. They were also generally approved in Europe until the
Council of Trent in 1563 started a movement against them by outlawing
them for Roman Catholics.

In America, different reasons brought about their practice. The many
miles that separated frontier dwellers from localities where those authorized to issue licenses and perform ceremonies resided, made it almost,
if not impossible, to conform to existing marriage laws. Consequently,
settlers in outlying areas preferred to authorize a young couple's marriage
on their own, rather than have them become guilty of fornication and produce children who would be considered illegitimate.

In today's American society there is no valid reason for allowing
common-law marriages, and a number of organized groups feel that they
should be prohibited in all states. Couples today who might be considering a common-law marriage should be made aware that such unions are
legally binding, and the usual court divorce procedures must be followed
in order to terminate them.

Secret Weddings

Couples of an impetuous nature who feel they are very much in
love often become frustrated when parental objections or the need to
take steps that can lead to a sound plan for marriage slow down or block

their desire to be together. So, they impulsively slip away, get married secretly, and assume that their hasty action will make everything all right. Some couples feel that one of the most glamorous ways to do this is to drive to a neighboring state where marriage laws are lax and it won't be necessary to arrange a lot of attendant details. Such a union is popularly called a Gretna Green marriage. The name comes from Gretna Green, a border town in Scotland which was a haven during the days of Queen Victoria for English lovers who were in a hurry to marry. Inasmuch as a waiting period was required in England, they would cross the border into Scotland where they could get married without waiting. No questions were asked, and all they had to do was take their marriage vows in front of two witnesses. It was not even necessary to have a clergyman present. Consequently, the town of Gretna Green did a flourishing marriage business from about 1753 until 1876, at which time Scotland enacted marriage laws which included a twenty-one-day waiting period.

Some cities in the United States have followed this Gretna Green pattern, and among those which have been popular as easy places to get married have been Las Vegas and Reno, Nevada, and Elkton, Maryland. Elkton dropped out of the competitive market when stricter marriage laws were passed in Maryland, but other easy marriage centers continue to flourish. In these cities where marriage is considered big business, everything is done to make hurried-up weddings enticing events. Attractive little wedding chapels which are often built with an adjoining motel display bold signs announcing that weddings are performed day and night. Price schedules are advertised, and package deals are featured that include witnesses, flowers, photography, music, and officiant all at a reduced price.

Several years ago, while on a family vacation in the western states, the writer and one of his daughters, who was seventeen at the time, entered a wedding chapel in Las Vegas, just to look around. A charming matron immediately appeared, showed us their pleasing accommodations, and quoted prices for a package wedding that included "everything." Then, she asked what time we would like to get married. She said, if we desired, they could arrange our ceremony at 3:00 o'clock that afternoon. Needless to say, the writer's daughter was indignant at the inference that she was planning to marry an older man. Fortunately, we left the chapel before she gave vent to her feelings.

The matron's behavior described above is typical of those engaged in the marriage business. Their watchword being, get all the customers you can with no questions asked.

The circumstances under which Gretna Green marriages take place are often far from glamorous. A number of students who have been married this way have told the author of their disillusionment. Mary reported an experience which was typical. She said: "I was so excited after Bill and I decided to drive out of the state to elope that I could hardly wait until we arrived in the town and found the office of the judge who would marry us. What a letdown!! It was a dusty old room, nearly bare except for an old-fashioned desk with a picture of Abraham Lincoln hanging above it.

"The Judge wasn't even dressed up. He wore rumpled trousers, a colored shirt with no tie, and an old jacket. He provided two witnesses, who acted bored, and slouched as they watched the ceremony, if you can call it that. The judge forgot to ask me to say, "I do," and he didn't even tell Bill to kiss me when we were pronounced man and wife.

"It didn't cost much—five dollars for the ceremony, two for the witnesses, but I really didn't feel married because the ceremony was over in two minutes. I felt so depressed, it was hard to keep from crying."

Jack told of a "run-away marriage" experience that illustrated the impulsive nature of such actions. He said:

"Joan and I decided to take off one morning after class, cross the state line, and get married. It was a hot day, and on the way we had a couple of beers so the heat wouldn't cut down our enthusiasm. By the time we got to the small marriage town, it was noon, and the city hall offices where we were to get married were closed until one o'clock. We got ourselves a hamburger and a malt and then sat in the car and waited for the offices to reopen.

"The heat was terrific, and while I was busy brushing away a bee that had zeroed in on me, Joan turned around and said, 'I'm bored. I just can't take waiting until one o'clock. Let's drive back home.'

"I protested, but secretly I was relieved, so we left for home. After we had driven awhile, we both agreed that running away to get married was not for us."

Of course, it is not necessary to drive to a distant place to have a secret marriage. Secret church weddings can be arranged, and some couples get a marriage license from a local county clerk or a probate judge with the accompanying pledge that their marriage arrangements will be kept secret. However, the fact remains that even secret church weddings can be disillusioning. A male student reported:

"I was best man for my buddy at a secret church wedding. They put boutonnieres on us, but the whole thing was horrible. We stood around and didn't know what to do after the ceremony, so we just walked out and that was it.

"I'll have other people at my wedding—even if I have to invite the bums in off the street."

Do secret weddings have a higher incidence of failure than those that are publicly planned and celebrated? Such statistics are difficult to obtain. Popenoe in a study of 738 elopements in Southern California found that 48 percent of the couples ranked their marriages as happy.[1] Landis and Landis report research indicating that elopements, or secret weddings have a higher rate of marriage failure than those that are openly planned and celebrated.[2]

Is there ever any justification for a secret marriage?

In all fairness, it should be stated that illness or other circumstances such as career prohibitions against marriages may sometimes make a secret marriage desirable. However, before undertaking such a step, the couple who is about to marry should consider all of the advantages of a publicly planned and publicly celebrated marriage.

Informal Weddings

At the present time there is a feeling among some people that they want to get married "the new, natural way" and avoid the traditional rites that have previously accompanied the wedding ceremony. Such thinking was recently reported by Kazickas as follows:

"Some brides today say 'I dig it' instead of 'I do,' walk barefoot in flowered peasant dresses through a park rather than march down a cathedral aisle in gossamer white, and celebrate with hot dogs and Coke instead of three-tiered wedding cakes and champagne.

"In a new movement to make their weddings more relevant, today's young are moving away from traditional ceremonies to 'celebrations' for

[1]Popenoe, Paul, "A Study of 738 Elopements," *American Sociological Review*, Vol. 3, February 1938, pp. 47-53.

[2]Landis, Judson T., and Mary G., *Building a Successful Marriage*, Englewood Cliffs, N. J.: Prentice-Hall, Inc., 1967.

which they write their own vows and speak them everywhere from mountain tops at dusk to beaches at sunrise.

"While many of these weddings are for the street people, the hippies of yesteryear who can't relate to anything Establishment, a growing number are middle-class youths who want something different or find traditional weddings hypocritical or boring.

"Many are of mixed religions who can't find the usual ministers to marry them."[3]

Studies show that individuals who arrange such ceremonies include those who have rejected the church and the state and want to control their own lives; those who have already been living together and want to publicly celebrate their commitment; and those who don't want to be bothered with planning and undergoing all the things a traditional wedding implies. Such weddings that often take place in the woods, on the beach or a majestic mountaintop, can be delightful events. Flowers in the form of baskets of daisies substituted for expensive bouquets, the strumming of guitars rather than the peal of an organ, and the serving of honey in the comb, peanuts, raisins and sunflower seeds in place of more expensive refreshments all combine to produce an aura of romance and peace.

MARITAL CONTRACTS

One part of these ceremonies which must be questioned is the involved couples' attitudes toward the traditional wedding vows. Jessie Bernard, the noted sociologist, says, "A write-your-own-ticket relationship replaces the traditional vows with a marital work contract."[4] Bernard thinks that one reason such contracts have come into being is because feminists feel that traditional marriage vows have not taken into consideration a life-style that is suitable for the woman as well as the man.

Typical of such marriage contracts was a three-page agreement recently drawn up by a couple which included the following:

"There will be hyphenating and combining of both surnames into one married name.

"There will be sharing of household tasks, mutually approved major expenditures, and maintaining a joint checkbook for two years.

---

[3]Kazickas, Jurate, Associated Press release, The Minneapolis *Tribune*, February 7, 1971.
[4]Bernard, Jessie, "A Look Into Your Future Marriage," *Today's Health*, April 1973, pp. 29, 60. The American Medical Association, New York.

"Social invitations, employment opportunities, etc., will not be accepted without prior consultation and consent of the other.

"Child care will be a joint responsibility of both partners.

"Physical affection will not be withheld from each other as a tool of punishment or communication of irritation or rejection of the other."

The contract also specified that its clauses would be reviewed in depth every two years, and unless expressly reaffirmed by both partners would expire with the ensuing joint responsibility of the partners to initiate divorce proceedings as soon as practicable.[5]

A careful study of this and similar marriage contracts causes one to infer that:

Attempts seem to be made to control emotions with intellectual reasoning, which is a worthy goal, but not always possible.

Possible changes in personality or circumstances are not carefully considered.

Spelling out all the ways involved couples are required to interact in their married relationship, somehow gives one the impression that the partners don't trust each other to exercise consideration, unless they put such an obligation down on paper.

Entering short-term commitments which are subject to review before being extended makes it more difficult to have long-range plans for a life together.

Feelings of insecurity may enter the relationship because partners seem to question whether they can maintain the necessary motivation to work out a satisfying married life together.

There is also some question about the legality of such marriage contracts. Looked at within the present framework of marriage laws, legal experts doubt whether they can be upheld in the courts.

One final word should be said about such marriage contracts. It could be that couples who sign them are more concerned with what they can get rather than what they can give in marriage. Jessie Bernard gives this advice to those about to marry:

"Don't choose a partnership as a means to make you happy . . . or entertain you . . . or provide for your needs.

[5]Zack, Marg, "Contract Spells Out Marriage Terms," The Minneapolis *Tribune*, December 17, 1972, Section 1E.

"Look to yourself for these things. Rather, choose a partnership with another giving person. Then, both of you will be free to build a rewarding life with each other."[6]

Suggested Readings

1. Eckhardt, Kenneth W., "Family Responsibility and Legal Norms," *Journal of Marriage and the Family,* February 1970, 105-109.

2. Goldstein, Joseph, and Katz, Jay, *The Family and the Law,* New York: The Free Press of Glencoe, 1965.

3. Jones, Wyatt C.; Meyer, Henry J.; and Borgatta, Edgar F., "Social and Psychological Factors in Status Decisions of Unmarried Mothers," *Marriage and Family Living,* 24:3 (August, 1962), 224-30.

4. Kephart, William M., *The Family, Society, and the Individual,* New York: Houghton, Miffin Co., 1972 (3rd ed.), Chapter 14, "Socio-Legal Aspects of Marriage."

5. Kephart, William M., and Strohm, R. B., "The Stability of Gretna Green Marriages," *Sociology and Social Research* (May-June, 1952), 291-96.

6. Kuchler, Frances W., *Law of Engagement and Marriage,* Dobbs Ferry, N.Y.: Oceana Publications, Inc., 1966.

7. Plateris, Alexander, "The Impact of the Amendment of Marriage Laws in Mississippi, *Journal of Marriage and the Family,* 28:2 May, 1966), 206-12.

8. Ploscowe, Morris, *Sex and the Law,* Englewood Cliffs, N.J.: Prentice-Hall, 1957.

9. Shipman, Gordon, "A Proposal for Revising Marriage Licensing Procedures," *Journal of Marriage and the Family,* May, 1965, 281-284.

---

[6]*Ibid.*

Chapter XII

The Traditional Wedding

HAVING A PREMARITAL CONFERENCE

One of the added advantages of having a traditional church wedding is that ministers usually require engaged couples to discuss their coming marriage with them. Even if this is not required, such a conference with a minister, marriage counselor, or doctor may provide the couple with needed information, clear up misconceptions, and allay anxieties about personality and sexual adjustment in marriage. As part of the conference it is advisable to have physical examinations. This should include:

A physical examination for both parties.

A discussion of diseases or defects that might be hereditary, and conditions that might affect childbearing.

A pelvic examination of the female.

Blood tests and venereal disease tests if they are not required by the state.

A brief explanation of the anatomical structure and physiological functioning of the male and female bodies, and if desired, the dissemination of reliable contraceptive information.

If the examining physician has been trained in psychological counseling, he may agree to conduct the entire conference. Otherwise, the discussion of personality and sexual adjustment can be conducted by a minister or marriage counselor. Some counselors have the couple fill out sex knowledge inventories; others chat informally and try to answer any questions that may arise. The important thing is that both partners feel free to bring up things that are bothering them regarding personality, sexual, or financial adjustments in their coming marriage. This can be done either in joint or separate interviews. The writer, in his premarital counseling practice, has learned that both men and women often do not understand the psychological or the physiological aspects of sexual adjustments in marriage. Sometimes, there is even vagueness as to what female orgasm is and how it is achieved.

In addition to playing the role of information giver, the counselor frequently discovers that counseling is needed because one of the partners may bring up some underlying resentment regarding the other's actions that has been suppressed due to fear of causing a break-up in the relationship. If such things are brought out into the open, and worked on objectively, many future conflicts in marriage may be avoided.

At the present time there is sentiment by some to make a premarital conference a prerequisite to receive a marriage license. Those opposed, claim it would deprive the individual of his rights. Only time will tell the outcome.

Today, Traditional Weddings Are in the Majority

Before discussing the traditional wedding, it should be pointed out that current statistics show that it is the most popular type of wedding taking place in the United States. A typical study of today's wedding practices is reported by Pauley who refutes the thinking that traditional weddings are on the decline.

She says: "Yes, there are some changes in the settings. Yes, there is some cohabiting without benefit of marriage vows. And yes, there is the commune culture.

"But by and large, people are getting married just as they did 150 years ago. The wedding is the acting out of a 'deep need for ritual in our lives,' says Marcia Seligson. 'There's an awful deep and fundamental emotion involved.'

"Miss Seligson gives us a look at the American way of marriage in 'The Eternal Bliss Machine' (William Morrow & Co., New York). Her new book is stuffed with facts on the marriage rite.

"To reinforce her premise that marriage continues as a healthy institution, Miss Seligson recites some statistics. Consider that in 1972, there were 2,269,000 marriages in the United States and that one percent of the population is getting married each year.

"Seven out of eight first-time couples are married in a church or synagogue. Seven out of eight first-time brides receive an engagement ring. About 85 percent of first-time brides wear a formal bridal gown.

And the wedding industry represents better than $7 billion a year in the U.S. economy."[1]

Planning a Wedding

The rule to follow in planning a wedding is to arrange a ceremony and reception which one will enjoy and one that will not place serious financial strain upon the concerned families. The reception may vary from a formal and elaborate affair to a simple, friendly gathering of families and relatives.

The following information may prove helpful to those who are planning a wedding. It is reproduced from a wedding booklet for brides and grooms which is dedicated to the bride.[2]

Wedding Plans

What kind of wedding should you have? This depends primarily on how much you wish to spend. Before deciding whether your wedding will be formal, semiformal or informal, you should obtain cost estimates of decorations, reception, wedding outfits, pictures, invitations and attendants' gifts. Then decide upon your wedding gown, the size of the bridal party, the elaborateness of the decorations, the kind of reception, and the number of guests.

Next determine the number of attendants you wish and invite them promptly. Be sure to tell your groom how many guests will attend, so that he will know how many ushers to ask (one for every fifty guests).

Visit the clergyman as soon as possible to engage the church for both the wedding and the rehearsal, and learn from him the rules and regulations pertaining to the ceremony. Ask about the organist and sexton and if there are any special charges for the use of the church.

When you engage the organist for the ceremony and the rehearsal, make an appointment to discuss with him the music that will mean the most to you and your groom.

Choose your florist early. He'll help you with church and reception decoration possibilities as well as your bridesmaid's bouquets. If you want

[1]Pauley, Gay. "Weddings Not Dying; She Can Assure You," New York, N.Y., (UPI), as reported in the Minneapolis *Star*, May 2, 1973.
[2]*Dayton's Wedding Book*, pp. 6-31 (printed here by permission of Dayton's of Minneapolis, Minnesota.)

candlelight, ask your clergyman if fire regulations permit the use of candles, particularly along the aisle.

Show your florist swatches of the attendants' dresses when you choose their bouquets. For a completely coordinated floral scheme, encourage your groom to select your bouquet, the mothers' corsages, and the ushers' boutonnieres from the same florist.

Engage your photographer early, too. If you want a formal bridal portrait, it will be taken before the wedding, probably at the photographer's studio. You'll want him for candid shots too, including a few before-the-wedding pictures. Ask your clergyman about the possibility of taking pictures at the altar after the ceremony.

The greatest expense of your wedding will probably be the reception. Many churches have facilities for receptions in the church parlors. And sometimes church women's groups provide reception food, beverage and service at nominal cost. If you are having your reception elsewhere, engage the place as soon as you've confirmed the availability of the church. If the place you choose does not have catering facilities, engage your caterer right away, too.

The reception menu can range from simple beverage and cake to an elaborate dinner, depending upon the time of your wedding and what you wish to spend. Cost estimates are usually given on a price-per-plate basis.

Invitations

Both families will have relatives and friends who want to come to the wedding. The size of the church limits the number to be asked to the ceremony. If both families live in the same city, the total number of guests should be divided equally between the bride's and the groom's friends. If the groom's family lives far away, friends of the bride and her parents will comprise most of the guest list.

The bride's family is responsible for invitations, including addressing and mailing.

Wedding invitations are traditionally engraved or embossed and issued in the name of the bride's parents. The invitation to a church ceremony reads:

Mr. and Mrs. John Edward Jones
request the honour of your presence
at the marriage of their daughter
Mary Lee
to
Mr. Thomas Henry Smith
on Saturday, the fifth of June
at four o'clock
Hope Church
Minneapolis, Minnesota

The customary card enclosed for those invited to the reception is:

Reception
immediately following the ceremony
in the Church Parlors
Please reply

Certain changes are required in the wording for special circumstances
. . . if for example, parents are divorced or deceased, if the couple issues
its own invitations, or if it is a second marriage. A Stationery Department
can tell you the proper form for a particular situation.

If the wedding will be small and informal, your mother or you can
write personal notes to the guests. The note is addressed to the wife of a
couple.

Announcements are sent after the wedding to those who did not
receive invitations.

The traditional announcement form reads:

Mr. and Mrs. John Edward Jones
have the honour of announcing
the marriage of their daughter
Mary Lee
to
Mr. Thomas Henry Smith
on Saturday, the fifth of June
One thousand nine hundred and seventy-three
Minneapolis, Minnesota

An At Home Card is often enclosed to inform friends where the couple will be living.

At Home

after the first of July

1860 Oak Lane

Minneapolis, Minnesota

Invitations should be mailed three weeks in advance of the wedding. Announcements are sent after the ceremony.

Expenses

The bride's parents underwrite the expenses of the wedding. As host and hostess, they pay for:

Invitations and announcements

Church decorations, aisle cloth, canopy (if used)

Organist, soloist, sexton

Transportation of wedding party to church and reception

Rental of reception place and equipment

Reception food, beverages, service, decorations, music

Wedding costume for the bride

Bridal attendant gifts and bouquets

Groom's ring (in a double-ring ceremony)

Bride's personal trousseau

Bride's household trousseau

The groom pays for:

Bride's engagement and wedding rings

Marriage license

Clergyman's fee

Bride's bouquet and honeymoon corsage

Corsages for the mothers and grandmothers

Boutonnieres for the ushers, fathers, grandfathers

Gifts for the ushers and best man (sometimes including their gloves and ties)

Personal gift for the bride

Transportation for himself and the best man to the ceremony

Wedding trip

The groom's parents may or may not host and pay for the bridal (or rehearsal) dinner.

The bridesmaids and ushers usually pay for their own outfits.

Clothes

For the three types of weddings, formal, semiformal and informal, you, the bride, set the pace for the entire party when you select your wedding gown. Whatever your choice, the wedding party should wear garments that complement your costume.

At formal daytime weddings all the men in the wedding party, including both fathers, wear cutaways with striped trousers, gray waistcoats, ascots or four-in-hand ties, and gray gloves. Single-breasted black or oxford gray coats with striped trousers are proper for semiformal daytime weddings. Navy blue or gray business suits are worn at daytime and evening informal weddings. (In summer, white coats with dark blue trousers are sometimes worn at informal weddings.)

At formal evening weddings, full evening dress (white tie and tails) is worn by the men of the wedding party.

At semiformal weddings after six p.m. the men in the wedding party wear tuxedos. (From Memorial Day to Labor Day, white dinner jackets and dark trousers are also acceptable.)

The above suggestions reflect the generally accepted dress in large cities.

Rehearsal

A smooth wedding requires that everyone knows what to do when. The clergyman has an opportunity at your wedding rehearsal (usually held the night before the wedding) to brief everyone on the procedures and details of the ceremony.

Ceremony

Your day of days has arrived. Allow plenty of time to dress; arrive at the church early; and enjoy leisurely each precious moment of your big day. The groom and the best man should arrive a half hour before the ceremony.

The ushers should arrive an hour in advance of the wedding and line up on the left side of the church door. They offer their right arms to the ladies as they enter the church.

Five minutes before the wedding the church doors are closed, and no more guests are seated. The groom's mother is then escorted to the front pew on the right side of the church. The usher then returns to escort the bride's mother to the front pew on the left side.

At the first notes of the wedding march, the clergyman, groom and best man, enter the chancel. Then from the vestibule the ushers enter in pairs, about five pews apart, followed by the bridesmaids, who may walk either singly or in pairs beginning with the smallest. The honor attendant comes next allowing a somewhat greater space between herself and the bridesmaids, then the ring bearer, the flower girl, and finally the bride, who enters on her father's right arm allowing a distance of about ten pews between herself and the last attendant.

The actual wedding ceremony varies widely. The basic requirement is that the couple conform to the law by both agreeing to the marriage covenant. Aside from this they may write their own ceremony or participate in a more ritualistic one which is prefaced by the licensed officiant giving them admonishment regarding the sacredness of the marriage covenant. After discussing the sacred nature of marriage and giving the couple any other advice he thinks necessary, the one performing the ceremony usually proceeds as follows:

Addressing the couple, he will say:

"You will please take each other by the right hand."

This done, the one officiating, addressing the bridegroom, will continue: "——————— (calling him by his full name) you take ——————— (calling the bride by her full name) by the right hand in token of the covenant you now enter into to become her companion and husband, to love, honor and cherish her as long as you both shall live. And you hereby promise to observe all the laws, covenants and obligations pertaining to the holy state of matrimony; and this you do of your own free will and choice in the presence of these witnesses and as if you were in the presence of God?"

Answer in affirmative.

The one officiating, addressing the bride will continue: "——————— (calling her by her full name) you take ——————— (calling the bridegroom by his full name) by the right hand in token of the covenant you now enter into to become his companion and wife, to love, honor and cherish him as long as you both shall live, and promise to observe all the laws, covenants and obligations pertaining to the holy state of matrimony, and this you do of your own free will and choice in the presence of these witnesses and as if you were in the presence of God?" Answer in affirmative.

Next the couple gives each other rings, or the man may just give the woman a ring. Then the officiant pronounces them husband and wife, gives them a blessing, and finally says, "You may kiss each other as husband and wife."

It must be noted that the foregoing ceremony is an example of one that illustrates the basic points that are covered when a couple take their marriage vows. A justice of the peace might eliminate the advice given before, and the blessing pronounced after. Whereas some religious faiths such as the Jewish, Roman Catholic, Methodist, and so forth, may include a number of different and symbolic rituals.

Despite all of the different types of marriage rituals, the essential elements of the marriage ceremony are taking the vows before witnesses and a licensed officiant. (Except in common-law marriages, and in those of some religious sects.)

Following the ceremony, the clergyman congratulates the happy pair, the organ peals forth the wedding march, and the bride and groom head the procession, followed by the flower girl, ring bearer, honor attendants, bridesmaids and ushers.

An usher quickly returns to escort first the bride's and secondly the groom's mother from the church before anyone else leaves.

Reception

Your friends and relatives want to wish you well, tell you what a beautiful bride you are, congratulate your husband on his good fortune.

The receiving line is formed at the back of the church if there is to be no reception. Otherwise, you wait until the reception to greet your friends.

Your mother is hostess and stands first in the receiving line. Next to her is the groom's mother. The fathers may choose to receive or circulate among the guests. In the line, the groom's father may stand next to your mother, followed by his wife, your father, you and the groom (you stand to his right), your maid of honor, and the bridesmaids. The ushers and best man do not stand in line.

After all guests have greeted you, you and your husband lead the way to the table where the wedding cake is to be cut. You cut the first slice and share it with the groom. You may also cut a piece of cake for each attendant, or you may have a friend or waitress continue cutting the the cake after the first "good luck" piece.

At a seated reception, dinner, or luncheon there may be a special bridal table for the wedding party. You sit to the right of the groom at the center of the table. On your right is the best man; on the groom's left is the maid of honor. Alternate the ushers and bridesmaids around the table being sure not to seat husband and wife next to each other. Should your parents be seated at the same table, we suggest that your mother sit at one end and your father opposite her at the other end. To the right of your mother, seat the groom's father; to her left, the clergy-man. On your father's right place the groom's mother; on his left, the clergyman's wife or a grandmother.

When you are preparing to leave the reception, remember to ask to see the groom's parents as well as your own. Thank your mother and father for the wonderful wedding. And send them a wire the next day, again telling them how much you appreciated the wonderful wedding they gave you.

Wedding Gifts

It is suggested that soon after you become engaged, you register preferences for china, silver, crystal, pottery, stainless steel, linens, and small appliances at a Bridal Gift Registry. This will help your friends select what you want, and eliminate duplicates. However, it is a bride's privilege to exchange her presents when she receives duplicates.

As you open each package, list the contents in a gift book and put a sticker with the corresponding number on the gift. Record the item you received, the name of the person who sent it, the date, and the store from which the present arrived. As you acknowledge the gift, record the date you sent the thank-you note with the previous information.

We suggest you write each note as soon as possible after the gift is received. Your thank-you notes should be completed two months after the wedding. Address the note to the wife of the couple who sent the gift.

Wedding gifts need not be displayed—but if you show your gifts, be sure to display all of them. It is better not to have the sender's card attached to the gift. Be sure to use sturdy tables covered by white cloths or inexpensive sheer pastel fabrics over sheets. Put similar types of presents together. You may prefer to display one complete table place setting—a table mat and napkin, silver, china and crystal. Shower gifts may be shown with wedding gifts. Put light bulbs in lamps and turn them on; use ferns or flowers in gift vases. Put some time and thought into attaining an artistic arrangement.

One way to acknowledge a money gift when you arrange your display is to write a white gift card, "Check for ten dollars" and omit the name of the donor. Make out a separate card for each check and place the cards among the other gifts.

Types of Gifts Which Mark the Celebration of Wedding Anniversaries

1st	Paper	14th	Ivory
2nd	Cotton	15th	Crystal
3rd	Leather	20th	China
4th	Silk	25th	Silver
5th	Wood	30th	Pearl
6th	Iron	35th	Coral or Jade
7th	Wool or Copper	40th	Ruby
8th	Bronze	45th	Sapphire
9th	Pottery	50th	Gold
10th	Tin or Aluminum	55th	Emerald
11th	Steel	60th	Diamond
12th	Linen	75th	Diamond
13th	Lace		

The Honeymoon

Some writers counsel against taking a honeymoon and state that the time and money could be used more effectively in other ways. Such thinking may arise because the honeymoon's purpose is misunderstood. Basically, the honeymoon is designed as a period of time during which the newly-married couple can get away from the routine of daily living and begin to understand their new roles without being influenced by their associates. It also provides a brief respite from the pressures of living during which the new husband and wife can devote their time to activities they mutually enjoy. If a honeymoon is taken with these things in mind, it should do much to further the new partners' understanding of each other.

The origin of the honeymoon dates back to ancient times, and it is said that newly married Northern European couples would drink a wine made from honey during the month following their wedding.

Thus, it is thought by some that "honeymoon" is really a combination of two words, "honey," signifying the sweetest food in existence, and "moon," which means month. Research discloses that in early American farming communities the word "honeymoon" was used to refer to the first month of marriage, which was considered to be the sweetest month in married life.[3]

Subsequently, by the early nineteen hundreds, it became the custom among the well-to-do to turn the honeymoon into a wedding trip of several days' duration, and today the practice has become so widespread that we all think of a honeymoon as a trip that a couple takes after the wedding reception so they can spend the first few days of their married life away from relatives, friends, and daily routines.

A question asked by many is, "Is this period a time in which the couple is expected to achieve perfect sexual adjustment and fulfillment?" This must be answered in the negative. This is *not* the purpose of a honeymoon. As was previously stated, its primary purpose or function is to provide a relaxed and pleasant setting in which a couple can begin to understand each other and learn how to be good partners, not only sexually, but also mentally and spiritually.

If couples would view the honeymoon period from this standpoint, they would not become unhappy and frustrated if their first experiences in living together are not what they had dreamed they would be. What can be done to make the honeymoon a happy experience? Naturally there is no magic formula to follow that will insure couples days and nights of ecstasy and bliss, but there are a few helpful hints that can start them in the right direction.

The following suggestions might be helpful to newlyweds.

1. Make all necessary arrangements in advance. Have reservations made, maps marked, your car serviced, and everything ready, so you can depart after your wedding without having to concern yourself with travel details. Having to do these things after your wedding reception may seem rather burdensome.

[3]Miles, Herbert J., "Honeymoon Trends" as reported in *Family Life* (Los Angeles), Vol. 26, No. 12 (December 1966).

2. Make your honeymoon a twosome. No matter how much you love your mother, or your father, or your best girlfriend, or your buddy— LEAVE THEM AT HOME. This is a time in your life when you want privacy. It should be a romantic period between the two of you, not a family or old friend's reunion.

The undesirable consequences of taking an extra person along were reported by an acquaintance who commented, "My wife's mother offered to pay for the gas and oil, so she could go along on our honeymoon to a famous resort. It was a mistake as my wife had to divide her time trying to make us both happy. Now we are looking forward to going away alone."

3. Don't travel too far or spend too much. Unless you have unlimited funds and can cruise the Caribbean on a yacht, it would pay to restrict your time and length of travel. After all, the honeymoon period is a time to get acquainted with each other, not to see the world.

A study by Herbert J. Miles of Carson-Newman College revealed that modern couples traveled an average of 74 miles to their honeymoon spot. It also disclosed that 77 percent of the couples spent their wedding night in a motel.

It may be concluded from these studies that if you follow the pattern of most couples, you will select a spot for your honeymoon not too far from home. It would also be wise to make it a place that provides interesting activities that you both will enjoy. This would be much better than attempting to complete an exhausting travel schedule that may make you both tired and tense and possibly lead to unhappy misunderstandings.

Such an outcome was reported by a married student who said, "We decided to spend our honeymoon at a cabin in the northwoods. We only had a couple of days, so we drove like crazy to get there as soon as possible. When we arrived, I was so bushed that I flopped on the bed and fell asleep. Man, was my wife mad the next morning. She said I didn't love her. It sure started our marriage off on the wrong foot." Finally, don't spend so much that it will burden you financially.

4. Be considerate in adjusting to each other's living habits. On the honeymoon you may learn for the first time that your wife spends hours each night setting her hair, or that your husband always leaves the cap off the toothpaste tube. Accepting these and other living habits

good-naturedly and in stride will help you to build a climate in which you both can feel comfortable with each other.

5. Be sensitive to each other's attitudes toward sex. The whole tone of your sexual relationship throughout married life can be set during your honeymoon days. Be patient with each other. Respect each other's attitudes toward modesty. Never ridicule or act disgusted with each other, but try to understand why you each feel as you do. Good sexual adjustment in marriage is a satisfying intimate relationship between two different personalities that often takes years to achieve. Don't spoil it at the start by demanding or rejecting sexual contact at the expense of your partner's feelings.

In summary, after considering the possible advantages of going on a honeymoon, it seems that, ideally, every couple should have one if they can in some way afford the time and the money.

Suggested Readings

1. Bowman, Henry A., *Marriage for Moderns,* New York: McGraw-Hill Co., 1970 (6th ed.), Chapter 9, "Beginning Marriage: The Wedding and Honeymoon."

2. Blood, Robert O., Jr., *Marriage,* New York: The Free Press (2nd ed.), 1969, Chapter 8, "Wedding and Honeymoon."

3. Dayton's *Wedding Book,* Minneapolis, Minn.: Dayton's, 1973.

4. Eichler, Lillian, *The Customs of Mankind,* Garden City, N.Y.: Doubleday, Page & Co., 1924, Chapter 8, "Marriage Customs."

5. Fishbein, Morris and Fishbein, Justin, *Successful Marriage,* Garden City, N. Y.: Doubleday & Co., Inc., 1971 (3rd revis. ed.), "The Wedding," pp. 116-122.

6. Riker, Audrey Palm, and Brisbane, Holly E., *Married Life,* Peoria, Ill.: Chas. A. Bennett Co., 1970, Chapter 10, "Weddings, U.S.A."

PART III

Building a Successful Marriage

Chapter XIII

Developing a Satisfying Marriage Pattern

All you need for marriage is—a man, a woman, a few children, a few things to eat with and sleep on, and maybe an animal or two. It is like the beginning of creation. And from the beginning of creation to the present day that is what it has always been—a man and a woman with a few things and a few animals in the marriage house. Fortunes have been made and lost, masses of human beings have covered the face of the earth and vanished under it, there has been a flood and a new earth, and always there has been this man and woman standing side by side with their children and a few things in the marriage house—the place one can return to again and again, the place one can set out from, again and again.[1]

The foregoing idealistic portrayal of what marriage might mean to each individual seems to have little impact upon many of today's wedded couples. As they hurry about trying to succeed in the world, and at the same time jealously guarding their individual marriage rights, their homes often become arenas in which they compete with each other rather than havens of security to which they can retreat from the outside pressures of their environment.

Why does this happen? Is it because marriage has ceased to be a popular institution? Apparently not, especially when current statistics suggest that in the seventies 97 out of 100 people in the United States will get married. There are other reasons for breakdowns in marriage. One is suggested by the noted clergyman, Norman Vincent Peale, who said, "One of the saddest facts about many marriages is that two people will share the most intimate relationship, yet know nothing about each other's outlook on life."

Paul Popenoe, widely quoted family life authority, says the greatest single cause of divorce is "failure to grow up emotionally." He adds,

---

[1]Max Picard, as quoted in Bovet, Theodor, *A Handbook to Marriage*, Garden City, New York: Doubleday & Co., 1969, p. 105.

". . . too large a part of the population has never attained the self-knowing, self-control and unselfishness that form a yardstick for measuring a mature personality."

These succinct statements citing emotional immaturity and marriage partners' lack of knowledge of each other's outlooks give the general reasons why marriages fail, but like the tip of an iceberg, they just describe what is visible above troubled matrimonial waters. It is necessary to study the marriage relationship in greater depth to learn what causes these disruptive factors to surface. Studies of marital adjustment disclose that the basic causes of marital failure seem to be associated with the following three aspects of the marriage relationship:

1. Marriage Expectations That Are Not Fulfilled

Couples enter marriage with specific role expectations. Each person expects to play his or her role in marriage in a certain way, and expects the wedded partner to play marriage roles in a certain way. When these expectations are not met, trouble results.

2. The Kinds of Personalities That Husband and Wife Bring to Marriage

When two people marry, each one brings a definite type of personality to marriage that does not change appreciably after the marriage vows are taken. If the husband was a domineering person during his boyhood and in his premarriage years, he will most likely be a dominating marital partner. And if the wife, before marriage, interacted with her parents in such a manner that she cried or had tantrums in order to get her own way, she will probably attempt to manipulate her husband by crying and having tantrums. This happens because married couples usually relate to each other the same way they related to people during their childhood and adolescence.

When informed of this, some people say, "So what's wrong with that? You should be yourself and not put up a false front when you are married."

Granted, but the trouble is that most of us do not always reveal our true selves before marriage, during casual relationships, or even during the engagement period, when we tend to "put our best foot forward." Consequently, our partner may marry us not realizing we tend to be a domineering despot or an occasional tantrum thrower. Thus, disillusionment may occur when our real self emerges.

3. Conflict Between Being Individualistic and Cooperative

Many problems in marriage stem from the fact that it is sometimes difficult for the involved pair to think in terms of the needs of two rather than those of one. This often happens because some individuals feel they will lose their individuality in a pair-oriented relationship. There is no valid reason why a married person cannot retain his or her individuality and be a good partner at the same time. However, such a state is difficult to achieve if either mate views marriage as a battle between the sexes rather than a complementary relationship.

In the ensuing discussions of marriage adjustment, some of the research and other factors related to these and other basic problems of marriage will be considered.

EXPECTED ROLE PATTERNS IN MARRIAGE

Once the honeymoon has become a memory and the newly married couple has passed through the early novelty stage of marriage, it soon becomes apparent that their continued adjustment will depend partly upon how they expect each other to play the roles of husband and wife and whether their expectations are similar. Several decades ago this did not pose a problem inasmuch as the husband's and wife's roles were clearly defined. The husband was considered the provider and contact with the outside world. While the wife's expected role was to stay home, bear children and perform the tasks necessary to keep the household running. Today, there are no clear-cut marriage roles that spouses are expected to play. Instead, each marriage partner has, through environmental conditioning, developed a concept of what kind of role he or she desires to play in marriage and an expectation of how the mate's role should be played. Because the husband and wife have been reared in different families and have had different life experiences, it is more likely than not that they will come to marriage with different ideas as to how the man's and woman's roles should be played. However, if each partner can perceive what the other expects and respond consistently to these role expectations, which are composed of a complex pattern, effective adjustment will be furthered. On the other hand, if either partner inaccurately perceives what roles are expected of him or her, marriage adjustment becomes more difficult.

Stuckert lists four significant components of marriage role perceptions.

1. ". . . the degree of similarity between the role concepts and expectations of one partner and the other's own role concepts and expectations.

2. ". . . the degree of similarity between the way a person perceives the
   role expectations of his marital partner and the partner's actual role
   expectations.

3. ". . . the degree of congruence between his concept of the marital
   role in general and his concept of his specific role, i.e., does he view
   his marriage as being similar to or different from most marriages?

4. ". . . the degree of similarity between a person's role expectations and
   his perceptions of the expectations of his spouse."[2]

In order to test these components of marital role perception, Stuckert
studied a group of newly married couples in Milwaukee. His findings
included the following:

Accurate perception may detract from marital satisfaction if the
two marriage partners have widely differing expectations of the roles
of husband and wife. On the other hand, inaccurate perception may
not result in dissatisfaction if the person defines his marriage as being
typical of marriages in general.

. . . The husband's role definitions and expectations may be more
important to the early success of a marriage than the wife's.

Family adjustment may be greatly affected by the extent to which
the husband and wife are oriented toward both actual and potential
role changes.

A number of individuals may question the suggestions that the husband's role definitions and expectations may be more important in early
marriage than the wife's. But a realistic look at the present American
culture shows that the husband is still generally considered the family
leader, and the wife usually has a greater proportion of her activities
centered around the family. Thus, because of more time spent with family
members, the wife would have more intra-family situations to accommodate herself to, and thus be required to make the greater adjustment
in marriage.

---

[2]Stuckert, Robert P., "Role Perception and Marital Satisfaction—a Configurational Approach." Lasswell, Marcia E., and Thomas E., *Love, Marriage, Family,* A Developmental
Approach, Glenview, Illinois: Scott, Foresman and Co., 1973, pp. 377-80.

What can be done to improve role perception in marriage? Luckey points out the need for the wife to be empathetic. She says, "It is to the benefit of the relationship if she knows what she is adjusting to! If she sees the husband as he sees himself, she is better able to make adjustments which bring more satisfaction to the marriage."[3]

If both the wife and the husband could always exercise empathy, which is the ability to perceive the feelings of others, marital harmony would be fostered. Unfortunately, emotional immaturity often gets in the way, and mates become so preoccupied with their own needs that they don't even hear what their partner says, let alone understand how he or she feels.

It often helps spouses to see each other's viewpoints if they put their role concepts and role expectations down on paper and then try to discuss them objectively. One way to get started is for both partners to take a separate sheet of paper and fill in their thinking under the following headings:

The Roles I Want to Play in Marriage

The Roles I Expect My Husband (Wife) to Play in Marriage

The writer has encouraged a number of dissatisfied husbands and wives to do this, and has heard one or the other say with amazement, "I didn't know you expected this of me. Why didn't you say so before?"

Using such a procedure as writing down and discussing role concepts and expectations is just a start toward developing more effective role perception, but with all of its limitations it is better than attempting nothing that will help remedy the situation.

Occasionally, one meets a couple who are married, or are about to be, who are able to communicate to each other how they feel about specific marital situations and can openly discuss their own role-playing concepts and what they expect of their partner.

This was true of Charles and Mary. Mary expressed the following thoughts in a counseling interview:

We discovered early in our relationship, during our engagement, that we could create and pretend we were in real life situations, and then discuss how each felt, what his or her role should be and what was expected of the other. For example, when it came to spending money,

[3]Luckey, Eleanor B., "Marital Satisfaction and Congruent Self-Spouse Concepts," *Social Forces*, 39, Dec. 1960, pp. 153-157.

Charles said he was an impulsive buyer and I revealed that I was careful in my spending. We agreed that we both had a right to feel the way we did, so we worked out an arrangement in which Charles expected me to check his impulsive buying, and in which I would realize that sometimes I was too conservative in my buying habits and expect him to show me some advantages of spending more freely.

We had the same type of discussion regarding sexual adjustment, in-law relationships, and bringing up children. Now that we are married, we continue talking about our roles, and it has really helped our adjustment.

It cannot be assumed that open sharing of feelings regarding role concepts and role expectations will always help marital adjustments.

Cutler and Dyer found in their study of seventy-five young married university students that nearly one half of them reported that open discussion of the violation of role expectations led to nonadjustment responses.

Their findings also showed other approaches the couples used to work on problems in role adjustment:

Some of them were:

A "wait and see strategy" with the hope that the situation would improve.

Different handling of problem areas. For example, husbands said they could talk openly about violations related to financial expectations, but not about sexual maladjustments.

Wives put more stress on spending time at home.

". . . in a large percentage of times, a negative reaction on the part of one partner does result in an adjustive response by the other."[4]

THE BALANCE OF POWER IN MARRIAGE

As married couples continue to move in the direction of what is called an equalitarian marriage relationship, more and more is being written about what is called the "family power structure"—the way decision-making and tasks are distributed within the family.

It seems strange, in a way, that two people who take their marriage vows and mutually profess their everlasting love, and vow to cherish

[4]Cutler, Beverly R., and Dyer, William G., "Initial Adjustment Process in Young Married Couples," *Social Forces*, 44, 1960, pp. 195-201.

each other, soon thereafter become concerned with who wields more power in the family. But this does happen, and often very early in marriage, and usually starts when conflicts in interests and desires develop. If the resolution of these conflicts is not approached with objectivity, their marriage interaction may become an emotional seesaw with the partner who carries more weight (ego strength) balancing things in his or her favor. Consequently, the marriage may then develop into a relationship that is husband-dominated, wife-dominated, or equalitarian. Naturally, the form the marriage will take does not develop overnight, but it gradually takes shape in accordance with how marriage partners respond to each other's desires. John Haley, director of the Philadelphia Marriage and Family Center, believes this adjustment takes place within the context of a message-sending, message-receiving relationship. His hypothesis is that either the husband or the wife will attempt to define how he or she would like a specific marriage relationship to be by sending out a message. Then the way the recipient accepts or rejects the message would determine how that relationship would be structured.

Just how are messages or marriage signals sent?

It is common knowledge that they can be verbal or nonverbal. But it is also important to realize that the situation in which the message is given has an effect upon how it will be interpreted. For example, in a verbal message the inflection of the voice could mean different things at different times. If a wife shouts at her husband, who is mowing the lawn, to come to dinner, the message would generally be given and received with small emotional overtones. But if he is sitting in the living room reading, and his wife shouts at him that dinner is ready, anger may color both the message and the response. Be that as it may, no matter where the transaction takes place, the wife soon learns from her husband's responses whether she can continue shouting or must modify her request to a gentle, "Dinner is ready, Dear, if it is convenient for you to come."

Nonverbal messages, such as a frown, a gesture, or a certain body posture are sometimes overlooked and often misinterpreted. Nevertheless, the way they are given and accepted, rejected or countered contributes to the balance of power between spouses. This was illustrated by the young wife who complained that every night her husband left his dirty socks lying on the living room floor. His nonverbalized message was, "You are in charge of dirty socks."

After describing the situation, her question was, "What should I do? Pick them up? Leave them there? Nail them to the floor? Or what?"

She finally decided to pick them up, which set the stage for her husband to continue exercising power in the dirty sock department.

It is easy to see that the ways in which the constant stream of messages of married partners are given and received will gradually determine who-decides-what in the family and who-decides-who-decides-what.

What other factors determine the power structure in marriage? Blood and Wolfe in a pioneering study reported in 1960 came up with some interesting answers.[5] They set up the study in order to learn something about "the structure of husband and wife relationships in terms of both the relative dominance of the partners in decision-making and the participation of each in household tasks." To accomplish this, they interviewed 909 white, middle-class families in the Detroit area. Among the many questions asked were two categories definitely related to family power structure. First, they asked how the family jobs were divided, and if they were performed by the:

1. "Husband always"
2. "Husband more than wife"
3. "Husband and wife exactly the same"
4. "Wife more than husband"
5. "Wife always"

Typical questions in this category included:

Who does the grocery shopping?
Who gets your husband's breakfast on work days?
Who does the evening dishes?
Who does the housework?
Who mows the lawn?
Who keeps track of the money and bills?

In the decision-making area, the same procedure was followed. The questions asked regarding who made the decisions related to:

What job the husband should take.
What house or apartment to take.
What kind of car to buy.

---

[5]Blood, Robert O. Jr., and Wolfe, Donald M., *Husbands and Wives*, Glencoe, Illinois: The Free Press, 1960.

How much money to spend on food.

Whether or not the wife should go to work or quit work.

Whether to buy life insurance.

Where to go on a vacation.

What doctor to call when illness occurs.

The answers showed that with these eight particular questions, the aggregate balance of power falls slightly in the husband's direction. After analyzing these and other answers, Blood and Wolfe characterized a marriage as "husband-dominated," "wife-dominated," or "equalitarian." Then the two research specialists set about to determine why one marriage partner wielded more power than the other.

First, certain subcultures were studied to determine if the power today's husbands exercise stems from continued belief in the patriarchal system which makes the husband the ruling power in the family. An examination of farm families, immigrant families, Catholic families, older generation families and poorly educated families showed that wives no longer subscribe to this thinking. Although Blood and Wolfe said there may be groups and individual families that are exceptions to this rule, they felt that the evidence they uncovered suggested that the principles of patriarchy no longer constituted a significant force in determining the family power structure.

Having discarded this theory related to family power, Blood and Wolfe, after scrutinizing the interaction in the sampled marriages, formulated the theory that "the balance of power in particular families and in whole categories of families is determined by the comparative resourcefulness of the two partners and by the life circumstances in which they live." The researchers then listed such resources as financial ability, education, competence, social status, and type of employment as factors that influenced the family power structure.

Although the Blood-Wolfe study is still widely quoted, current researchers have refined and added to its basic concepts. Other resources associated with wielding power in the family that have been added are:

Physical attractiveness

Illness (an ailing spouse can often have a partner do his or her bidding)

Confidence in ability to adjust if the marriage is dissolved. For example, a wife with small children would find possible divorce a threat inasmuch as opportunity for remarriage or obtaining needed employment might be limited.

As one ponders these resources writers list which are associated with exercising power in the family, it becomes apparent that the power struggle in a marriage can result in partners playing games to manipulate each other and assuming roles similar to those of politicians who take the posture, "If you scratch my back, I'll scratch yours." When such a marriage climate prevails, the wife may, for example, in the area of sex, withhold or grant sexual favors in relationship to how her husband meets her demands for new clothing or other material desires. And the husband may threaten divorce, or suggest that he will seek sexual satisfaction elsewhere, if his wife doesn't "shape up" and participate in amorous activities which she might consider repugnant. Such manipulatory devices may be used in all areas of their adjustment until the marriage deteriorates into a cold war.

At this point in the discussion, it seems that the logical question to ask is, if playing power politics in marriage leads to marital disruption, and is basically an exercise in futility, what can a couple do to avoid becoming entangled in such a marriage structure?

First, it might be well for them to recall the marriage vows in which they agreed to love, honor and cherish each other. If the words, "love," "honor," and "cherish" were said with sincere intent, then the husband and wife should take a good look at their marriage and determine how they can order their relations with each other on the basis of love rather than on the basis of power.

What would this mean? The term love is an intangible, and difficult to define, so it might be more meaningful to use the phrase "a love relationship," and consider what goes into it.

It would seem that married people should like their mates well enough to want to do something for them, rather than be preoccupied with getting something from them. Simply put, have a giving rather than a getting attitude. If such were the case, their concern with having equal power would vanish. In such a marriage, a wife would do things for her husband such as laundering or mending his clothes because she wanted to, and her husband would take his wife out to dinner because he liked to do things for her that she enjoyed.

Things that needed to be done in the partnership would be accomplished with no thought that one was doing more than the other. Gone would be the use of power politics in which pressure would be applied to get one's way by withholding something that the mate needed or desired. Marriage partners would strive to more fully understand each other, and with selfless giving move toward their mutual goals.

In conclusion, it should be stated that because all people are subject to human frailties, there is probably no relationship, marriage or otherwise, which is completely free of some kind of jockeying for power. Nevertheless, as the marriage partners' capacity to love each other grows, the use of power politics should diminish.

Suggested Readings

1. Bird, Joseph and Bird, Lois, *Marriage Is for Grownups,* Garden City, N.Y.: Doubleday & Co., 1971.

2. Bovet, Theodor, *A Handbook to Marriage,* Garden City, Long Island, N.Y.: Dolphin Books, 1960.

3. Ligon, Ernest, and Smith, Leona, *The Marriage Climate,* St. Louis, Mo.: The Bethany Press, 1963.

4. McGinnis, Tom, *Your First Year of Marriage,* Garden City, N.Y.: Doubleday & Co., 1967.

5. Moss, Joel J. and Moss, A. C., *Moss on Marriage,* Provo, Utah: Brigham Young University Press, 1968.

6. Nelson, Elof G., *Your Life Together,* Richmond, Virginia: John Knox Press, 1967.

7. Peale, Mrs. Norman Vincent, *The Adventure of Being a Wife,* Englewood Cliffs, N.J.: Prentice-Hall, Inc., 1971.

8. Williams, Mary, *Marriage for Beginners,* New York: The Macmillan Co., 1967.

Chapter XIV

Learning to Adjust in Marriage

A husband who kisses his wife good-bye in the morning—lives five years longer—earns 25 to 30 percent more—is 50 percent more effective on the job—has fewer car accidents.—From a 1973 statistical report.

These statistics were given wide coverage by the news media as symbolizing the results of successful marriages. However, the complex, and often painful process, of adjusting positively in marriage which leads to sincere and affectionate good-bye mate kisses is rarely publicized and is often overlooked. Instead, the negative aspects of adjustment are frequently stressed. For example, various observers of the American marriage scene have from time to time commented that our form of marriage is difficult for individuals to adjust to. Margaret Mead, noted anthropologist, has this to say:

"The American marriage ideal is one of the most conspicuous examples of our insistence on hitching our wagons to a star. It is one of the most difficult marriage forms that the human race has ever attempted, and the casualties are surprisingly few, considering the complexities of the task. But the ideal is so high, and the difficulties so many, that it is definitely an area of American life in which a very rigorous reexamination of the relationship between ideals and practices is called for."[1]

Although each marriage partnership is unique, and it is possible that there are as many different kinds of adjustments as there are marriages, Cuber and Harroff provide an interesting framework for studying marital adjustment by dividing it into five general types. They decided on these typologies after interviewing 107 men and 104 women "whose marriages had already lasted ten years or more and who said that they had never seriously considered divorce or separation."[2]

---

[1]Mead, Margaret, *Male and Female, A Study of the Sexes in a Changing World*, New York City, N.Y.: William Morrow and Co., 1949, p. 342.
[2]Cuber, John F., and Harroff, Peggy B., *The Significant Americans, A Study of Sexual Behavior Among the Affluent*, New York: Appleton-Century Crofts. 1965.

They suggested that these five types of marriage relationships exist:

1. The Conflict-Habituated

A relationship in which conflict and tension color the marriage. Nevertheless, the married pair stay together by controlling their emotions well enough to avoid divorce and also present the picture of a fairly successful marriage to their close friends and relatives.

2. The Devitalized

A marriage in which the partners have arrived at the stage of disenchantment. The husband and wife look back with nostalgia on the earlier years when they were "deeply in love." They get by with " a little affection and occasional attention," and often falsely assume that this is the general pattern of marriages in the middle and later years.

3. The Passive-Congenial

A marriage in which the participants have never expected anything very exciting. They avoid discussing their differences and live together mostly as a convenience. They also enjoy a great deal of personal independence and get satisfaction from putting emphasis on other "civic and professional responsibilities . . . property, children, and reputation."

4. The Vital

A partnership in which the spouses get more joy from engaging in activities together than alone. Recreation, careers, hobbies, civic service, and so forth, are more enjoyable when closely shared. ". . . the mates are intensely bound together psychologically in important life matters. Their sharing and their togetherness is genuine. It provides the life essence for both man and woman."

5. The Total

This type of marriage is more multifaceted than any of the others. ". . . in some cases all of the important life foci are vitally shared." Differences of opinion have always been settled or are settled as they arise with no stress on who is right or who is wrong, but on how the problem can be "solved without tarnishing the relationship." The couple feels natural together, happy with each other, and has no need to employ pretense between themselves or to the world outside. The husband usually looks upon his wife as "his friend, mistress, and partner."

Cuber and Harroff in describing the total relationship say, "This kind of relationship is rare, in marriage or out, but it does exist and can endure. We occasionally found relationships so total that all aspects of life were mutually shared and enthusiastically participated in. It is as if neither spouse has or has had, a truly private existence."

In commenting on these five types of relationships, the research team makes some interesting observations. Briefly summarized they are:

The classification was made in order to understand similarities and differences in various types of enduring marriages.

"The typology concerns relationships, not personalities. A clearly vital person may be living in a passive-congenial or devitalized relationship and expressing his vitality in some other aspects of his life—career being an important preoccupation for many."

The five types are not "to be interpreted as degrees of marital happiness or adjustment. Persons in all five are currently adjusted and most say they are content, if not happy. Rather, the five types represent different kinds of adjustment and different conceptions of marriage."

There may be movement from one type to another, but such changes are relatively infrequent as the "relationship types tend to persist over relatively long periods."

The partners of such marriages experience common conditions. "Infidelity, for example, occurs in most of the five types, the total relationship being the exception." The authors point out, however, that infidelity would occur for different reasons. In the conflict-habituated—as an outlet for hostility. The passive-congenial—to relieve boredom. The devitalized —to recapture the lost mood. The vital-infidelity is often considered as a basic human right which either partner should be allowed to have.

Divorce and separation occur in all five types of marriages, but for vastly different reasons. For example, even in the total relationship a divorce might take place after many years of happiness, if for some reason one partner is unable to continue a rich and deep sharing relationship.

Cuber and Harroff in reporting their findings have made a significant contribution to marriage adjustment analysis in pointing out that marriages can endure and the partners be content within the frameworks of various types of adjustment patterns. Nevertheless, it seems logical to assume that Americans have been conditioned to look upon marriage as a means to greater happiness and fulfillment of needs, thus, it is probable that very few would enter marriage with thoughts of settling for a relationship that was conflict-habituated or passive-congenial. Consequently, on the assumption that the majority of persons who are married or plan to marry desire a relationship that is both enduring and deeply satisfying, the following discussion of marriage adjustment is oriented toward the "Total Marriage."

MEANING IN MARRIAGE

The writer spent several months counseling two marriage partners who were extremely unhappy. They were both intelligent, attractive, in good health, and as a couple, had no financial problems. Nevertheless, they were bored with their life together and their marriage had gone flat. One day during a joint counseling session, they were asked what their marriage meant to them—what the purpose of their life together was. Both, with puzzled looks, replied that this was something they had never thought about, and they countered with, "Does marriage need to have a purpose?"

After it was pointed out to them how the lack of purpose affects a marriage, and the advantages of having a mutual long-range goal were discussed, they formulated a mutual long-range goal of their own, and their adjustment began to improve.

A marriage, to be successful, must have meaning, and although it might be unrealistic to "hitch one's marriage wagon to a star," it must be hitched to something that transcends ordinary daily routine, or it will lack direction. Although each couple must ultimately decide what the purpose of their marriage is, help in making such a decision can be obtained from such sources as the teaching of the church, the thoughts of great leaders, or one's family heritage.

EARLY ADJUSTMENT PROBLEMS
Learning to Get Used to Each Other's Living Habits

As soon as the wedded pair crosses the threshold into their new home, the physical sharing of the same living space may cause problems. Different ways of doing things, and individual living habits may trigger conflict. The sheer closeness of the new mate who is still a stranger in many ways takes some getting used to, and sharing living accommodations can lead to tension caused by such ordinary things as who gets to sit in the most comfortable living room chair.

Bedroom and bathroom behavior can often cause embarrassment or resentment, and may even foster hostility, if the partners are not sensitive to each other's temperaments and attitudes. Some of the complaints spouses have expressed to the writer regarding their mate's bedroom behavior are:

Husband	Wife
"She won't even undress in the bedroom. Instead she takes her clothes off in a closet and acts like I'm a wild animal about to pounce on her."	"He struts around in the nude like a peacock. I wish he'd be more modest."
"She rolls up in the blankets, and I spend half the night trying to pull some back over on me."	"Even if it's 20 degrees below zero, he has to have all the bedroom windows wide open."
"I get my own breakfast every morning while she slumbers on."	"He never hears the alarm, and I get tired of having to wake him up."

The bathroom, perhaps more than any other place, seems to be the center where differences in cleanliness, neatness, and consideration for each other soon become evident. Squeezing the toothpaste tube in the middle or at the end, leaving the bathtub with a ring or leaving it clean, putting used towels in a hamper or dropping them on the floor are all conflicting patterns of behavior that may rub one partner or the other the wrong way. One suggested solution, if it is economically feasible, is to have separate bathrooms, "His" and "Hers." But, even this will not alleviate the problem, if one has to tidy up the other's messy room, or either mate follows a lengthy ritualistic pattern in the bathroom which might delay planned mutual activities. For illustration, one husband said, "When we are getting ready to go somewhere, my wife has to take at least an hour in the bathroom to fix her face and hair even if it makes us late. She finally comes out looking like a model from Cosmopolitan magazine, but all I can think of is how she's kept me waiting."

Coping With Tremendous Trifles

Spouse's irritating behavioral activities, such as the above, are often called "tremendous trifles" because notwithstanding the fact that they are tremendously significant to the irritated partner, they seem to be but mere trifles to the offending mate as well as to outsiders. What can be done to minimize them as problems?

The offending spouse, in many cases, refuses to try to change, and might say, "I did things this way at home when I was growing up, so don't blame me. You'll have to accept me as I am—my parents did!"

Research studies of predictive factors associated with successful marital adjustment have repeatedly shown that individuals with this "You-must-take-me-as-I-am" attitude usually had trouble getting along with their parents. A typical study by Goodrich, Ryder and Raush shows this relationship between childhood and marital happiness.[3] In a study of 50 average middle-class marriages, their findings suggested "that wives who report problems with their families in childhood and adolescence are to be found among those early marriages reporting unhappiness, doubt and conflict."

Regarding husbands, they reported the following:

For the husbands who report emotional strain or problems in childhood or in adolescence, a particular stage-specific and sex-specific set of influences appears to be operating to support certain defenses against the overt enactment of conflict. ". . . these husbands have tended to marry maternal, home-centered wives and to have invested themselves singlemindedly in matters of occupational ambition . . . This is a pattern of traditional role orientation, with husbands expressing less interest in housework and wives expressing less interest in working outside the home."

In putting their results together, the research team conjectured that "the economic constraints on the husband or . . . occupational opportunities provided to him" caused him during the newlywed stage to suppress the overt expression of inner conflict. "On the other hand, the troubled wife, who may be seen as the emotional center of the family, or at least more confined to the home, expresses her conflicts from the past more openly within the family."

Of course, knowing that one's mate's background influences his or her marital behavior does little to eliminate the irritation produced by "tremendous trifles." As one couple said, "We both *know* that our family backgrounds and premarital experiences have shaped our temperaments differently so we are in conflict. But just knowing this does not help. We need some help learning how to adjust."

Suggestions to consider in learning how to adjust which were discussed with this couple and have also been discussed with a host of others are given below.

LEARNING HOW TO ADJUST

Try to Become Genuinely Aware of One's Mate's Presence

Some married people live as if they were all by themselves on a remote island. Typical are the spouses who take long baths while their partners may need their help to do things in order to meet certain schedules. Or those who spend long periods of time on the telephone at inopportune moments, seemingly insensitive to the fact that their mates are feeling like neglected bystanders. Other inconsiderate acts reported by counseling clients include such things as reading in bed while their mates struggle vainly to get some much needed rest, or dropping their clothing or other personal effects all over the house after their partners have just finished tidying up.

Married persons need to develop the awareness that their spouse is usually affected in some way by how they behave in the home. Then they should learn to almost automatically ask themselves, "If I do this, how will it affect my mate?" Developing such sensitivity to the other's presence and to the interaction between the two partners would eliminate many conflicts.

Avoid Working at Changing One's Mate

Partners in marriage should strive to understand and please each other, but if one starts a crusade to change the other with the desire to have him or her conform to a certain mold, trouble may be in the offing. Leopards don't usually change their spots, and neither do people. But sometimes individuals will, if they are handled with diplomacy. Constant nagging at one's partner to change may result in the other's reluctant compliance, but at the same time there is the possibility that the couple's marital interaction may be made artificial, and each mate will become self-conscious around the other. On the other hand, if the criticized mate seems unable to throw off his or her supposedly offensive habits, the crusader for change may begin to feel like a martyr or eventually play the role of a tyrant and try to force change with barbed attacks or spiteful nagging. Then the relationship may deteriorate into one of open hostility, or it may be colored by moodiness, sarcasm, or sexual coldness.

Out of Sight, Out of Mind

Sometimes couples can close the door on irritations with careful structuring of physical facilities. Separate bedrooms, separate bathrooms, and separate work or study rooms can eliminate facing the offensiveness of such things as snoring and untidiness even though they still exist. However, if such segregation is used to avoid trouble, the couple would be wise to make a pact that each will be responsible for the cleaning of his or her quarters, or if this is not feasible, agree to hire a cleaning person.

Sublimate Negative Feelings

Individuals who work outside of the home are often required to suppress or sublimate their negative feelings toward fellow employees. Instead of giving vent to their irritation in direct confrontation, they will channel it so it finds an outlet in a less offensive way, such as becoming more involved in the task at hand or clothing their resentment with humor.

Married couples can also drain off negative feelings in this manner. However, caution should be exercised in using humor to reduce tension. An insecure spouse may not be able to take any kind of joking, and may misinterpret it as an attack on his or her personal worth. So if partners cannot laugh together about a problem without one mate feeling that he is also being laughed at, it is better to employ other ways of controlling negative feelings.

Going for a walk may help, if it takes place at a natural time, but some spouses go for a stroll at the most unusual hours—say at 1:00 a.m., or right at mealtime. Such activity usually aggravates the situation, because it is an obvious way of showing displeasure for the other mate's behavior. Having hobbies or other interesting activities that one can turn to when the other spouse's behavior is causing negative feelings can help to dissipate them. Married people who play musical instruments, enjoy working with their hands, and like to get outdoors and exercise find that such activities help them in controlling undesirable feelings toward their mates.

Develop Flexibility

Perfectionistic partners who have an either-or-attitude toward everything usually have to overcome their rigidity before they can become more tolerant and thus able to compromise in adjusting to their mate's living habits. Learning to tolerate the other's irritating behavior can be worked at. First, it may be necessary to reduce expectations and realize that the mate may not have the temperament or the capacity to live up to the perhaps unrealistic image that one has set. Gaining self-insight and learning that one may be hypersensitive to certain behavioral patterns because of childhood conditioning may also help. It can happen that as a person lives longer with a spouse who is loved, the offending mate's irritating mannerisms and behavior may cease to bother and be accepted as a natural part of living together. Individuals who reach the stage at which they can accept their mate's ingrained behavior as the possible result of childhood conditioning and learn to look at the total picture of their life together, often decide that the benefits of their marriage far outweigh the irritating things that their mate does.

ADJUSTING TO EACH OTHER'S PERSONALITIES

As was stated in Chapter Three, the personalities that mates bring to marriage have a great bearing on the kind of marriage that will result. And mutual efforts to understand and adjust to them help make the partnership more stable and satisfying. To do this, married pairs should strive to learn all they can about each other's total selves which are made up of thought patterns, moods, emotions, overt behavior, attitudes, hopes, fears, and every other characteristic that has to do with physical, mental and moral characteristics.

Mature Empathy

A marriage partner who learns as much as he can about his mate's personality is in a better position to use empathy, which is usually defined as the process of feeling what the other person feels. Janis, Mahl, Kagan and Holt make some interesting observations on how empathy works. They point out, "that a very young baby will grow tense and restless if the mother holding him is, herself, anxious; this process has been called emotional contagion." Then they continue: "Empathy, the mature version of emotional contagion, makes it possible for one person to know some things about another on rather brief acquaintance . . . it is not present in everyone to the same extent, nor is it infallible. The main information empathy gives us is emotional; it can tell us nothing about how intelligent a person is and can give us no specific facts about his background or history . . . and little information about the way his thinking is organized. But through empathy it is possible to tell how friendly or hostile, tense or relaxed, interested or bored, open or defensive, hopeful or bitter, self-confident or doubtful a person feels; how he enjoys life; and even how sick he is."

The authors then list the prerequisites for exercising mature empathy.

A Secure Sense of Identity

The individual must have a secure sense of identity so he can "be willing to let go of his own immediate interests and participate imaginatively in someone else's world with the security of knowing that he can slip comfortably back into his own skin." It also requires the ability to tolerate enough delay in getting satisfaction of one's own needs to be able to consider those of others, which in turn means being able to imagine the future and overcoming the urgency of getting what he wants when he wants it.

Genuine Communication

The ability to talk, listen and respond so genuine interaction takes place.

Practice

Be willing to consistently attempt to respond to what the other person is trying to communicate and thus become more alert to others' "subtle cues, complex states of mind and feeling."

Caring About Other People

"Clearly, affection and empathic perception are closely connected." Individuals who "lack the capacity to care about others will be sealed off from understanding them fully."

The Ability to Experience Emotions

Individuals must be able to identify sufficiently with the other person to be open to his emotions without losing control of their own. People whose defensive make-up is so rigid as to shut them off from fully experiencing their emotions lack the empathy that would enable them to get along with others easily.[4]

---

[4]Adapted from Janis, Irving L., Mahl, George F., Kagan, Jerome, and Holt, Robert K., *Personality-Dynamics, Development, and Assessment*, New York: Harcourt, Brace and World, Inc., 1969, pp. 583-584 and 610-613.

Undoubtedly, marriage partners who can both exercise mature empathy in their interaction with each other have a strong base from which to work out personality adjustments.

This was learned early in marriage by Richard, a married student who said:

> The first morning after our honeymoon, I got up for work, and as I have done for some time, I began preparing my lunch items. My wife had a fit. She got so depressed and sad, and she could not look in my eyes without crying. She thought (evidently) that it was her duty to make my lunch and nothing I could say would make her feel differently. She now makes the lunches. I learned right then to try to sense how she felt about things so I could prevent her from shedding tears. She tries to do the same with me, and it's helped our adjustment.

Complementing Each Others' Needs

Reference has already been made to Winch's Theory of Complementary Needs in Mate Selection, however, it should also be pointed out that maintaining a pattern of complementing each other's needs in marriage aids adjustment. The adjustment may not be the best and could result in neurotic interaction, but it still merits attention as one way of adjustment.

One of such complementary need patterns not mentioned in Chapter Nine that illustrates such adjustment is:

Nurturance	Succorance
The need to protect and aid a weak, helpless or ill person.	The need to be helped, nursed or protected by a sympathetic person.

It follows that a wife who loves to nurse and fuss over her husband will get along in great fashion with her mate, if he enjoys having her nurse and fuss over him. The weakness in such an adjustment pattern is that it might hinder the personal growth of both partners and could lead to conflict if one of the spouses' needs were to change.

Domination

Adjustment can occur rather quickly if one partner dominates and the other submits. However, domination is usually unhealthful. Either partner may tend to gain the upper hand by such devices as instilling fear or guilt in the other by resorting to physical force or the shedding of tears.

Developing Mutual Interests

Married partners who develop mutual interests and enjoy being companions in doing a number of things often find that positive thoughts replace their negative thinking and their adjustment improves.

One of the author's married students, in fulfilling a written assignment, turned in a vivid account of the damaging effects of lack of mutual interests in marriage. She wrote:

> This brings me to the point I wish to discuss, probably because it is still a total enigma to me. Why we should be able to make a success of marriage is a point that seems almost worthless to discuss. We have absolutely nothing in common. He is instinctively bright and perceptive, but we cannot carry on a conversation about anything that I know well—books, poetry, philosophy, art. And, I don't know his music (or appreciate it as I should). His greatest ambition in life is to gain what I walked away from—suburban house, two cars, two fireplaces, etc. His main focus in life is not his family, but the almighty corner, "where the action is." He cannot plant a garden, ski, bowl, play bridge—nor does he care to. His idea of "class" is a diamond ring and a Cadillac—mine is bare feet and an M.G. He would leave a party if he were under-dressed, I would leave if I felt too dressed up.
>
> Of course we fight. We have both given up the ship 100 times. Somehow, though, strong bonds have arisen between us that have been too much to break. We both love the children and want to do the best for them—he in his way, me in mine. We love each other and are trying to see through the fog that shrouds what is important to him, what is important to me.

This young wife's expressed need for companionship in her marriage is representative of the thinking of many of today's wives. Blood learned this in a study of urban and rural wives in Michigan when they were given a choice of five valuable aspects of marriage:

1. Companionship in doing things together with the husband
2. The chance to have children
3. The husband's understanding of the wife's problems and feelings
4. The husband's expression of love and affection
5. The standard of living—house, clothes, car, etc.

Companionship was chosen as the most valuable aspect by 55 percent of the farm wives and 48 percent of the city wives. The husband's expression of love and affection, which is heavily stressed by many in contemporary society, ran next to last (standard of living) with only 9 percent of farm wives and 10 percent of city wives choosing it as most valuable.[5]

Although the author is not aware of any corresponding study discovering what husbands prize most in marriage, the emphasis our culture puts on companionship in dating, and the apparent growing need that individuals have to associate with people who care about them make it seem probable that companionship is the most highly prized aspect of today's marriages in the minds of both husbands and wives.

It is quite obvious that married partners won't be satisfying companions to each other unless they have mutual interests. Blood, on the basis of past research, suggests that the most happily married couples experience most of their companionship at home, the most popular activities being "TV watching, radio listening and reading."[6]

Although many couples may be content with these stay-at-home activities, marriage companionship usually is more stimulating if the husband and wife together periodically do things outside of the home such as attending cultural or sporting events. Associating with mutual friends on a regular basis is also important. Zimmerman and Cervantes found in their survey of more than 60,000 American families that those making the most successful adjustments associated regularly with about five other families whose members had similar ideals and characteristics. These associations and sharing of values not only provided the involved families with interesting activities but also gave them the stability to resist the influences of outsiders who held dissimilar and often undesirable values.[7]

Creative Cooperation

One of the most reliable indications that a married couple is making a satisfactory adjustment is their ability to operate on the level of creative cooperation—a stage of socialization which gives them the insight to view the needs of their partnership as more important than their own individual needs. Such personal growth enables the husband and wife to cooperate creatively in meeting family needs, achieving family goals, and solving family problems.

---

[5]Blood, Robert O. Jr., *Marriage*, New York: The Free Press. Second Edition, 1969, pp. 279-280.
[6]*Ibid*, p. 282.
[7]Zimmerman, Carle C., and Cervantes. Lucius F., "Successful American Families," New York: Pageant, 1960.

How does creative cooperation work? Here are some illustrations from the writer's counseling practice:

Meeting Needs

Husband (to salesman), "Sure you have a good price on that fishing tackle, but right now we are spending our money to get my wife a new summer outfit. The fishing tackle isn't that important to me."

Achieving Goals

Wife, "Rod and I are both working all the overtime we can get. No, it isn't any strain. We both feel lucky we can do it, because we'll soon have enough saved to buy a house."

Solving Problems

Husband (John), "We've finally learned how to solve our problems. When something is bothering us, we get it out in the open and look at it together to see what has made it develop."

Wife (Mary), "Yes, and then we are able to talk about it without blaming the other for causing it. John used to get mad, and I'd cry, but we don't anymore because we've quit trying to decide who is to blame. We just look at the problem as something that's come up between us, and then work out a compromise solution to it that we both like. This way, we're both winners and neither of us has hurt feelings."

Couples who have acquired this ability to isolate their problems and look at them creatively and objectively without placing blame or incurring hurt feelings, have developed one of the most satisfying methods of adjustment that can be used in marriage.

It should be pointed out in summary that learning to adjust in marriage is a never-ending process. However, those husbands and wives who face their adjustments with an attitude of creative cooperation will find themselves growing closer to each other in a richer and more satisfying marriage relationship.

Suggested Readings

1. Bower, Robert, *Solving Problems in Marriage,* Grand Rapids, Michigan: Wm. B. Eerdmans Publ. Co., 1972.

2. Brothers, Joyce, *The Brothers System for Liberated Love and Marriage,* New York: Peter H. Wyden, Inc., 1972.

3. Burns, Robert W., *The Art of Staying Happily Married,* Englewood Cliffs, N.J.: Prentice-Hall, Inc., 1963.

4. Clinebell, Howard J. and Clinebell, Charlotte H., *The Intimate Marriage,* Chicago: Harper & Row, 1970.

5. Evans, Louis H., *Your Marriage: Duel or Duet?,* Westwood, N.J.: Fleming H. Revell Co., 1972.

6. Fisher, Esther Oshiver, *Help for Today's Troubled Marriages,* New York: Hawthorn Books, Inc., 1968.

7. Lobsenz, Norman M., and Blackburn, Clark W., *How to Stay Married,* New York: Cowles Book Co., 1969.

8. Mace, David R., *Success in Marriage,* Nashville, Tenn.: Abingdon Press, 1958.

9. Otto, Herbert, *More Joy in Your Marriage,* New York: Hawthorn Books, 1969.

Chapter XV

Communication and Married Love

She loves me,
She loves me not;
She loves me,
She loves me not;
She loves me—
Or does she?

A married man who cannot communicate with his wife is about as uncertain of her love for him as the lovesick swain who resorts to plucking a daisy's petals one by one with the hope that the last one will tell whether his sweetheart loves him.

Husbands and wives have no way of knowing whether they really love each other, unless each can learn what is going on within the other mate's inner self. But they can find out by communicating with each other, and the opportunity to do so is present in all of their interaction together. Bach and Wyden affirm this when they say, "Intimates usually fail to understand that the language of love does not confine itself to matters of loving and other intimate concerns. It permeates all communications between lovers." They also point out the contrast between the communication of lovers and that of ordinary business acquaintances. "For example, if one business acquaintance says to another, 'I'm hungry,' this message almost certainly needn't be weighed for emotional implications. It can be taken at face value and acted upon accordingly. However, if an intimate sends the same message to another intimate, he may be engaging in several activities:

1. expressing a private sentiment, perhaps feeling out loud, just to gauge whether the partner's reaction is sympathetic or indifferent;

2. appealing emotionally to the partner in order to persuade him to do something (perhaps, 'Come on, let's go to the coffee shop.');

3. transmitting meaningful information (perhaps, 'I'm starved, but I can't stop to eat now').[1]

This researched observation that the "language of love permeates all communication between lovers" and that it is loaded with emotional implications makes it extremely important that married couples learn all they can about communication, if they wish to grow in their love for each other.

McGinnis stresses the importance of communication in marriage with the following statement:

> You must have free communication in order to love each other. You want to love your mate for his or her self alone; but how can you tell what his true self is if you never learn what is going on inside of him? You want your mate to share your inner joys and sorrows, your secret hopes and fears; but how can he do this unless you tell him what your joys and sorrows are? Only when you really know another person—not only what he thinks, feels and does, but also why —can you understand him and therefore really love him.[2]

The following discussion of communication is oriented toward the improvement of understanding and the development of a love relationship between husbands and wives. However, the basic principles that are outlined would apply to any individual who wishes to improve his communication with others.

WHAT IS COMMUNICATION?

Many people think that communication is talking with someone, but there is far more to it than just talking. Burgess, Locke and Thomes give an incisive definition of communication and how it helps a marriage partnership grow. They say, "Communication is a process of symbolic interaction between a sender and a receiver in which the sender is also a receiver and the receiver is also a sender. The messages sent and received may be about feelings, attitudes, values, aspirations, expectations, convictions, conceptions, factual information and the like. Sensory reception and interpretation of messages and the transmission of messages in response leave some residues within the communicating persons. Moreover, if traces of another person's message occur repeatedly and over a

---

[1]Bach, George R., and Wyden, Peter, *The Intimate Enemy*, New York: Avon Books, 1970, pp. 122-123.
[2]McGinnis, Tom, *Your First Year of Marriage*, Garden City, New York: 1967, p. 29.

long period, ways of behavior of the other person or persons become increasingly imbedded within one. At the same time one becomes increasingly a part of the person with whom communication is taking place."[3]

Janis and his associates[4] feel that communication is an integral part of mature empathy in that empathy "is trained and refined by the interplay of communication." They write further, "When young people first play together, they are properly described as playing *alongside* one another."

Piaget called their conversations "collective monologues."[5] Janis said further, "Some people never wholly outgrow this phase; although they seem to be animated conversationalists, they do not listen, so that genuine interaction with them is not possible. The attempt to talk with such a person, even if it is merely to pass the time of day, can be extremely, frustratingly annoying. Why should that be? Apparently, a normal person feels a need to establish some emotional contact with anyone he meets and to communicate, if only by exchanging conventional symbols of friendliness and of caring about one another's welfare. But by failing to supply the expected feedback, an unempathetic person thwarts this need."

There are several important points in these two statements which are associated directly with the building of married love. In the Burgess, Locke, Thomes definition the phrase stating that "Communication is a process of *symbolic* interaction between a sender and a receiver" extends the scope of communication beyond verbal interaction, inasmuch as not only words, but signs and tokens are considered to be symbols. Webster's Dictionary states that a symbol can also be a "visible sign of something invisible." Thus "symbolic interaction" between married partners implies that they reveal their innermost thoughts and attitudes to each other by the means of verbal messages and non-verbal signs. Consequently, they should grow in their love and become increasingly part of each other because the residues of their exchanged messages that were left in each person would tend to modify their behavior and lead toward a fusion of their attitudes.

[3]Burgess, Ernest W., Locke, Harvey J., and Thomes, Mary M., *The Family—From Traditional to Companionship*, New York: David Nostrand Reinhold Co., 1971, 4th Edition, p. 367.
[4]*Ibid.*
[5]Piaget, J., *The Language and Thought of the Child*, New York: Harcourt, Brace and World, 1926.

The Janis statement suggests that genuine communication in marriage would cause the involved partners to avoid marital monologues. Instead, they would listen carefully to each other, so there would be perceptive feedback in their exchange of ideas and opinions. Such an empathic relationship in which the spouses should be better able to understand how the other felt, would aid them in overcoming the problems that were blocking the building of a love relationship.

COMMUNICATION BEFORE AND AFTER MARRIAGE

"It's almost impossible for me to understand how a man who talks so sweetly to you before marriage can get so stubborn after he becomes your husband. Now, all we have is hard-nosed discussions."—Bride of three months.

Complaints similar to this young bride's are often expressed by husbands and wives, although usually not quite so soon after marriage. Recent studies made at Cornell University suggest that during the first year or so of wedded life, marriage talk reaches an all-time high. Then it gradually begins to drop. Why? First, it should be stressed that couples who talk freely to each other are not necessarily communicating. They may simply be talking at each other. Even so, inasmuch as talking is one aspect of communication, it is interesting to learn why this verbal conversation dwindles. To begin, a look at the premarriage or courtship stage might be helpful. Dating couples who are deeply involved with each other gradually build special vocabularies known only to the two of them, and often make up terms of endearment (including baby talk) that outsiders might consider absurd. The writer recalls one couple who engaged in baby talk, and were completely oblivious to the reactions of those who overhead them. Their expressions such as, "Oo is my ittle sugar plum," "Did I hurt my itsy bitsy dolly," "Dive ums ittle baby a dreat big kiss," often caused their companions to suffer attacks of nausea. Evidently, their love talk didn't hold up, because the couple went to the divorce courts several years after getting married.

The use of terms of endearment, including baby talk, is perfectly all right if such expressions are symbols that express the couple's innermost feelings. But in many cases they do not, and lovers and newlyweds who feel they can communicate beautifully with each other about parties, friends, sex, religion, or whatever comes to their minds, may be talking

COMMUNICATION AND MARRIED LOVE

freely and easily because they are unconsciously avoiding each other's tender spots. When these sensitive areas become noticeable during the subsequent adjustments of marriage, conversation may become more guarded and lose much of its spontaneity. Marriage counselors frequently meet with married clients who have had little or no conversation with each other for weeks or even months, and have a ready list of reasons for living in such a conversational vacuum. Some random examples are: "We have nothing to talk about anymore." "He never listens to me, why should I talk?" "I keep still, because if I say what I think, it always leads to a fight." "I'd just as soon talk to a blank wall." "She never means what she says." "He doesn't love me, why waste words on him?"

Having clients recall their past marital experiences in an effort to put their fingers on the event that seemed to start their conversational difficulties brings out some interesting things. Often one partner remembers a marital quarrel that the other has completely forgotten. Such was the case with Joe and Betty as was revealed in a joint counseling session.

They expressed themselves as follows:

Joe: "I'll admit I don't talk to Betty like I used to, but why should I, she doesn't love me anymore."

Betty: "Now, Joe, don't be silly! I've always loved you. What makes you say a thing like that?"

Joe: "You don't know?"

Betty: "I haven't the slightest idea."

Joe: "Man, you sure have a short memory. You mean you don't remember what happened five years ago when we argued about whether we should go to my folks or yours for Christmas dinner? You got so mad that you called me a stupid clod. Then you threw our wedding picture at me and smashed it to bits. Right then, I knew you didn't love me anymore."

Betty: "Why Joe! So that's what's been bothering you all of this time. Why didn't you tell me? You know I didn't mean it. When I get angry, I often say and do stupid things that I don't really mean. You should know that's the way I am, by now."

Joe: "Yes, I suppose I do know that's the way you are, Betty, but that doesn't make the things you say hurt me any less. I guess I'm the kind of person who never forgets a mean thing that was said to him."

It's not necessary to report more of the Joe-Betty dialogue to show what was one cause of their difficulties in communication. Betty was a person who ventilated her emotions, got what was bothering her off her chest, and then forgot the whole thing.

Joe, unlike Betty, was an individual who could not get things off his chest. Instead, he would nurse his emotional hurts, and rather than verbalize his negative feelings, would take out his displeasure toward his spouse in other ways, such as not talking to her.

It would be unfair to say that either Betty or Joe was to blame for their lack of communication. Both were following their natural pattern of behavior. In an effort to help them, the writer tried to get Betty to "think before she spoke," and attempted to counsel Joe in the need to "forgive and forget." However, it was evident that the couple had a long struggle ahead of them before they could reach such goals.

Difference in temperament such as displayed by Joe and Betty constitutes one of the basic causes of poor communication in marriage. And the only way it can be eliminated is for married partners to try to understand how each reacts to emotion-laden discussions and then try to avoid the reactions that aggravate problems.

As was said before, conversation also drops off because spouses are not diplomatic in discussing sensitive areas that pertain to each other's personal characteristics or to certain aspects of the marital relation. Naturally, the degree of sensitivity differs in various people, but there are some general topics that, if commented on negatively, often provoke marital quarrels or result in hurt feelings.

Wives are generally sensitive to remarks about their figures, and husbands who say, "My, you're fat," or "I wish you'd take some exercises to develop your bust," are asking for conversational difficulties.

Husbands are quite often sensitive about their thinning hair, or their inability to perform sexually, and wives who remark, "Hasn't that guy got the most gorgeous hair" or say, "A man your age shouldn't be slowing down sexually," can in turn so affect their husband's ego, that he will become silent at home, and talk with women who make him feel more important.

Insensitive remarks about in-laws often trigger negative feelings in both spouses.

Some married partners seem to be almost gleefully sadistic when talking to their mates—perhaps to get back at them for some previous hurt. The writer recalls a husband at a social gathering whose chief topic of conversation was his wife's forthcoming session with her dentist.

"Cathie's going to have all of her teeth yanked next week," he said. "You'll be brave, won't you, dear?" he went on. "You'll look funny with false teeth, but after all, you're getting on."

Cathie took the sarcastic barbs without talking back, but it was apparent that several of the group would have liked to have told her husband to "knock it off."

Insensitivity to the mate's temperament and lack of diplomacy in presenting one's opinions are personal traits that affect marital conversations negatively.

Studies show that the longer the marriage exists, the more likely that disenchantment and disengagement may cut down the amount of conversation.

HOW DISENCHANTMENT AND DISENGAGEMENT MAY CUT DOWN CONVERSATION

Disenchantment

Many couples lose their initial enthusiasm for marriage, after they have been married awhile. What was once romantic, may become prosaic. Unrealistic anticipations that are never fulfilled often result in disillusionment. And couples who rely upon the novelty of sexual intimacy and other discoveries in their new life together to make their marriage a success soon learn that they may gradually begin taking each other for granted unless they work at building their marriage. Ardent love for each other can also wane, and marriage might begin to seem less permanent for those couples who don't try to meet the challenges of marriage. Pineo in a 20-year follow-up of the engaged couples in the Burgess and Wallin study, found that over a 10-year period, the husbands and wives gradually had less love for each other and felt increasingly insecure in their marriages.[6]

If couples are disenchanted with each other and take each other for granted, it follows that their conversational interaction will suffer.

[6]Pineo, Peter C., "Disenchantment in the Later Years of Marriage," Marriage and Family Living, 1961, 23:3-11.

Disengagement

Couples who are disenchanted with each other usually engage in fewer social or leisure-time activities together, and even get so they can sit in the same room and ignore each other's presence. A common complaint that disillusioned wives make is, "After dinner, my husband watches television until bedtime, then climbs into bed and promptly falls asleep. I may as well be living with the sphinx as far as conversation goes."

Disenchanted husbands often say, "When we were first married, my wife liked to hear about what I did at work. Now when I'm talking, she'll even pick up a magazine and start reading it. Maybe I'm boring, I don't know, but our marriage has surely lost its spark."

Naturally, if couples quit doing things together, they won't have as much to talk about. Some disengagement may also occur as a result of parenthood.

The dependency of the baby may cause each partner to focus attention on its needs, and become so engrossed in its care, that little time is left to give to the mate. Subsequently, if more children come, both husband and wife may be so busy doing things for them that their one-to-one relationship as husband and wife scarcely exists. Although conscientious parents should most assuredly provide for their children's needs, they should also avoid marital disengagement during the child-rearing years by saving regular periods of time for each other to enjoy the intimacies of a one-to-one relationship both within and outside of the home. If this is not done, when the children grow less dependent and finally leave home, the couple may find that they have grown so far apart that they are unable to resume satisfactory interaction with each other.

Feldman's study showed how the advent of the first child cut husband and wife conversation. His findings revealed that the coming of the first baby cut their conversation time almost in half from an average of two hours a day to about one. Moreover, the content of the conversation shifted to talking about the child.[7]

So far in the discussion, an attempt has been made to show why the amount of conversation between husbands and wives gradually declines. In the rest of the chapter an effort will be made to show how it might be maintained and also improved.

---

[7]Feldman, Harold, 1960. Preliminary research report "Why Husbands and Wives Can't Talk to Each Other," written by John K. Lagemann, Redbook, December, 1960.

IMPROVING COMMUNICATION IN MARRIAGE

"Lord, fill my mind with worthwhile stuff and nudge me when I've said enough!"[8]

The Ability to Communicate

If individuals want to communicate with words, it's important that they have something to say, and then know how to say it. Everyone wants to put in "his two cents worth" when a conversation starts, but sometimes the thoughts expressed are not worth much more than two cents.

Married partners should try to keep their minds filled with interesting thoughts. This can be done by keeping abreast of current events and making a practice of reading, observing and reflecting upon varied and interesting things. Spouses who engage in mutual activities that are satisfying to both add to this fund of thoughts. Such activities should enable them to avoid routinely turning to discussions of babies' formulas and describing their latest operations because they can think of nothing else to talk about.

The Use of Words

It must be remembered that having a fund of thoughts does nothing to aid communication unless they are put into words. Few people can read others' minds, so it is extremely important to develop the ability to express one's thoughts in words that are both interesting and understandable to one's listeners. Words are powerful things and can do much to change the lives of those who utter them and those who listen to them. However, problems may occur when words are used. One of them is that the same words may mean different things to different people. For example, today's teen-agers use words in a frame of reference that is foreign to the older generation. Consequently, when older and younger persons converse, although they may use the same words, the different interpretations they place on them may interfere with communication.

The same thing also happens to husbands and wives. Masculine and feminine subcultures attribute different meanings to certain words which may cause mates to discuss some incident with both having a different picture in their minds of what has happened or is happening. Take for illustration a case when a wife says to her husband, "I left the bridge club

[8]Goates, Les, *Master of Ceremonies*, Salt Lake City: Deseret Book Company, 1964, Earl J. Glade, p. 39.

and came home early because Sue and Tom were having a horrible fight." The listening husband may think, "I'm surprised at Tom hitting his wife." While what his reporting wife really meant was that Tom had criticized Sue for not having his shirt pressed.

If a speaker has the feeling that a listener's background of experience might cause him to misinterpret some words that he uses, there is no harm in saying, "By that statement, I meant . . ." or "putting it in other words, I mean."

Husbands and wives can also do this without either one losing face, and there is in addition absolutely no harm in one mate stopping the other in the midst of a conversation and asking, "What do you mean by that word?"

The Desire to Talk

"My husband is the strong, silent type. Years ago, I was afraid we would eventually run out of conversation, so I tried to get him interested in folk dancing, bridge and a great books club, so we would always have something to talk about. But you know he'd rather tinker with his car in his spare time. He doesn't like to talk much. He's not mean to me, but I'm dying inside for lack of conversation. What can I do?"

This type of complaint, which is commonly registered with marriage counselors, bears closer examination. First, it should be realized that some people are not as talkative as others, and they may get more satisfaction from creating or building things with their hands. Then other factors should be considered. One is sex differences. Studies by Anastasi[9] and others show that girls generally tend to start talking earlier and are more talkative than boys, and that differential conditioning causes women to be more interested in interpersonal relationships than men. Consequently, husbands tend to talk more about sports, business and hobbies, while wives like to talk more about people.

Applying this information to the above case, it is interesting to note that the wife tried to get her husband to become involved in the things that were of interest to her—not to him, and she wrongly expected him to be talkative because she was.

[9]Anastasi, Anne, *Differential Psychology*, New York: Macmillan, 1958, 3rd Edition, pp. 472-473.

Another reason that one partner may talk less than the other is that some spouses learn early in marriage that their mates can outtalk them, so rather than engage in a verbal argument and come out the loser, they remain silent, and unconsciously retaliate in other ways. As one husband said, "I can't compete with my wife's stream of words, so I quit talking. Then I try to get back at her in other ways."

Many individuals lose their desire to talk to certain people because they feel insecure in their discussions with them. They have learned that it is safer to remain silent than to speak out and be ridiculed or punished in some way for expressing their honest thoughts. Thus a wife or husband may often say things to their friends that they wouldn't dare mention to their mate.

This lack of security in conversation may be a result of the personalities of both the speaker and the listener. The listener may try to compensate for his or her own feelings of inner inadequacy by criticizing the speaker. On the other hand, if the speaker does not have the necessary ego strength to take the criticism, he may withdraw into himself, and never again venture an open expression of opinion in the presence of that particular person.

It is highly possible that many husbands and wives never reach a stage in their communication with each other in which they feel completely secure in expressing themselves, but nevertheless the more nearly secure they do feel, the more likely they are to understand each other.

Harper says, ". . . the heart of communication as I see it (is) a situation of safety for the individual to express his true feelings; a sense that the person to whom he is relating genuinely understands his feelings; and the knowledge that in this relationship of safety and understanding, he is truly loved."[10]

Selectivity in Communication

"My wife and I have been in the 'quiet stage' for five days. She drove the car without oil and wrecked the transmission. It burned me up. But yesterday somebody hit me and wrecked the car body, so I guess I can talk to her again."

Some married couples wait for an incident such as the above to occur which makes it obvious that one or the other will be in a talking

[10]Harper, Robert A., "Communication Problems in Marriage and Marriage Counseling," *Marriage and Family Living,* Vol. 20, No. 2, May, 1958, p. 107.

mood. Their communication would run more smoothly if they would learn to gear it to the right time and place, the right thing to talk about, and the right way of talking about it.

Parents caution their children against talking out of turn with such admonitions as, "Don't ever say you have to go to the bathroom in front of company." "Don't bother your father when he is tired." "Don't you dare tell Mrs. Brown that she is getting fat!" Yet, the same husbands and wives will often select an extremely inopportune time to say the most inappropriate things to the other.

A case in point was the wife who always greeted her tired husband when he arrived home from work with a long list of the day's problems, such as the washing machine breaking down, coupled with the insistence that he do something immediately to rectify them. When they came for counseling, the husband, Henry, was beside himself. He said, "If Janet (his wife) doesn't stop meeting me at the door with problems every night, I'm going to start working overtime, and not come home until she's in bed."

Janet, a woman quivering with nervous energy, said, "I thought you liked me to share our problems with you, Henry. After all, I don't know how to fix the stupid things."

After they had both calmed down, Janet agreed to tell Henry the day's problems after he had been fed and rested, and also to quit nagging him about things she felt needed fixing. Henry, in turn, said he would try to keep things around the house in better repair, if his wife would "get off his back" and let him do things when he was in the mood.

After two weeks had elapsed, the couple returned to report their progress. When asked how things were going, Henry replied, "Awful, I'm about ready to climb the walls. I can't take it much longer."

"Haven't you kept your part of the bargain, Janet?" the writer asked.

"Of course," Janet replied sweetly, "I haven't said one word during the past two weeks to Henry about repairing or doing anything around the house."

Henry exploded, "It's true, she hasn't said a word for two weeks, but do you know what she has done? She's written things that she wants me to do on a bulletin board and there they are hanging on the wall staring me in the face every time I sit down to relax."

The above story illustrates the need for selectivity in verbal and nonverbal communication. Married partners who practice it, don't—

criticize each other in front of their friends.

point out that other individuals are more attractive or more skilled than their mates.

say, "I told you so," when the other was mistaken in his or her judgment.

constantly send out nonverbal signals indicating their displeasure with their partner.

Married couples who learn when, and when not to talk, what, and what not to say, and how and how not to say things are learning to be better communicators.

How to Talk

"A word fitly spoken is like apples of gold in silver . . . By long forbearing is a prince persuaded, and a soft tongue breaketh the bone."
—Book of Proverbs—The Holy Bible

An individual may practice repeating such phrases as "The rain in Spain stays mainly on the plain," dozens of times in order to improve his enunciation until it becomes crisp and precise, but if he expresses his thoughts without warmth and enthusiasm, his words will still have little impact.

Lawrence M. Brings, well-known publisher and noted speech professor who has taught scores of distinguished citizens to express themselves effectively and eloquently, has the following to say about the use of words in communication.

"How are words created? Out of human experience, of course! Words are the re-creation of physical and mental existence. How would you transform words into reality? You must *see* what you are saying! If you want to speak with authority, you must learn to re-create reality—with all its drama and shades of meaning."[11] Professor Brings adds that in re-creating reality you must speak naturally and with enthusiasm.

Naturalness

Too many people attempt to put on a facade of sophistication when they speak. Such artificiality and affectation fails to engage the listeners'

---

[11]Zehnpfennig, Gladys, *Lawrence M. Brings—Book Publisher,* Minneapolis: T. S. Denison & Co., Inc., 1973, pp. 70-71.

minds. Instead, their thoughts will wander to something more pleasant, or they will not hear a thing that is being said while they await their turn to speak.

How reassuring it is to have someone speak to you naturally and from the heart. You sense that he really cares about you, and is not trying to impress you with his importance. Married couples who can talk to each other in this manner are usually more relaxed in each other's presence.

Enthusiasm

Almost everyone will shout "fire" with enthusiasm in order to warn the neighborhood of a threatening conflagration, but very few people bother to put the same kind of enthusiasm into their daily speech. If a husband doesn't talk enthusiastically to his wife about his job, how can he expect her to get interested in it? If a wife is trying to persuade her reluctant spouse to go to a ball, she will more likely succeed if she describes the coming event with enthusiasm.

The enthusiasm that the speaker has usually rubs off on the listener, and may motivate him to action or lift his spirits.

How can enthusiasm in speech be acquired?

Married people, as well as all others, are usually more enthusiastic in their speech if they talk about things they know something about, or really like. Allowing then for individual differences, what do married couples who enjoy communicating with each other usually talk about?

Feldman in his study of 862 married couples of all age groups, reported their most frequently discussed topics:

Their work and current events (about once a day)

Children and friends (several times a week)

Sports, religion, and sex (several times a month)

Husbands' favorite topics—news and sports

Wives' favorite topics—homemaking and religion[12]

BEING A GOOD LISTENER

Listening has already been mentioned as an integral part of good communication, and two important aspects of listening, being empathetic and furnishing perceptive feedback to the speaker have also been stressed. Therefore, just a brief list of suggestions pertaining to good listening will be presented here.

---

[12]Feldman, Harold, *Development of the Husband-Wife Relationship*, Cornell University, research report to National Institute of Mental Health, Grant M-293. 1965, p. 13.

Good listening involves hearing what is said and at the same time being aware of nonverbal cues. Consequently, it includes an awareness of and sensitivity to the speaker's tone of voice, his facial expressions, and bodily mannerisms. For example, if the listener fails to observe the speaker's hand gripping or foot tapping that may be indications of inner tensions, he is not in communication with the total person.

Good listening also includes overt reaction. The listener's facial expressions, bodily posture, and the fact that he is looking at or away from the speaker all have effect on the tone of the conversation.

The good listener should also be enthusiastic in reflecting the speaker's thoughts or in commenting on particular things that are said. Such simple comments as, "I'll bet that was wonderful!" or, "Well, you don't say!" let the speaker know that the listener is an interested participant in the conversation.

Finally, it should be remembered that when people have something to say, they want others to listen, and there is no doubt that one reason that many individuals marry a certain person is because they feel that he or she is interested in what they have to say. Consequently one of the most depressing things a married person who is talking can experience is to have the spouse yawn and say, "I'm sorry, Dear, I didn't hear you. I'm really too tired to listen. Why don't you tell me about it tomorrow?"

It should be pointed out again, in summary, that effective communication in marriage can lead to greater understanding between partners, improve the quality of their relationship, and build unity in their marriage. Studies show that couples who communicate effectively don't always have the best marriages. But it is quite obvious that those couples who don't learn to communicate are overlooking an opportunity to improve their relationship and learn the true meaning of married love.

Suggested Readings

1. Bach, George R., and Wyden, Peter, *The Intimate Enemy,* New York: William Morrow & Co., 1969.

2. Blood, Robert O. Jr., and Wolfe, Donald M., *Husbands and Wives,* New York: Free Press, 1960.

3. Dahlquist, Albert B., *Conversation Today,* Chicago: Nelson-Hall Co., 1960.

4. Dahms, Alan M., *Emotional Intimacy,* Boulder, Colorado: Pruett Publ. Co., 1972.

5. Fast, Julius, *Body Language,* New York: M. Evans & Co., 1970.

6. Flinders, Neil J., *Personal Communication,* Salt Lake City, Utah: Deseret Book Co., 1966.

7. Henry, Joseph B., *Fulfillment in Marriage,* Westwood, N.J.: Fleming H. Revell Co., 1966.

8. Howe, Reuel L., *The Miracle of Dialogue,* New York: The Seabury Press, 1963.

9. Jackson, Don D., *Communication, Family and Marriage, Human Communication,* Palo Alto, Calif.: Science and Behavior Books, Inc., 1968, Vol. 1.

10. O'Neill, Nena and O'Neill, George, *Open Marriage,* New York: M. Evans & Co., 1972.

Chapter XVI

Sexual Adjustment in Marriage

When the urge toward physical union arises out of the mutual desire to do that which will serve the highest welfare of the other, and because of a sense of kindred closeness, of mutual understanding and appreciation, and because of the sense of blessed nearness as bodies blend together—then is known true intercourse. In this lovely interchange of thoughts and feelings there is a harmony of communication—physical, mental, spiritual. Husband and wife are themselves at their best. They achieve the height of life's meaning on earth. . . . To the degree that a man and a woman achieve this realization, the value of a marriage is measured.[1]

The above description of "true intercourse," may sound like a lofty relationship which few married partners can achieve. But if it is studied objectively, it becomes quite apparent that couples who can reach such a state in their sexual interaction are meeting that challenge of marriage, that of integrating the physical, mental, and spiritual aspects of their marriage to produce a union in which each mate relates to the total self of the other. Couples who live such a life together have developed a unique relationship that goes beyond the closest friendship.

Those partners who have difficulties in the area of sex adjustments gradually learn that trying to improve their sexual performance by working on techniques of arousal and experimenting with different coital positions does not help the situation very much unless they also work on their total personality adjustment. This is so, because just as lack of sexual satisfaction can cause partners to be irritable and moody, personality grievances can also create obstacles to sexual satisfaction. Wives and husbands who feel they love and understand each other have a better chance to develop a satisfying sex relationship. Chesser found that the

---

[1]Henry, Joseph B., *Fulfillment in Marriage*, Westwood, New Jersey: Fleming H. Revell Co., 1966, p. 88.

wives he studied showed a close correlation between love for their husbands and sexual satisfaction.[2]

Clark and Wallin learned that marital happiness and sexual responsiveness in wives were also closely related. In a study of 397 wives, the number of happy wives who were sexually responsive increased from 82% for under three years of marriage to 88% for five or more years of marriage. On the other hand, the number of unhappy wives who were sexually responsive decreased from 65% to 56% for the same married periods. Sexual responsiveness was defined as "usually or always achieving orgasm in intercourse.[3]

If sexual difficulties can harm an otherwise good marriage, and satisfactory sexual adjustment can help adjustment in other areas of marriage, then the study of how to improve sexual adjustment in marriage can only be made by looking at the total relationship, physical, mental, and spiritual. Humans, unlike animals, whose sex function, with rare exceptions, is determined by mating seasons and stimuli over which they have little control, have the power of choice in determining what their sexual behavior will be. They can make the sexual relationship a casual encounter or one that involves their total being.

Rollo May writes, "It is possible to have sexual intercourse without any particular anxiety. But by doing this in casual encounters, we shut out, by definition, our eros (the experiencing of the personal intentions and meaning of the act) that is, we relinquish passion in favor of mere sensation; we shut out participation in the imaginative, personal significance of the act . . . eros drives us to transcend ourselves, to leap barriers, to unite with another person in relation to whom we discover our own real self-fulfillment. Eros—not sex—enables us to realize the deepest meaning of love."[4]

It may be said, in summary, that those married couples who want to make the most satisfactory sex adjustment must explore the attitudes that influence their relationship. Thus the discussion will proceed in that direction.

---

[2]Chesser, Eustace, *The Sexual, Marital and Family Relationships of the English Woman*, New York: Roy Publishing Co., 1957.
[3]As reported in Blood, Robert O. Jr., *Marriage*, New York: The Free Press, 1969, 2nd Ed., p. 295.
[4]May, Rollo, *Love and Will*, New York: W. W. Norton & Co., 1969, pp. 72, 105.

UNREALISTIC EXPECTATIONS

Many young couples who enter marriage without previous sexual experience expect to have an earthshaking adventure the first time they have coitus. They have been so conditioned by novels and articles describing sexual climax as an "out of this world experience" that if they aren't swept into ecstasy, and don't see colored lights, and don't tremble with emotion as if they were experiencing a California earthquake, they think something is wrong with them, and usually consult the most available marriage manual. Such disillusionment is not uncommon, and Mark Twain, even in his day, when commenting on the typical honeymoon said, "The second biggest disappointment is Niagara Falls."

Other unreasonable expectations about sex can cause discontent in marriage far beyond the honeymoon years. For example, some husbands and wives expect the same type of affectionate expression every time the sex act takes place. One wife said, "I always want to be held close, kissed, caressed and told how much I am loved." On the other hand, some husbands feel that their masculinity suffers if their wives, despite a long, tiresome day of doing the washing and settling disputes between their children, don't eagerly accept their advances and perform like nymphomaniacs.

Couples who make a good sex adjustment come to realize that they do because both have a deep and abiding love for each other and thus accept the fact that it can remain constant even though their overt sexual expression may vary from time to time and run the gamut from wild abandonment to simply lying close and holding each other.

CONDITIONING AND ATTITUDES TOWARD SEX

One of the problems of sex adjustment is that men and women tend to come to marriage with different attitudes toward sex. Although little research has been done in this area, there is general agreement that wives are more concerned than husbands with the emotional setting in which sex takes place.

Kinsey reports that "the average female marries to establish a home, to establish a long-time affectional relationship with a single spouse, and to have children whose welfare may become the prime business of her life. Most males would admit these are all desirable aspects of marriage, but it is probable that few males would marry if they did not anticipate that they would have an opportunity to have coitus regularly with their wives. . . . Conversely, when a marriage fails to satisfy his sexual need, the male is more inclined to consider that it is unsatisfactory, and he is more ready than the female to dissolve the relationship."[5]

Another facet of the different attitudes between males and females is that some wives seem to be able to tolerate going for longer periods of time without sex than their husbands.

Female Sexual Conditioning

There has been some debate as to whether these different male and female attitudes toward sex are the result of conditioning or innate characteristics. Experts in human physiology agree that nearly all females are born with the potential capacity for sex desire, but studies also suggest a relationship between low sex desire and physical abnormality. Landis reported a relationship between low sex desire and menstrual irregularities, including the late onset of menstruation.[6] However since the menstrual period can be affected by psychologic factors, no definite case can be made linking its physiological functioning to low sex desire.

In the American culture, different social conditioning of the sexes often causes mates to bring different sex attitudes to marriage. As girls are growing up, they are generally looked upon with a protective attitude by parents. Without meaning them harm, their mothers and fathers often try to tell them as little as possible about sexual functions, exercise rigid control over their social activities and punish them severely if they "get into trouble" sexually. Consequently, many women become inhibited in their sexual feelings, and enter marriage with apprehensions regarding sexual intimacy with their husbands. But then, as soon as the marriage vows have been taken, their husbands, parents, and society expect them to cast off all of their sexual inhibitions, and respond freely to their mate's sexual overtures, and as one husband put it, "become a delicious animal between the sheets."

Sexual experiences while growing up can also shape a woman's attitude toward sex in marriage. The writer counseled one coed who could not even "bear the thought of having intercourse with a man." One of the reasons was that when she was a small girl, her father would come

[5]Kinsey, A. C., Pomeroy, W. B., Martin, C. E., and Gebhard, Paul H., *Sexual Behavior in the Human Female*, Philadelphia: W. B. Saunders Co., 1953, p. 684.
[6]Landis, Carney and Agnes T., and Bolles, M. M., *Sex in Development*, New York: Hoeber-Harper, 1940.

to her bedroom in the nude, stand in the open doorway, and fondle himself. His actions so repelled her that she grew up thinking all men were beasts.

Dating experiences in which sexual problems arise, can also cause girls to develop positive or negative attitudes toward sex in marriage. They can influence them to look eagerly forward to more opportunities for sex in marriage or enter married life with the feeling that sex is all that husbands think about. A traumatic sexual experience can most certainly shape female attitudes in different ways. One would think that being raped would usually cause a girl to have some anxiety about having coitus in marriage, but there seem to be individual reactions to such an experience. One college graduate in recounting her experience with a dating partner said:

"I had never dated Bill before, but he was so much fun during the movie, I thought to myself, 'Man, he's a sharp guy.' But then, when we were parking after the movie, he wanted to make love. Being that it was our first date, I didn't want to be too intimate. Well, he couldn't get what he wanted on the back seat, so he dragged me out on the ground and raped me. A strange feeling came over me at the time. I was frightened, but at the same time I kind of felt that it was an exciting adventure."

This girl developed no subsequent sexual hangups because of the experience, dated and showed natural affection toward other fellows, and is now a happily married mother.

In recent years, a new attitude has emerged that many women (especially middle-class) bring to marriage, namely an open expression that they have a right to expect sexual fulfillment in marriage. This often brings mental conflict to those who have been emotionally conditioned negatively toward sex, but still intellectually accept the thinking that every wife has a right to sexual satisfaction in marriage.

Male Sexual Conditioning

As boys grow and develop, they are usually allowed greater social freedom than girls. The results of sexual experimentations are not considered as potentially hazardous for them. Usually they are encouraged to be aggressive, and parents often wink at behavior which they would punish in their daughters. Boys' playmates, and later those in their teen peer groups may make them concerned about their boyhood and masculine images, which are related to sexual behavior, and cause them to behave in undesirable ways. Naturally, there are differences in home training, but by and large the male is not subjected to the protective attitude which is afforded the female.

The dating structure also allows the male more initiative and freedom in dating. Consequently, if a female dating partner dislikes his sexual behavior, he can much more easily arrange to date someone else than the girl who displeases her boyfriend, who usually has more difficulty getting back into the dating game.

Of course, there is a wide variety of sex attitudes that men bring to marriage, ranging from complete lack of sex interest to great sex desire with few inhibitions. Generally speaking, however, males because of different conditioning seem to bring fewer sex inhibitions to marriage than do females.

The thinking is often advanced that a male who has had a variety of premarital sexual experiences will be in a position to help his wife work out a better sexual adjustment in marriage. A study by Landis and Landis refutes this idea. In their study of 581 married couples, they found that "the men who had been promiscuous—in that they reported having had coitus with as many as nine women before meeting the one they married—were twice as likely after ten years of marriage to report sex to be a serious problem in their marriages as were men who had not been promiscuous." They concluded, "This finding is open to a variety of interpretations, but one conclusion can be drawn: Premarital experience with many or several people is not necessarily adequate preparation for marital success. Men and women who at marriage have open minds and are willing to learn and to work at reaching a good understanding will achieve success more readily.[7]

UNDERSTANDING MALE AND FEMALE SEXUAL DIFFERENCES

It helps in marital adjustment if each partner, both husband and wife, understands the sexual differences of the male and female. A brief summary will be given below.

The Sex Drive

A man's sex drive (desire and or ability) usually peaks at about age eighteen, and then gradually declines. It doesn't necessarily cease in

[7]Landis, Judson T. and Mary G., *Building a Successful Marriage*, Englewood Cliffs: Prentice Hall, Inc., 1973, 6th Edition, p. 277.

the later years, as some studies of men over 75 show that the majority reported coital activity about four times a month.

A woman's sex drive usually peaks in the late twenties or early thirties and remains stable until late in life.

Married couples who are aware of these differences can be more understanding if there is disparity in their desire for frequency of intercourse. Thus the wife, in the later years of marriage, would be less likely to berate her husband, if he could not perform as frequently as she desired.

One question that arises concerns the strength of the sex drive. It is commonly thought that the male has a stronger drive than the female. No studies substantiate the fact that either sex has greater capacity for potential sex drive. The female's natural desire may be more inhibited due to cultural conditioning. Also the aspect of timing enters into sex desire and response. Inasmuch as the husband is customarily the initiator of the sex act, it may be that he approaches his wife when her body metabolism is not conducive to sexual response.

Differences in Responsiveness to Sexual Stimuli

Males seem to respond more sexually to visual and auditory stimuli than do women. A summary of Kinsey's studies shows the following responses to stimuli:[8]

Differences in Responsiveness to Sexual Stimuli

	Percentage of Those Aroused	
	Male	*Female*
Observing opposite sex (clothed or nude)	72	58
Nude photographs and drawings	54	12
Observing commercial motion pictures	36	48
Watching burlesque and floor shows	62	14
Observing portrayals of sexual activity	77	32
Fantasies (thinking of opposite sex— a specific person or in general)	84	69
Reading literary materials	59	60

The Female's Periods of Greatest Sex Desire

Something that husbands often fail to realize is that their wives have a heightened interest in sex that usually occurs at a certain time

[8]*Ibid*, pp. 651-671 Adapted.

during their menstrual cycle. Most wives who have been questioned about it (about half) say it occurs just before the menstrual period. Others say it occurs directly afterward or in the middle of the cycle.

If the married pair are aware of this, both partners can be sensitive to the fact that mutual sexual satisfaction is more likely to occur at this time. And there is surely nothing wrong with the wife letting her husband know when she is in this sexual mood.

STEPS IN SEXUAL ADJUSTMENT

The Time Element

Inasmuch as psychic and emotional factors have much to do with sex adjustment, many couples realize that it takes time to work out a mutually satisfying relationship. Consequently, spouses should not become impatient if first sexual experiences leave something to be desired. Landis and Landis in a study of 409 couples found "that one eighth needed weeks or months, but reached a sexual adjustment they considered satisfactory within a year. One tenth of them required an average of six years to work out this part of their marriage, some as long as twenty years. . . . In the average marriage, a measure of uncertainty, awkwardness, and even tension in sex life is likely at first. . . . Happily married couples report that their sex adjustment becomes an increasingly satisfactory bond in their marriage as years pass."[9]

Necessary Anatomical and Physiological Knowledge

Marriage partners should have some knowledge of the anatomical structure and the physiological functioning of the male and female bodies which would include the facts needed to understand techniques of stimulation, how intercourse takes place, and the external manifestations of male and female orgasm. The names of the various organs and the structure and functions of the reproductive systems are given in the chapter "The Male and Female Reproductive System," so the same information will not be repeated here.

Response to Sexual Stimulation

Sexual adjustment is furthered if each partner learns what parts of the body the other wants to have touched. Nudity during love play makes it much easier to learn which of these areas evoke the greatest

[9] Ibid, p. 275.

response. The entire body can be sensitive to sexual stimulation, but generally speaking, there are some parts that produce greater sensations. In the female, the tongue, lips, ears, neck, arms, breasts, and thighs are all sensitive, with the genital area, particularly the clitoris, being highly sensitive. Masters and Johnson assign a dual role to the clitoris during sexual excitation, that of "a receptor and transformer of sexual stimulation." They state further that its primary function is to stimulate female sexual tensions, and that despite what has been commonly thought, "there is no relation between the size of the clitoris and the effectiveness of its role in female sexual stimulation."[10]

These sensitive areas, called erogenous zones, are basically the same in the male, with the penis being the focal point of stimulation. However, inasmuch as the male's sexual sensations seem to be more localized than the female's, he is generally aroused more quickly and with less stimulation.

It must be kept in mind that there is a psychologic aspect of sex arousal, and if couples develop certain ritualistic sex foreplay that touching a certain part of the body can trigger sexual response. As the Hegelers say ". . . we must bear in mind that erogenous zones can be cultivated. If a man, for instance, always begins by patting his loved one on the tip of her nose by way of leading up to further caresses and their whole sex life . . . is a matter of pleasure to her—this pat on the nose will soon become a signal, a sign that something good is on its way—and thus will become an erogenous zone in the person concerned."[11]

In addition to becoming acquainted with their erogenous zones, it is also important for married partners to learn what type of touches or caresses are most desired. Some individuals prefer firm caresses, while others respond more to a light touch or a combination of both firm and tender. An illustration of the importance of touch is that of caressing the clitoris, an area where firm or even light continuous stroking may cause irritation. To produce best results, both sex partners should discuss and experiment with the best techniques.

If the couple is forearmed with the above knowledge, their first act of intercourse in marriage should go more smoothly. Above all, they should be considerate of each other. It often happens that the bride is

---

[10]Masters, William H., and Johnson, Virginia E., *Human Sexual Response*, Boston: Little, Brown & Co., 1966, p. 56.
[11]Hegeler, Inge and Sten, *An ABZ of Love*, London: Neville Spearman Ltd., 1963, p. 82.

eager for the first sexual union with her husband and her expectations have been built up to a romantic peak. A husband should sense this and never show lack of interest or desire.

One young bride said:

I was completely crushed on our wedding night. I put on my most attractive nightgown, got into bed, and waited eagerly for my husband to start making love. Instead, he went into the bathroom and went through such a long ritual of getting ready for bed, that I finally sensed that he couldn't care less whether he had intercourse with me that night or not. I've since learned that he was shy and was anxious about approaching me sexually, but this knowledge has never erased the disappointment of my wedding night.

It also occasionally happens that wives are insensitive to their husbands' feelings and accuse them of being animal-like in their sexual approach, instead of realizing that their awkward behavior may be due to lack of knowledge or nervous tension.

If the wife has had no previous sexual experience, she may be worrying about the rupture of her hymen. If such is the case, it pays to have a previous pelvic examination so the doctor can reassure her that everything is normal, or if necessary stretch or instruct her how to stretch the obstructing membrane.

ACHIEVING MUTUAL SATISFACTION IN INTERCOURSE

It would naive to say, "Now follow these directions and sexual intercourse will be satisfying to both partners," which incidentally is what many marriage manuals do. Following such advice would be more likely to turn the sex act into a mechanical ritual that would be devoid of any emotion and lacking in spontaneity. However, there are some general things to consider, which, if adapted to the unique circumstances and personalities of the couples, may help in achieving mutually rewarding intercourse.

An illustration of one result of following directions was the expression of the married college student who came to the author for help because as he said, "Our sex life has become a bore, it has become so dull that we both get more enjoyment out of taking in a movie."

After some discussion, it was learned that he, John, and his wife, Marsha, had fallen into the habit of having sex on Monday, Wednesday, and Friday nights at the time they went to bed. It was pointed out that such a routine practice would probably blunt most couples' sexual appetites. So it was suggested that he vary his sexual approach to Marsha, and at some unscheduled time get her into the proper mood by dimming the lights, turning on soft music, and whispering words of love to her. Then as his desire built up to a passionate crescendo, sweep her into his arms, carry her to the bed and make love to her. He left, agreeing to try the experiment.

A week later, he returned with a beaming countenance and said, "Man, your advice was great! I followed your suggestions and we both got more excited sexually than we have for months. In fact, we got so carried away that Marsha said afterwards, 'Golly, what got into you. I didn't realize you could be such a romantic lover.' So I told her I was following your directions."

Of course, John spoiled the incident for Marsha in retrospect, but even if he had not told her he was following directions, repeating the same approach, in the future, would have eventually brought sexual boredom again. So, in presenting the following ideas, it must be remembered that they cannot take the place of creative thinking or spontaneous behavior on the part of the involved couple.

Attitudes

The couple who looks upon the sex act as a natural, beautiful and joyous thing have made a start toward developing a rewarding relationship. Unfortunately, some individuals cannot do this. One young wife said that when she was growing up her mother had given her so much sexual misinformation and punished her so severely when she had shown affection for the boys she dated, that every time she had intercourse with her husband, she felt like her mother was looking over her shoulder ready to reprimand her.

A young husband, because of childhood conditioning, said he felt intercourse with his wife was simply a husband's duty, and he got it over with as quickly as possible.

The Approach and the Setting

When and where should a husband or wife approach his or her partner for sex? Answer—when and where either or both are in the mood. Much is written about having sex in an attractive bedroom with a comfortable bed and subdued lighting. However, it might occasionally be even more romantic to make love on the shore of a rippling lake or in an out-of-the-way motel. Masters and Johnson write that the male cannot instinctively "discern exactly what a woman wants sexually, and when she wants it" and they add, "no woman can know what type of sexual approach she will respond to at any given opportunity, until faced with absence of a particularly desired stimulative factor." They stress spontaneity and say, "spontaneous sexual expression which answers the demand to be sexually needed and gives freedom for comparable male and female interaction, is universally the most stimulating of circumstances. Here the (mutual) signal systems (a combination of verbal and non-verbal communications, through which individual feelings, reactions, and preferences of sexual importance may be shared and understood) lead each partner toward and into the specifics that are desirable at a particular time."[12]

Personal appearance is also important for most people in contributing to the setting in which coitus takes place. Cleanliness of the total body is important and many individuals are also affected by odors, sight and sound. One woman who was deeply in love with her husband said, "When Richard makes love to me, I want to feel that I'm kissable all over."

Sexual Union

Masters and Johnson have divided sexual response in intercourse into four phases: excitement, plateau, orgasm, and resolution. Very briefly, their manifestations are:

Excitement Phase

Male	Female
Erection of the penis	Stimulation of the erogenous zones —moistening of the vaginal area

Plateau Phase

Male	Female
Increased rate of breathing and heartbeat—sex flush may appear on the back, abdomen, breasts	Increased rate of breathing and heartbeat—sex flush—breasts may increase in size—nipples become erect

---

[12]Masters, William H., and Johnson, Virginia E., *Human Sexual Inadequacy*, Boston: Little, Brown and Co., 1970, pp. 86, 87.

Orgasm Phase

Male	*Female*
Contractions of the penis and ejaculation of semen	Acute increase in pulse rate and breathing (these occur in a lesser degree in the male), muscular contractions of the vaginal area— they number three to twelve, about one second apart, marked distentension of the deeper part of the vagina closest to the uterus

The Resolution Phase

(Return to Normal Physiological Functioning)

Male	*Female*
Erection of penis usually subsides, male cannot perform again for several minutes to several hours as related to health and age	Detumescence of the clitoris (5 to 30 minutes), general relaxation, usually capable of almost immediate rearousal

It should be stated that although many partners feel relaxed and fall asleep after intercourse, a number of wives feel the need to be fondled, and held close during their period of detumescence. If their husbands perform to climax, and afterward promptly fall asleep, the wives often feel that their bodies have been used for sexual gratification without consideration for their personhood.

Other Things to Consider

1. It helps in adjustment, if partners can talk about their sexual feelings. It can not only heighten erotic desire, but also help each one learn what caresses and attitudes the other most readily responds to. Many couples have difficulty in discussing their sex needs with each other, perhaps because of lack of proper vocabulary, or because they feel that talking about needs will put either one of them in a vulnerable position. Many wives who would readily ask their husbands to rub their backs and specifically direct them to the sore spot, hesitate to tell the same mate which areas of their body are most sensitive to manual stimulation. When asked why, they often answer, "Goodness, he should know where to touch me, after all these years."

Some couples even talk awkwardly when discussing engaging in possible intercourse. A husband may come home in the mood, and say,

"How about it?" to his wife, and receive the reply, "How about what?" Such verbal skirting of needs and desires can often lead to cynicism or bitterness.

2. A couple should not become anxious if they don't use all of the coital positions suggested by marriage manuals. A recent best seller which has been purchased by nearly two million people contains over 420 photographs of artists' mannequins, showing the male and female separately in every imaginable coital position. Taking such suggestions seriously would cause some couples to feel that they should forego sex entirely unless they were skilled gymnasts.[13]

It is true that there are many possible positions that might be used in intercourse, but it is up to each couple to experiment and employ those which give the most pleasure to both of them. To illustrate, the position with the male above, will not be mutually pleasant unless he is able to rest his weight on his elbows. If he is physically incapable of doing this, his wife may have difficulty participating actively in the sex act because she has been rendered immobile by her partner's weight.

3. Wives usually take longer to become aroused sexually than do husbands. Consequently, patience and understanding should be exercised in this respect. Couples may also mistakenly measure their sexual success in marriage in terms of frequency of contact. Trying to perform according to the frequency of reported averages is unrealistic. Perhaps the only guideline to be conscious of is that as men get older their capacity to perform frequently gradually diminishes. Thus, frequency should be regulated by the physiological and psychological needs of the couple.

4. The wife does not always have to have an orgasm in order to enjoy intercourse. Many report that much satisfaction can be gained from caresses, being loved, and meeting their husband's sexual needs. Various studies estimate that about 10 percent of the mature women in the population have never experienced orgasm, although a correlation has been found between rarely experiencing a marital orgasm and unhappiness[14] the situation might be turned around and the hypothesis advanced that unhappiness blocks orgastic response. Couples who feel that

[13]Kokken, Sha, *A Happier Sex Life*, Robert Y. Tatsuoka, Sen Kozuka (trans.) Tokyo: 1964. Ikeda Publishing Co., U.S. Edition by Sherbourne Press, Los Angeles, 1967.

[14]Gebhard, Paul, "Factors in Marital Orgasm," *Journal of Social Issues*, 22: 88-95, 1966.

they must experience simultaneous orgasm to be successful sexually are also unrealistic in that very few partners can achieve this goal.

5. Other things to know are:

a. Fatigue can hinder adjustment.

b. Studies show that intercourse during menstruation is not harmful if it is aesthetically desirable to both partners.

c. Masters and Johnson suggest that certain traditional time periods during which intercourse is prohibited during pregnancy may do more harm than good. Since there is no consensus on this among obstetricians, the individual woman should be guided by the obstetrician's knowledge of her particular condition.

d. Husbands' egos are also involved in the sex act and they derive more pleasure from intercourse if they know their wives love and respect them and respond to their lovemaking.

FACTORS THAT CAUSE INADEQUATE SEXUAL RESPONSE

Fears and Negative Comments

Fears—Common fears that may interfere with sex adjustment are:
fear of pregnancy
fear of not satisfying the partner
fear of being overheard when making love (children's feet pattering in the hall)
fear of pain
fear of being considered unladylike
fear of giving oneself freely, and thus remaining a spectator to the sex act

Negative Comments:
"I can stand it."
"You're hurting me."
"I love you, but I don't desire you."
"My you've put on weight."
"My first husband was more tender."
"Why can't you cooperate?"
"Why aren't you in the mood? I am."

SOME PROBLEMS

Female Problems

Frigidity

The word frigid should be replaced by Masters and Johnson's phrase, "A prevailing inability or subconscious refusal to respond sexually to effective stimulation." When this condition, which may be caused by a number of physical and emotional factors, is present, professional treatment should be obtained.

Female dyspareunia
                    (Painful sexual intercourse)

Possible Causes

Physical

An intact hymen—bruised vaginal tissues, clitoral irritations—vaginal infections and irritations.

Psychological

Insufficient lubrication of the vaginal passageway due to fear, hostility or conflict.

Treatment Needed

Medical treatment and psychotherapy.

Inability to achieve orgasm

Medical treatment and psychotherapy should be sought.

Vaginismus

Involuntary spasms of the vagina and muscular constriction of the vaginal outlet.

A psychosomatic condition that should be treated. Often caused by the psychic trauma of rape or painful previous coital experience.

Sagging of the Pubococcygeus Muscle

The sagging of this thick pelvic muscle which acts as a platform to support the vaginal canal and the other organs of the pelvis can reduce sensations in the vaginal passageway. A medical examination to determine its condition, and subsequent exercises to improve muscle tone can increase sexual response. A woman can learn to contract and exercise it at home if she is able to interrupt the flow of urine by a willed effort which is an indication that the P.C. has been contracted.

Male Problems

Male dyspareunia

Pain during intercourse which may be caused by infection, scars in or a stricture of the urethral passage; bacteria or infections within the wife's vagina; phimosis (an abnormally tight foreskin that cannot be pulled back from over the glans of the penis).

Medical treatment needed.

Impotence

The inability to have an erection and maintain it long enough to enjoy intercourse.

Physical and psychological causes can be treated.

Premature Ejaculation

Ejaculating and losing an erection before the partner is satisfied. Might be caused by too prolonged foreplay, having no sexual contacts for a long period of time, or the husband's fear that he will not be able to perform adequately. Can also take the form (ejaculatory incompetence) of inability to ejaculate within the vagina.

Can be treated.

THE USE OF DRUGS

So much that is controversial has been written about the effect of drugs on sexual intercourse that only a brief summary will be quoted here. Kogan says:

"Examples of drugs that indirectly stimulate sexual activity by releasing inhibitions are relatively small doses of alcohol and barbiturates. Those that directly stimulate sex activity include the amphetamines and cocaine. Marijuana may fit into both groups. Difficult to categorize are the psychedelic drugs, particularly MDA.

"Drugs that decrease sexual activity may do so by either diminishing desire or (with the male) by decreasing potency. Heroin and high doses of either barbiturates or alcohol are examples. . . . By diminishing coordination and concentration, LSD may interfere with consummation of sexual intercourse."[15]

It must be stated that the above discussion is a generalization on the effects of drugs, so it should be remembered that certain individuals may react differently.

---

[15]Kogan, Benjamin A., *Human Sexual Expression*, New York: Harcourt Brace Jovanovich, Inc., 1973, p. 346.

Some people attempt to increase sex desire with the use of aphro-disiacs (foods or drugs that stimulate erotic feelings). Experts generally agree that no known food is in itself a sex stimulant. Some of the drugs that have recently been reported as possible aphrodisiacs are Dexedrine, Methedrine, Ritalin, Preludin, L-Dopa (L-dihydroxyphenylalanine) and PCPA (p-chlorphenylalanine), and Cyclazocine.[16]

Suggested Readings

1. Bell, Robert R., *Marriage and Family Interaction,* Homewood, Ill.: The Dorsey Press, 1971 (3rd ed.), Chapter 15, "Marital and Extramarital Sexual Expression."

2. Bird, Joseph W., and Bird, Lois F., *The Freedom of Sexual Love,* Garden City, N.Y.: Doubleday & Co., 1967.

3. Calderone, Mary Steichen, *Release From Sexual Tensions,* New York: Random House, Inc., 1960.

4. Curtis, Lindsay R., *Sensible Sex: A Guide for Newlyweds,* Salt Lake City, Utah: Publishers Press, 1968.

5. Davis, Maxine, *Sexual Responsibility in Marriage,* New York: Dial Press, 1963.

6. Deutsch, Ronald M., *The Key to Feminine Response in Marriage,* New York: Random House, Inc., 1960.

7. Hastings, Donald, *Sexual Expression in Marriage,* Boston, Ma.: Little, Brown & Co., 1966.

8. Mace, David, *Sexual Difficulties in Marriage,* Philadelphia, Pa.: Fortress Press, 1972.

9. Masters, William H., and Johnson, Virginia E., *Human Sexual Response,* Boston: Little, Brown & Co., 1966.

10. ———, *Human Sexual Inadequacy,* Boston: Little, Brown & Co., 1970.

11. Otto, Herbert A., and Otto, Roberta, *Total Sex,* New York: Peter H. Wyden, Inc., 1971.

12. Rainer, Jerome and Rainer, Julia, *Sexual Pleasure in Marriage,* New York: Simon and Schuster, 1969.

13. Stone, Hannah and Stone, Abraham, *A Marriage Manual,* New York: Simon and Schuster, 1968 (rev.).

14. Wrage, Karl, *Man and Woman: The Basics of Sex and Marriage,* Philadelphia, Pa.: Fortress Press, 1966.

---

[16] *Ibid,* p. 348.

Chapter XVII

Managing Family Finances

MARITAL CONFLICTS

Managing the family's income is one of the major areas of conflict in marriage. Blood and Wolfe in their study of marital disagreements as evidence of stresses found money to be the chief disagreement among middle-class urban families. The following table shows its relationship to other areas:

Some Major Areas of Disagreement in Urban Families[1]

Type of Disagreement	Percentage of Wives Mentioning	
	First	At all
Money	24%	42%
Children	16	29
In-laws	6	10
Religion, politics	3	4
Sex	*	1

*Less than ½ of 1 percent

The Family Service Association of America, in a more recent study, shows a much higher percentage of couples reporting money as a major area of disagreement in marriage, and also indicated that the way money is used rather than how much is available is the major factor in causing problems. It was reported:

"In a study of requests for counseling made to various Family Service agencies, more than half the couples reported severe problems with the money aspects of their marriage. Yet only a tiny proportion of them, six percent to be exact, were in difficulty because of inadequate income or financial need. Most couples were in trouble for two other reasons:

---

[1] Adapted from Blood, Robert O. Jr.. and Wolfe, Donald M., *Husbands and Wives— The Dynamics of Married Living*, Glencoe: The Free Press, 1960, p. 241.

1. Immature or unrealistic attitudes toward the earning, saving, or spending of money;

2. The emotional use of money either as a weapon with which to control or punish a spouse or as a way of compensating for inadequacies, guilt, or the inability to give love."[2]

Immature or unrealistic attitudes and the use of money as a weapon against the spouse seem to be factors in many marriages where there is disagreement regarding management of finances.

The statement of the following husband is representative:

Since we have been married, we have had trouble managing our money wisely. At first, we also ran into trouble about whom the money belonged to. We were continually buying things we really didn't need. By buying these things we didn't need, we were letting things we did need wait. I used to do things like going out and buying a new motorcycle when the stuffing in the chair was coming out. We also never kept ourselves on a budget. We figured that if there is something we wanted to do or get, what the heck, let's do it or get it.

It didn't take long to find out that my wife did a better job of paying the bills and more or less managing the money, so we somewhat adjusted to part of our money management this way. We also started budgeting ourselves somewhat and this has helped also. We, however, still have an adjustment problem as far as buying things that we want and like rather than buying something for the household which should be of more priority. The only other problem we have as far as money adjustment goes is that we still tend to argue once in awhile about the way the other one spends money on themselves. As of right now, we are still trying to work on a solution.

Some Reasons Why Couples Disagree

One does not have to look far to learn why husbands and wives often disagree when it comes to handling money. In the first place, partners usually come to marriage with different attitudes toward handling money. These have been shaped by some of the following things:

The attitudes and spending patterns of their parents. The wife may say, "My parents always paid their bills promptly and in cash. I feel that is what we should do, but my husband won't cooperate." Or the husband

[2]Lobsenz, Norman M., and Blackburn, Clark W., *How to Stay Married—A Modern Approach to Sex, Money and Emotions in Marriage*, New York: Cowles Book Co.. Inc., 1969, p. 89.

may remark, "Dad always handled the money in our family. It's a man's job. Why can't Mary realize it?"

These different "inherited" attitudes toward handling money often cause disagreement.

Another factor which may contribute toward financial management attitudes is the subculture in which the individual has grown up. Both husband and wife will often arrange spending priorities the way their associates did. For example, different groups of people may place importance on using money for completely different things; cars or concert tickets, clothes or tools, houses or trips abroad. Consequently, if husbands and wives have grown up in different subcultures, they are likely to assign completely different priorities to the spending of money.

Personality differences in the spouses can also cause disagreement regarding the handling of money. For illustration, the insecure wife who has a tendency to worry about the future may be constantly upset by her optimistic and adventurous husband's risk-taking ventures. Thus, if he speculates in the stock market and loses, she may vehemently denounce him and say that he has no concern for his family's security.

As was said before, the immature use of money in order to give vent to one's emotions or manipulate the other partner is also a contributing factor to disagreement. The use of money can be linked with the entire gamut of emotions, and can represent in turn, love or hate, fear or calmness, recognition or revenge, satisfaction or retaliation.

One young wife confided how her emotional state affected her spending habits. She said:

> Every time my husband goes on a hunting trip, he refuses to take me along. It makes me furious to think of all the money he is spending, so I get even by going downtown and buying myself an expensive new dress.

THE ALLOCATION OF MONEY

It seems that the only way a married couple can get rid of disagreements over the use of their money entails doing two things. One, knowing how much money is available to use. Two, agreeing on how it is to be used. Some married partners don't have enough faith in each other to reveal what their individual and collective financial resources are. A typical example was the husband who refused to tell his wife what his salary was. He said, "It's better to keep her in the dark, because she always spends right up to the limit of what she thinks I earn. So, if I get a raise and don't tell her, I can put a little money away without her feeling she's being deprived."

It also happens that a wife may not have enough faith in her husband's financial judgment to reveal that she has some money that could help defray family expenses. Nancy B. felt this way. "My husband, Don, is such an impulsive buyer," she exclaimed, "that I don't dare tell him that my father left me some money and that I have a secret bank account. Why, if Don knew about it, he would nag me to spend it, and it would be gone in no time. This way, I'll always have something to fall back on if things go wrong or we should get a divorce."

Both of these married partners were not happy in their mate relationships because their lack of trust in their spouses was stopping them from developing a cooperative attitude—a "we" rather than an "I" approach to doing things.

Once couples can overcome this reluctance to disclose their financial resources to each other and "put everything on the table," they are in a position to decide what system of allocation to use. Any system can be fairly effective if the couple uses it with the attitude that it is an agreed-upon way of allocating "our money."

It should be mentioned that even when a family agrees on a certain system of allocating money, some discontent on the part of one mate or the other may still exist. For example, some husbands even though they agree to let their wives handle the money may feel that their masculine image is impaired in the process, and the wife in turn may begin to feel that she is carrying a burden that should rightfully be assumed by her husband. Landis and Landis found in a study which included 1,022 couples who were either engaged, married, or divorced that the engaged couples had the highest percentage of agreement on how money was spent, 41%. Married couples, 18%. Married couples having marriage counseling, 8%. And divorced couples, 3%.[3]

Duvall and Hill list five of the more common ways to allocate money which they call "the dole system, the family treasurer system, the division of expenses system, the joint account system and the budget system."[4]

[3]Landis, Judson T. and Mary G., *Building a Successful Marriage*, Englewood Cliffs: Prentice Hall, Inc., 1973, 6th Edition, p. 323.

[4]Duvall, Evelyn M., and Hill, Reuben, *Being Married*, Boston: D. C. Heath and Co., 1960. p. 251.

These systems are set up as follows:

The dole—One person controls the money and uses his or her discretion in handing out money to meet family members' requests.

The family treasurer—The family agrees on a system of allowances, and then turns over the bill paying and most of the buying to the member whom everyone feels is most capable of handling the money. The treasurer still consults family members regarding major outlays of money, and the others are usually relieved to be free of the routine matters associated with buying and the payment of bills.

Division of expenses—Husband and wife agree on the amounts needed to cover specific expenses, and then make each one responsible for paying certain things. The method of payment of unforeseen or unusual expenses is decided by joint decision.

The joint account—All moneys are put into a common checking account which both partners use to pay expenses. However, one partner would not draw an unusually large sum from the account without consulting the other.

The budget—Families plan ahead on how their money will be used, and then try to operate financially within their agreed-upon framework. Inasmuch as the budget system seems to be the most effective method for most families to use, it will be discussed in greater detail.

Someone has said, "A budget, strictly enforced, is like long underwear. If you need it, you'd better have it. If you don't, it scratches." Certain types of individuals do get tense if they try to account for every cent they spend, consequently, a budget should be flexible enough so it can serve and not dominate married partners.

Robert Frost referred to this weakness in keeping track of money in his poem entitled "The Hardship of Accounting":

> Never ask of money spent
> Where the spender thinks it went.
> Nobody was ever meant
> To remember or invent
> What he did with every cent.

Steps In Setting Up a Budget

Step 1: Your Income. Write down how much the family expects to receive from all sources during a twelve-month period. This would include wages and salaries (minus payroll deductions), and income from investments.

Step 2: Your Weekly Set-Asides. Put down all of the fixed obligations that must be met during the twelve-month period. This would include such things as rent, payments on mortgages, life insurance, taxes over and above the payroll tax, church contributions, installment payments, and so on.

If it helps, indicate what month these outlays will come due. Don't write down any expense you can't estimate very closely but include every kind of fixed expense or obligation you can estimate. Total all these fixed items and divide by 52.

The answer you get will be your weekly set-aside, and it will be the heart of a workable plan. Every week you will put your set-aside in the bank or in a special fund; every time one of your fixed items comes due, you will pay it out of this fund. If you do this and your original estimates were correct, there will always be enough in the fund to meet your obligations once your system is well under way.

Step 3: Your Emergency fund. To make your financial plan work and to meet unexpected expenses—and they come to every family—you will need a reserve fund. It doesn't need to be a large amount of money, but it should be enough to tide you over bad weeks or even months.

Do not confuse your emergency fund with saving. The purpose of the emergency fund is not to advance your family, or to buy things sometime in the future, or to provide for your family's long-term security. It is simply a fund to tide your family over temporary emergencies. Be conservative in estimating how large a fund you need. Some people suggest a sum equal to one, two or three months' income, but even three months' income, from all indications, seems to be more than most families have in cash and saving bonds and savings accounts.

When you have figured out how much you want to try to put into your emergency fund every week, write this down and add it to your weekly set-aside. Every week put it in your bank or special fund. If it should ever happen that you have an emergency fund which you think is big enough, stop putting any more money in it. Instead increase your life insurance or regular savings program, add to your investments, or put the money to some other use.

Step 4: Your Living Expenses. When you take your weekly income and subtract your allowance for set-asides and your allowance for your emergency fund, you will have a weekly figure with which to pay all your day-to-day expenses. This means food, clothing, home upkeep, automobile maintenance and other transportation, personal allowances, ordinary medical care, education, recreation and so on. To know whether your plan will work you must estimate all of these items as closely as you can and check the total with the amount you have put down for them. If it isn't enough you must go back and refigure the provision you have made for other things.

In controlling your living expenses, it will be a good idea to portion out the amount of money you have among the people in your family. Mother, for example, may have "x" dollars for food and "y" dollars for everything else in her particular domain—laundry, dry cleaning, and so on. Father may have an allowance for car expenses, another allowance for his lunches and transportation. The children may have an allowance for school expenses and incidentals. Everyone in the family, in addition, may have a small "spend-as-he-pleases" allowance and there may also be a "go-to-the-bank" allowance for vacation or Christmas savings.

In dividing your day-to-day living expenses, you will probably want to end up with a general "household" or "incidental" fund. A few families, extremely conscious of their responsibilities, allocate money clear across the board—so much a week for routine medical expenses, so much a week for minor clothing expenses, so much a week for household supplies, and so on. The majority of families, however, don't figure this closely and don't need to.

Whatever plan you adopt, what is left after expenses will be the amount you have for regular savings. This will determine the rate of your progress toward future family goals.

If a family wants to determine if it is spending a disproportionate amount of money in any one area of its needs, it is helpful to compare expenditures with those of families who have a comparable income. The following table shows the average amounts spent for different items.

Dividing the Urban Family's Dollars

	Lower-Income Family	Middle-Income Family	Higher-Income Family
	Percent of Annual Budget		
Food	27.9	23.2	19.8
Housing	22.0	24.6	25.6
Transportation	7.5	9.6	8.6
Clothing and Personal Care	11.8	10.8	11.1
Medical Care	8.0	5.3	3.8
Recreation, other "Consumption"	5.0	6.0	7.4
Gifts and Contributions	2.5	2.8	3.8
Personal Life Insurance	2.0	1.8	1.8
Job Expenses	0.8	0.9	0.7
Social Security, Disability Taxes	4.5	3.3	2.3
Personal Taxes	8.0	11.7	15.1

Source: Bureau of Labor Statistics, U.S. Dept. of Labor, Computed for 1967.
Reprinted from U. S. NEWS & WORLD REPORT, March 24, 1969.

MAJOR FAMILY EXPENDITURES

There are certain types of expenditures that may occur very few times during the family's life cycle. But their effects can often influence the family's life-style for many years after they are made. Among the major expenditures are family funds spent for housing, and life and other types of insurance.

Obtaining Housing Facilities

The Decision to Rent or Buy a House

The question, "Should we rent or buy a house?" confronts most couples even before they make the trip to the altar. The answer to this query must come from the couple—no one else. They must decide what course to follow by discussing the needs and aspirations of the two of them and by engaging in realistic thinking about the number of children with whom they eventually hope to share their home. A sound decision cannot be made without first acquiring information and gathering facts. The decision to buy or to rent should be made after considering the following information.

Reasons for Renting

1. A newly married couple should usually rent until they have determined how long they intend to live in a certain locality.

Typical questions should be: "How long do we plan to stay here?" "Will a desire for additional schooling make it necessary to move?" "Will frequent company transfers make buying a house a costly venture?"

2. It would be wise to rent until they are prepared financially to assume a long-term fixed obligation. Renters are only obligated for the period of their lease, whereas home owners assume a much longer obligation and also will be affected by changes in property values, the need to sell, and so forth.

3. Renters usually have much smaller expenditures related to maintaining the property. Avoiding these costs may make it possible to pay for further education.

4. If a couple does not have the time, desire, or aptitude to repair and improve property, they will usually find renting less costly than homeowning.

5. If they rent a house that is adequate for their present needs, they should be able to save and accumulate more funds for future investments.

6. Renting affords an opportunity to evaluate different kinds of living accommodations and to study the community. This should enable the couple to be better judges of what kind of house they will later want to buy and what sort of community they will be the happiest living in.

7. Renting provides much more flexibility of movement. If a neighborhood begins to deteriorate, the couple can leave it without the need to sell their property.

Some Ways to Save on Rent

Married college students have reported the following ways to cut down on rental costs:

Be caretakers for an apartment building and receive their own apartment rent free in return.

Manage an apartment complex which includes enough units to enable the owners to give them a free apartment plus a salary.

Provide security for a church building by seeing that doors are open for, and locked after meetings, as well as guarding against vandalism, in exchange for a free apartment in the church.

Rent furnished rooms from a family whose home has become too large for their own needs.

Reasons for Buying a House

1. As soon as a couple knows where they want to settle down and are prepared to assume a long-term financial obligation, buying a house can bring a greater sense of permanency to their relationship.

2. Pride in owning a home usually motivates persons to make improvements and, consequently, the home will increase in value.

3. Buying a home, in normal times, is a sound investment. Studies show that during the past two inflationary decades the purchase of a home has enabled many families to improve their financial positions.

4. Home owners can gradually acquire better furnishings and more conveniences, because they can plan these improvements over a period of years.

5. Home owners are given some consideration related to income tax and are allowed deductions for property taxes and interest paid on mortgages.

6. Living for an extended period in the same community provides individuals with the opportunity to acquire a circle of lasting friendships. Children will also feel more secure, because they can progress through their different stages of schooling without the interruptions that make new adjustments and the seeking of new friends necessary.

7. Home owners have opportunities to engage in more community and civic activities, which in turn may lead to greater development as individuals.

Buying a House—The Important Question—"Is the Price Right?"

Thousands of houses change ownership in our culture. In fact, some studies show that many families move about every five or six years. The most important question to be answered when buying a home is, "Is the price right?" If the price is right, both buyer and seller will benefit from the transaction. If it is not, someone will suffer financially. The family that suffers may have its entire financial structure undermined and spend years trying to recover.

A Brief Summary of Things to Consider

Dealing With Owners or Realtors

The couple should look at owner advertised houses first because of the possibility that they might get a reduced price by avoiding the realtor's commission. However, it should be kept in mind that experienced realtors can render many helpful services and best buys can also be made through them. Buyers should avoid having two real estate salesmen show them the same house because if it is later purchased they may have to pay two fees.

Obtaining a Mortgage Commitment

Before spending a great deal of time checking everything concerning the house, it is wise to see what kind of financing is available. An appraiser from a bank will, on request, evaluate the house and determine what kind of conventional mortgage commitment can be made on it. Buyers can also contact the Federal Housing Administration and Veterans Administration to obtain appraisals of the house and learn if they can qualify for either an FHA approved loan or a GI approved loan. It pays dividends to become conversant with procedures and costs related to these different types of loans and then use the type best suited to one's needs.

A mortgage commitment is also one criterion to use in deciding if the house is priced fairly, inasmuch as the lender will designate if the sales price of the house is out of balance with the percentage he is willing to lend on it.

It is also sometimes possible to buy a house on a contract for deed from the owner.

It is extremely important to check the property taxes and any special assessments that have been or might be made against the property. Special assessments might include things such as curbing and surfacing streets, and hook-ups to water, gas, or sewage lines. Unusually high taxes may make the house a dubious investment.

A Study of the Neighborhood

A couple should take time to ride, or if possible walk around the neighborhood, to observe general conditions and note the architecture and appearance of surrounding houses. If the area is composed of uneven streets (those on which the houses are not of comparable value), the price offered for the house should be reduced. Buying a house that is much larger and more expensive than the other homes in the immediate area is not a judicious investment, inasmuch as there will be a limited number of interested buyers, if it is later put up for sale.

Learning if the home is so located that there is convenient access to schools, churches, shopping centers and transportation facilities is also important.

General Construction and Condition of the House
Things to check:
Foundation above grade to avoid dampness in basement.

No loose bricks or cracks.

Tile or slate roof.

Flashings in good shape.

No attic leak stains.

Is cellar beam sagging?

Any termite damage?

Rigid floors or squeaky?

Hardwood floors.

Test water pressure by turning on several faucets at the same time.

Interior Arrangements and Conditions

Things to look for:

If under 1200 sq. ft. house should be on one floor.

Closets, adequate? Does it have tile floor in entrance hall?

Interior walls, plaster best, may crack first year, hunt for any wall mildew.

Fireplace, blackened, then it works well. Chimney lined.

Doors and windows, weatherstripped, screened, doors stick, rotted wood.

Floors, oak, stairs 9" tread and 7" riser.

Bathroom, tile floors and walls.

Is the house insulated?

Are the following adequate and in good condition: electrical wiring, heating system, water pipes?

Suggestions for Closing the Deal
If in doubt about the price, have a separate appraisal made by a non-lender.

Make a bid lower than 80% of the asking price, possibly two-thirds of the asking price.

If bid is rejected, wait a few days before submitting another one.

Raise bid in 2½% increments.

If bid is rejected, one is no longer obligated until a new bid is made.
Older houses cost a lot less to build and they may take a low bid.
Sales pitch—there is always "another customer" who is looking at
the same house.

Remember that earnest money is a binder or check given with the
earnest money contract when the deal is agreed upon to force the
buyer to go through with the deal or suffer a loss.

Have a lawyer draw up the purchase agreement contingent upon
the type of purchase mortgage desired (FHA) (VA) and at the
bank that one desires. Put in writing all things such as copper
pipes, drapes, carpeting, etc., the seller claims go with the house.

A real estate contract should never be entered into without sound
legal advice. And one should never put his name on the dotted line until
an attorney has checked the abstract of title (the historical description
of the transactions that have taken place concerning the house and lot)
and been told that the title is clear.

Building a New House
Selecting the Lot and Neighborhood:

Buy a lot just before you need it, to avoid paying extra taxes.

Lot should not exceed 20% of the total house-lot value.

Size of lot—consider maintenance and recreational aspects.

Location and convenience of lot.

Neighborhood—stable, improving, etc.

Zoning.

Assessments—property and special taxes.

Topography.

Elevation and drainage, soil test.

Trees and landscapping.

Dealing With a Building Contractor

Go over all plans and specifications with him to be sure they include
everything you want.

Sign a written agreement which contains a fixed price and a specified
completion date.

Check construction periodically to be sure all specifications are being
followed.

PROTECTING THE FAMILY'S FINANCIAL STRUCTURE WITH INSURANCE

Life Insurance

Any qualified life insurance agent can tell a couple all they want to know about insurance, but it is still wise to become acquainted with a few basic principles, so insurance can be purchased wisely.

General Guides for Buying Life Insurance

1. Usually the average family should not spend over ten percent of its income on life insurance. Families with low incomes should not spend over five percent for this purpose.

2. The greatest amount of insurance should be carried on the family breadwinner.

3. It is generally less expensive to take out insurance early in life.

Six Basic Kinds of Life Insurance

1. Industrial Policies—These policies are straight life insurance written for small amounts. The coverage is low in proportion to their cost because the premiums are collected weekly or monthly by agents going from door to door. The costs of collections and bookkeeping for these policies are so high that customers get very small coverage for their money. These policies are usually bought by low income families with the thought of cashing them in for several hundred dollars when their sons or daughters need extra money for college expenses. Couples who buy such policies are not making the best use of their money.

2. Term Insurance—Provides financial protection only (for beneficiaries, in event of policyholder's death)—is relatively inexpensive as to annual premium—average cost about 7-8 dollars per $1,000.00 coverage. *Decreasing term insurance*—Premiums are relatively low because the face value of the policy gets smaller each year and falls to zero at the end of a specified period of time. Its low cost and the fact that the coverage is heaviest when the need for protection is the greatest makes this type of policy attractive to young family men. Group, renewable term insurance is the best buy. In this type, the premium does not rise, and insurance can be renewed without additional physical examinations.

3. Ordinary or Straight Life Insurance—A permanent lifetime policy —annual premium must be paid as long as one lives or until about 85—

premiums vary, but average (if policy taken out at age 23) cost is about $15.25 a year per $1,000.00 coverage. One may borrow against built-up cash value of policy or cancel policy and get cash value back.

4. *Limited Payment Policy (20 Years)*—Same features as Ordinary Life—paid up in 20 years—average premium about $27.25 a year per $1,000.00, if taken out at age 23.

5. *Endowment Policy (20 Years)*—Same features as Limited Payment Policy—additional feature, after 20 years one receives full payment in lump sum or monthly installments—average premium $47.10 a year per $1,000.00, if taken out at age 23.

6. *Family Income Plan*—A type of insurance estate—a combination of ordinary life and decreasing term insurance—policy usually written to cover family needs in case of death or disability of family breadwinner—face amount and premiums decrease as children become self-supporting.

Other Insurance

Other types of insurance necessary to safeguard financial stability are:

1. Health and medical insurance to cover costs of hospitalization, surgery, and maternity.
2. House insurance for protection against fire, storm, or other hazards.
3. Personal property insurance.
4. Automobile insurance.
5. Personal liability insurance for protection against visitors' accidents on the insured's property.

Space will not be given to a discussion of these types as there are so many varieties.

USING MONEY WISELY

Resisting Pressures to Buy

Married couples are under continuous pressure to buy things. The mass media are constantly telling them what they should have to enjoy life, and persuasive salesmen get many of them to buy beyond their means.

Advertising appeals to the human ego, and persons struggling to gain a sense of identity will frequently buy expensive products just to prove to themselves that they are as good as anyone else. Cosmetic products are sold by the millions to individuals who believe that using a certain kind of toothpaste, hair rinse, or perfume will make them more attractive to their associates. Husbands and wives can help each other curb such undiscriminating and impulse-buying if they will recognize their mate's natural attractiveness and help him or her to suppress the supposed need to buy certain products in order to become more desirable.

Children can also cause pressure to buy things. Some parents have a relationship with their children in which they feel unable to meet their needs. Consequently, they may resort to buying things for their sons and daughters in an effort to show them love, and win their approval. Using money as a bargaining agent to gain love, cooperation or approval can become a two-way street, and parents and children can in turn manipulate one another to gain certain needs. During the growing-up years when children usually want to meet their peer group's standards of dress and behavior, their parents may find spending for certain things getting out of hand, unless they can build pride in their own family's standards and have children realize they can be popular without imitating the dress and manners of their associates.

EMPLOYING SOUND SPENDING PRINCIPLES

The following principles should be useful for any kind of buying:

1. Don't be pressured to buy by the dealer who lures you into his place with an attractive ad and then tries to sell you a higher-priced article.
2. Don't be dazzled by "bargains" offered at unrealistic prices.
3. Don't be fooled by phony mark-downs of overpriced items or the substitutions of poorer quality merchandise during sales.
4. Don't buy something because the salesman tells you it is a "golden opportunity that will never come again."
5. Don't allow door-to-door salesmen to leave merchandise with you "on approval" before you determine what obligations you have to pay, whether you keep the merchandise or not.
6. Don't buy things to meet your ordinary needs until you learn to read and understand labels on all products, so you will be in a position to compare their quality and quantity with those of similar commodities.
7. Never sign a contract before reading and understanding all of its terms.[5]

---

[5]Adapted from Saxton, Lloyd, *The Individual Marriage, and the Family,* Belmont, California: Wadsworth Publishing Co., 1972, 2nd Edition, p. 324.

Buying Food

Buying food takes a good share of the family's dollar, and the astute buyer tries to develop the judgment necessary to buy those commodities that best meet the family's psychological and nutritional needs. Some families are satisfied with hamburger, while others will settle for nothing less than caviar. Both groups will be satisfied psychologically if they can get the desired product at what they think is the right price.

Here are a few suggestions to help cut the family grocery bill:

Plan the week's menus ahead and make a list of food needs, so shopping for items will be coordinated, and not simply random buying.

Avoid buying convenience foods—frozen dinners, add-milk-or-water mixes and so forth. Cooking from scratch cuts the costs of involved foods one-half or more.

Read labels and buy foods on the basis of price per quantity.

Save money by purchasing advertised weekly specials and shopping at discount stores.

Learn more about less expensive and equally nutritious cuts of meats, and purchase them by the cost per cooked portion.

Compare the quality of private brands with nationally advertised goods. If the family likes them, money will usually be saved.

Learn something about and experiment with meat substitutes.

Study and act on the best seasonal buys on all foods.

Save money by buying food in quantity—cases of canned vegetables, milk in gallon containers, and so forth.

Buying Clothing

Families should plan basic wardrobes for their members, and then try to complete them by comparison shopping and taking advantage of off-season sales.

To save money, it is important to read labels, learn something about fabrics, and buy clothing that can be used with more than one function in mind. For example, a raincoat with a detachable lining that can be used in mild or cold weather.

Buying basic styles in clothing is less expensive than trying to keep up with the latest fads.

Money can also be saved by purchasing clothing in standard sizes— small, medium or large. Buying garments that have specific neck and sleeve sizes costs more. Shoes have gradually become more expensive, but their costs can be cut if they are purchased during the seasonal sales of January and July, and if one chooses simple traditional styles and colors. It is less expensive to buy a new wardrobe piece by piece at sales, than buying everything all at once.

Knowing the Best Periods of the Year to Buy Specific Merchandise

Like clothing, all commodities needed by the family can be purchased at savings, if they are obtained during the period of the year that they are available at off-season sales. These periods can be determined by watching for inventory sales, buying items just before new models come out, and shopping for things at the times of the year when they are not generally needed.

MAKING THE MOST OF CREDIT

Some couples believe in paying cash for everything. Their life is lived on the pay-as-you-go-plan, and if they don't have the money to buy something, they do without it. This is a commendable, but also somewhat unrealistic practice. Take for example, the purchase of a house. Very few families can buy one without the help of a mortgage loan. Should the pay-as-you-go couple wait twenty years until they have saved the full amount needed to buy a house before making a purchase, their children might be grown up and married before the family had a home of its own.

Obviously, the use of credit has a definite place in family buying, at least for major expenditures, and often for other things. The important factor is that it is used with discretion. Several ways to purchase with credit are:

Open-account credit—usually limited to a certain sum—no interest if paid in full within 30 days (furniture or clothing often allowed 90 days).

Revolving charge account (open-end credit)—usually limited to about 20 percent of total income—requires a monthly payment at a specified rate. Interest rate—usually 1½ percent per month (18 percent per year) on the unpaid balance.

Credit card—an all-purpose charge account—revolving (open-end) credit—no interest if bill paid by a specified time—after that about 12 to 18 percent annually on unpaid balance.

Installment credit—borrowing a specified amount to be paid off in monthly installments at a fixed interest rate which is usually computed on the total sum borrowed.

Securing loans to pay bills

Small-loan companies—no collateral needed to secure the loan —interest rates about 2 to 3½ percent per month on unpaid balance.

Commercial bank loans—when collateral is available, interest rates lower than loan companies—rates vary with the state of the economy, 11.5 percent to 13.5 percent (in 1971) a year—rates computed on the whole sum.

Credit unions—a cooperative approach in which members are allowed lower interest rates on loans than are generally available, 10 to 12 percent (in 1971) a year—no collateral necessary on loans up to about $2,500.

Life insurance loans—anyone with a life insurance policy that has a cash surrender value can borrow up to 95 percent of that amount— 5 to 6 percent interest rate will vary with the state of the economy.

LONG-RANGE GOALS AND THE FAMILY'S FINANCIAL LIFE CYCLE

When two people get married, they hope and expect to share a life together that will be filled with the satisfactions that come from achieving individual and mutual short-term and long-range goals. One factor that will contribute to the fulfillment of such hopes and aspirations will be the establishment of a sound financial structure, an operational framework in which they can envision their family's activities and needs as they progress through each stage of the family life cycle. A brief look at these stages reveals how planning ahead and a careful study of the cycle will help meet problems that might arise at each stage.

STAGES IN THE FAMILY'S FINANCIAL LIFE CYCLE

1. **The Establishment Stage**—the financial honeymoon period—majority of wives are working—broad policies of financial management are instituted—expenses at a minimum—with careful planning, couple should be able to save for coming periods requiring heavier expenses.

2. **The Child-bearing and Preschool Stage**—living costs gradually increasing—possible unpredictable expenditures for medical care and un-

expected needs—necessary to explore and decide on enrollment in health plans and learn about family service facilities—decision to be made about the wife continuing in a job outside of the home.

3. **The School-Years Stage**—expenditures for food, clothing, and other needs gradually increase—peer group pressures may cause children to ask for a variety of material things—as children get older, mother may be able to go back to work—the teen-agers may supplement the family income with part-time jobs.

4. **Launching Young Adults Stage**—family expenses usually at highest level—college students and young marrieds may need financial assistance—family income usually at peak—after children become established, family costs rapidly decline—husband and wife may be able to save in order to supplement future retirement incomes.

5. **Retirement Stage**—living and clothing costs low—couple free to pursue hobbies, travel, etc., if careful planning ahead has taken place at other stages, should be a period without financial tensions.

Suggested Readings

1. Bratton, Esther Crew, *Home Management Is . . .,* Boston, Ma.: Ginn and Co., 1971.

2. Britton, Virginia, *Personal Finance,* New York: American Book Co., 1968.

3. Cavan, Ruth Shonle, "Unemployment—Crisis of the Common Man," in *People as Partners,* Wiseman, Jacqueline P. (ed.), 392-402, New York: Harper & Row, 1971.

4. *Consumer Reports,* "How to Buy Life Insurance," Part I, 32:1 (January, 1967), 14-25; "Should Your Policy Also Be a Savings Account?"; Part II, 32:2 (February, 1967), 100-107.

5. Cutright, Phillips, "Income and Family Events: Marital Stability," *Journal of Marriage and the Family,* 33:2 (May, 1971), 291.

6. Garrett, Pauline and Metzen, Edward, *You Are a Consumer of Clothing,* Boston, Ma.: Ginn and Co., 1967.

7. Hastings, Robert J., *How to Manage Your Money,* Nashville, Tenn.: Broadman Press, 1965.

8. Kirkman, William C., *Dollars and Sense in Marriage,* Jericho, N.Y.: Exposition Press, 1972.

9. Ludwig, Amber, *The Bissell Guide to Housekeeping for Young Homemakers,* New York: Bantam Books, Inc., 1967.

10. Margolius, Sidney, *The Great American Food Hoax,* New York: Walker Co., 1971.

11. Nickell, Paulina, and Dorsey, Jean Muir, *Management in Family Living,* New York: John Wiley and Sons, 1967.

12. Wilder, Rex, *The Macmillan Guide to Family Finance,* New York: Macmillan Co., 1967.

PART IV

Parenthood

Chapter XVIII

The Biological Aspects of Family Life

Married couples who desire to meet the responsibilities of parenthood must acquire certain basic information related to how life begins. To do this they should first understand the structure and functions of the male and female reproductive systems. If a clear understanding of these parts and processes is gained, superstition and hearsay will no longer cause confused thinking, and problems associated with menstruation, conception, pregnancy, and childbirth will be met with greater objectivity. The purpose of this chapter will be to present briefly and as clearly as possible the facts needed to gain this understanding.

GAMETES, CHROMOSOMES, AND GENES

Life begins when two reproductive cells of the parents unite. These tiny specks of living matter are called gametes. The male gamete is named a spermatozoon and the female gamete an ovum.

The spermatozoon is so tiny that it cannot be seen without a microscope. It is shaped somewhat like a tadpole and contains an oval head, a middle piece, and a tail, all of which make up a structure about 1/500 of an inch in length. The more than 3 billion sperm cells needed to produce the world's population could easily be held by the cap of a toothpaste tube. The sperm moves by lashing its long tail. It is a vigorous swimmer and when its relative size is compared with that of a man, it makes about a five-mile swim upstream from the vagina to one of the Fallopian tubes in order to meet and fertilize an ovum.

The ovum, a globular-shaped cell, is much larger than the sperm but still is not quite 1/200 of an inch in diameter. It is nonmotile (cannot move by its own power). Although the ovum is the largest single cell in the body, the number needed to produce the world's population could be held by a container the size of a hen's egg. In each of these cells, both the sperm and the ovum, is a small body, generally oval in shape, called a nucleus. The nucleus contains twenty-three rod-shaped bodies of chromatin which are termed chromosomes. The chromosomes, in turn, have minute bodies within them which are arranged in the order of a string of beads and are named genes, which are the complex molecules of deoxyribonucleic acid called DNA. These produce certain hereditary characteristics in each individual.

Consequently, when fertilization takes place and the genes of the sperm and ovum unite, a combination of genes is effected which produces a new individual who inherits traits that come from the biological backgrounds of both father and mother.

THE MALE REPRODUCTIVE SYSTEM
Structure
The male reproductive system is made up of the following structures:

Two testes, two epididymides (plural of epididymis), two vasa deferentia (plural of vas deferens), two seminal vesicles, the prostate gland, the penis, and the scrotum.

These parts are organized into the reproductive system in the following manner:

Two testes, each about the size of a walnut, are housed in the *scrotum,* a sac which hangs behind and underneath the penis. These male sex glands usually descend about two months before birth from the abdominal cavity into the scrotum. It is extremely important that this happens before adolescence. Crawley, et al., say, "To avoid this impairment, glandular injections (gonadotropins) are given between four and five years of age. If there is inadequate response, an operation is performed to assist the testes into the scrotum when the boy is about five to six years old." If only one of the testes descends, the individual is usually fertile, however, if both testes remain in the abdominal cavity, he will be sterile. Surgery and hormone injections have been successful in treating this condition.

The reason that the testes must descend into the scrotal sac is because the temperature of the abdominal cavity is too warm to allow the development of the sperm cells in the testes. They can only develop in the cooler temperature provided by the scrotum. Thus, this containing sac which hangs beneath the penis keeps them at a cool, even temperature with the aid of a muscle (cremaster) which pulls the testes and scrotum close to the warm body when the outside temperature is cold, and

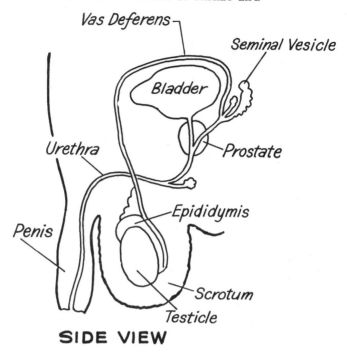

SIDE VIEW

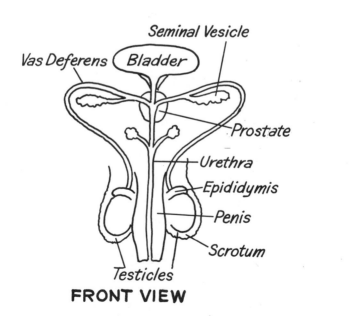

FRONT VIEW

PLATE I
THE MALE REPRODUCTIVE SYSTEM

extends and allows them to hang farther away from the body when the outside temperature is warm. The testes are extremely sensitive to pain and injury, and it has long been debated as to whether taking excessively hot baths could be used as a contraceptive technique by destroying sperm production. Crawley and his collaborators comment: ". . . to serve this purpose they would have to be taken longer and hotter than is practical. When a male is troubled by low fertility, however, he is sometimes advised not to wear tight underwear because holding the testes close to the heat of the body may further impede already poor or inadequate sperm production and motility (the ability to move spontaneously)."[1]

McCary has this to say, "However, although a 2 °C to 3 °C increase in temperature does in fact occasionally result in temporary sterility, fertility returns in a short time. There is little evidence that taking prolonged hot baths is an effective contraceptive technique, despite the fact that one researcher reported that heat which is tolerable to the hand can, in a 30-minute period, arrest the testicular manufacture of sperm for weeks."[2]

This sac also contains the two *epididymides,* tightly coiled tubes about twenty feet long which run along the side of each testis. These tubes join the two *vasa deferentia,* ducts which are partly contained in the scrotum and then continue through the inguinal canal and into the abdominal cavity. The two vasa deferentia continue in the abdominal cavity until each meets a *seminal vesicle,* two glands which secrete fluids. Then these two ducts (the vasa deferentia) pass through the tissue of the *prostate gland* which lies between the bladder and the bodily end of the penis, and finally enter the urethra. The *urethra* is a canal in the center of the penis through which urine is passed and also is the channel through which semen is expelled during sexual intercourse.

Physiological Functioning

These reproductive organs begin their full functioning when the male reaches puberty at the average age of about fifteen. At this time, the anterior lobe of the pituitary gland secretes hormones which initiate two processes in the testes. One starts the production of sperm cells and the other stimulates the interstitial tissue, which is scattered among the

[1]Crawley, Lawrence Q., Malfetti, James L., Stewart, Ernest I. Jr., Vas Dias, Nina, *Reproduction, Sex and Preparation for Marriage,* Englewood Cliffs: Prentice-Hall, Inc., 1973, 2nd Edition p. 5.
[2]McCary, James Leslie, *Human Sexuality*—A Brief Edition, New York: D. Van Nostrand Co., 1973, p. 33.

elements of the tubular tissue, to produce *testosterone* (the male hormone) which in turn promotes the development of the secondary sex characteristics such as the growth of the beard, change of voice, and so forth.

The sperms form within tiny coiled tubules in each testis. If these tubes were straightened out, they would measure several hundred feet in length. While the sperm cells are still developing, they are moved by ciliary action into each epididymis. They continue to mature there for about two to six weeks, and then go into the two vasa deferentia, the tiny tubes which are about eighteen inches long and run into the lower part of the abdominal cavity. During this stage the sperm are nonmotile and are thought to be moved along in the tubes by tubular contraction and the motion of tiny hairlike protuberances that line the tubes and are called cilia. When they arrive in the lower part of the vas deferens, they are stored until sexual excitation and ejaculation take place.

During excitation the sperms are moved by contractions of the vasa deferentia toward the urethra. At this juncture they mix with fluids from the seminal vesicles and the prostate gland. They also become active at this time and move in the fluid by lashing their tails. The contractions of the vasa deferentia, seminal vesicles and prostate gland all play a part in sending the combined fluid and sperm cells through the urethral passageway until the mixture (semen) is expelled from the head of the penis.

It should be remembered that the male urethral canal provides the passageway that both the semen and urine use to leave the body through the head of the penis. However, the two fluids do not pass through the canal at the same time. Before ejaculation of the semen begins, ringlike muscles (sphincter) close the exit of the bladder, so urine cannot enter the urethra during the ejaculatory period, and the openings of the vasa deferentia also close during urination. During sexual excitement, two other accessory reproductive glands, the Cowper's glands, secrete an alkaline mixture that neutralizes the acidity in the urethral canal and prepares the way for the semen to flow through safely. The fluid from the Cowper's glands emerges at the head of the penis before ejaculation takes place, and because it often contains sperm cells, the man's female sex partner could be impregnated by penetration of the penis even though ejaculation has not taken place.

The Structure and Functioning of the Male Penis

The mechanics of erection of the penis make an interesting study. Structurally, this male organ is made up of the urethra and surrounding muscles and spongy erectile tissue which contain a large number of blood vessels. During sexual excitation, the penis enlarges because these vessels receive an increased amount of blood. Its size increases as long as the inflow of blood into its tiny arteries exceeds the outflow through its veins. It remains rigid when the inflow and outflow become and remain equal. Penile erection can be caused by several things. It can be triggered by the higher brain centers or physical stimulation. But it also can be caused by heavy lifting, an erotic dream or anything that excites its nerve fibers. When ejaculation occurs, hundreds of millions of sperm cells may be contained in the teaspoonful amount of seminal fluid that is expelled. If this takes place during sexual intercourse, the sperms move into the vagina in all directions. Usually some go into the uterine cavity and may continue their journey up to the Fallopian tubes where if an ovum is present, fertilization may take place.

Some men are quite concerned about the size of the penis, having grown up thinking that a large penis is associated with strength, masculinity and sexual prowess. Research has proved such thinking to be false, and has also shown that the size of the penis has no relationship to the pleasure partners may enjoy in coitus. "Recent investigations . . . have indicated that abnormally small adult penises caused by hormone deficiency usually can be increased to normal size within a few months by hormonal treatment."[3]

There are some misconceptions regarding circumcision (removal of the foreskin from the head of the penis). It is thought by some that circumcision dulls the sensitivity of the penis, and that the uncircumcised male has more control of his ejaculations than the circumcised. Research dispels such thinking and discloses that the foreskin of the uncircumcised male retracts to such a degree during intercourse that the penis reacts much like that of the circumcised male. The chief advantage of circumcision is that it is easier for the male to maintain good personal hygiene.

---

[3]*Ibid*, p. 35.

Inability to Produce Sperm Cells
Mumps

Although several conditions may cause inability to produce sperm cells, probably the one most commonly talked about is the effect of mumps. Studies show that mumps occurring before puberty, have no injurious effects on the male testes. However, if contracted after puberty, the possible effects can be severe. The results may be painful swelling of one or both testes, shrinkage, atrophy, destruction of active germinal tissue, and partial or complete loss of the ability to form sperm cells. Light cases may only cause a slight decrease in the production of sperm cells, or only one testis may be affected.

Mumps do not affect hormone production or cause a decline in sex drive.

Castration

If for some reason it becomes necessary to remove the testes (castration) the affected male will become sterile because he can no longer produce sperm cells. However, he will still retain the ability to have intercourse and ejaculate. Inasmuch as he will produce but small amounts of testosterone (some by the adrenal gland) his male secondary sex characteristics will be affected. If castration occurs before puberty, he will never have his voice deepen or a beard grow. If it happens after puberty, these and other male secondary sex characteristics may regress, but not necessarily disappear.

THE FEMALE REPRODUCTIVE SYSTEM
Structure

The female reproductive system contains the following organs:

The vulva, an external structure, which consists of two labia majora, two labia minora, and the clitoris. The internal organs are the uterus, two Fallopian tubes, two ovaries, and the vagina.

Before summarizing the physiological functioning of these organs, desired clarity makes it necessary to describe their structure. Let's start with the vulva. First, there are the liplike folds of tissue between the thighs which help to cover and protect the inner parts of the genitals. The larger lips (*labia majora*) are two vertical cushions or folds which enclose the other more delicate structures of the vulva. In young unmarried women they almost meet in the center. As a girl's body begins

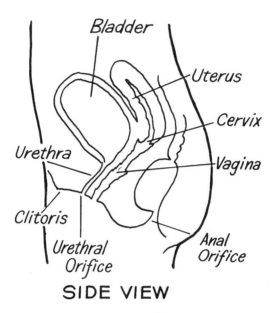

SIDE VIEW

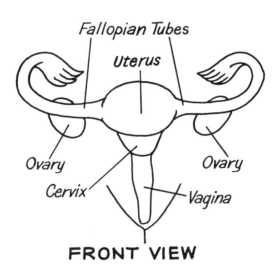

FRONT VIEW

PLATE II
THE FEMALE REPRODUCTIVE SYSTEM

to develop, at about the age of nine or later, hair begins to grow and cover them (pubic hair).

The smaller, inner lips *(labia minora)* lie parallel between the outer lips. Their inner surface is very sensitive and if it is touched, they may become firmer and more erect. The inner lips at their upper end form a cover somewhat like a hood which protects a tiny, pea-shaped organ called the *clitoris.* The clitoris is supplied with nerves and blood vessels that cause it to enlarge during sexual excitation. It is extremely sensitive and it responds to the touch or thoughts about sex by becoming firm and erect almost like a small penis would. When sexual intercourse takes place, the sensitivity of the clitoris plays a very important part in the sexual response and excitement of the wife. The entrance to the vagina is situated about an inch below the clitoris. In the virgin's body it is partially closed by a thin sheetlike layer of tissue called the *hymen.* The hymen is usually ruptured during the first coital relationship. It was formerly believed that if the hymen were stretched or absent that a girl was no longer a virgin. Now it is known that it can be stretched by such things as the continual use of tampons. Because of this and many normal variations in the structure of the hymen, it is quite difficult to determine whether an enlarged opening has been caused by sexual intercourse or something else. The *vagina,* which connects with the uterus, is a passageway shaped like a sheathlike tube which averages about three and a half inches in length. It can stretch like a balloon and adjust its size so that even a baby which weighs as much as twelve or fifteen pounds can pass through it when it is born. So it is also named the birth canal. The vagina is also the passageway into which the erect penis is placed during sexual intercourse. At the vagina's upper end, it is closed all around except in the center where the neck of the uterus enters it.

The internal organs possess the following characteristics. The *uterus* (normally about three inches long and two inches wide) is shaped like a pear and is located inside the body in what is called the pelvic or abdominal cavity. It is suspended in an upright position with its larger part at the top and its smaller tapering neck *(cervix)* at the bottom. This tiny neck enters the vagina. In its center, the neck has a mouth *(external os),* a tiny opening which ordinarily is only about a fifth of an inch in diameter. At the upper end of the uterus are two ducts that branch out on either side and are named *Fallopian tubes.* These tubes, which are 4 to 6 inches long are lined with tiny hairlike structures called *cilia*. At the tubes' ends, which are the closest to the ovaries, they have funnel-shaped mouths which are made up of finger-like appendages named *fimbriae* which are also lined with cilia. Attached to each side of the uterus are the two almond-shaped *ovaries*, each about an inch and a half long, an inch wide, and half an inch thick which are the female sex glands They have two functions. The ova grow in them and they also secrete hormones which produce sex characteristics, such as female breast development and the widened pelvis.

Physiological Functioning

As is the case with the male, the anterior lobe of the pituitary gland in the female starts the full functioning of her reproductive system. It secretes hormones beginning with the onset of puberty (average age about 12.5 years) which induce the ovaries to produce hormones of their own. These hormones cause the development of the secondary female characteristics (the development of the breasts and so forth) and contribute to the processes which establish the menstrual cycle. The ova contained in the two ovaries also respond to the hormones secreted by the pituitary gland and begin the process of maturation. The maturation of the ova and their later extrusion from the *Graafian follicle* (ovulation) is brought about by two special types of hormones. The first type, the follicle-stimulating hormone (FSH), is secreted by the anterior lobe of the pituitary gland (influenced by chemicals from the hypothalamus) and released directly into the venous bloodstream, and it then reaches the ovaries. The FSH causes the ovarian follicles and the ova within them to begin maturing and increasing in size. When the Graafian follicle matures and its ovum is ready to leave the ovary, the second type of hormone, the luteinizing (LH) is released by the anterior lobe of the pituitary gland into the venous blood and it causes the Graafian follicle to rupture and release the ovum.

Ordinarily, once every month a "ripe" ovum appears on the surface of either ovary in this sac, the Graafian follicle. This follicle, in addition to housing the ovum, secretes a hormone called *estrogen,* which causes changes in the lining of the uterus *(endometrium)*. Finally, the follicle bursts and the ovum is extruded (the process of ovulation) and is drawn into the nearest Fallopian tube. Evidence suggests that the ovum is attracted into the tube by suction and the wave-like motion of the tiny cilia which line the fimbriae and the tubes. It is also thought that the ovum is moved along in the tube by the cilia and tiny muscular contractions of the tube (peristalsis).

Crawley[4] says: "If one ovary is defunct or removed the other usually produces sufficient hormones to maintain the secondary female characteristics, sexual desire, and the menstrual cycle. If surgical removal of both ovaries is necessary, the woman undergoes those changes associated with menopause. . . . The incidence of two-egg twin and multiple births indicates that one ovary can produce more than one egg or that both ovaries can produce eggs in one cycle. Some women do not know when they ovulate; others may experience some symptom—a slight pain . . . or a slight mucus discharge from the vagina."

Before following the pathway of the ovum, something should be said about the Graafian follicle which has discharged this cell. After the ovum has left this protective sac, the cells of the empty follicle undergo a change and are transformed into a yellow body named the *"corpus luteum."* This newly developed body secretes a hormone called *progesterone* which produces further changes in the uterine lining (endometrium) that prepare it for the reception of the fertilized ovum. Inasmuch as the changes which take place when the ovum has been fertilized are discussed in the chapter on pregnancy, the events which occur if fertilization does not take place will be discussed here.

The Cause of the Menstrual Flow

Generally speaking, if conception does not take place, all of the special preparations that have been made which are necessary to the implantation and continued growth of the fertilized ovum are no longer needed; consequently, the process of preparation breaks down. The corpus luteum degenerates, and ceases to secrete the estrogen and progesterone which have been influencing the uterine lining. This withdrawal of estrogen and progesterone causes the specially prepared uterine lining to begin deteriorating and in the process open some blood vessels. The lining and the blood which are discharged are the menstrual flow. Thus the preparations for the reception of a fertilized ovum are discarded, and the reproductive system begins new preparations for the ovum that might be fertilized during the next cycle.

---

[4]*Ibid*, p. 17.

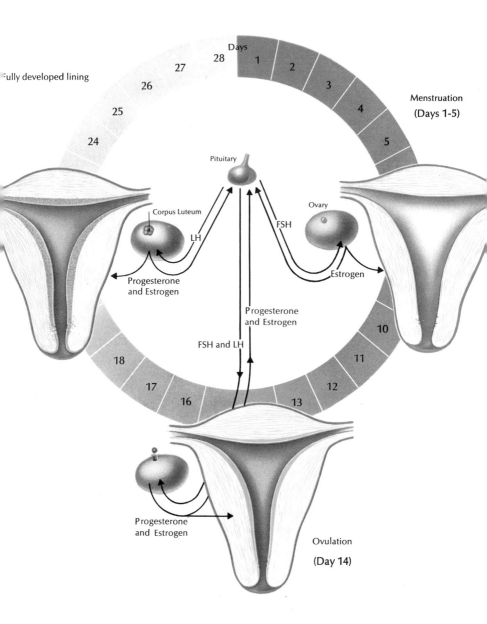

PLATE III

SUMMARY OF THE MENSTRUAL CYCLE

FSH—Abbreviation for Follicle Stimulating Hormone.
LH—Abbreviation for Luteinizing Hormone.

DEVELOPING POSITIVE ATTITUDES
TOWARD MENSTRUATION

For many years the menstrual process was a thing of mystery and superstition. Some individuals built up an eerie connection between the menstrual cycle and the cycle of the moon. In primitive cultures the menstruating woman was not only considered "unclean," but also dangerous. Inasmuch as it was felt that her influence was damaging to crops, domestic animals, and especially to men, she was often required to isolate herself from the community.

Many individuals today still misunderstand and fear menstruation despite the fact that medical science began building a body of reliable scientific information explaining the process ninety years ago.

Today, informed individuals realize that the menstrual period is a normal function which should be free from discomfort. Studies show that the *menarche* (the first menstrual flow) begins at the average age of 12.5 years in North America, occurs in the majority of women in cycles averaging 28.6 days, and does not cease until an average age of 48.[5]

The average woman should try to contemplate this 36-year period in her life with a positive, rather than a negative attitude.

Individuals who look upon menstruation as "the curse" or "a cross to bear" are approaching this time of the month with an attitude that may contribute to their discomfort. Some women experience discomfort preceding menstruation which may occur because the body tissues tend to retain fluids that cause a temporary weight gain that in turn produces feelings of pressure and tension. Bowman says this is part of the premenstrual syndrome and states further that writers estimate that about 60 percent of women mention the following conditions: ". . . headache, anxiety, restlessness, inability to relax, lethargy, inability to concentrate, depression, emotional outbursts, crying spells, hypersensitivity, unexplainable fears, imperative ideas, insomnia, contrariness, exaggeration of trifles, loss of inhibitions, cruelty, and a host of other symptoms." He states further, "In a sense, such symptoms are uncontrollable by the woman herself. At the least, the feelings are uncontrollable; their expression may be controlled to some degree."[6]

[5]Ellis, Albert, and Abarbanel, Albert, *The Encyclopedia of Sexual Behavior*, New York: Hawthorn Books, 1961, Vol. 2, "Menstrual Cycle," G. W. Corner, Jr.
[6]Bowman, Henry A., *Marriage for Moderns*, New York: McGraw-Hill Book Co., 1970, 6th Edition, p. 442.

Doctors who have commented on this premenstrual syndrome say that with most women it is not a serious problem and can be helped by anticipating the time these feelings will arrive and planning some interesting activities in order to divert the mind to other things. It must be remembered that the number of premenstrual symptoms listed by Bowman constitute a compilation of conditions mentioned by *some* individuals, and it is highly probable that the majority of today's young women treat menstruation as a normal bodily function that has little effect upon their everyday activities.

Painful menstruation (dysmenorrhea) is not uncommon. Crawley gives the following reasons for this. He says: "The uterus becomes engorged with dilated blood vessels during this period, and if it is 'tipped' so that the menstrual flow cannot easily get through the cervical canal, or there is a tight cervical muscle, or marked nervous tension resulting in spasm, discomfort might well result. The woman in a generally poor physical condition may find the congested pelvic organs unusually burdensome, and other symptoms of menstruation may further debilitate and incapacitate her already weak organs and system. But severe and prolonged menstrual cramps, nausea, vomiting, and other marked symptoms should be investigated. Although normal menstrual functioning is closely related to good physical health, the mental set of the woman is important . . . her acceptance of her role as a woman with creative reproductive powers of which the menstrual cycle is a physical manifestation help to offset whatever discomfort there might be."[7]

Activities During the Menstrual Period

Many women are confused in relationship to activities which may be engaged in during the menstrual period. A study made by Rogers[8] bears this out. An analysis was made of 232 discussions on menstruation given in 21 states and the District of Columbia during a 4-year period. The 2,032 questions asked during these discussions by junior and senior high and college students, as well as teachers and other adults, showed the following questions as causing the greatest concern:

1. Is it all right to swim during the menstrual period?
2. Is it all right to wash our hair during the menstrual period?

[7]*Ibid*, pp. 26, 27.
[8]Rogers, Martha E., "Responses to Talks on Menstrual Health." *Nursing Outlook*, Vol. 1, May 1953.

3. Is it all right to take a bath during the menstrual period?

4. Is exercise harmful during the menstrual period?

Doctors now advise that all of the above activities may be engaged in, providing that extremes are avoided. Ordinary exercise tends to increase circulation and prevent congestion, which is one of the causes of discomfort. Bathing may also be engaged in as long as excessively hot or cold baths are avoided.

In conclusion, emphasis must be given to the fact that it should always be remembered that menstruation is a normal function which is one evidence that the female's reproductive system is operating as it should.

HOW SEX IS DETERMINED

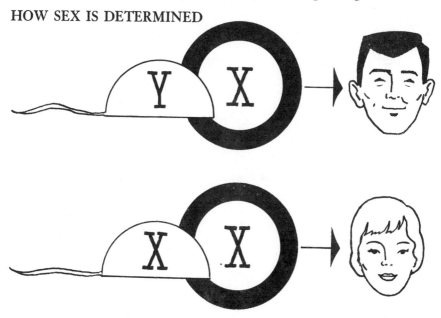

PLATE IV
HOW SEX IS DETERMINED

It has been a custom in some cultures for a husband to harshly reprove his wife or even divorce her if she seemed incapable of bearing him a male heir. The assumption was made that it was the woman who determined the sex of the child.

Baby girls were so unpopular in times past, that in religious writings, such as the Jewish Talmud, one reads, "When a girl is born, the walls are crying." The Holy Book of Islam states, "When an Arab hears that a daughter has been born to him, his face becomes saddened." Female infanticide was practiced in certain regions in China, India, and New Zealand, and numerous tribes looked upon baby girls as liabilities. Consequently, many curious practices developed which were considered helpful to the couple who desired a baby boy. Some of the most unusual were advising the husband to bite his wife's ear during the sex act, counseling the husband to keep his boots on during the marital embrace, and guaranteeing a male heir if the husband would hang up his pants at the right side of the bed.

Despite all of these superstitious beliefs and negative attitudes toward having baby girls, it is now known that sex is determined by the type of sperm cell which fertilizes the ovum. Sex determining chromosomes which are contained in the sperm and the ovum are designated as either X or Y. All ova carry only the X chromosome. Sperms vary in that they carry either an X or a Y chromosome.

When fertilization takes place, if an X-bearing sperm fuses with the ovum the resulting combination is XX, which produces a girl. If the Y-carrying sperm fertilizes the ovum, the YX combination results in a boy. Ever since this has been discovered, studies have been undertaken in an attempt to control the process. None has reported completely positive results. One theory has been proposed by research people which has aroused considerable interest. Operating on the premise that the Y-carrying sperm is smaller and swims faster than the X-bearing one, it is thought that if the married couple determines the precise time of ovulation in the wife and has coitus during this period, the faster-swimming Y-carrying sperm will reach and fertilize the ovum first. On the other hand, it is suggested that if a girl is desired, intercourse should take place long enough before ovulation occurs so that the slower-moving and perhaps longer-living X-carrying sperm will reach and fertilize the ovum. It is also suggested by Dr. Landrum B. Shettles of Columbia University's College of Physicians and Surgeons that "Male offspring are favored by the use of an alkaline douche . . . preceding intercouse, by the woman's achievement of orgasm, and by deep penile penetration. . . . Female offspring are favored by using an acid douche before coitus, lack of orgasm in the woman, and shallow penile penetration."

Although this and other theories are interesting, it should be noted that nature does fairly well in regulating the present sex ratio at birth.

It is 105.5 boys to 100 girls. The higher mortality rate of the male plus exposure to greater occupational hazards and so forth, combine to affect this ratio so that at the marriageable age of about 20, it approximates 100 to 100.

In the final analysis, the basic desire of the parents should be not what sex the baby is, but that it is normal and healthy.

MULTIPLE BIRTHS

Research scientists do not know all of the reasons why some mothers have more than one baby at a time. In fact, all that can be said is that

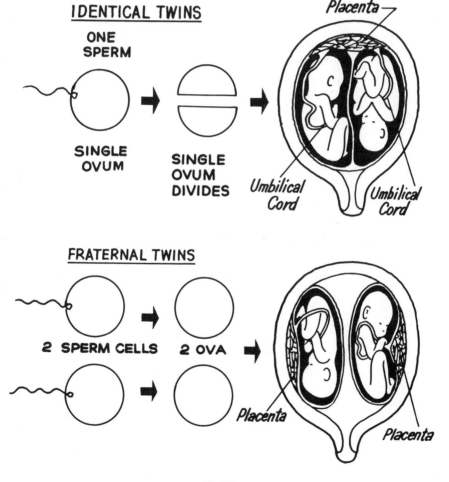

IDENTICAL TWINS

ONE
SPERM

SINGLE
OVUM

SINGLE
OVUM
DIVIDES

Placenta

Umbilical
Cord

Umbilical
Cord

FRATERNAL TWINS

2 SPERM CELLS   2 OVA

Placenta

Placenta

PLATE V
HOW TWINS DEVELOP

studies suggest that bearing twins seems to run in families. There is some information as to the frequency of multiple births, and data reveal that twins occur about once in 100 live births. Triplets are much rarer, and the chance of having them is only once in about 10,000 births. Quadruplets occur about once in 1,000,000 live births. (U.S. Department of Health, Education, and Welfare, October, 1967.) Quintuplets are so rare (about once in 50 million births) that a couple who has them becomes a center of curiosity, a source of national pride, and the recipients of many gifts.

Multiple births are of three kinds: identical, fraternal or a combination of the two.

Identical twins occur when one fertilized ovum seems to split at a very early stage and develops into two individuals. Such babies usually share a common placenta and chorionic membrane, but possess separate amniotic sacs and umbilical cords. They are always of the same sex and usually are similar in appearance. (Siamese twins develop if the ovum does not completely divide.)

Fraternal twins are the result of two ova being fertilized at about the same time. They have separate placentas, cords, amnions and chorionic membranes. They may be of the same or different sexes, and do not necessarily look alike as they are no more closely related than are other children of the same parents.

A multiple birth could be made up of a combination of individuals developing from one fertilized ovum (egg cell) and other ova (egg cells). For example, quadruplets could develop from one, two, three, or four fertilized ova. All four could develop from a division of one ovum, two could come from each of two fertilized ova, two could develop from one ovum and two each from separate ova, or all four could develop from four separate ova.

New drugs to stimulate ovulation (fertility pills) have had some effect upon multiple births. Crawley says: "It is not unusual for the ovaries to react to the fertility pill by maturing several eggs at the same time, and for multiple births to result. In spite of carefully controlled dosages, triplets or quadruplets are becoming increasingly common. The fertility pill is in no way similar to the contraceptive pill. The former stimulates ovulation, the latter suppresses it."[9]

---

[9]*Ibid*, p. 79.

THE RH FACTOR

Many expectant parents are unduly concerned about the Rh factor. Those who feel some anxiety in this respect, will benefit from reading the following discussion by Dr. G. Albin Matson, internationally recognized authority in the field of blood studies.[10]

"SOME FACTS ABOUT RH"

What Is Rh?

The Rh factor is a substance which is present in or on red blood cells. It is called Rh because of its chemical relationship to a substance present in the red blood cells of the Rhesus monkey (Rh for the first two letters of Rhesus). It is also present in the red blood cells of about 85% of white people. Those individuals who possess the Rh factor in their blood cells are called Rh positive. Those who lack this factor, about 15% of white people, are called Rh negative. Among peoples such as the American Indians, Hawaiians, Eskimos, Paupauans, Filipinos, Chinese and Japanese, the Rh factor is present in almost 100% of the population. Ninety-three percent of Negroes are Rh positive.

Antibodies Are Formed

Now, those who lack the Rh factor are capable of becoming "sensitized" against it, that is, they may produce antibodies against this factor if they are exposed to it. This exposure in Rh negative people may occur in one of two ways.

One of these ways is by transfusion in which the Rh negative person receives Rh positive blood. If an Rh negative person should receive a transfusion of Rh positive blood then the Rh factor so introduced would stimulate the production of antibodies against Rh in much the same way as an inoculation of typhoid vaccine would stimulate the production of antibodies against the typhoid organism. Should such a person later receive another transfusion of Rh positive blood it is likely that a transfusion reaction would result, due to the reaction of the Rh antibodies in the patient's blood against the Rh factor introduced by the transfusion into the bloodstream of the Rh negative patient. It is, therefore, necessary to accurately determine the Rh type of any patient requiring a transfusion.

[10]Matson, Albin G., "Some Facts About Rh," Minneapolis War Memorial Blood Bank, 1959. Reprinted here by permission of the author.

Ideally, all Rh negative patients, regardless of sex, should be given only Rh negative blood.

The other way in which Rh negative individuals may become sensitized against the Rh factor is in women during pregnancy while they are bearing an Rh positive fetus. This can only happen if the father is Rh positive and the fetus inherits the Rh factor from the father.

The blood in the fetus begins to be formed about the second month of fetal life. During this time, however, the blood sinuses (dilated cavities and channels containing blood) are small and centrally located in the placenta. About the third trimester of pregnancy, however, a radical change occurs. The blood sinuses now become enlarged and they approach more nearly toward the surface of the placenta. The fetal blood is at this time separated from the maternal circulation only by a thin membrane. During the latter part of pregnancy this membrane is only one cell in thickness. It has been shown that, at this time, small amounts of fetal blood may get across the placental barrier into the circulation of the mother, and since the mother does not possess the Rh factor, the presence in her circulation of these red blood cells which have the Rh factor stimulates the cells of her body to produce antibodies against it.

The blood of each of us contains many kinds of antibodies. We have antibodies against childhood diseases which have protected us during our lives so that we have had the disease only once. We have antibodies against other diseases and infections which we have experienced during our lifetime, and against vaccinations for smallpox, diphtheria, etc. These antibodies serve a useful purpose. If we should later become exposed to an organism or virus which originally gave rise to antibodies, these antibodies react with and destroy such viruses. In this way, protection is offered to the body against disease.

Before the baby is born, antibodies possessed by the mother pass across the placenta membrane into the circulation of the baby. It is in this way that the infant is offered for its first few months of life the same antibody protection that the mother possesses, and thus the baby is aided in getting a start in life.

The Effect of Rh Antibody on the Baby

Now in the mother who is "sensitized" against the Rh factor, Rh antibodies pass from her circulation across the placenta membrane into the circulation of the fetus along with other antibodies so transported. The Rh antibodies, however, serve the fetus no useful purpose. Indeed, these antibodies are produced against a factor present in the baby's own blood and, therefore, they react with the Rh factor in the baby's blood and tend to destroy the red blood cells in the baby. For this reason, the baby may be born anemic, or jaundiced, or if the destruction goes far enough, even still-born. At the same time that the blood is being destroyed, the spleen, which is the principal blood-forming organ in the fetus, becomes enlarged. This is a compensatory mechanism which functions to restore more blood to the circulation of the fetus for that which is being destroyed. For the same reason immature red blood cells known as erythroblasts are thrown into the bloodstream. The liver also may become enlarged due to the additional burden forced upon it as a result of the products of red blood cell destruction.

We have now presented the mechanism which causes the disease known as erythroblastosis fetalis or hemolytic disease of the newborn. This is the worst side of the Rh problem. In this connection it is important to know that once a mother becomes sensitized against the Rh factor and does produce an erythroblastotic baby, then the chances are greater that subsequent Rh positive babies born to that mother will be affected.

There Is a Brighter Side

These unfavorable aspects of the Rh problem have been emphasized in popular magazines and journals so much that it is not surprising that an altogether bizarre conception of Rh and hemolytic disease of the newborn has been gained by many people. Furthermore, the amount of misinformation about Rh and hemolytic disease of the newborn is positively astounding. Many young women have had their peace of mind disturbed by the erroneous notion that *any* baby born to an Rh negative mother is doomed to be affected with hemolytic disease. There *is* a most encouraging side to the problem, which we are now ready to consider:

1. In the first place it must be remembered that the Rh factor is hereditary in the same way that brown eyes or black hair or any other physical characteristics are inherited. Therefore, *simply because a woman is Rh negative does not mean that she will produce affected babies.* Her husband may be Rh negative also, in which case, all offspring from that union would be Rh negative and therefore normal so far as hemolytic

disease is concerned. If a wife is found to be Rh negative, it therefore becomes important to determine the Rh of the husband.

2. If the husband is found to be Rh positive, then it becomes important to know whether he is pure (homozygous) Rh positive or whether he is what is known as heterozygous Rh positive and is capable of transmitting the Rh negative condition to his offspring. *Remember, only Rh positive babies may be affected.* If the husband is pure (homozygous) Rh positive and married to an Rh negative woman, then all of the offspring will be Rh positive. If, however, he is heterozygous (not pure) Rh positive, then with each pregnancy there is an even chance of the offspring being Rh negative, which will be normal so far as hemolytic disease of the newborn is concerned.

In about one half of all marriages of an Rh positive man and Rh negative woman, the husband is heterozygous Rh positive, and therefore some Rh negative children may be born which do not sensitize the mother. This heterozygous condition of the husband can be determined in most instances by laboratory tests in a good Rh laboratory.

3. It is important to know that although in about one marriage in ten among white people the wife is Rh negative and the husband is Rh positive, *yet only about one in twenty-five* of this group has any complications due to Rh.

4. *The first baby is nearly always normal.* Unless the mother has at some time earlier in her life received a transfusion of Rh positive blood or has received intramuscular inoculations of Rh positive blood so that there has been some opportunity to expose her to the Rh factor, there would have been no stimulus to the cells of her body to produce antibodies. In other words, *it takes at least one pregnancy and sometimes several to sensitize the mother.* We know of several families in which the mother is Rh negative and the husband a pure (homozygous) Rh positive so that all of the offspring have been Rh positive, and although seven or eight children were born, it was only the last of these children who were jaundiced. In these families it took six or seven pregnancies to sensitize the mother.

5. *The Rh factor is not a powerful antibody producer.* Although one could inoculate typhoid vaccine into almost anyone and produce antibodies, the Rh factor, on the other hand, requires many stimuli over a

long period of time. This is so because the chemical structure of the typhoid organism readily stimulates cells of the body to produce specific antibodies and is, therefore, known as a strong antigen, whereas the Rh factor is a weak antigen.

6. *The ability of an individual to produce antibodies is an extremely variable factor.* It seems, therefore, that barring previous sensitization by transfusion, *only in those mothers who are good antibody producers and who receive adequate stimulation does the second or third baby become affected with hemolytic disease of the newborn.*

What to Do About It

We have now discussed the general aspects of the Rh problem. A consideration of more precise procedure may now be in order.

First—The first time the expectant mother presents herself at the doctor's office, her doctor will draw a specimen of blood. This he will send to the laboratory for determination of Rh.

Second—If the blood is found to be Rh negative, the Rh of the husband is then determined. If he is found to be Rh negative also, there is no problem.

Third—If, however, the husband is found to be Rh positive, then there is no cause for alarm. The doctor will take a specimen of the wife's blood which is to be tested for the presence and concentration of Rh antibodies (especially if she has had one or more previous pregnancies) to see whether she has been sensitized against the Rh factor by previous pregnancies or in some other way.

Fourth—More tests for antibodies will be ordered by the doctor during pregnancy to determine if and when antibodies begin to be formed. A report of these titrations is sent back to the doctor, who uses this information to aid him in managing the case. If antibodies do not appear, there is no reason to be concerned.

Fifth—*If antibodies do appear,* it is a signal to the doctor that antibodies are being formed and that those antibodies *may* cause some difficulty in the baby. Remember, however, that *the later during pregnancy that the antibodies appear in the expectant mother, the less likely are symptoms of hemolytic disease to appear in the baby.* It is also important to know that *the presence of Rh antibodies does not mean that the fetus is Rh positive or that it will be affected.* In any event, the doctor will keep a watchful eye on the health of the mother and that of the baby and will have Rh negative blood on hand to transfuse the infant when it is born if it is Rh positive and appears to need a transfusion.

Sixth—Sometimes the doctor will perform a simple transfusion in the infant. At other times he may do an exchange transfusion by which the infant's blood is drawn a little at a time as more and more blood is being added until finally a large portion of the baby's own blood is replaced with Rh negative blood. This Rh negative blood is not affected by the antibodies which the baby has in its blood stream. Therefore, this blood will tide the baby over until the antibodies in the baby's blood have been eliminated through its own kidneys and until its own blood-forming organs have caught up on their much needed rest.

From the above facts it is abundantly evident that all except the occasional Rh negative woman have an excellent chance of having normal babies so far as Rh complications are concerned.

* * *

Crawley and Bowman report some recent developments regarding treatment of the Rh factor which make the prospects for its control even more favorable.

Crawley[11] says, "Fortunately, this is now largely a correctable problem through use of an anti-Rh 'antibody.' Within forty-eight hours after the delivery of her first Rh positive baby, an Rh negative woman is given an injection of this anti-Rh preparation. (". . . the nonsensitized woman is injected intramuscularly with a special anti-Rh gammaglobulin preparation procured from the blood plasma of Rh negative women who had developed a high concentration of antibodies," Bowman.[12]) If she has any fetal Rh positive red blood cells in her system, the preparation neutralizes them and her own antibody system is not called upon, thus making things safer for her next positive pregnancy. This same procedure should be followed . . . for live births . . . abortions and miscarriages to Rh negative women. . . . The same anti-Rh preparation is given after the birth of each subsequent Rh positive child . . . the Rh negative mother already sensitized by Rh positive pregnancies resulting in live

---

11*Ibid*, pp. 63, 64.
12*Ibid*, p. 537.

birth, miscarriage or abortion should not be given the anti-Rh preparation, for this would increase risk to the unborn child. Remedies are being sought for her situation."

Crawley also reports that it is now possible if a pregnant mother's blood shows a potentially dangerous level of antibodies, to examine the amniotic fluid and assess the actual danger to the fetus accurately. (Amniocentesis—withdrawal of amniotic fluid through a needle inserted through abdominal and uterine walls.)

Suggested Readings

1. Bowman, Henry A., *Marriage for Moderns,* New York: McGraw-Hill, 1970 (6th ed.), Chapter 14, "Pregnancy and Childbirth."

2. Crawley, Lawrence, Malfetti, James, Stewart, Ernest I., Jr., and Vas Dias, Nina, *Reproduction, Sex, and Preparation for Marriage,* Englewood Cliffs, N.J.: Prentice-Hall, (2nd ed.), 1973.

3. De Merre, Leon J., *The Female Sex Hormones,* New York: Vantage Press, 1954.

4. Diamond, Milton, *Perspectives in Reproduction and Sexual Behavior,* Bollmington, Indiana: Indiana University Press, 1969.

5. Gifford, Jones W., *On Being a Woman: The Modern Woman's Guide to Gynecology,* New York: Macmillan Co., 1971.

6. Kogan, Benjamin A., *Human Sexual Expression,* San Francisco: Harcourt Brace Jovanovich, Inc., 1973.

7. McCary, James Leslie, *Human Sexuality,* New York: D. Van Nostrand Co., 1973 (2nd ed.).

8. Reed, Sheldon C., *Counseling in Medical Genetics,* Philadelphia: W. B. Saunders Co., 1963 (2nd ed.).

9. Scheinfeld, Amram, *Your Heredity and Environment,* Philadelphia: J. B. Lippincott Co., 1965.

Chapter XIX

Family Planning

Family planning and controlling conception are not new ideas. In fact, some people have been practicing contraceptive techniques for hundreds of years. Papyrus rolls dating back to 1850 B.C. contain instructions for inducing abortion. The ancient Hebrews practiced coitus interruptus. And primitive tribes such as those in Africa and the Achinese of Sumatra attempt to curb population growth by using withdrawal during intercourse (coitus interruptus) or placing substances in the vaginal orifice that destroy sperm cells. Despite this long and widespread interest in birth control, it has only been in the past two decades that research and mass education concerning conception have been encouraged. Previous opposition to such measures resulted in such leaders as nurse Margaret Sanger being in constant trouble with the law and even jailed (New York, 1915) because of her writings about contraception.

Today, attitudes have changed regarding public discussion of birth control. Concern with the growing world population has caused many individuals to openly express their opinions as to whether the birth rate should be curbed. Sides have been taken regarding whether the world's space and food supply can meet the needs of its potential future population, and debate has raged over the moral and psychological aspects of specific methods of birth control. Some say that diminishing natural resources make it imperative that each couple produces no more than two children. Others contend that proper distribution and utilization of the world's natural resources and geographical areas would make such limitation of children unnecessary.

There are no conclusive studies to prove either side right inasmuch as the hypotheses are based on what *might happen* in the future. Consequently, the positions that individuals take are probably based more upon their philosophy of life or their religious belief than the ability to prove statistically what the condition of the world will be in the future.

A recent Gallup poll, reported February 24, 1971, disclosed that representative samplings of Americans show a decided drop in the desire for large families as compared with the sixties. For example, in 1960, 45 percent felt four or more children was the ideal family size. In 1967, 40 percent felt the same way. But in 1971, the percentage who considered four or more children ideal, was only twenty-three. One must not be hasty in assuming that this change was caused solely by anxieties over survival of the world population, inasmuch as such factors as the emerging independence of women, changing sex roles, and the desire to do more for their children have caused many couples to limit the size of their families.

Before describing the methods of birth control that are used today, it should be stated that proponents of contraception have unrealistically believed that an effective birth control method, such as the use of the pill, would liberate women both married and single so they could express their sexual urges freely without fearing possible pregnancy, and be as "unrestricted as men are in making love." Because of this thinking, the advent of the pill caused many people to believe that it would usher in a new era of sexual harmony between the male and female, both within and outside of marriage. This seemed to be true at first, but as the use of the pill was gradually adopted by millions of women, marriage counselors and expert observers began to realize that the use of the pill frequently increased rather than reduced sexual problems between couples. The following brief summary of the representative thinking of individuals and experts in the field of sexual adjustment is a combination of the writer's observations and an adaptation of an article by Ostermann and Arnold.[1]

When the pill was first introduced some typical comments were as follows:

Dr. Gregory Pincus and Dr. John Rock, two of the pill's originators, said its use would cause couples to have "anxiety-free sexual intercourse."

One husband said, "With my wife on the pill . . . any moment was the right moment for love."

A wife who started using the pill commented as follows on the sex

---

[1] Ostermann, Robert and Arnold, Mark R., "*The Pill and Its Impact*," Newsbook published by the *National Observer*, Dow Jones and Company, Inc., Silver Springs, Md., 1967, as printed in Bowman, Henry A., *Marriage for Moderns*, New York: McGraw-Hill Book Co., 1970, 6th Edition, pp. 499-505.

act, "I had never known anything like it . . . It was like I have never made love before."

Studies made in 1962 and 1963 confirmed such individual comments. For example, "In San Antonio, Texas, Dr. Joseph W. Goldzieher and several colleagues found that the majority of 210 women studied for 43 months experienced an increased interest in sex."

However, as the years have passed, and more individuals and therapists have commented on the psycho-sexual effects of the pill, it has become evident that different individuals will be affected in different ways by this method of birth control. The writer, in his counseling practice, has encountered several young wives who were on the pill who said they had lost their love for their husbands and could not stand to have them touch them. When, after counseling, they were advised to, and subsequently stopped using the pill, their sexual desire and love for their mates returned. One young wife said, "I used to cringe when my husband touched me. Now it thrills me."

Doctor William Masters, noted director of the Reproductive Biology Research Foundation in St. Louis, refuses to accept women with sexual problems for therapy who are taking the pill unless they stop using it. He says, "Responsiveness usually returns . . . after they have ceased taking the pill," and adds, "Comprehensive studies would be needed, before we can say we know what it means or what causes it."

Other comments are now coming in from lay people and experts which suggest that there are many and varied psychological results of using the pill that have negative effects on sexual adjustment. Both husbands and wives are complaining that their sex life "has become flat," and that they "feel they are on trial to perform satisfactorily in bed." Some husbands feel their wives have become too available sexually, are too demanding and independent. Among the professionals, doctors and therapists are beginning to agree that the total personalities of husband and wife should be studied before the pill is prescribed, and more attention given to "the psycho-sexual effects of the pill in long-term use."

One of the most realistic statements concerning the use and results of the pill which probably summarizes the current thinking of many experts has been made by Dr. Howard McQuarrie, a Salt Lake City gynecologist, who has done research on patients using the pill. He says, "The pill is a . . . good contraceptive. That's all it is. Let's leave it at that until we know more."

KINDS OF BIRTH CONTROL
Methods Without the Use of Devices or Chemicals
Abstinence

Abstaining from sexual intercourse is the simplest method of birth control. Whether it is the best is open to question. Surely, there are times in marriage when abstaining from coitus makes sense. Logical examples would be when either partner is ill, during the later stages of pregnancy, and for a period of time after childbirth. If the husband and wife talk things over frankly, and both agree on abstinence, there should be no problem unless their sex drives differ markedly in intensity. If they do, then there is the possibility that either or both may chafe under the agreement, with the one who has strong sexual urges feeling like a martyr, and the other leaning toward the thinking that the mate is animallike. Of course, either partner might, during the period of abstinence, obtain involuntary relief of sexual tensions by experiencing orgasm in dreams, but this in turn might create greater desire for contact with the mate.

The difficulty in practicing abstinence is that biological sex urges might occur regardless of what the couple has decided to do. Some couples provide such urges with an outlet through manual stimulation. Others frown upon such a practice.

One wife whom the writer counseled was embittered by the fact that although she was ill, her husband demanded and would accept no other form of sexual relief except intercourse, claiming it to be his legal right.

Needless to say, the only way abstinence can be practiced successfully in marriage is when the partners achieve mutuality in their thinking and learn to exercise empathy toward each other.

Coitus Interruptus

Coitus interruptus, a contraceptive technique that dates way back to antiquity (Genesis 38:8-10) and is used by many, is a practice in which the male withdraws his penis from the vagina just before ejaculating, and expels his semen outside of the woman's body.

Some of its claimed advantages are:

It can be used without instructions from a clinic or a physician.

It costs nothing.

No advance preparation is necessary.

There seem to be no harmful effects to either husband or wife when it is used, even over a long period of time.

Couples who use it generally have confidence in its effectiveness.

Its stated disadvantages are:

Pre-ejaculatory secretions of the penis may contain sperm cells that might possibly cause fertilization.

Withdrawal may not be timed properly.

It puts the husband under tension because he is solely responsible for its satisfactory outcome.

Some wives report feelings of deprivation when complete intercourse does not take place.

Husbands also report less satisfaction than that derived from complete intercourse.

Coitus Reservatus

Coitus reservatus is an unusual method of contraception in which couples, although they remain joined sexually, learn how to stop their movements during intercourse so the male can avoid ejaculating. By alternating periods of activity and rest, they are able to be together sexually for several cycles of rest and activity until the penis becomes flaccid and they are required to separate. Although some individuals report satisfaction from the use of this method, it has never been widely used.

Breast Feeding

Some mothers attempt to prevent the conception of another child by breast feeding their baby. Members of the La Leche League International, have the following to say about this method of child spacing:

"Studies have shown that complete breast feeding (no solids or supplements) for the first four to six months also has a definite effect on the natural spacing of children, since it usually tends to postpone the resumption of ovulation and the menstrual cycle for seven to fifteen months. The babies are then usually born about two years apart. It is *not* true that you cannot become pregnant as long as you are nursing, but pregnancy is extremely unusual before the first menstrual period, if you are *completely* nursing your baby. This means extra time in which to enjoy and pay special attention to your baby before the next comes along —and extra time for the baby to develop the security that comes from individual maternal attention."[2]

Hubbard presents a slightly different viewpoint regarding breast feeding as a contraceptive measure:

"Immediately after childbirth women will have, on the average, 6 to 8 weeks of amenorrhea (absence of menstruation) and during that time, will not release a mature ovum. Most women can prolong this . . . period by continuing to breast feed. It sometimes can be prolonged for a year or more. After the menses return, there are usually one or two menstruations that are not preceded by ovulation. Unfortunately, the return of the menses does not always precede return of ovulation. For this reason, breast feeding is not a reliable means of contraception when depended upon beyond the 6th week of childbirth . . . a woman wishing to avoid a subsequent pregnancy should resume the use of a contraceptive method by the end of the 6th week after a birth, whether she is breast feeding or not."[3]

Using a Douche

Some individuals who have scant knowledge of how conception occurs think they can prevent fertilization of the ovum with the douching technique (wash the seminal fluid out). This method is totally unreliable for several reasons:

1. Sperm cells may be ejaculated directly into the mouth of the uterus.

2. Studies show that some sperm cells have moved from the vagina into the uterine cavity within 90 seconds after the discharge of the seminal fluid. And inasmuch as the efficacy of douching is limited to the vaginal canal, sperm cells already in the uterus cannot be affected by the douching procedure.

3. Several studies have shown that the douching substance might even push sperm cells toward the uterine cavity, rather than render them ineffective as it is intended to do.

---

[2]*The Womanly Art of Breast Feeding*, Franklin Park, Illinois: La Leche League International, 1963, Second Edition, pp. 9, 10.
[3]Hubbard, Charles William, *Family Planning Education*, Saint Louis: The C. V. Mosby Co., 1973, p. 85.

It is also hazardous to use some of the highly-advertised "feminine hygiene" products for internal cleansing in order to insure feminine daintiness or prevent conception. They often contain chemicals that some individuals cannot tolerate. The internal organs of the healthy woman cleanse themselves, and the external organs need only the application of soap and water to be kept hygienically acceptable.

The Rhythm Method

The basic concept upon which the rhythm method of contraception rests is that each woman has a "safe period" in her monthly cycle during which there is no ovum present that might be fertilized. Theoretically, this is true, but the problem lies in finding when this "safe" or infertile period occurs, and then confining sexual intercourse to that time.

The first thing to do is to determine when ovulation occurs. On the average, ovulation usually takes place about fourteen days before the menstrual period begins, so if the woman has a regular twenty-eight day cycle, she will usually ovulate around the fourteenth day, counting from the first day of her period. Inasmuch as this time cannot be pinpointed, three days should be allowed for the variation in the possible time of ovulation. Next to be considered is the life span of the ovum which is thought to be twenty-four hours, which would mean adding one day on each side of the possible ovulatory time. But still another computation must be made which considers the effective life of the sperm. This is thought to be forty-eight hours, so two days must again be added on each side of the time of ovulation. Once these computations are made, it would be assumed that the fertile period would be from the ninth through the eighteenth day of the cycle and the infertile ("safe") periods would

The Theoretically Safe Periods During a Regular Twenty-eight Day Menstrual Cycle

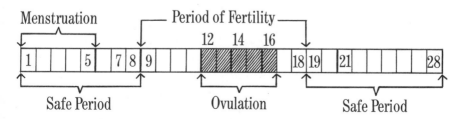

occur from the first through the eighth day and the nineteenth through the twenty-eighth day. The diagram depicts these periods.

It must be stressed that this computation of "safe" periods assumes that the woman has a *regular* twenty-eight day cycle. However, the problem is that very few women are that regular. Even though she may keep a record of her cycles for several months and assume it is regular, the individual's cycle may be changed by illness, shock, emotional stress or some physical ailments. Consequently, it is considered more helpful to try to determine the precise time of ovulation than to keep track of cycles. This is done by recording the basal body temperature over a period of time. It is known that this temperature rises several tenths of a degree after ovulation. If the woman can determine this time and then abstain from intercourse for 72 hours afterward, the ovum that is supposedly present should no longer be fertilizable. The suggested procedure for finding this temperature requires the wife to take and record her temperature each day on awakening, and at approximately the same time. Hubbard says it should "be recorded after a person has been at rest (sleeping) for 6 hours or more . . . on a specially designed rectal or oral thermometer, called a rhythm, ovulation, or basal temperature thermometer. A reading is taken by the woman immediately after she awakens and before she does much moving, uses any tobacco, takes a drink of water, or makes a trip to the bathroom."[4]

Needless to say, this procedure does not always work because basal body temperature can be elevated by other things. There are other ways of determining the ovulatory time. Some women know when it occurs because they have a twinge or pain in the pelvic area at that time of the month. Others notice an increased secretion of mucus from the cervix. However, these detecting practices are also not completely reliable.

A possible test for detecting the time of ovulation is being studied by the Food and Drug Administration. A strip of treated paper has been produced that the woman puts into her mouth daily, and changes in her saliva cause the paper to change color two or three days before ovulation begins. It is assumed then that if she abstains from intercourse for at least 5 days, conception can be avoided.

---

[4]*Ibid*, p. 31.

Oral Contraceptives—The Pill

Individuals who decide to use man-made contraceptive methods should be provided with a contraceptive that is readily available, simple and easy to use, inexpensive, and effective. In addition, it should be aesthetically acceptable to both partners, not interfere with the pleasure of the sex act, and produce no harmful side effects. Finally, it should in no way affect future chances for pregnancy if the couple desires to discontinue its use.

Although the pill is now used by millions of persons, it does not meet all of these requirements.

There are about 30 different brands of pills available in the United States today, and they are all made up of different proportions of synthetic hormones that are designed to suppress ovulation. The two types most widely used are certain combination types and the sequential types. One of the most popular of the combination types is a pill composed of synthetic estrogen and synthetic progesterone that is taken, (one daily) beginning with the fifth day counting from the first day of menstruation for twenty days. These pills stop the ovaries from releasing an ovum during that month, so the woman is unable to conceive. She then begins the procedure again on the fifth day of the next menstrual period.

When the sequential type of pill is used, the woman, beginning with the fifth day of menstruation, takes one pill containing synthetic estrogen daily for fifteen or sixteen days (depending on the brand) and then takes one pill made up of synthetic estrogen and synthetic progesterone daily for five or six days.

If both types of pills are taken regularly, as prescribed, they are nearly 100 percent effective. Kogan says, "Except for total abstinence or surgical sterilization, the combination pill is the most effective contraceptive known to man. Failures numbering . . . less than 1 per 100 women per year. The sequential pill . . . is only slightly less effective, with failures of about 1.4 per 100 women per year."[5]

A woman should never take the pill before a physician obtains her medical history, gives her a physical examination, and then approves its use. Reexaminations are usually performed at about 6 to 12-month intervals in order to determine if the pill is having any adverse effects.

---

[5]Kogan, Benjamin A., *Human Sexual Expression*, New York: Harcourt, Brace, Jovanovich, 1973, p. 110.

Side Effects

Everything that is taken internally by a large number of people will cause side effects in some of them. Oral contraceptives are no exception. The most common problems which, if severe enough, would make it inadvisable for a woman to continue using the pill are weight gain, nervousness, dizziness, persistent fatigue, bleeding between menstrual periods, breast soreness and a general state of irritability or depression. Mothers who want to nurse their babies are counseled not to use the pill after childbirth as it suppresses milk production.

Long-Term Effects

There have been many debates about the possible long-term effects of using the pill. Unfortunately, nothing definite can be said about this until studies have been made of a large number of women who have used them for about 20 or more years. Some conditions that have been attributed to the use of the pill, but which have not yet been confirmed by adequate data are blood clotting (especially in the veins of the legs), an increase in the incidence of cancer in women who have a predisposition toward cancerous growth, and liver injuries.

Chemical Contraceptives

The principles governing the use of chemical contraceptives are that they should be substances that do not harm body tissues but are still able to render sperm cells incapable of fertilizing the ovum. The failure rate of these methods is high, with the foam, the most effective, averaging a failure rate of 28 per 100 women per year.[6]

Their psychological drawbacks are that they must be used shortly before intercourse and might affect the mood surrounding the sex act, another application must be made for each sexual union, the woman must restrain her movements to intercourse, otherwise her body will not retain the chemical used, and protection only lasts about one hour.

Creams and Jellies

Vaginal creams and jellies are packaged in toothpaste-like tubes and are placed in the vagina with an applicator, a small plastic syringe mechanism. The creams seem to disperse, coat vaginal surfaces, and destroy sperm cells more effectively than the jellies.

---

[6]*Ibid*, p. 112.

Foams

There are several different kinds of foams. A foaming tablet that is inserted with the fingers. Powdered and liquid foams that are put into a sponge that is inserted. Aerosol vaginal foams that are packaged with an applicator for insertion. This type is considered the least troublesome to use.

Suppositories

Vaginal suppositories are usually made from vegetable fats, gelatin, and soft soaps. After these cone-shaped objects are inserted into the vagina, they take about 15 minutes to melt before they can be effective during intercourse. They provide protection for about one hour.

Mechanical Contraceptives
The Condom

The condom is a widely used device that was the most popular method used in many countries until the pill became available in 1960. It is a thin rubber sheath, shaped like a finger, that is pulled over the erect penis. Many brands of condoms are available without prescription and some are so packaged that they can be stored for five years under normal temperatures. Thus, many people keep them on hand to use when other methods of contraception may not be available. The condom may be prelubricated at the factory or at the time it is used with a vaginal jelly. Problems with its use occur when it contains a defect, such as a tiny hole, tears, or slips off the penis too soon, allowing seminal fluid to escape. Some couples refrain from using it because lovemaking must be interrupted while it is placed on the penis and because some men feel it cuts down their sensations during the sex act. Kogan lists its failure rate at 16 failures per 100 women per year.[7]

Diaphragm

A diaphragm is a thin rubber device designed like a dome-shaped cup which has a collapsible metal outer edge. When fitted properly it covers the mouth of the uterus (in the cervix). To be an effective contraceptive it must be coated inside and around its edges with a spermicidal cream or jelly before it is put into place in the vagina. This forms a mechanical and chemical barrier between the sperm and the ovum. It

---

[7]*Ibid*, p. 113.

must be fitted by a physician, who also shows the patient how to coat it with jelly and cream, and insert and remove it. Inasmuch as the involved internal dimensions of the woman are subject to change, it should be refitted every two years and after each pregnancy. The diaphragm may be inserted anytime up to six hours before intercourse and should be left in place at least six hours afterwards. It may be inserted with the fingers or a plastic inserter. It is highly reliable when used properly and is prescribed by many physicians. Some couples don't like to use the diaphragm because they think it is difficult to insert and remove. They also feel that it interrupts or destroys the spontaneity of the sex act. One young wife voiced a typical complaint when she said, "I went through all the bother of putting my diaphragm in place before my husband came home, so we could have a romantic evening. Then what did he do, but roll over and fall asleep as soon as he climbed in bed. Men! I could have killed him!"

Such incidents should not happen, if couples who use the diaphragm can learn to pick up nonverbal clues from each other which indicate whether either is in the mood for making love.

Cervical Cap

A cervical cap is shaped much like a diaphragm, but is made of rubber or plastic, and is smaller, thicker, less flexible than a diaphragm and is more difficult to insert. After initial physician fitting and instruction, some patients have the dexterity needed to insert it themselves, others do not. It can be used with or without a jelly or cream, left in place 24 hours at a time, is highly reliable, and has no side effects.

The Intrauterine Contraceptive Device (IUD)

Intrauterine devices to prevent pregnancy are not a recent development. Over two thousand years ago, Hippocrates wrote about a contraceptive device that was placed in a woman's uterus through a hollow lead tube. For hundreds of years, the idea was used to protect animals from conceiving, for example, ancient camel drivers would insert small pebbles into their camels' uteri. German gynecologists used combinations of silkworm gut in the uterine cavity that were attached to buttons or discs that hung over the mouth of the uterus. However, because of numerous infections and the lack of antibodies to treat them, the IUD method did not gain widespread acceptance until the early 1960s. This was precipitated by favorable reports in 1959 from Japan and Israel and the availability of suitable and inexpensive plastics and metals that could be used for manufacturing IUDs. Today, there are several million users throughout the world, and the IUD is considered second only to the pill as a reliable contraceptive method. At present, there are a number of kinds of IUDs available, usually made from plastic or a nickel-chromium alloy.

The IUD must be inserted into the uterus by a physician, and after it enters the uterine cavity, it opens up into its original shape. It does not interfere with menstruation or ovulation and can be left in the uterus indefinitely.

"This plastic is nontoxic and is well tolerated as a 'foreign body' by the uterus. It has a 'built-in memory' so that when loaded and inserted from a straight tube that carries it past the cervical canal it resumes its original shape when it emerges in the cavity of the uterus. The IUD is most effective when placed high in the uterus. The plastic material is impregnated with a radio-opaque material so that it can be seen by X-ray. A nylon thread attached to the device runs through the cervical canal and can be felt by the woman. This assures the woman that it is still in place and operative."[8]

There are many types of IUDs. Some commonly used are the Lippes loop, the Marguiles spiral, the Birnberg bow, the Ota-type ring, the Saf-T-coil, and the Dalkon shield. The type used depends upon the physician's recommendation and the patient's tolerance. It is considered about 97 percent effective. It is not known precisely how the IUD prevents conception. Currrent theories are:

1. It speeds the zygote (fertilized ovum) through the Fallopian tube and into the uterine cavity before it is mature enough to implant itself in the uterine lining (endometrium).

2. Its contact with the surface of the endometrium starts a foreign antibody reaction which produces materials that destroy either the sperm cells or the fertilized ovum.

3. It prevents the sperm cells from moving up into the Fallopian tubes and fertilizing an ovum.

4. It causes the uterus to expel the zygote.

---

[8]Crawley, Lawrence Q. and Associates, *Reproduction, Sex, and Preparation for Marriage*, Englewood Cliffs: Prentice Hall, 1973, 2nd Edition, p. 195.

Some question has arisen as to whether the IUD is a contraceptive, if it affects the implantation and growth of the ovum after it has been fertilized, or if it is an abortifacient (that which induces early spontaneous abortions). The only answer that can be given is that it depends upon the individual's concept of when life begins. Those who believe it begins when the sperm meets the ovum would consider the prevention of implantation by the IUD as abortive. Those who think that life begins with implantation would not. The individual's religious belief has much to do with his concept.

Physicians say there are a number of conditions that would make the insertion of an IUD inadvisable. Some of them are: Suspected pregnancy, infections of the cervix, pelvic inflammation, tumorous growth in the uterus, and a history of heavy bleeding between periods.

Problems and Side Effects

Some problems that might occur are the unnoticed expulsion of the IUD, possible pregnancy if the IUD used is too small for the particular woman, and a remote possibility of perforation of the uterus (about one in one thousand insertions). The most common side effects include excessive bleeding and pain during and between menstrual periods, and inflammation of the endometrium.

RESEARCH ACTIVITIES IN PROGRESS WITH EXPERIMENTAL CONTRACEPTIVE METHODS

Extensive research to develop new contraceptive methods is going on throughout the world. A few of those which hold greatest promise are listed below:

For the Female

The "Mini-Pill"

Studies of oral pill usage have disclosed that most of its adverse side effects have come from the estrogen it contains. Consequently, experiments are being made with a pill which contains tiny quantities of synthetic progesterone. This pill, which must be taken at the same time every day, eliminates most side effects and does not disturb ovulation or the menstrual cycle. What it *does* is thicken the mucus of the cervical canal so sperm cells cannot penetrate it. It also produces changes in the endometrium which discourage the reception of a fertilized ovum.

A Progesterone Capsule Implant

The need for taking daily doses of progesterone can be avoided if the woman has an inch-long spaghetti-like progesterone capsule inserted under her skin (arm, leg or groin). The capsule contains a year's supply which is periodically released to prevent conception. The doctor can easily remove or insert it.

"Morning-after" Pill

This pill contains a large amount of synthetic estrogen called diethylstilbestrol. It should be taken within twenty-four hours after coitus, and has been effective 3 to 5 days after, in some cases. However, it sometimes causes illness from induced menstrual changes and precipitates staining and bleeding.

A recent study by Dr. Lucile Kirtland Kuchera of the University of Michigan Health Service proved the morning-after pill to be 100 percent effective in 1,000 women who volunteered for the experiment. "One thousand women of childbearing age were given, within 72 hours of sexual exposure, 25 mg. (milligrams) of diethylstilbestrol twice daily for five days. No pregnancies resulted and there were no serious adverse reactions."[9]

The results of the study were impressive because most of the women had engaged in coitus at the mid-point of their menstrual cycles, a time at which the risk of conceiving is the greatest. Despite the results of this test, the "morning-after" pill is still advised for emergency use only.

A Progesterone Uterine Packet

Another device under study is a packet with enough progesterone in it to prevent pregnancy for a year that is inserted into the uterus by a physician. The progesterone that is released alters the hormone balance within the uterine cavity, so the endometrium rejects the implantation of a fertilized ovum. It has no reported side effects.

GRF

Another experimental method recently reported involves a chemical called Gonadotropin Releasing Factor (GRF) which is produced in the hypothalamus of the brain. The GRF causes the pituitary gland to release hormones that stimulate ovulation in the woman. Steps are being taken to

[9]Kuchera, Lucile Kirtland, "Postcoital Contraception With Diethylstilbestrol," *Journal of the American Medical Association*, Vol. 220, No. 8, (May 22, 1972), pp. 1061-65.

produce a synthetic GRF that would block the pituitary gland from releasing the hormones that precipitate ovulation. Thus, there would be no ovum (egg cell) available to be fertilized. Studies show that such a method, it if becomes workable would produce no side effects.[10]

For the Male

The development of male contraceptives has been difficult because interference with male reproductive functioning can only be approached in three ways, namely, to control sperm production, maturation, or transportation. Present research includes:

Experiments to Impede the Maturation of Sperm Cells

Undesirable side effects include the reduction of male sex drive, possible feminizing effects, and problems if alcohol is consumed.

Research to Affect the Chemistry of the Seminal Fluid

Efforts are being made to develop a substance that can be added to the seminal fluid that will in turn render the sperm cells ineffective. The problem is to find a nontoxic agent that can be ingested or injected.

Impeding Sperm Transportation

Such experiments include inserting a plug that can be easily removed into the canal of the vas deferens.

Summary

It should be emphasized that the above described methods of contraception are still in the experimental stage. And if the time comes when they have been sufficiently tested to be placed on the commercial market, they should only be used under the direction of a physician who predetermines their suitability for each individual.

STERILIZATION

At the present time, because of their concern regarding the increasing population, many individuals are resorting to sterilization as a form of birth control. The primary thinking is that they can undergo simple surgery and be forever freed from worrying about incurring future pregnancies. Inasmuch as the technique for sterilizing the male is the least intricate procedure, this operation, called a vasectomy is becoming increasingly popular.

---

[10]Blakeslee, Alton, "GRF, the New Contraceptive," The Minneapolis *Star*, Aug. 9, 1971. p. 1B.

Vasectomy

The vasectomy can usually be performed in a doctor's office, using a local anesthetic. Its purpose is to cut and tie the sperm duct (vas deferens) that extends from each testicle, so the sperm cells can never pass from the testes, where they are produced, to the urethral canal through which they can be expelled from the penis. Incisions are made high on the scrotum (on each side) where it joins the body, and the two tiny tubes (vasa deferentia) are cut and tied. After surgery, the patient is advised to go home and rest for a short time and to avoid sexual or hard physical activity for at least 3 days. He is also advised to use a contraceptive during intercourse for 8 weeks or longer after surgery as he still may have sperm cells present in the body above the blocked area that can cause a pregnancy. Inasmuch as vasectomy has no effect upon erection, ejaculation, or sexual climax, there is no functional body change. Although it is claimed that it does not reduce the sex drive or sexual pleasure, psychological studies suggest that although the capacity for these manifestations remains, the individual's mind-set may have some effect upon them. Doctors are divided in their thinking regarding the psychological effects of vasectomy. Landis in a study of 887 doctors in California reports that 40 percent opposed the operation chiefly on the basis "that the man might later change his mind."[11]

Slovut reports the attitudes of an eminent urologist at the Mayo Clinic which illustrates his concern with the psychological implications of a vasectomy. He writes:

Doctors differ on how liberal they should be in performing the sterilization operation—whether, for example, one should be done on a bachelor. Each doctor has to make up his own mind.

Dr. Laurence F. Greene, a urologist at the Mayo Clinic in Rochester, Minn., says the decision to go ahead is fairly easy in the case of a couple with an already large family.

He won't necessarily refuse to do the operation, he says, if the parents have an apparently stable marriage and they have decided their family is complete.

There are conditions, he says, in which he will perform a vasectomy

---

[11]Landis, Judson T., "Attitudes of Individual California Physicians and Policies of State Medical Societies on Vasectomy for Birth Control," *Journal of Marriage and the Family,* 28:3 (August 1966), pp. 277-283.

on a fairly young man in a childless or one-child marriage if the marriage is stable, but:

"I do not perform vasectomy on the husband whose wife is pregnant. I prefer to await the results of the pregnancy.

"I do not perform vasectomy on young single men because, first, I am not convinced that the 'confirmed bachelor' is truly confirmed and, second, the wishes of a future spouse must be safeguarded.

"Similarly, I refuse to perform vasectomy on a man contemplating marriage; I insist that the marriage be consummated and vasectomy be requested by both partners.

"Finally, I believe that vasectomy to 'save a marriage' rarely succeeds."[12]

Interviews with patients who have undergone vasectomy reveal that the majority of them feel their sex life has improved with more frequent coital activity and over half of their wives obtaining climax more easily.[13] However, psychological studies suggest that some men worry about being demasculinized and seem to be scrutinized by themselves or others afterwards for possible loss of masculine characteristics.[14]

It is evident from these statements that there should be counseling of and agreement between husband and wife before a vasectomy is performed.

Another possibility that might help to avoid later problems is to learn how to make the operation reversible. Surgeons have attempted to do this by avoiding cutting of the tubes, and instead using clamps, valves or plugs to block sperm transportation that could all be removed later to restore fertility. None of these procedures has been completely successful. A possible usable technique is now under study. ". . . A mechanical device made of gold and stainless steel . . . is permanently implanted in the vas deferens and has a tiny faucet-like valve that may be set on or off. A second operation is necessary to change the position of the valve."[15]

[12]Slovut, Gordon, "Vasectomies for Bachelors? Some Doctors Won't." The Minneapolis *Star,* August 16, 1971, p. 4B.

[13]Ferber, Andrew, and William L., "Vasectomy," *Medical Aspects of Human Sexuality,* Vol. 2, No. 6 (June 1968) p. 34.

[14]Ferber, A. S., Tietze, C., and Lewit, S., "Men With Vasectomies: A Study of Medical, Sexual and Psychosocial Changes," *Psychosomatic Medicine,* Vol. 29, No. 4, (July-August, 1967), p. 354.

[15]Kogan, Benjamin A., *Human Sexual Expression,* p. 120.

Tubal Ligation

Sterilization in the female is a procedure which involves cutting and tying the Fallopian tubes, so that no ova can enter them and become fertilized. This used to be expensive, had to be done in a hospital, and meant making an incision in the abdominal wall, removing a small section of each tube, and then tying off their remaining ends. Such an operation has been nearly always irreversible.

Recently, newer and simpler techniques have been developed. They include:

Laparoscopy

Two small incisions are made in the patient's abdomen. A laparoscope, a tube carrying a light, is inserted into one incision and an instrument carrying a blade and an electric cautery is inserted into the other. A segment of each tube is then cauterized and severed near the middle of the segment. This causes the end of each tube to become sealed with scar formations. This procedure has become known as the "Band-Aid Operation," as the incisions are so small that they can be covered with Band-Aids, and the woman can leave the hospital after becoming fully awake.

Reversible Sterilization

Closing the Fallopian tubes with clips that can be easily removed.

Culdoscopy

Tubal sterilization with a vaginal approach. A culdoscope (instrument for viewing the body cavity) enables the surgeon to see, cut and tie the tubes.

Summary

As is the case with male sterilization, in these operations the ova, like the sperm cells, are blocked from passing to areas where fertilization can take place and instead are absorbed by the body. Sterilization does not affect female physiological functions, and many report increased sexual pleasure. However, there are some who feel "less of a woman" afterwards, and the inability to reproduce or a feeling that they have violated their religious convictions may cause negative emotions.

ABORTION

There is no accurate way of determining how many abortions are being performed in contemporary society. Estimates vary from several hundred thousand to one or two million a year. It should be remembered, however, that all abortions are not brought about by deliberate interference with pregnancy in order to satisfy the expectant mother's desires. Some of them are spontaneous and others are medically necessary. Before discussing the three types, the term abortion should be defined. Medical terminology defines it as the termination of a pregnancy before the fetus becomes viable (capable of living after birth), which is usually designated as before the beginning of the seventh month of gestation. It should be emphasized that birth control and abortion are not the same. Birth control is taking deliberate action to prevent the sperm and ovum from meeting. Abortion is a condition or an act which stops the new life from developing after fertilization has taken place.

Spontaneous

A spontaneous abortion usually happens without any outside influence. In other words, it is brought about by some condition in the mother or fetus. Although all the reasons for its happening are not known, some that are given are:

Hormonal imbalance in the early stages of implantation.

Faulty germ plasm.

Defects in the sperm, ovum or developing embryo.

Glandular imbalance.

Some types of infections and diseases.

Physical stress or injury. (Usually when the fetus is not firmly anchored in the uterine cavity.)

Nutritional deficiencies.

Some progress had been made in cutting down the incidence of spontaneous abortions, by the attending physician stressing adequate diet, treating hormone imbalance, and being alert to toxic conditions in the expectant mother.

Induced Abortions

Therapeutic (Legal)

Until a short time ago, an induced abortion, to be legal, could only be performed after two or more doctors had agreed that continued pregnancy would place the health or the life of the expectant mother in jeopardy. At the present time, a recent decision by the United States Supreme Court, on January 22, 1973, ruled that in the first trimester of pregnancy (13 weeks) the decision to have an abortion must be left to the pregnant woman and her doctor. During the second trimester the state may regulate abortion procedures "in ways that are reasonably related to (protecting) maternal health." In approximately the last three months of pregnancy, the state may, if it chooses, regulate and even prohibit abortions to preserve the expectant mother's life or health. This new ruling has stirred up much controversy, with its proponents praising it and its opponents seeking legal ways to modify it.

This new framework of legality in which the pregnant woman operates has now caused her, if she is considering an abortion, to be required to make a value judgment regarding when human life begins and how important it is. Each person can answer such questions only after giving careful thought to the principles of her religious belief or her philosophy of life. Needless to say, if the decision is made to have an abortion, it should be performed by an experienced and knowledgeable physician who is in a position to provide his patient with post-abortion care. Different techniques used to perform an abortion depend upon how long the pregnancy has progressed and the decision of the doctor and the patient. They include dilation and curettage ("D and C"), and vacuum aspiration (until the twelfth or thirteenth week). After that, the saline method of injection is generally used.

Illegal Abortions

Illegal or criminal abortions are those performed contrary to abortion laws, and usually by unqualified individuals whose usual motive is financial gain. The risks of undergoing such an abortion are great, chiefly because the need for secrecy may produce conditions in which proper facilities are not available. Also, unqualified practitioners who are usually more interested in money than the patient and often provide no post-abortion care add to the hazards of the operation. Landis reports that, "One-third of all maternity deaths are the result of abortions. Where death does not result, the effect of the illegal abortion may be permanent impairment of health, or sterility."[16]

---

[16]Landis, Judson T., *Journal of Marriage and the Family*, 28:3 (August 1966), p. 437.

General Attitudes Toward Abortion

Despite the recent liberalized abortion laws, there are many people who do not consider abortion acceptable as a form of birth control. Their numbers include not only lay persons and religious leaders, but also a sizable group of obstetricians and gynecologists. There is also evidence that some women have abortions for additional reasons added to the practice of birth control. Downs and Clayson report that "among women who have abortions, pregnancy is 'initially more wanted than unwanted.' Far from being accidental, it represents a subconscious effort to cope with extreme emotional stress."

In a study of 108 patients in a New York hospital, they learned that 79% of their abortion patients had personality problems, and that "85% of the group had suffered either a personal loss or grave psychiatric disturbance, or both, in the months just before conception . . ." Downs and Clayson conclude that the women they studied had unconsciously "chosen" pregnancy as a way of reparing "a threatened or damaged psyche." They needed their supposedly unwanted pregnancies at least for a while, "to prove something to themselves"—perhaps that they were truly feminine, or that they were whole enough to create or that they need not be entirely alone.[17]

It seems from the above study and the controversy that is continuing over liberalized abortion laws, that society as a whole must devote much more painstaking thought to the practice of abortion than has been the case so far. It should also be remembered that liberalized abortion laws will never change the thinking of many individuals who feel that planned and unplanned children should not be denied the right of birth and life.

Suggested Readings

1. Adams, John E., and Kim, Hyung Bok, "A Fresh Look at Intercountry Adoptions," *Children* 18:6 (Nov.-Dec. 1971), 214-21.

2. Angrist, Shirley S., "Communication About Birth Control: An Exploratory Study of Freshman Girls' Information and Attitudes," *Journal of Marriage and the Family* 28:3 (August 1966), 284-86.

---

[17]Downs, Lawrence, Clayson, David, a paper presented to the American College of Obstetricians and Gynecologists, as reported in *Time* Magazine, May 29, 1972.

3. Barber, Hugh R. K., Graber, Edward S., and O'Rourke, James J., *Are the Pills Safe?*, Springfield, Ill.: Charles C. Thomas, 1969.

4. Blake, Judith, "Abortion and Public Opinion: The 1960-70 Decade," *Science* 171 (February 12, 1971).

5. Bracher, Marjorie J., *SRO—Overpopulation and You*, Philadelphia: Fortress Press, 1966.

6. Brown, Harrison and Sweezy, Alan, *Population: Perspective*, San Francisco: Freeman-Cooper & Co., 1972.

7. Bumpass, Larry, and Westoff, Charles F., *The Later Years of Childbearing*, Princeton, N.J.: Princeton University Press, 1970.

8. Calderone, Mary Steichen, *Manual of Family Planning and Contraceptive Practice*, Baltimore, Md.: Williams and Wilkins Co., 1970 (2nd ed.).

9. Callahan, Daniel (ed.), *The American Population Debate*, Garden City, N.Y.: Doubleday & Co., 1971.

10. Ehrlich, Paul R. and Ehrlich, Anne H., *Population/Resources/ Environment: Issues in Human Ecology*, San Francisco: W. H. Freeman and Co., 1970.

11. Feldman, David M., *Birth Control in Jewish Law: Marital Relations, Contraception, and Abortion,* as set forth in the Classic Texts of Jewish Law, New York: New York University Press, 1968.

12. Finegold, Wilfred J., *Artificial Insemination,* Springfield, Ill.: Charles C. Thomas, 1964.

13. Gillette, Paul L., *Vasectomy: The Male Sterilization Operation,* New York: Paperback Library, 1971.

14. Kaufman, S. A., *New Hope for the Childless Couple: The Causes and Treatment of Infertility,* New York: Simon & Schuster, 1970.

15. Pohlman, Edward H., and Pohlman, Julia Mae, *The Psychology of Birth Planning,* Cambridge, Ma.: Schenkman, 1969.

16. Williams, Glanville, *The Sanctity of Life and the Criminal Law,* New York: Alfred A. Knopf, 1970.

Chapter XX

Pregnancy and Childbirth

ATTITUDES AND ADJUSTMENTS

Married couples are becoming increasingly aware of the fact that planning to have a baby and adjusting to its coming is a shared experience in which both partners must exercise maturity and understanding. This growing trend has caused many husbands to attend classes with their wives where marital adjustments during pregnancy, the process of birth, and the care of the newly-born baby are discussed. Such involvement on the part of the husband removes him from the role of a passive bystander, an individual who has participated for a brief moment in the beginning of a new life and then has been relegated to the sidelines. If he is encouraged to continue as an active partner in the challenging and joint adventure of bringing a new member into the family and prepares himself so he can help care for the baby's needs after it is born, there is much less likelihood that he will behave in a manner that will make the period of pregnancy a difficult time for either himself or his wife.

It seems that ancient cultures and some existing primitive peoples have sensed the husband's need for recognition and involvement before and after the birth of the child, and have met it by practicing a custom known as *couvade*. Marco Polo observed the practice among the mountain tribes of China, and reported that after a baby was born, the father stayed in bed 40 days, during which time all of his relatives paid him a visit. Diner says couvade is still practiced today among some primitive peoples, and expectant fathers complain of nausea and pain, and when the child is born, writhe and groan in misery, and require weeks of bed care to recover.[1]

Many of today's American husbands suffer adverse effects during their wife's pregnancy. Some become ill, others jealous of the new baby, and still others experience a change in attitudes toward their wife. Le-

---

[1]Diner, Helen, *Mothers and Amazons*, New York: 1965, p. 113.

Masters in his study of 46 couples reported that 38 (83 percent) said they experienced "extensive" or "severe" crisis in adjusting to the birth of their first baby.[2]

Such problems of adjustment won't be solved by the husband taking to his bed as those who practice the couvade do, but many of them can be worked out if the man of the house realizes the tremendously important psychological and economic functions he might perform during pregnancy and after the child is born. During those nine long months, and even after the baby is born, he can lend a hand with the housework. Washing the dirty dishes in the sink or tidying up the house cheerfully and without being told to, can often convey more than the words, "I love you," the vital concern and deep affection he has for his wife. The husband who is a real partner in the having-a-baby enterprise will plan interesting things that he and his wife might do in their leisure time. And, of course, he will learn with his wife all he can about the prenatal period, the process of birth and child care. An understanding husband also takes care of the financial side of having a baby, and through his attitude lets his wife know that money is of small importance when compared with her's and the baby's welfare.

Couples who are planning to have a baby should both strive to be in good health, and the wife's readiness for childbearing should be determined. If she undergoes a thorough physical examination, and in a frank discussion tells her doctor all about her past illnesses and physical problems, he can determine if there is any past or present condition that might make a pregnancy inadvisable.

PRESUMPTIVE SIGNS OF PREGNANCY

Couples who have been hoping to have a baby, eagerly await any indications that conception has taken place. The first signs that appear are called presumptive signs, because although one may assume when these are present that a new life is beginning, it is not an established fact. Some of the manifestations which should be watched for are:

1. *A missed menstrual period.* This sign is not reliable because menstruation may be delayed by emotional upset, illness or changes of climate.

---

[2]LeMasters. E. E., "Parenthood as Crisis," *Marriage and Family Living,* 19:4 (November 1957) pp. 352-355.

2. *"Morning sickness" or nausea.* More than half the number of pregnant women report experiencing nausea during the first three months of pregnancy, after which it usually disappears.

3. *Changes in the breasts.* The breasts become larger, more tender, and seem fuller. The tiny pigmented ring (the aureola) surrounding the nipples darkens; and there are also some prickling or tingling sensations.

4. *The need to urinate more frequently.* This is due to congestion in certain blood vessels.

5. *A tendency toward brownish pigmentation of the skin.*

6. *Changes in color of the vagina and the vulva.*

7. *A sustained elevated basal body temperature* (taken in the morning before getting out of bed).

8. *Softening of the cervix.*

If the combination of these signs is present, it is wise to consult a doctor to ascertain the true situation, because, although conception may have occurred, one is not positive. In fact, some wives who have an intense desire to have a baby may experience a false pregnancy (pseudocyesis) with which they insist that they feel life; and they may also exhibit some of the presumptive signs.

POSITIVE SIGNS OF PREGNANCY

1. *Hearing and counting the rate of the fetal heartbeat.* This can be heard with a stethoscope during the fourth or fifth month.

2. *The outline of the fetus may be felt through the abdominal wall.*

3. *Feeling the movement of the fetus in the uterus.* This can be done during the fourth or fifth month.

4. *Making an X-ray photograph of the fetus.* This is possible only in late pregnancy.

TESTS FOR PREGNANCY
Tests Using Animals

If the husband and wife are extremely anxious to know if pregnancy has occurred, certain tests can be made to determine this in advance of the appearance of positive signs.

Some tests which show a high degree of accuracy, if administered properly in the period beginning about one to two weeks after conception, are the following: the Aschheim-Zondek test which uses mice; the Friedman test which uses rabbits; tests using female rats, and tests in which female and male frogs or toads are used.

The biological tests all work on the same principle. When conception occurs, an increased pituitary-like hormone is contained in the urine. If a specimen of urine is taken and injected into the animals, which must be either immature females or those which have been isolated from males for a period of time, obvious changes take place in their ovaries. Injection of the female frog or toad causes expulsion of eggs; and injections of the male frog or toad results in the discharge of spermatozoa.

Tests Using Chemicals

Several chemical tests for pregnancy are available which are based on the presence of a hormone in the urine and body fluids of the pregnant woman. It is called HCG (human chorionic gonadotropin), is produced by the placenta, and is detectable in the urine about 10 days after ovulation. A drop of urine, which can be used in different types of tests, is mixed with certain chemicals, and if the woman is pregnant, no agglutination or clotting occurs. If she is not pregnant, agglutination does occur. This test has become very popular. These tests can be made anywhere from four to fourteen days after a missed menstrual period, and are highly reliable (about 97%), with results being available within as few as three minutes.

There are also less reliable tests in which progesterone tablets are taken orally. These tests which have no negative effects on the pregnancy, cause a reaction when the dosage is discontinued. If the woman is not pregnant, vaginal bleeding takes place. If she is assumed to be pregnant, no menstrual flow occurs.

At the present time, there is no test for detecting pregnancy that is perfect, but continued research will undoubtedly improve test accuracy.

ASCERTAINING THE SEX OF THE BABY BEFORE BIRTH

Some couples who are expecting a baby are eager to know its sex before it is born. Curiosity and the advice of friends may cause them to make diagnoses that are based upon superstition and hearsay. Consequently, the wife may say, "We know it's a boy. He kicks on the right side and I'm carrying him high. Also, I prefer sour foods and have considerable nausea." And on the other hand, she may think, "Our baby must be a girl because she is so calm and peaceful and I have such a craving for sweets."

Medical scientists have engaged in considerable research in order to help inform curious parents, and have devised many tests in an effort to determine the baby's sex before its arrives. However, nearly all of them have been unreliable.

One accurate method of determining the sex of the fetus has been developed, but it is generally used in hospitals for research purposes only. This is so, because the procedure poses hazards which can be minimized only when highly experienced persons are in charge. This procedure, called amniocentesis, requires inserting a needle-like instrument into the uterus through the abdominal wall, with which a sample of the amniotic fluid which surrounds the unborn baby is withdrawn. The research people then examine cells present in this fluid which have been shed from the baby's skin. This enables them to count the number of so-called "sex chromatin bodies" in the cell nuclei. The presence of certain numbers of these bodies reveals whether the baby is male or female.

Another test which is still in the experimental stage has been reported by Simak, " 'The sex of a child, based on maternal blood tests, can be determined in the 13th week of pregnancy,' Dr. J. de Grouchy, research director at the National Scientific Research Center in Paris, France, told Medical Report. The investigation, he said, was carried on in collaboration with Dr. Claudine Trebuchet.

"He explained that his research was carried on in the belief that fetal cells can cross the placental barrier as early as the 13th week of pregnancy and can be found and identified in the mother's blood. He claimed that in his research the sex of the child was correctly forecast in 14 of 21 pregnancies."[3]

Considering everything, it is wiser for expectant parents to wait until the baby arrives to learn its sex.

CHOOSING AN OBSTETRICIAN

Finding a suitable obstetrician is easier if the married couple remains in their home town, and have a family doctor who is acquainted with the

[3]Simak, Clifford, "Medical Report." Minneapolis *Tribune*, Nov. 28, 1971.

wife's background and personality. He will usually either accept her as a maternity patient or refer her to an obstetrician with whom he feels she can establish rapport. However, if the couple has recently settled in a strange and different area, the task of selecting a doctor may be a bit more difficult. If newly found friends have no recommendations, they may turn to their county medical society for help or go to the public library and consult the "Directory of Medical Specialists." It must be remembered that these sources will not select a doctor, neither will they evaluate him. They will simply provide lists of certified doctors and their affiliations. What guides should be used then in making a choice? There are three important things to consider:

The doctor's training.

The number of successful deliveries to his credit.

How his personality affects them. It should be one that inspires confidence and helps the wife feel comfortable.

Some might like a doctor who converses freely, others may prefer one who is noncommunicative. But in either case, the wife and husband should certainly have a good talk with him before she places herself in his care. It should be learned how he feels about "painless" childbirth and "natural" childbirth. The anesthetics he will use and how the couple feels about them should be frankly discussed.

The doctor should be questioned regarding the frequency of visits to his office; how long he provides care after the baby is born, and what hospital he uses. The couple should be sure to ask the doctor what his fee is, and be frank in telling him how much they can afford to pay for his services. If this is done, and his fee seems too high, he will usually be willing to refer them to someone else whose prices fit their budget. On the other hand, if he is told that his fee is satisfactory, he has the assurrance that his bill will be paid. After such things have been arranged with mutual satisfaction, the doctor will schedule the wife's initial visit to him. It should be stressed once more that establishing rapport with the obstetrician so that a mutually satisfying relationship exists will contribute significantly to making pregnancy and childbirth a more pleasant experience.

THE FIRST VISIT TO THE OBSTETRICIAN

At the first visit the doctor will do the following things:

1. *Get a complete medical history of the wife's past,* which will include illnesses, menstrual history, operations, and accidents.

2. *Give her a complete physical examination.* Of special importance is the blood test to detect possible syphilitic infection, blood type, and presence or absence of the Rh factor.

3. *Determine her pelvic measurements* and make an internal examination of the vagina, cervix, and uterus.

4. *Give an estimated delivery date.* This is done by adding seven days to the first day of the previous normal menstrual period and then counting ahead nine months. For example, if the first day of his patient's previous normal menstrual period was July 10th, the baby would be due April 17th of the following year.

5. *Set up a schedule for subsequent visits,* at which time he will carefully check weight, blood pressure, and urine.

6. *Suggest a proper diet to follow.* Incidentally, this does not usually mean eating more food, but it does mean adhering to a balanced diet with emphasis on certain foods. The doctor will not only recommend holding weight gain to about two pounds a month or a total of not over 20 to 25 pounds for the nine-month period, but he will also be critical if the expectant mother gains too much. She should not be hurt and consider him an old "fuddy duddy." He will only be doing this for her own good and she will love him later because he did scold her.

SUGGESTIONS FOR ENJOYING PREGNANCY

Ignoring Rumors and Superstitions

In order to keep herself free from the influence of rumors and superstitions, the wife should bear in mind that she has engaged her doctor to answer any questions that may arise to disturb her. She should avoid well-meaning friends who say, "My aunt's doctor told her . . ." or "Virginia Green had a baby and she says . . ."

She should also accept the fact that medical science says that the mother cannot mark her baby during pregnancy. If a rabbit startles her, the baby will not appear with a rabbit's outline on his shoulder, or if she eats too many strawberries, her darling daughter will not carry a strawberry mark on her thigh. She should forget such fears and realize that if the baby does appear with a rabbit or a strawberry marking, the birthmarks will be due to faulty pigmentation or a tangled mass of blood vessels, rather than anything she has done.

Controlling "Morning Sickness"

Although the doctor is the one to consult if there is excessive nausea, there are some things which the pregnant woman can do to help herself. A few simple helps are to:

Eat something in the morning before getting out of bed. Suggested foods are Melba toast, salty crackers or oatmeal.

Avoid getting overhungry. Nibble on crackers or cookies.

Not let herself become too tired, as fatigue will aggravate a nauseous condition.

Diet and Weight Control

Even though the obstetrician has prescribed a proper diet, his patient must use judgment in avoiding certain foods. Sweets, starches and fatty foods can easily balloon her figure.

There has been some controversy regarding the amount of weight the woman should gain during pregnancy. Certain obstetricians set the limit at about 10 to 14 pounds which the National Research Council says is too low. In their detailed study of dietary habits during pregnancy, the following things were stressed:

A weight gain during pregnancy in the range of 20 to 25 pounds was recommended.

Evidence suggested a possible link between the practice of drastically limiting weight gain and high perinatal (time span before and immediately after birth) and infant mortality rates.

". . . the risks of pregnancy for both mother and child were substantially greater when the expectant mother was younger than 17 years old . . . (because) most girls under 17 had greater nutritional requirements in proportion to body size than older women, and the additional demands of pregnancy may compromise their continued growth and increase their risks."[4]

---

[4]"How Many Added Pounds for Pregnancy?" Report by the National Academy of Sciences—National Research Council, New York Times Service, reprinted in the Minneapolis *Tribune*, August 9, 1970, p. 17.

Obviously, weight control is necessary even if the woman is allowed to gain 25 pounds. The developing baby puts additional demands on the mother's heart, liver, kidneys and circulation, and the excessive burden of weight gain might lead to complications. Although each mother should be individually advised by her obstetrician, medical men generally agree that continuing one's normal diet without desserts is sensible.

The question is often asked if the use of tobacco and liquor during pregnancy is harmful. As has already been reported in Chapter Three, studies dating from 1960 and on indicate that expected babies of smoking mothers have a lower birthrate and a higher rate of prematurity than babies of those mother who do not smoke. "Alcohol used to excess may have a depressant effect unfavorable to the fetus' normal functioning after birth."[5]

Bathing and Rest

Doctors feel that bathing (shower or tub) is usually not harmful; but they caution against becoming overheated or chilled. If any problems occur, the doctor should be contacted. The mother may need extra rest at night and naps during the day. She should avoid becoming overtired.

Sexual Relations

Obstetricians generally advise that sexual relations can be enjoyed during pregnancy. In fact, some wives enjoy them even more than at other times, because they now "have no fear of becoming pregnant." Doctors have conflicting opinions when it comes to linking sexual relations with possible miscarriages. Dr. Seidman makes a very interesting observation concerning this problem. He says case histories show that the pregnant wives of servicemen, whose husbands were ordered to overseas duties, showed symptoms related to threatening miscarriage due to being emotionally upset. He states that women ". . . who have shown some tendency to premature labor or miscarriage . . . 'should' . . . keep all forms of sex stimulation to a minimum. This is because strong emotions of any kind seem to have the ability to stimulate uterine contractions. This can sometimes result in the threat of miscarriage."[6]

Doctors disagree as to whether engaging in intercourse is unsafe during the final weeks of pregnancy, consequently, the wife should dis-

---

[5]Bowman, Henry, *Marriage for Moderns*, New York: McGraw Hill, 1970, 6th Edition, p. 468.
[6]Seidman, Theodore R., and Albert, Marvin H., *Becoming a Mother*, Greenwich, Conn.: Fawcett Publications, Inc., 1963, p. 112.

cuss this carefully with her obstetrician. However, there are some points on which there is general agreement.

1. If bleeding, pain, or cramps follow intercourse, it should be discontinued until the doctor is consulted.

2. Gentleness should be exercised in intercourse at the time when menstruation would normally occur.

3. During the later stages of pregnancy, coital positions should be adjusted to avoid causing the wife discomfort.

4. Both the wife's and husband's sexual desire might increase during the third to sixth months of pregnancy and wane during the last three months.

5. Loss of sex interest on the part of either partner should be discussed frankly between the couple, so it will not be misinterpreted as a loss of love.

Clothing

Yesterday's grandmothers used to go into seclusion when pregnancy occurred. This was partly because they were embarrassed and also because "they did not have a thing to wear." Today there is no reason for such behavior.

Surveys show that the maternity clothes of today are extremely chic. Some of the dresses can be made larger with the pull of a seam string. These same seams can be restitched later to make a smart postmaternity outfit. Nearly three fourths of today's maternity apparel is one-piece. The remaining two-piece outfits feature short jackets which can be used as plain overblouses after the baby is born. Loose clothing is recommended for better circulation.

The woman's wardrobe should also contain articles that safeguard her from strains and falls. Unless there are unusual foot problems, firm shoes with medium heels will give adequate support and minimize the likeliness of losing balance and falling. Backaches can sometimes be eased by using a maternity girdle that lifts up and reduces the strain on the muscles of the back.

Social Activities

If the expectant mother is in average health, mild exercise will help her relax physically and buoy her up emotionally. Walking, playing golf, easy swimming, and moderate dancing are all splendid forms of exercise. The rule to apply when engaging in these activities is to avoid anything too vigorous that might cause fatigue.

The wife and her husband should go out socially and keep themselves alert and interesting. Travel is permissible, mostly during early pregnancy, but long, bumpy, tiring trips should be avoided. The doctor should be consulted before taking a trip by air.

Positive Thinking

There are two schools of thought regarding the wife's moods and whims during pregnancy. One is that now she knows she can be catered to and get her own way. The other is that for the good of her body and soul she needs unusual foods and tender care.

It is at this time that her husband will play one of his most important roles. If he is oversolicitous, he may weary his wife and make her feel sorry for herself with his repeated "Be careful, dear! Remember your condition. Are you all right?"

On the other hand, he must realize that his wife may need more affection than usual and also may have become a bit more sensitive in developing hurt feelings. Dr. Caplan, in discussing the pregnant wife's emotional attitude, says, "Instead of being the giving person in the home, actively attending to the needs of others, she feels that need to sit around and be waited on. . . . If she receives enough affection during pregnancy, she can give out enough affection to the baby. Those women who are deprived during pregnancy later have a tendency to deprive their babies."[7]

So, the husband, although he may think his wife's behavior is a bit peculiar, should give her plenty of affection. If she asks for difficult-to-get strawberries at 2 a.m., he should do his best to satisfy her (unless he feels she is downright cranky). Above all, he should let his wife know how delighted he is that she is carrying his baby and pay serious attention to the things that worry and concern her. He should let her know that she is still his attractive sweetheart even though her figure *is* losing its curves, and tell her, as some Indian tribes believe, that she is not losing her figure at all, but is simply "standing behind her baby."

---

[7]Caplan, Gerald, M.D., "Practical Steps for the Family Physician in the Prevention of Emotional Disorder," *Journal of the American Medical Association*, July 25, 1959.

HOW THE BABY GROWS IN THE UTERUS

When a new life starts to develop within the wife's body, it sets off a marvelous series of events. This process begins when two tiny specks of living matter unite. The ovum, which is about the size of a pinpoint or even tinier than the specks in a sunbeam which float through a window, is met in one of the Fallopian tubes by a cell which is so small that it cannot be seen by the naked eye. This sperm cell, an infinitesimal bit of life, has undergone a rigorous and a tortuous journey in order to meet the ovum. After having been deposited in the vagina with several hundred million other sperms, it and some others have found their way into the mouth of the uterus and waged a valiant battle to survive and reach their destination. Since a comparatively small number of sperm cells reach the ovum, it is understandable why a large number must be deposited in the vagina for fertilization to occur. Most of the sperms die before ever getting past the vagina. After one sperm has reached and penetrated the ovum, the others present are usually stopped from entering and they gradually disintegrate.

The Zygote

The fertilized ovum is called a zygote. The fusing of the nuclei of the two cells forms a combination of genes that possess all of the potential qualities with which parents can endow their child. These genes found in the twenty-three chromosomes of each nucleus determine the baby's sex, the color of its hair and eyes, the shape of its nose, and all other individual characteristics.

Next, the zygote begins to divide, first into two cells, then into four, eight, sixteen, and so forth (a process called mitosis). As it divides, it is moved along in the Fallopian tube by the whip-like motion of tiny hair-like cilia which line the tube's interior surface. There is also a theory that the ovum is moved along by peristalsis (tiny muscular movements of the tube). By the time the fertilized ovum reaches the uterus (an estimated three to seven days) it has become a cluster of cells called a morula. When it reaches the uterus, it remains free for a few days. However, processes are at work which are dividing the cell cluster into specialized parts.

The Placenta and the Umbilical Cord

One layer of cells becomes a disk-like structure called the placenta. The root-like projections of the placenta (villi) imbed themselves in the

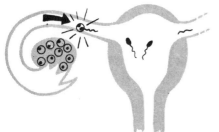

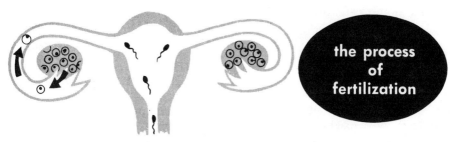

the process of fertilization

1. Egg cell leaves ovary   *2. Sperm cells enter uterus*

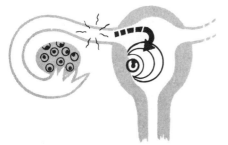

4. Sperm enters egg

3. Egg cell and sperm unite in tube   *5. Fertilizes egg in tube*

6. Fertilized egg enters uterus, attaches to wall   *7. Cell begins to divide and grow into baby*

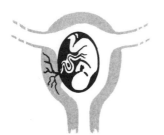

8. Baby grows, fed by placenta

—Illustration taken from "What Teenagers Want to Know" by Levinsohn and Kelly. Published by Budlong Press Company, 5428 North Viriginia Ave., Chicago, Ill. 60625.

PLATE VI

uterine lining (endometrium). Oxygen and nutritive substances from the mother's blood pass through the villi into the baby's blood to provide for the child's growth and development. The waste products of the developing infant are also disposed of through a reversal of this process and are removed from the mother's body by her excretory organs. The connecting channel between the mother and the baby through which food and waste products move back and forth is the umbilical cord. This cord is made up of two arteries and one vein which are enclosed by a membrane.

The Protecting Sac

The embryo develops from the center cells, the so-called formative cells. These are the *endoderm* (inner layer cells) which contributes to inner body parts such as the respiratory and digestive systems; the *ectoderm* (outer layer cells) which will develop into skin, hair, and nervous tissue; and the *mesoderm* (middle layer cells) which will become blood, marrow, bone, muscle, kidney, and gonad. Then a membrane encircles it which is called the amniotic sac. This sac fills with from 1 to 4 pints of amniotic fluid. Thus, the fetus lives in an aquatic state and is anchored by the umbilical cord and the placenta. The fetus is further protected by the chorionic membrane and the placenta which combine to form the outer wall of the sac within which it develops. Consequently, the baby as it grows and develops is guarded from outside shocks by the amniotic fluid and the sac which surrounds it. They also keep the baby in a constant temperature.

Progressive Development of the Baby

The growth of the baby is a fascinating process which will be summarized very briefly. When the new life is at the two-week stage, it is named an embryo. After two months it is called a fetus.

Pattern of Development

One Month—Size about ¼ inch long. Weight, tiny fraction of an ounce. Growth characteristics—heart beginning to form and beat—blood circulating—eyes and ears beginning to develop.

Two Months—Size about 1¼ inches long. Weight about 1/14 ounce. Growth characteristics—big head, face more nearly human with eyes, nose, and mouth—limbs, fingers and toes beginning to form—genital organs have appeared.

Three Months—Size slightly over 3 inches long. Weight about one ounce—teeth are developing—vocal cords are formed.

Four Months—Size, 6 to 8 inches long. Weight about 5½ ounces. Growth characteristics—hair beginning to grow on skin and perhaps on head. Eyes, ears, and nose are well formed. Eyebrows and eyelashes appear. Doctor can detect heartbeat with stethoscope. Mother may feel fluttering of its tiny limbs.

Five Months—Size, 10 to 12 inches long. Weight about 1 pound. Growth characteristics—further refinement of features. Mother can feel baby move.

Six Months—Size about 14 inches long. Weight about 2 pounds. Growth characteristics—has the appearance of a baby. Skin wrinkled, due to lack of fat deposits.

Seven Months—Size about 16 inches long. Weight about 3 pounds. Growth characteristics—central nervous system developed enough so that survival is possible if birth should occur.

Eight Months—Size about 18 inches long. Weight about 6 pounds. Growth characteristics—skin has smoothed out.

Nine Months—Size about 20 inches long. Weight, 7 to 8 pounds. Growth characteristics—baby fully developed. Full term is 280 days.

DIAGNOSIS AND TREATMENT OF THE BABY BEFORE BIRTH

Great progress has been made in the treatment of the unborn baby since such procedures as amniocentisis have been developed. This process involves inserting a needle through the walls of the abdomen and the uterus in order to withdraw a sample of the amniotic fluid and examine the cells that it contains. Such conditions as Rh blood disease, respiratory difficulties and genetic disorders can be detected, and possible treatment instituted.

Two severe conditions that can be diagnosed by amniocentisis are Tay-Sach's Disease, a genetic disorder characterized by mental retardation and blindness and a chromosomal aberration called Down's syndrome (Mongolism).

Other conditions present in the unborn baby can be detected with newly developed methods of obtaining and staining chromosomes for

PLATE VII
THE GROWTH OF THE BABY DURING THE
NINE MONTHS OF PREGNANCY

(Actual Size)

(Actual Size)

The First Two Weeks   The First and Second Month

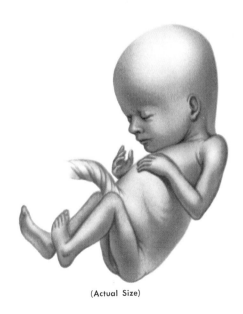

(Actual Size)

The Third and Fourth Month

The Fifth and Sixth Month

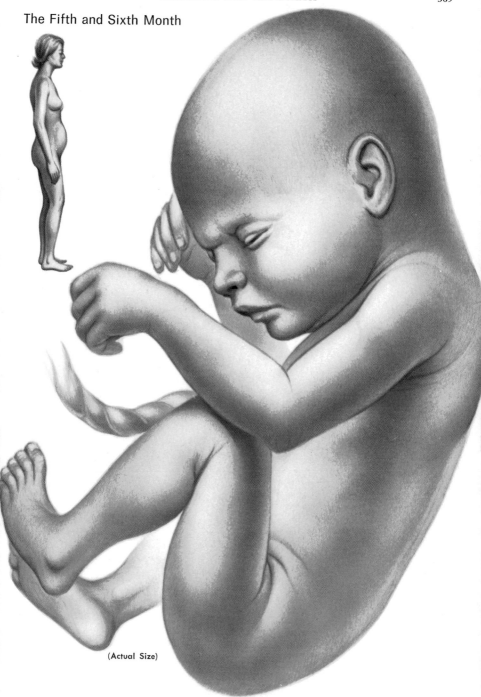

(Actual Size)

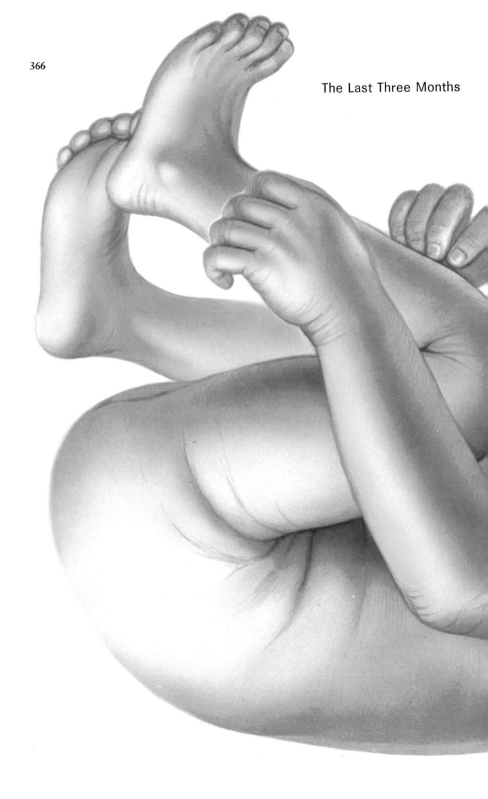

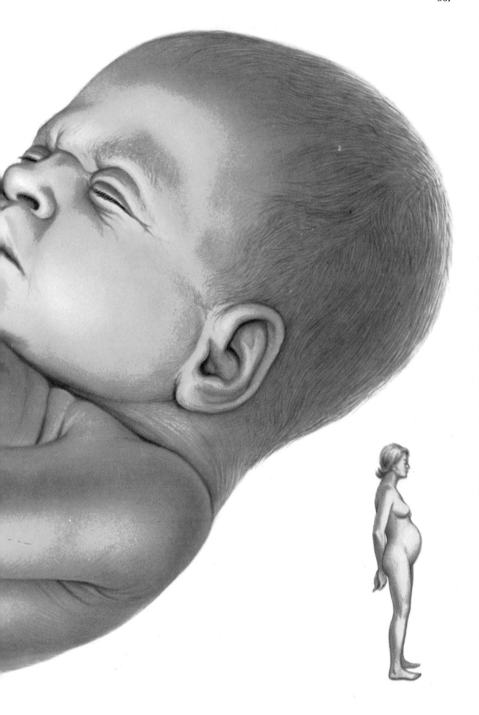

study. One that has attracted considerable attention is an abnormal arrangement of chromosomes in which a fertilized ovum has an XYY syndrome. Kogan states that the tentative results of recent research "indicate a startling association between the XYY disorder and criminal insanity. Richard Speck, the 1966 murderer of eight Chicago nurses was found to have the XYY disorder. . . . Only a portion of XYY males develop criminal behavior. But it does appear much more commonly in prison populations." He states further, "Fathers and children of XYY are no more likely to have abnormal chromosomes than the average person in the population. The condition is innate, but not hereditary." Kogan emphasizes that such findings are tentative and "all that can be now indicated is this: possibly some people with an XYY chromosomal structure may be more susceptible to certain kinds of social stress than people without such a chromosomal structure."[8] Continued research in this area of diagnosis and treatment of troublesome conditions in the unborn baby should gradually make it possible to eliminate many of the childhood disorders that have previously been present at birth.

THE BIRTH OF THE BABY

The full-term fetus takes about 280 days (10 lunar months) to develop. About two weeks before the onset of labor, it settles down lower in the pelvis and begins to enter the birth canal. This process is called "lightening." By this time, the structures in the lower part of the woman's body will have become less rigid, so that they will not be so resistant to the dilation of the cervix. It is thought that hormones and other factors cause the longitudinal muscles of the uterus to begin contracting and pushing the baby down against the cervix. These first contractions may be very slight and cause little discomfort. The wife should call her doctor when the contractions have become established or if the sac of water breaks. He will usually advise her to go to the hospital if he feels that the described condition indicates imminent presentation.

Registering at the Hospital

The husband can be of considerable help when the time comes to go to the hospital. He can make the necessary financial arrangements with

[8]Kogan, Benjamin A., *Human Sexual Expression*, New York: Harcourt Brace Jovanovich, 1973, pp. 155, 156.

the office and attend to all of those little details that are necessary to help smooth the procedure.

Occasionally, a young husband becomes a bit too objective in thinking about childbirth and does not give his wife all of the emotional support which she needs. The writer remembers a graduate student who drove his labor-involved wife to the curb of the hospital grounds, kissed her good-by, said "Good luck, Honey," and drove back home to resume his sleep. His anxiety or interest was sufficient to motivate his phoning his wife the following afternoon to inquire if the baby had arrived. Fortunately, it had, without undue complications. However, his young wife carried a hurt look in her eyes for weeks after the incident.

THE THREE STAGES OF LABOR
First Stage

During the first stage of labor, the cervix must dilate sufficiently until the mouth of the uterus is open enough for the baby to pass through. This can be a trying period for the wife, as she may feel frustrated because she seems unable to speed things up. However, she will have an experienced team of doctors and nurses attending her, who will do everything possible to assist in delivering the baby. But, she will also be able to do *something*. First, she should remember that during this stage of labor, two sets of involuntary muscles in her uterus will be busily engaged in helping the baby come into the world. The longitudinal muscles will be contracting, in order to push the baby down to the birth canal. The sphincter muscles, which make up a circular band of involuntary muscles in the cervix that helped to keep the baby safely in the uterus while it was growing, will now be reversing their role. They will respond to the pressure of the baby by relaxing and allowing the mouth of the uterus to open up, if the wife can relax along with them. However, if she becomes tense and afraid, these muscles will tighten. She should try to remember what her doctor told her during pregnancy regarding meeting a contraction by lying back, relaxing and engaging in deep, slow abdominal breathing. Such behavior should make the birth easier.

Second Stage

When the second stage of labor begins, the cervix opens up completely and the baby is ready to leave the uterus and pass through the birth canal and be born. He usually proceeds with his head first. (About

95 percent of babies do.) The other 5 percent enter the canal feet or buttocks first, or in some other manner (breech presentation).

Normally, the baby cries as soon as it is born, which in turn fills its lungs with air. Whether the baby cries because it is happy to be outside of its mother's body or because it fears facing the cruel world, no one really knows. A number of theories have been presented to explain the baby's thinking when he first makes his debut; but, until we are clever enough to produce babies who can talk at birth, we will have no definite answer. If the baby does not cry spontaneously, the obstetrician has modern scientific ways to start its breathing without resorting to spanking, plunging it into hot and cold water or using other antiquated methods.

Shortly after the baby is born, the doctor ties or clamps the umbilical cord in two places near the baby's body and severs it between the two ties. Silver nitrate or an equally effective substance is put into its eyes to guard against infection. He or she is cleaned up, so a proper introduction can be made to relatives and friends. Also, identification steps are taken so the parents won't get their child confused with someone else's baby.

Third Stage

Anywhere from a few minutes to a half an hour after the baby is born, some more contractions occur and the rest of the cord and the placenta (afterbirth) are discharged from the uterus. The doctor examines the placenta carefully to be sure that it has all been expelled. Then he performs any other necessary details and the new mother is wheeled back to her room.

Methods of Relieving Pain

Many women fear childbirth because they feel anxious about the possible pain they may experience. It would be unrealistic to state that an obstetrician can guarantee his patient complete absence of pain during delivery, but he can assure her that many things can be done to make her as comfortable as possible. Ever since society decided that it isn't woman's lot to suffer pain during childbirth (in 1561, in Scotland, a woman named Eufaine MacLayne was put to death because she employed medicine to relieve pain during childbirth) efforts have been made to develop pharmaceuticals to control pain. There are four general types available. Analgesics, that relieve pain; amnesics which help the patient to forget pain; anesthetics which produce insensitivity to pain and often unconsciousness; and sedatives which induce sleep and may also produce amnesia. These

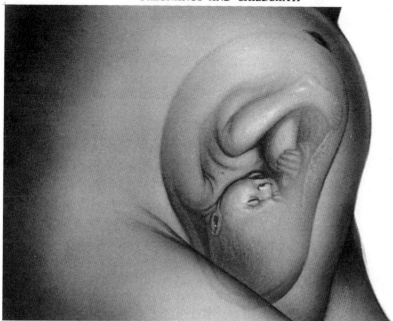

PLATE VIII

THE POSITION OF THE BABY IN THE UTERUS

PLATE IX

BEFORE LABOR BEGINS

LABOR · CERVIX DILATING
and BAG OF WATERS

PLATE X
LABOR—FIRST STAGE

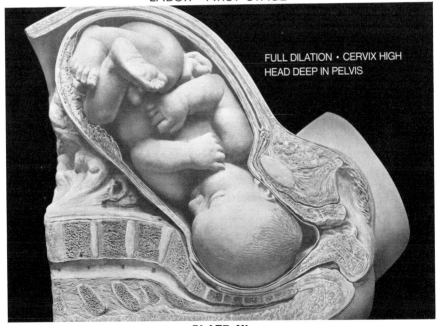

FULL DILATION · CERVIX HIGH
HEAD DEEP IN PELVIS

PLATE XI
LABOR—SECOND STAGE

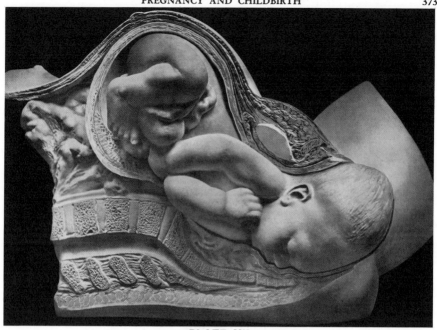

PLATE XII
LABOR—CROWNING OF BABY'S HEAD

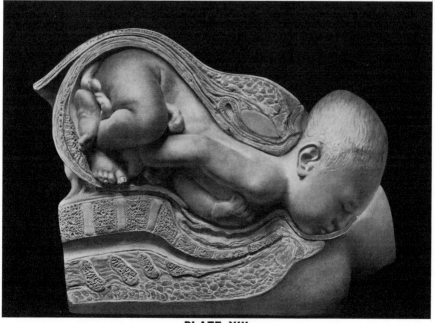

PLATE XIII
LABOR—SECOND STAGE—NEARLY COMPLETED

PLATE XIV
BIRTH

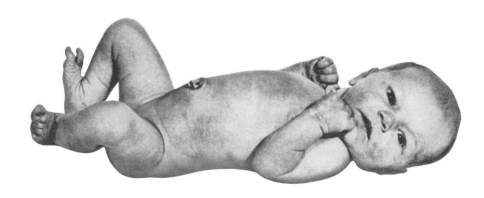

PLATE XV
NEWBORN BABY

drugs are administered by inhalation or injection. When injection is used, different areas may be desensitized such as the cervix, vagina or spinal region. The obstetrician should explain the technique he feels would be most suitable during the woman's prebirth visits to him, and a mutually satisfying procedure should be agreed upon.

In recent years, it has become common to use other methods in addition to drugs in order to relieve the pain of childbirth. The pioneer in this field was Grantley Dick Read who believed that dispelling the fear of childbirth by teaching the wife what was happening to her body and instructing her in how to breathe, relax and control the muscles involved with delivery would eliminate much of the pain. His concept called "natural childbirth" suggests that delivering a baby is a natural function that should not require the use of drugs.[9]

Read's ideas started other approaches such as hypnosis and group therapy as preparation for childbirth. At the present time, the approach which seems to be growing in popularity is patterned after a method introduced to our culture in 1951 by Dr. Ferdinand Lamaze. This method sees the wife and husband as a team who participate together in the birth experience. They attend prenatal classes together and learn about exercises, breathing and muscle control during labor and delivery. The husband stays with his wife during labor and in the delivery room and uses his knowledge in practical ways. All obstetricians do not go along with this method as some feel the husband "gets in the way" more than he helps.

Summaries of the philosophies and the procedures used by the maternity divisions of two hospitals that have adopted the husband-wife participation method are reprinted here to show the possible advantages of such an approach.

The Abbott-Northwestern Hospital, Minneapolis, Minnesota[10]

PHYSICIAN BELIEVES TEAM CONCEPT OF CHILDBIRTH STIMULATES GROWTH IN MARRIAGE

Hospitals house many of the experiences that once took place in the home. Childbirth was in days past characterized by the complete exposure

[9]Read, Grantley Dick, *Childbirth Without Fear*, New York: Harper and Row, 1944.
[10]Grosscup, Jeffrey P., "Physician Believes Team Concept of Childbirth Stimulates Growth in Marriage," *The Consultant*, Abbott-Northwestern Hospital Corporation, January 1972, p. 8. Reprinted by permission.

of children and relatives to the events of labor and delivery. As medicine became more sophisticated, childbirth went to the hospital.

Dr. Henry C. Meeker, obstetrician on the Abbott-Northwestern Staff, believes that though childbirth belongs in the hospital, hospitals and physicians need to give back to the family some of the human elements formerly associated with childbirth. He does this, as do other physicians, by allowing husband and wife to participate together in the tremendous experience of birth.

Labor and delivery rooms, once the exclusive preserve of the wife and her attendant medical personnel, have, in recent years, frequently seen the husband who has been extremely helpful during labor and delivery in being able to keep his wife calm. To do this the husband has been seated at the head of his wife during childbirth.

The question of allowing fathers in the labor and/or delivery room is still a matter of controversy among physicians.

Dr. Meeker said that Abbott was one of the first hospitals in this area to allow the father to participate in childbirth. He said that several of the dozen or so obstetricians then on the Abbott Staff had worked with fathers in the delivery room at the University of Minnesota Hospital and, because of their favorable reaction to it, the obstetrics department members at Abbott agreed among themselves to allow it.

Dr. Meeker feels that for a hospital to individualize obstetric care and allow fathers to participate in delivery, requires excellent nursing care and a high nurse/patient ratio. He added that it requires more time and added effort on the part of doctors and nurses to get the father set up for delivery and among other things, time to answer their questions.

Dr. Meeker feels that it can be a meaningful experience for a husband to witness the birth of his child, particularly if the husband has gone through a childbirth education course with his wife, is knowledgeable about the events of delivery and can actively participate and give support to his wife.

In his practice Dr. Meeker said that the husband's presence and witness to the birth has generally been a heart-warming experience for the couple.

If the woman is not put to sleep during childbirth, the ease with which she has the delivery depends on her proficiency in breathing techniques and relaxing exercises. The psychology is that by concentrating on relaxing, a woman's fears and associated tensions of labor are reduced and in doing so the pain is reduced.

According to Dr. Meeker, the husband can be given an active role of coaching his wife in breathing techniques, timing the contractions and keeping her as comfortable as possible. Subconsciously his job is to keep the level of distractions high to keep his wife's mind off the contractions. Through conversation and his reassuring words this is attained.

Dr. Meeker believes that allowing the husband in the labor and delivery room is a privilege extended to them and not a requirement. He allows it only when husband and wife earnestly desire it and when he thinks they will find the experience meaningful.

He has found that when the husband witnessed the delivery, his dramatic involvement helped him to better identify with his newborn. Dr. Meeker also finds the team concept of childbirth stimulates growth in the marriage since the husband and wife are working together towards a successful goal.

"I believe it helps marriages," said Dr. Meeker. "In some cases it is the first active partnership they have engaged in during their marriage and as such I think it prepares them to reach other goals that they share."

Of the five percent of births that result in complications, Dr. Meeker said that the husbands attending such deliveries generally were confident that everything possible was being done to fight off the complications.

Dr. Meeker stressed that the husband's presence at childbirth is uniquely the decision of each couple. He encourages the father to join his wife on an office visit in order to meet him and be assured that he isn't being coaxed into something he doesn't particularly want to do. Also, many women would just as soon go through childbirth without the husband physically there.

For many couples there has been no greater joy than to witness together the birth of their child and to hear its first cry. Many women would have been unable to deliver their children while awake and to actively participate had it not been for the support, encouragement and guidance of their husbands.

The University of Minnesota Hospital, Minneapolis, Minnesota
Parent Education Program[11]

"Our philosophy and objectives are based on the belief that having a baby is a shared and prepared experience. Our primary emphasis is on the family-centered approach. Much class time is discussion of both the mother's and father's roles during pregnancy, labor and delivery, in the hospital and in return to the home as a new family unit."

—Betty Lou Hogberg, *Staff Member*

Note: Much additional helpful material is given to the prospective parents that is not printed here, the entire approach is oriented toward informing them about what happens during labor and delivery and what procedures are used in the hospital, so they both will feel comfortable and happy with the experience.

UNIVERSITY OF MINNESOTA
PARENT EDUCATION PROGRAM
LABOR AND DELIVERY GUIDE FOR EXPECTANT PARENTS

This guide is a basic fact sheet on labor and delivery, including the normal physical and emotional changes experienced by many women during this phase of the maternity experience. The expectant mother may not feel all of these reactions but it will give you some idea of what to expect during labor and delivery. It will also serve as a guide and reference for the father-coach or coach. We hope it will be of value to you as you participate in this very exciting and unique experience.

BEFORE LABOR BEGINS

You may notice:

1. *Lightening*—The baby will "lower" or settle down into your pelvis; you may notice that it is easier to breathe but there is more pressure on the bladder. With first babies, this may occur 2-4 weeks before the baby comes, with subsequent pregnancies this comes closer to labor.

2. *Braxton-Hicks contractions* may increase. (These are painless uterine contractions felt over the lower abdominal area, occurring all during pregnancy but may be felt more in last months of pregnancy.)

---

[11]Reprinted by permission of the Parent Education Program of the University of Minnesota Hospital. Material made available by Betty Lou Hogberg.

3. *Suggestions:*

    a. Be sure your suitcase is ready.

    b. Try to have a relaxed schedule and get plenty of rest in the last weeks of pregnancy.

    c. Do exercises *DAILY* as taught in class.

LABOR

Labor is the process in which the cervix is opened by periodic, rhythmical contractions and the baby, placenta and membranes are expelled.

SIGNS OF LABOR

The following should help you distinguish between *false* and *true* labor.

False Labor is identified by the irregular, intermittent contractions (Braxton-Hicks) which become stronger and may cause discomfort. These may occur as early as 3-4 weeks before the end of pregnancy. The false labor contractions are felt mainly in the lower part of the abdomen and groin and do not increase much in intensity, frequency or duration. They may sometimes be relieved by walking.

True Labor is characterized by:

1. Regular contractions (may be felt as menstrual cramps, gas, backache, pelvic pressure, or tightening down low in the area of the pubic bone). The contractions may start by being thirty minutes apart *or* fifteen/to twenty minutes apart *or* even start as close together as ten *or* five minutes apart. Early contractions usually last about 15-30 seconds. As contractions continue, they will come closer together (the interval between will shorten), they will last longer in duration (30-45-60 sec.) and increase in intensity (more discomfort.)

2. *Rupture of membranes or breaking of the bag of water.* (This may occur either as a sudden gush or as a slow trickle of fluid). The fluid is odorless, clear and the breaking does not cause any pain. (There may be a feeling of release of pressure in the vaginal area.) Rupture of membranes may or may not be accompanied by contractions and sometimes membranes do not rupture until later in labor or may be ruptured by the doctor. You should always call and come to the hospital when membranes rupture.

3. A pinkish discharge of blood-tinged mucous may appear. This occurs as the mucous plug is released from the opening cervix and is a sign that labor may soon begin. (The discharge sometimes is confused with normal increased vaginal discharge during last month of pregnancy. You don't have to come to the hospital, just be aware of condition). Any significant amount of bleeding should be reported to your doctor or call the hospital.

Comments:

1. Do *not* eat any solid foods after labor has begun. You may have clear liquids such as water, tea, plain jello, broth, or coffee.

2. If this is your first baby, you should call and come to the hospital when your contractions are 5 minutes apart. For second and subsequent pregnancies call and come in when contractions are about 10 minutes apart, or as directed by your doctor.

3. When labor starts, complete the packing of your suitcase and put it by the door. If labor starts at night, mother should try to continue resting. If labor begins during the day, do relaxing and diversional things such as watch TV, read, knit, etc. It is important to conserve energy and strength for labor and delivery.

STAGES OF LABOR

1. *First Stage* is from the onset of labor to 10 cm. or complete dilatation of the cervix. This subdivides into three (3) phases:

    a. Early or latent phase—0-4 cm. dilatation

    b. Accelerator—4-8 cm. dilatation

    c. Transition—8-10 cm. dilatation

2. *Second Stage* begins with the complete dilatation of the cervix and ends with the delivery of the baby.

3. *Third Stage* is the delivery of the placenta and "afterbirth."

4. *Fourth Stage* is the immediate postpartum period.

LABOR ROOM CARE

The expectant mother and father will be welcomed to the labor and delivery room area by one of our nurses. All procedures will be explained to you and our immediate care will consist of obtaining information on your labor. Care will consist of your temperature, pulse, respirations, blood pressure, baby's heart tones, a one third or one half perineal shave according to doctor's orders, and an enema (depending on your progress). A vaginal exam will also be done to evaluate progress. The nurse or the doctor on call will want to know when your contractions began, how frequently they are coming, how long they last, if bag of water is broken, the last time you ate, allergies or sensitivities, if you are planning to breast or bottle feed, room preference, religion. The fetal monitors will be explained to you (see reference sheet on the monitors) and will be put in place as labor progresses. An intravenous feeding will also be started according to doctor's orders, to supply fluids for your body as labor progresses.

The nursing and medical staff will be close by and continually checking your progress and assisting you as labor progresses. Please feel free to ask any questions or let us know in any ways in which we can be of assistance to you.

GUIDE FOR THE HUSBANDS—COACH
Prepare—Practice—Plan Ahead

1. Learn and practice relaxation techniques with your wife. Know how to check for relaxation. Study how each breathing technique looks and sounds so you will be able to coach, encourage, and advise her during labor.
   Exercise should be practiced *every* day the last two months before delivery.

2. Encourage your wife to get plenty of sleep and rest the last weeks before her due date. Try to do things together which will be fun and relaxing but not too tiring.

3. *If labor begins at night,* encourage your wife to relax, rest, and sleep. A backrub or cup of tea may be soothing. You should rest some also. *If labor begins during the day* and your wife is well rested, she may continue with light activities.

4. *Help time the contractions.* Determine the *frequency* (the number of minutes from the beginning of one contraction to the beginning of the next) and the *duration* (the number of seconds each contraction lasts). Call your private doctor and report on what is taking place.

IN THE HOSPITAL—LABOR AND DELIVERY

1. Our labor area nursing staff will always be close by while your wife is in labor. Many times they will come into the labor room to sit with you both during labor but they may also be assisting other mothers and will need to assist you on a less continuous basis. During this time the nurses will assist in making the mother more comfortable, assessing the state and progress of the labor and the baby's progress. The nursing staff are there to help in every way possible to see that labor and delivery will be a safe and satisfying experience for you both. Feel free to ask any questions or express your feelings.

2. Try to remain with your wife during labor, if at all possible, since she will need companionship and encouragement; she should not be left alone for any length of time. Assist her through *Progressive Relaxation* and coach her on breathing techniques. Keep track of frequency and duration of contractions, sharing the information with your wife. During a contraction, tell her when 15-30-45-seconds, etc., are over.

3. *Encourage, praise,* and *reassure* her. She will need reminders in spite of long hours of practice.

   A calm, subdued atmosphere will foster relaxation. Try to remember to talk quietly but in a firm and caring way.

4. Many mothers become very warm and dry in the mouth during labor. A light sponging of her face and neck with a cool, moist washcloth will often feel good. Sucking on a wet washcloth, ice chips or sour lollipop, is helpful for mouth dryness as is chapstick, Vaseline, etc., for dry lips.

5. If the mother is having backaches or back labor a good firm hand massaging this area often feels good. (Talcum powder or lotion will prevent skin soreness.)

   Encourage her to be relaxed by utilizing comfortable positions. (The supported back relaxation or ¾ side rest positions as taught in class.)

6. *Emotional reactions* change during labor; in early labor, your wife will probably remain cheerful and enjoy talking between contractions; as labor progresses, she will become more serious and may not

wish to talk. Respect her moods since a woman in labor is very sensitive to those around her.

7. If your wife needs something to help her to relax or to help relieve pain, be sure to communicate this to the nurse or doctor. They will be happy to assist, and may administer a safe dose of medication which can help make her more comfortable.

   After medication, many women doze between contractions and may be confused when the contractions begin again. She should be spoken to in a calm manner.

8. If your wife gets the "urge to push," call the nurse so she can check your wife's progress in labor. Then she will let her know when she may begin to push.

9. When your wife goes to the delivery room, you may wait in the father's waiting room unless you are planning on accompanying her. The staff will keep you informed of her progress.

10. If you choose to be with your wife during delivery, you will be required to change into a "scrub suit," cap, and mask. In the delivery room you can observe and assist as needed at the head of the delivery table, beside or behind your wife's head. You will be able to support her back as she pushes, if desired. You may be given a stool on which to sit. Remain in the place designated for you until requested to move.

    We sincerely hope this will be a satisfying and happy experience for you both. Your comments and suggestions are always appreciated.

LABOR AND DELIVERY GUIDE FOR EXPECTANT PARENTS

STAGE	PHYSICAL CHANGES— WHAT IS HAPPENING	MOTHER'S REACTION/ PARTICIPATION	COACHING—SUPPORT— OTHER HELPS
FIRST STAGE Early or latent Phase Cervix effacing 0-2-3 cm.	Contractions are regular and progressive. Come to hospital as directed.	Excitement, relief, may be talkative—should rest between contractions, may read, watch TV during contractions, use slow deep breathing.	Help time contractions. Husband or other companion offers diversion and calm, relaxed environment.
3-4 cm.	Contractions becoming stronger and closer together. Approximately 5 min. apart lasting 30-60 sec.	Becoming more uncomfortable. She becomes more preoccupied with self and labor. Little or no talking or walking desired. More dependent on helpers. Use total relaxation and slow, abdominal sleep breathing or abdominal "bulge" techniques. Side or back relaxation positions as desired. Effleurage as helpful.	Needs continuous companionship, much reassurance and encouragement. Keep environment quiet and relaxed. (Backrub—low—may feel good.)
Approximately 8 Hours			May use pillows as needed.
Acceleration or **LATE First Stage** 4-8 cm.	Contractions build up faster to peak, longer duration and closer together. (Approximately 3 min. apart, lasting 50-60 sec.)	She doubts her ability to cope with contractions. Should continue to use relaxation. Breathing techniques which may be used: a. steady rate chest br. b. acc-dec. chest breathing. c. some may find abdominal bulge helpful.	She needs **frequent** encouragement **and** firm, calm coaching on relaxation and control of breathing. Cool cloth on face feels good—lips moistened—medication as needed. Offer back rubs and/or pressure **as** mother desires. Remind mother to: a. rest/relax completely between contractions. b. take full cleansing breaths before/after each cont. c. take one contraction at a time. d. change position frequently and **empty** bladder frequently.
Approximately 4-3 Hours			

8-10 cm. (Shortest Phase)	Contractions are long, strong and close together (may seem almost continuous).	Mother **may** be hypersensitive, irritable, short tempered, restless, discouraged, uncommunicative, bewildered, lose modesty, unable to relax. She **may** have trembling of extremities, momentary nausea with vomiting, leg cramps, hiccups, perspiration, backache, may feel hot or cold, cheeks may appear flushed.	Coach **should accept** any of the mother's reactions in a calm manner. **She needs constant** reassurance and encouragement, through each contraction.
Nearing the end of transition.	May feel "urge to push" before fully dilated or low rectal pressure may be falsely interpreted as urge to push.		Remind her to: a. keep eyes open and concentrate. b. blow or puff out to prevent pushing. Notify staff about her pushing urge.
Approx. ½-1 Hour		May be confused, overwhelmed or frightened about push sensation. Use pant-blow techniques to combat urge to push by increased concentration.	
SECOND STAGE Pushing or Expulsive stage (Delivery)	Baby moves gradually through birth canal. Contractions remain strong, but slightly further apart (3-5 min. lasting 60-90 sec.) Rectal bulging.	She may have irresistible urge to push, grunting on exhalation.	Rest between contractions. Needs guidance with contractions and pushing.
	As baby's head moves down birth canal, may produce feeling of tremendous fullness, groin pressure, burning feeling or splitting sensation.	Push with contractions as directed—remember to relax pelvic floor.	**In Delivery Room**
	If first baby move to delivery room when crowning about 2 cm. If second, or more, mother moved to del. room when about 8 cm. dilated or before complete.	Pressure on rectum may cause anxiety and reluctance to push.	Remind her to: a. relax perineum. b. pant when instructed to stop pushing.
	As baby's head crowns it causes numbing of the perineum by pressure on the area and slowing of circulation.	Totally absorbed in job of pushing-relaxing, excited, impatient, may be strong desire to push. Pant as directed by doctor, may watch in mirror.	
	Episiotomy performed.		
	Head born, shoulders delivered one at a time and baby slides out easily.	Relief, joy; Wants to know: 1. "What is it?" (sex) 2. "Is it OK?" (Order may be reversed!)	Share mother's joy and excitement. Praise her accomplishments.

STAGE	WHAT IS HAPPENING	MOTHER'S REACTIONS/ PARTICIPATION	COACHING—SUPPORT— OTHER HELPS
THIRD STAGE Placental stage	A few more contractions and the placenta is delivered. (Usually 5-10 min. after delivery of baby.)	May need to push as directed. Usually tired but happy — thirsty — may be hungry — eager to see baby.	Observe mother, see baby.
	Medication given which helps uterus contract down. Episiotomy repaired.		
FOURTH STAGE Postpartum observation	Moved to Recovery room for 2 hours. Blood pressure, tone of uterus, stitches and blood flow checked frequently.	Rest. Urine voiding checked.	May visit with wife. Rest.
	May have something to eat and drink per doctor's order.	Thirsty, perhaps hungry.	

SUGGESTIONS FOR "BACK LABOR"

1. Your breathing techniques should remain the same whether labor is in the abdomen or back.
2. You will find that the side lying position is more comfortable than back lying because it removes the weight of your baby from your spine. (Lie on your side, with knees bent, with top leg supported by a pillow and drawn up slightly higher than the other leg.
3. You may want to sit up at a 90° angle or lean forward over a pillow.
4. Pelvic rocking may feel good.
5. Husbands—coaches can apply firm pressure to lower back by using palm of hand or a fist. Massage using talcum or lotion may feel good.
6. Warm, moist cloths may be applied to lower back.

SUGGESTIONS FOR HYPERVENTILATION

(Rapid, deep breathing in which too much carbon dioxide is being exhaled.)

To *prevent* hyperventilation, breathing should be kept shallow, in upper chest, throat and mouth.

Signs of Hyperventilation are:

1. Tingling of hands and feet, which can progress to muscle spasms in hands.
2. Feeling of dizziness or of being "lightheaded."
3. Blurring of vision.

Ways to correct hyperventilation:

1. Slow down your breathing, especially on exhaling.
2. Hold your breath for a few seconds after a contraction.
3. Breathe into your cupped hands or into a small paper bag.
4. Hold your breath for a few seconds after exhaling.

UNUSUAL DELIVERIES

In about 4 percent of deliveries the baby's position is reversed so that the buttocks rather than the head are facing downward in the uterine cavity. Such a birth is called a breech presentation and presents more problems than the head first presentation. If necessary, the obstetrician uses forceps, or version (external manipulation to turn the baby) to help and guide the baby in getting through the vaginal outlet.

If it appears that delivering the baby through the bony opening in the mother's pelvis would be impossible or hazardous, a Caesarean section may be performed. This is a surgical procedure in which incisions are made in the abdominal wall and the uterus, and the baby is lifted out. This method of delivering the baby poses more risks than having it pass through the vaginal canal. However, when performed by a skilled physician, unfavorable outcomes are now extremely rare. Physicians differ in their opinion as to how many Caesarean deliveries may be used safely with the same mother. Some say 2 or 3, others 5 or 6. The debate centers around how strong the scar tissue is that develops after closing the uterine incisions. There is general agreement that it is not as strong as normal tissue in bearing up under the expansion and contractions of the uterus.

Extremely rare is a condition called ectopic (displaced pregnancy). In this situation implantation of the fertilized ovum takes place outside of the uterus, for example, within a Fallopian tube or the abdominal cavity. Usually, surgical intervention is necessary long before the fetus nears full term. However, there are cases on record of healthy babies who have developed this way in the abdominal cavity and have been delivered by opening the abdominal cavity.

GIVING BIRTH AT HOME

At the present time, there is an apparently increasing number of women who want to give birth to their babies at home. Some feel that treatment afforded in hospitals is too impersonal, has a dehumanizing element and deprives the mother of satisfactions she could experience in her own home. Typical of their comments are the following:

A hospital is dehumanizing to a mother at the time she is feeling the greatest womanly dignity. . . . There's much more to birth than the physical aspect. It's also an emotional and spiritual occasion. Women are giving birth at home because of the lack of emotional and spiritual fulfillment in the hospital.—A mother (4 children—3 born in hospital) and medical technologist.

I stayed home to have the peace, beauty and joy of birth.—Mother of eight (the first six born in hospitals).[12]

The baby should always be with the mother, so you can hold it whenever you want to. Putting the baby behind glass in a nursery is barbaric.—Mother of two (1 in hospital) and music teacher.[13]

The specific complaints of these and other mothers include the following:

. . . they don't like the separation of mother and child, not being allowed to breast feed the child immediately after birth, separation of the father from the experience, being given drugs they don't want and having an episiotomy.[14]

Physicians are concerned with the physical risks accompanying childbirth which they feel cannot always be dealt with adequately at home. They say the principal ones are possible hemorrhaging in the mother and

---

[12]Zack, Marg, "Giving Birth at Home," Minneapolis *Tribune*, Feb. 8, 1972, p. 1E.

[13]Slovut, Gordon, "They Are Against Putting Baby Behind Glass in the Hospital," Minneapolis *Star*, Feb. 14, 1972, p. 1B.

[14]*Ibid*, p. 7E.

failure of the baby to breathe and "the less obvious problems of insufficient oxygen."

Hospital administrators have sensed the discontent of some mothers with their procedures and have instituted such practices as the team concept and parent education program previously described. Another experiment undertaken in an attempt to make the hospital stay less impersonal has been a plan called "rooming in." In this plan, babies remain in the same room with their mothers and the mothers are encouraged to breast feed their babies and do just as much as they want to in taking care of their needs. It is thought that the emotional and mental health of both mother and child will be furthered by the practice. Mothers' reactions to the plan vary. Some are enthusiastic about it and others feel that it robs them of a much needed vacation and a rest from the duties of child care.

It remains to be seen whether giving birth at home will become widespread. If it does, perhaps the European system of home delivery will be adopted with a physician or a specially trained nurse-midwife in attendance and a mobile emergency unit standing by.

Note: The above discussion is based on the two newspaper articles previously cited.

NURSING THE BABY

The decision to breast feed or bottle feed her baby must be made by each individual mother. In this age of all sorts of formulas and highly improved infant foods, she need not feel guilty if she decides not to nurse her baby. Many pediatricians feel that breast feeding is the ideal method. Some reasons they give are: It is the completely natural way of feeding the baby. It is also a pleasant experience. Mother and child develop closer emotional relationships with breast feeding. There is some evidence that the baby who is given foreign proteins early in life may be more likely to develop allergic conditions. Crawley makes the following observations on the assumed advantages of breast feeding. "Nursing is without question the best thing for the baby. As a baby nurses, the stimulation of contact with his mother's body—especially the stimulation to his face, lips, nose, tongue, and mouth during suckling—is important in improving his ability to breathe and get more oxygen into his blood. At the same time he is ingesting colostrum (a watery substance) from his mother's breasts. While colostrum production lasts only two days, its mild laxative action helps to establish the baby's elimination processes, and it favors the growth of desirable bacteria in his gastrointestinal tract." He states further that breast feeding can contribute to providing the baby with "an emotional environment of security and love."[15]

Members of the LaLeche League International, a group of mothers who are staunch advocates of the advantages of breast feeding to both mother and child, have compiled a book on the advantages of breast feeding. A typical statement that they cite from a nursing mother reads:

"On days when so many things have gone wrong and my own performance has not been creditable, I get renewed and refreshed when I am nursing my baby and realize that with all my faults she loves me and needs me just the way I am. When I finally put her down, I find I am calm again and kinder to the rest of the family."[16]

Some mothers refuse to nurse their babies because they fear it will impair the appearance of their breasts. This should not happen if the doctor's instructions are carefully carried out. Other reasons given are: "It is inconvenient," "a revolting practice," "I am too tired." Aside from fatigue, the other reasons against breast feeding depend upon attitudes. There is some evidence that if the mother is overtired or under emotional stress, her milk will suffer adverse effects. Of course, if this should happen or if her doctor discovers there are medical contraindications to her engaging in breast feeding, it would be folly to persist in nursing her baby.

AFTER-THE-BABY DEPRESSION

There is considerable popular talk concerning the mother's emotional state after the baby is born. Some mothers report feeling blue and depressed. There can be physical as well as emotional reasons behind this feeling. The woman must remember when she becomes pregnant, that it may take some time for her body to adjust to the chemical changes taking place, but after the first three months she will usually feel better.

After her baby is born, her body will again undergo a period of adjustment and it may take some time for her glands to get back to the functioning of their earlier state. These changes, coupled with the introduction of a new member into the family group which may require

---

[15]Crawley, Lawrence Q., et al, *Reproduction, Sex and Preparation for Marriage*, Englewood Cliffs: Prentice-Hall, 1973, 2nd Edition, p. 50.
[16]*The Womanly Art of Breast Feeding*, Franklin Park: LaLeche League International, 1963, 2nd Edition, p. 13.

many modifications in the routine of living, may cause her to become depressed very easily. She may discover herself crying over all sorts of trivial things. She may think that her husband does not understand her and that she never will feel well again. If this happens (many mothers escape this period), the wise thing to do is to remember that it is simply a postpartum symptom and that the feelings should vanish within a few weeks.

The husband should also realize that this moody, irritable behavior of his wife is a temporary thing and help her through it by being loving and thoughtful.

Professional people who are interested in discovering some of the problems of adjustment which occur after the baby is born are engaging in research to bring information that will be of additional help during this period. A brief summary of two of the most informative studies follows:

LeMasters,[17] in a study of 46 couples, reported that 38 (83 percent) said they experienced "extensive" or "severe" crisis in adjusting to the birth of their first baby. By the term, crisis, LeMasters means an event which forces a reorganization of the family social systems to the extent that it is "any sharp or decisive change for which old patterns are inadequate." (Reuben Hill's definition.)

The majority of the couples in the study had planned for or desired their babies and they also considered their marriages "good." But the interesting fact is that all of the couples felt that they had scarcely any effective preparation for their future parental roles. Aside from knowing where babies come from, they were totally ignorant of how to care for a baby.

During this period of crisis both partners stated they suffered loss of sleep, felt constantly tired, and developed tensions from the loss of social contacts and increased financial pressure.

The encouraging note that came from the study was that nearly all of these couples eventually made a seemingly successful adjustment to parenthood.

The results of this study give additional emphasis to the recommendation that expectant parents should prepare for and learn all they can about fulfilling their future parental roles in an effective manner.

---

[17]*Ibid*, pp. 352-355.

A study by Bernstein and Cyr[18] which explored prospective fathers' feelings and their later reactions to the birth of the baby is also interesting. In this research, a number of husbands from a group of sixty-nine cases was seen in an interview both before and after the birth of the baby. The aim of the study was to determine how young husbands would react to the first pregnancy and the subsequent birth of the child. It is interesting to note that these young men had not reached occupational stability and had not experienced satisfactory relationships with their own parents during their childhood.

The social workers, in the interviews, give the husbands general information about pregnancy, hospital routines, and postpartum care of the baby. They also discussed such problems as finances, housing, work, and so forth.

Apparently the interviews had a beneficial effect inasmuch as the husbands' reactions to the birth of the baby and their participation in its care were more positive than the case workers had expected. All of the fathers were delighted with the baby, participated actively in caring for it, and in some cases showed greater skill in handling the child than their wives.

Although both of these studies were conducted with relatively small groups of parents, the results definitely indicate that expectant parents do a much more effective job when the baby arrives if they have had prenatal instruction.

GIVING THE BABY A GOOD START
Choosing a Name

Surely a name should be chosen that gives each child a sense of individuality. The author dislikes the practice of naming a child after a parent or a close relative. Usually this results in designating the identically named persons as big and little Mary, and so forth. Bizarre names should be avoided as in many cases they severely test the ego strength of the concerned individual.

Establishing a Healthful Routine for the Baby

The new baby should get plenty of fresh air and sunshine. His progress should be checked by the doctor at frequent intervals. He should

---

[18]Bernstein, Rose, and Cyr, Florence E., "A Study of Interviews With Husbands in a Prenatal and Child Health Program." *Social Casework* 38 (November 1957), pp. 473-480.

have a feeding and sleeping schedule based upon a rhythm of his own, which can be learned after careful observation. Both the father and mother should cooperate as partners to guide him in achieving his potential. If they are interested in his development as compared with other children, there are many books which disclose what degree of development can be expected at a certain age level. There are also a number of excellent books on baby and child care that can be obtained in pocket book form.

INVOLUNTARY CHILDLESSNESS

There is no precise information concerning how many couples are involuntarily childless, but estimates place the figure at about 10 percent. There is a confusion of terms when the subject is discussed, as some persons equate relative infertility or relative fertility with sterility. Strictly speaking sterility means the individual lacks the capacity to reproduce, while fertility or infertility relate to the degree of ability to have children.

If a husband and wife are both under 30 and want children they should attempt to effect conception (without using any contraceptives during the period) for at least one year before enlisting medical assistance. Couples who are over 30 should usually wait no longer than six months.

There are a number of things that contribute to infertility. Some of the most common are:

In both—ill health, age, mental and emotional condition, maldevelopments of the genitals, overexposure to X rays or radium, glandular disorders, inadequate nutrition, and certain infectious diseases In the woman—excessive acidity in the genital tract, closed or obstructed cervix, closed Fallopian tubes, abnormal position of the uterus. In the man—low sperm count, defective sperm cells.

Procedures to Aid Conception

In the male, if a semen analysis discloses deviations from normal, some corrective measures would include building general health, better nutrition, recommended physical exercises, treatment for glandular deficiencies and diagnosis and treatment for possible blockage of transportation of sperm cells.

In the woman, tests are made and suggestions are given to determine the possible time of ovulation (see Chapter 19) so coitus can be engaged in then, and improve chances of conception. If ovulation is not taking place, hormone or drug therapy is used to stimulate ovulation. If the Fallopian tubes are found to be closed, treatment to blow them open or remove the blockage is given. The cervical canal may be treated to make it more receptive to the sperm cells. Corrective surgery may be performed to eliminate growths or cysts that may be interfering with fertility. Of course, as with the man, treatment to improve general health and mental attitudes is given.

Artificial Insemination

If tests determine that the wife is apparently fertile and the husband is either sterile or for some reason his fertile sperm cannot be delivered or received to effect conception, the couple may employ artificial insemination. This is a process in which some of the sperms of the husband or the sperms of an unknown donor are introduced by syringe into the vagina or uterus of the wife about the time that ovulation is thought to occur. If the semen of a donor is to be used, the husband and wife should carefully consider how it might affect them from a religious, psychological, physiological and legal standpoint before a decision is made to go ahead. It should never be done without a written agreement signed by both. Successful inseminations have been made using sperm cells which have been frozen and stored in a sperm bank for as long as four years. (Sherman, 1964.)[19] It is highly possible that such sperm banks will be used more in the future as one of the aids for childless couples.

ADOPTING A CHILD

Attitudes toward adopting a child have changed. In the past, it was considered a magnanimous gesture with which the couple chose a child they liked and gave it a much needed home. Today, the emphasis has shifted to finding a suitable family for the child. Current social conditions have made finding a child to adopt difficult. More unwed mothers are keeping their babies, the availability of contraceptives and possibilities of legal abortion have reduced the number of unwanted children that are born, and many persons who are concerned with problems of overpopulation prefer to adopt rather than produce children of their own.

Adoptions are usually arranged through a social agency or by direct contact with the child's natural parents or their representative. The ad-

[19]Sherman, J. K., "Research on Frozen Human Semen: Past, Present and Future," *Fertility and Sterility*, Vol. 15, No. 5, September-October, 1964, pp. 485-499.

vantages of adopting through a licensed agency are: The agency usually has the facts about the child's background and information about any defects it may have. The child is placed with the prospective adoptive parents on a probationary status of several months, so it may be returned to the agency if defects or problems develop. The identities of the natural and adoptive parents are not revealed to the others, so no claims may be made for return in the future.

Questions to be Asked Before Adopting a Child

Couples planning to adopt a child should carefully consider their reasons for wanting an additional member in their family. Answering the following questions may help them gain insight into their motivations:

Do we desire to adopt a child because our marriage has become dull and we want to inject new life into it?

Do we feel that adopting a child will put a stop to our bickering and improve our adjustment?

Does our desire stem from certain ego needs such as having a son to carry on with the family business or a daughter who will be expected to accomplish what we failed to do?

If the foregoing reasons are prompting them to adopt a child, it would be well to rethink the project. A period of serious reflection may help them to realize that neither the child nor they would be happy unless their adoptive attitude changes to one of approaching the step from the standpoint of what they can do for the child. If this occurs then they should ask themselves:

Are we youthful enough in attitude to enjoy helping with the developmental conflicts through which a growing child must pass?

Are we mature enough to be sensitive to the child's needs, understand his temperament, and patiently guide him in achieving his potential?

Adoptive parents will find after they have adopted their child that he will become theirs if they strive to meet his basic emotional needs. He will not really belong to them unless they build a relationship in which he feels that he belongs.

The baby should be told as soon as he can understand that he is adopted. However, it should be done in a natural manner without placing undue emphasis upon it. Although it is important for the child to understand how he came to the family, it is of greater importance that his adoptive parents develop good relationships with him.

The writer has learned in counseling contacts with adopted college students that their concern with where and how they were obtained is of little importance to them if they enjoy their associations with their adoptive parents.

Suggested Readings

1. Bean, Constance A., *Methods of Childbirth: A Complete Guide to Childbirth and Maternity Care,* Bellevue, Wash.: International Childbirth Education Association, 1972.

2. Birch, William G., *A Doctor Discusses Pregnancy,* Chicago: Budlong Press, 1963.

3. Bulmer, M. G., *The Biology of Twinning in Man,* New York: Oxford University Press, 1970.

4. Fielding, Waldo L., *Pregnancy: The Best State of the Union,* New York: Thomas Y. Crowell Co., 1971.

5. Gebhard, Paul H., Pomeroy, Wardell B., Martin, Clyde E., and Christianson, Cornelia V., *Pregnancy, Birth and Abortion,* Chicago: Harper, 1958.

6. Genne, William H., *Husbands and Pregnancy,* St. Meinrad, Ind.: Abbey Press, 1970.

7. Guttmacher, Alan F., *Pregnancy and Birth,* New York: New American Library, 1970.

8. Hungerford, Mary Jane, *Childbirth Education,* Springfield, Ill.: Charles C. Thomas, 1972.

9. La Leche League International, *The Womanly Art of Breastfeeding,* Franklin Park, Ill.: La Leche International, 1963.

10. Maternity Center Association, *Guide for Expectant Parents,* New York: Grosset and Dunlap, 1969.

11. Read, Grantley Dick, *Childbirth Without Fear,* Chicago: Harper & Row, 1972 (rev. ed.).

12. Roberts, Robert W., and Pappenfort, Donnell M., *Maternity Homes: Programs, Services and Physical Plant,* Chicago: Florence Crittendon Association of America, Inc., 1970.

13. *Smoking and Pregnancy,* Washington, D.C.: Health Services and Mental Health Administration, Public Health Service, HEW, 1971.

14. Wright, Erna, *The New Childbirth* (the Lamaze Technique), New York: Hart Publishing Co., 1967.

Chapter XXI

Understanding Human Sexuality

I could never ask my parents questions about sex without the fear of being laughed at or feeling ashamed. This left me with an embarrassed and nasty feeling toward sex. It wasn't until I'd been married for several years that I realized sex was a natural part of life.

Two basic things must take place before an individual can understand the role of human sexuality in life. First, accurate information must be obtained about the sexual make up and sexual functions of the body. Second, a sexual life-style must be adopted and maintained which gives him or her a sense of personal worth, accords the same status to others, and is in harmony with his or her value system and goals. It is possible to experience the first by obtaining the necessary factual information in the home and from educational institutions. However, the second and more complicated achievement, that of developing and maintaining a satisfying sexual life-style is a never-ending process that is subject to the interplay of many influences throughout the various stages of the individual's life. There is general agreement that education for human sexuality begins in the home, consequently, what each person learns in the family circle during the childhood years constitutes a major part of the foundation of attitudes and information upon which the rest of his or her life is built.

THE IMPACT OF THE EARLY FAMILY YEARS ON HUMAN SEXUALITY

Nature and Objectives

The child's education in sexuality begins at birth. If it is born into a home free of tension, and the emotional climate is one of loving and accepting others, the chances are good that it will consider home a pleasant place to be, and as it grows up to look upon the family group as a social unit which contributes much to the satisfaction of individual needs.

In addition to developing positive or negative attitudes toward family life, other things happen very early in the child's development that contribute toward the shaping of attitudes toward human sexuality and the life-style he will adopt. The child's interaction with his parents will also affect the attitudes he has regarding heterosexual associations later in life. Broderick, in summarizing current research, suggests four family-related factors which help bring about average heterosexual development in the individual:

"First, the parent or parent-surrogate of the same sex must not be so punishing on the one hand or so weak on the other hand as to make it impossible for the child to identify with him. Second, the parent or parent-surrogate of the opposite sex must not be so seductive, or so punishing, or so emotionally erratic as to make it impossible for the child to trust members of the opposite sex. Third, the parents or parent-surrogates must not systematically reject the child's biological sex and attempt to teach him cross-role sex behavior." The fourth factor Broderick mentions is . . . "the necessity of establishing a positive conception of marriage as an eventual goal."[1]

Accepting One's Sexual Classification

Recent studies suggest that when the baby is born it does not have the psychosexual status of either a male or female, and that its psychosexual development can be shaped in either direction by parental, family, and cultural influences. This susceptibility to being molded to play a defined or assigned sex role has been demonstrated in studies of hermaphroditic children, those born with external sex organs that cannot definitely be defined as male or female, and who possess a mixture of male and female components. Brown and Lynn in a summary of current studies say that such children "usually grow up as masculine or feminine depending on the sex assigned to them and the sex role in which they are reared." Research also suggests, however, that at least as far as sex role identity is concerned, this plasticity does not persist beyond early childhood; once a masculine or feminine sex role is established, it may be extremely difficult for this pattern to be changed or reversed in later life.[2]

---

[1]Broderick, Carlfred B., "Sexual Behavior Among Preadolescents," *The Journal of Social Issues*, Vol. 22, No. 2 (April 1966) pp. 6-21.

[2]Brown, Daniel G. and Lynn, David B., "Human Sexual Development: An Outline of Components and Concepts," *Journal of Marriage and the Family*, Vol. 28, No. 4 (November 1966), pp. 465-70.

This research with hermaphrodites, combined with other studies, suggests that men and women do not automatically play masculine and feminine roles as they grow to adulthood, but that their behavioral patterns are the result of familial and cultural influences.

The results of these studies and others show how important parental models are in influencing children toward a certain sex role. Lynn in a summary of hypotheses related to the child accepting his sexual classification contrasts the difference between parental identification and the child's identification with the role considered typical of his own sex in his culture. He states that the child might identify with his same-sex parent (internalize the parent's personality characteristics and unconsciously react in a similar manner) and be poorly identified with the culture's concept of what the masculine or feminine role should be. "An illustration might be a girl who is closely identified with her mother, who herself is more strongly identified with the masculine than with the feminine role. Therefore, such a girl, through her identification with her mother, is poorly identified with the feminine role."[3] Lynn also postulates that due to a shortage of male models and the father's time spent away from home that "males tend to identify with a culturally defined masculine role, whereas females tend to identify with their mothers."

One must remember, as these influences are discussed, that the child's mind is constantly sorting out and accepting desirable or undesirable thinking about sexuality, and that he is continuously learning. So, when certain things are mentioned as contributing to sex attitudes, they should just be considered as landmarks along the path of the individual's continuing development.

ATTITUDES TOWARD THE HUMAN BODY

Very early in life, the baby is sensitive to the attitudes his parents display in ministering to his bodily needs. If his mother shows disgust when changing his diaper, or his father scolds when the bed is wet, the infant may begin to feel that certain bodily functions are not nice. He may build up his own feeling of nastiness toward that part of the body that will later be involved in mating relations and the birth of babies. Years later, as an adult, he may view sexual intercourse in marriage and the reproductive

[3]Lynn, David B., "The Process of Learning Parental and Sex-role Identification," *Journal of Marriage and the Family*, Vol. 28, No. 4 (November 1966) pp. 465-70.

process with a feeling of disgust. Much more desirable attitudes will be developed in the child, if his mother and father communicate the thinking that the entire body is good, and that all of its parts and functions play important roles in contributing to healthful living.

It is quite natural for babies to explore their bodies as they develop an awareness of self. In this process of discovery, the genitals may be touched and evoke pleasurable sensations. Parents should not become alarmed at such casual handling of the sex organs. If the child persists in touching this area of his body and seems to be forming a habit, angry disapproval and severe punishment do not constitute the best parental approach to the problem. The first thing the parents should do is ask, why? A physical examination may disclose that the boy needs to be circumcised. The girl may have irritating adhesions of the clitoris which can be taken care of medically. On the other hand, there may be no physically irritating condition present, and the baby may be indulging in excessive self-handling out of sheer boredom. Putting the child to bed when he is ready to sleep and having toys in his crib to divert attention from his body may be the only measures needed to break the habit.

Accepting Sexual Differences

As the infant grows older, he will become more observant of others and become curious about bodily differences in boys and girls. If parents answer the child's questions frankly and allow him the opportunity to see bodily differences in natural settings, he will be much less likely to undress other children in order to investigate these differences.

For some reason, a number of parents seem to think that small brothers and sisters should keep their bodies hidden from each other and learn about sexual differences when their mother and father think the time is ripe to explain such matters to them. The parents will then conduct a one-time lecture and perhaps use pictures and charts and say, "Johnny, it is time now for you to know how Mary's body is built," or "Mary, now you are a big girl, you have a right to know something about Johnny's body."

The two weaknesses in such a procedure are that first, the parents are arbitrarily setting the age at which they think their children should have such information. The parents' timetable may vary from six to sixteen years of age. Second, they take the information out of the context of human interaction and wind up giving their children a lesson in anatomy. Of course, correct anatomical information is a good thing to have, but such knowledge is not beneficial unless it is used in the proper way, and children are much more likely to use it in the proper way if they acquire the same information colored with attitudes of respect for each other as they are living and growing together from babyhood on. How can this be accomplished? One way is for parents to let their small children of both sexes bathe together. At such times they can observe bodily differences and can be told the reason for them. Some mothers say they don't dare do this because their children would become sex-minded. If the bathing is done naturally and casually, this should not happen. The following incident illustrates children's casual attitudes toward sexual differences.

A young mother said: "I bathed our three children together for months. One day, out of a clear blue sky, one daughter asked, 'Mommy, how do you know Tommy is a boy?' Her sister inquired, 'Is it because he wears long pants?'

"I got hold of myself and replied as casually as possible. 'Your little brother's body is made differently. Haven't you noticed?'

"They both looked at me, then at his penis, then again back at me, and said almost with contempt, 'Oh, that!'"

Sometimes the age difference between brothers and sisters is so wide that it would be impractical to bathe the children together. When this is the case, mother can let the older child watch and sometimes help bathe the new baby.

Children, as they get a bit older, do become more curious about basic body differences, and parents should always impart sound information in explanation, so that fears about the different body structures do not develop. For example:

Cathy's mother's answer made her small daughter confused and fearful when her four-year-old pointed to her little brother Robert's penis and asked, "Mom, why don't I have a fancy thing like Bobby? I wish I had a peanut." Mom replied, "That is called a penis, Cathy. You're a girl and don't need one, so the doctor cut yours off before you left the hospital."

The mother could have prevented Cathy's worries if she had said, "That is called a penis and when your brother grows up he will be a man like his father. But your body is just as fancy as Bobby's. You as a girl have a vagina, a very special part inside your body and when you grow up you will be a woman like Mother."

So far, all of the examples related to helping children accept sexual differences have involved small children of the same family. But such practices cannot be used by all parents. What can be done if the family does not have children of both sexes? What if they have one small boy? Or three little girls? What then?

One possibility is to arrange for their children to see opposite-sexed babies of relatives or friends in natural settings, such as in their early morning bath. If this is not possible, other alternatives are to take children to museums to view nude statues or to show them books which contain drawings or pictures of children's bodies which are presented in good taste. If none of these things is possible, some parents feel that natural acceptance of sexual differences will come if nudity is practiced in the home.

Nudity in the Home

There are differing opinions among professionals regarding the possible attitudinal effects of nudity in the home. Bowman[4] reports typical conflicting opinions of two psychiatrists:

My experience as a child psychiatrist has convinced me that exposure to parental nudity any time after the first three or four months of infancy is always severely disturbing to children. Exposure to the nude body of the parent of the opposite sex is the more disruptive experience. It results in the development of severe anxiety together with excitement, envy, and aggression. All these strong feelings give rise to further anxiety because of their intensity." Cyril Phillips, M.R.C.S. (Eng.), L.R.C.P. (Lond.), associate professor of child psychiatry and director of child psychiatry training, Tulane University School of Medicine, New Orleans, La.

The reaction to physical undress among parents and children should be as natural and unselfconscious as that between the healthy, happy man and wife. However, even the intimacy of marriage deserves moments of privacy, and above all, respect for the wishes and desires of the other person. To become well balanced, a child must

---

4Bowman, Henry A., *Marriage for Moderns*, New York: McGraw-Hill. 1970, 6th Edition, pp. 560-562.

be exposed both to the familiarity and the discipline of family inter-relationships. . . . In a close-knit family at ease with one another, the unconcerned familiarity between the states of dress and undress results in a familial relationship given no more attention or concern than the many other areas of intrafamily activity. As puberty is entered, the natural urge for independence, individualism, and privacy develops insidiously, resulting in a modesty appropriate to age and environment. — Doris A. Howell, M.D., professor and chairman of the Department of Pediatrics, Woman's Medical College of Pennsylvania, Philadelphia.

There are no well-known up-to-date studies that report the extent of nudity practiced in American homes, however, a summary by Elias and Gebhard of previously unpublished data collected by Alfred Kinsey and his co-workers (before 1955) for the Institute for Sex Research discloses a relationship between occupational level and the practice of nudity in the home. They say that nudity in the lower-income home "is more the exception than the rule for both girls and boys; in the upper-income home almost the reverse is true." They also state that "as a rule, boys are allowed more nudity than girls, except in homes where nudity is a common practice—in which girls report a higher incidence of nudity." They conclude, "This upper-class permissiveness regarding a sex-related behavior, nudity, fits nicely with our finding that upper-class parents communicate more freely on sexual matters with their offspring."[5]

Interviews with today's parents make it obvious that they are also in conflict regarding the practice of going without clothes in the family circle.

One mother said: "In our family we have always looked upon the human body as a natural and beautiful thing. Consequently, we never attempted to hide or cover up when another member walked in when we were bathing or disrobing. Today, our two sons are seventeen and nineteen, and we walk in and out of the bathroom without the slightest embarrassment when one or the other is showering."

Another mother stated: "I'd die of shock if one of our children saw me in the nude. My body is not for display and I don't care

[5]Elias, James and Gebhard, Paul, "Sexuality and Sexual Learning in Childhood," *Phi Delta Kappan*, Vol. 50, No. 7 (March 1969), pp. 401-405.

whether my kids are six or sixteen, they're never going to catch me undressed."

The results of these and other interviews suggest that each family will probably make its own ground rules regarding nudity within the family group. Consequently, a few general suggestions will be given here that might help regardless of what the family's attitudes are:

1. *Small children react casually to nudity among themselves.* Children up until the ages of about seven or eight usually seem quite unconcerned about bodily modesty or leaving the bathroom door open. However, at these ages they may begin to demand privacy, and their wishes should be respected. This should be done because although bodily modesty is not innate in children, it is brought about by their being conditioned by the social codes of the society in which they live, and so far, wearing clothes is the practice in our culture, no matter what attitudes are revealed by comparisons with other cultures. Thus, when children enter school the practice of nudity in their home may be in conflict with the teachings and associations of the classroom.

2. *Nudity between parents and children poses many questions to consider.* Some are: Will the sight and acceptance of their parents' bodies help small children to understand and regard sexual differences in a different light? Or will seeing their parents' nude bodies stimulate sexual excitement and desire in the child?

Can a father allow his four-year-old daughter to shower with him and then be calm and casual if she wants to touch his penis? If he allows her to, what will be the result? Or if he refuses will their natural relationship become strained?

Should a mother let her small son handle her naked breasts? What will be the results of her allowing or refusing such contact?

These and many other questions are extremely difficult to answer, chiefly because the personalities of all individuals who may be involved are so different. Perhaps the best generalization that can be made is that the revelation of the human body should not be considered shameful if a child should happen to see his parents in the process of bathing or undressing.

On the other hand, all modesty should not be cast aside and the body should not be exhibited with no sense of propriety. Everyone loses, when the needs and rights of every individual for a certain amount of personal privacy are not recognized and respected. Even though a small child's curiosity about the human body should be recognized, he should also be taught that his parents and other family members need a certain amount of privacy.

ANSWERING SMALL CHILDREN'S SEXUAL QUESTIONS

When children reach the age of about two or three they generally begin to ask specific questions about everything around them. And parents usually enjoy answering their barrage of "Whys?" "Whats?" and "Wherefores?" as long as they are not about sex. Mothers and fathers usually do their best to explain "Why the sky is blue" or "How bread is made." But when the small boy asks sex questions and points to a part of his body such as his penis and asks, "What's this?" The mother may blush and say primly, "We don't talk about such things." And if the father is caught with such a question, he often says, "I'm sorry, son, I'm busy now. Ask your mother."

Answering children's questions will be easier if parents know what kinds of questions to expect. Their inquiries about sex usually fall into the following general categories:

Bodily Organs and Their Functions—"What is this? What is it for?"

Physical Differences—"Why is Tommy's body different from mine?"

Origin of Babies—"Where did I come from?"

Father's Role—"Does Daddy help start a baby?"

Process of Birth—"How does the baby come into the world?"

Several things should be kept in mind when answering the child's questions:

The parents should be sure they know what the child is inquiring about. This might be done by asking, "What do you think about it?" Or saying, "Tell me again what you mean."

Parents should always give truthful answers, but also gear them to the child's readiness to understand. Short, simple, accurate answers can always be built upon and added to later as the child grows and is capable of and wants more detailed explanations.

It is not always necessary to answer a child's question on the spot. For instance, if the father is rushing out of the door to get to work on time or the mother is in the middle of a bridge game with visiting friends, it might be impractical to answer right then, and might even do more harm than good if a hurried answer is given. Either parent could say, "That's a good question. Let's talk about it tonight after dinner." Then the promise should be kept.

Questions should be answered in a relaxed and natural manner. If the parent shows tension or is abrupt when answering, the child may turn to another source of information.

It is not always necessary to wait for the child to ask questions before sexual information is given. Commenting on or asking the child how he feels about some sex-related occurrence such as the family cat having kittens might lead to a fruitful discussion.

Vocabulary

Occasionally, parents will refrain from talking to their children about sex because they feel they lack the necessary vocabulary. On the other hand, those who do feel adequate may either convey their information in slang terms or technical terminology. Although some fathers or mothers say they feel more comfortable using "baby talk" or "street language" when discussing sexual matters, they will probably find their channels of communication difficult to keep open when their children get older, learn correct terminology at school, and possibly assume that their parents are ill-informed. Using such simple terms as breast, nipple, penis, and vulva right from the beginning should make communication with children less awkward as they grow older. If individuals think some technical terms are too cold or too harsh, using a few substitute terms that do not detract from personal dignity such as substituting the word "mating" for "intercourse" may aid in more relaxed communication.

It will probably be helpful to children in keeping things clear in their minds if they have a simple vocabulary of terms before they enter school. Younger children should be told the correct words for the parts of the body which they see and the terms needed in relation to elimination. Other terms can be given later as the occasion arises.

Parts of the Body

Breasts, Nipples, Navel, Abdomen, Penis (circumcision), Testicle, Scrotum, Vulva, Genitals, Buttocks, Anus, Rectum.

Terms of Elimination

Urinate and Bowel Movement.

Note: The word "genitals" is included because it can be used as the term for the external sex organs of both sexes. The word "circumcision" is listed because small boys often notice the difference between circumcised and uncircumcised males and think that one or the other is defective.

Typical Questions and Answers

Bodily Organs and Their Functions

Question (Child pointing to navel): "What's that funny thing?"

Answer: "It's your navel. Everyone has one."

Child: "What's it for?"

Answer: "It has no special use. In fact, it's just a scar."

When the child is older, the answer must be more complete. Sometimes, parents give false answers in an attempt to satisfy their child's curiosity.

An illustration of one parent giving false information that resulted in problem behavior is that disclosed by one mother who was completely upset because her five-year-old Tommy kept pulling up his T-shirt and ". . . showing off his belly button to his playmates."

Tommy's mother was beside herself until she discovered the reason for Tommy's exhibitionist behavior, namely, that his dad had told him that his navel was a scar left from a bullet wound, which Tommy naturally took great pride in displaying.

Physical Differences

Question: "How do you know the baby is a boy or a girl?"

Answer: "Because their bodies are built differently. A little boy has a penis and a scrotum. A little girl has a vulva."

It should be stressed that the different type of sexual organs that male and female possess are of equal importance in fulfilling life's functions.

Origin of Babies

Question: "Mommy, where do babies come from?"

Answer: "Babies begin to develop from the joining of two cells (tiny bits of living matter). One grows in the father's body and one grows in the mother's body. When these two cells come together in the mother's body, a baby starts growing."

The origin of a baby is a fascinating story and one of the ways a parent can impress a child with its implications is by saying, "Just think, when these tiny specks of matter unite in the mother's body, a baby starts to grow; a baby who can some day become a star football player, a beautiful movie actress, or even the president of our great nation."

Father's Role

Question: "How does the father cell get into the mother's body?"

Answer: "Because father and mother love each other, they often draw very close when expressing their affection. At this time, the father cell finds its way through the special passageway up into mother's body."

As the child grows older, the parent can be more specific and explain how the father's sex organ is placed in the special passageway in the mother's body.

Process of Birth

Question: "How does the baby come into the world?"

Answer: "When the baby is big and strong enough to live in the world, the opening in mother's vulva enlarges so it is large enough for the baby to come into the world; then the opening closes again."

The birth of the baby is quite easy to explain if parents have taught the proper vocabulary. Otherwise it can be quite difficult. Even without the correct terminology, they can tell the child about the passageway (vagina) the baby is pushed along in toward the special opening in the vulva.

SEXUAL SOCIAL AND EMOTIONAL DEVELOPMENT
Middle Childhood

There is some thinking which has been promoted by Freud and other writers that children between the ages of about five and eleven lose interest in sex and go through a period of latency during which their psychosexual development stops and they temporarily quit moving toward heterosexual associations. This is one reason why some people have opposed sex education on the early levels in the public schools. They have contended that children should not be instructed in sexuality until the teens when their preschool sexual interest supposedly becomes reawakened. However, as far back as twenty-five years ago, Strain produced research findings indicating that there is no sexual latency period, and children continue without interruption through successive stages of heterosexual socialization.[6]

More recent research of Broderick and others confirms Strain's findings and suggests that there is no age level in the middle school years when the majority of boys and girls lose interest in the opposite sex. Broderick also indicates that heterosexual socialization follows the following steps: Having marriage as a goal—having an emotional attachment to a member of the opposite sex (girlfriend or boyfriend)—"confess having been in love"—"preference for a cross-sex companion . . . when going to a movie"—"actually going out on a date."[7]

It is extremely important that adults communicate effectively with younger people during the middle childhood years. The child's repeated exposure to new situations outside of the home and the increasing influence of age-mates can cause confusion in his thinking unless he has a dependable source of information to turn to. Unfortunately, past studies show that parents and educators have not made up this source. Gebhard and his associates reported that 90 percent of the young men in their study received most of their knowledge about sexual behavior from their friends, peers, or their own experiences.[8]

Burchinal found in a study of girls that only 39 percent had received adequate sex information from their mothers, and a small 15 percent from their fathers.[9]

If sex education is given in an effective manner in the public schools, parents and teachers should be able to cooperate in furnishing information about sexuality in such a way that greater numbers of young people will turn to them for knowledge rather than to their peers. Discussions involving personal concepts such as the development of masculinity or femininity can be discussed in the home, and discussions regarding group interaction or those requiring films, slides, models and other audiovisual aids can be entered into at school.

Masturbation

Childhood masturbation is a sexual activity that some parents have

[6]Strain, Frances B., *The Normal Sex Interests of Children*, New York: Appleton, Century, Crofts, 1948.
[7]*Ibid*, pp. 6-21.
[8]Gebhard, Paul H., et al., *Sex Offenders*, New York: Harper & Row, 1965, p. 469.
[9]Burchinal, Lee G., "Sources and Adequacy of Sex Knowledge Among Iowa High School Girls," *Marriage and Family Living*, 1960, Vol. 22, pp. 268-269.

difficulty dealing with. Research has proved that past fears associating masturbation with stunted growth, round shoulders, pimples and so forth are false. Today's medical opinion is that masturbation in and of itself causes no physical harm. However, the individual family's attitude toward the activity will depend upon their religious belief and their philosophy of life. Some families consider it a sin. Others look upon it as a harmless part of the growing-up process. Still others consider it a factor that contributes to a self-centered personality pattern. Despite these differences in thinking, parents should approach the matter calmly and objectively if they learn that their child masturbates.

Some things that parents might do are:

1. Discuss the situation calmly and listen to the child's viewpoint.

2. Never make the child feel evil or threaten him with punishment. If this happens, the child will possibly find a place to masturbate where it is less likely that discovery will take place.

3. Try to find out why a child is masturbating excessively. He may be attempting to compensate for a feeling of rejection and loneliness by getting pleasure by himself. If this seems to be the case, parents should try to help him find congenial companions and encourage him to engage in interesting activities.

4. Be patient, and realize that even if he wants to, the child cannot be expected to drop the habit overnight.

5. Develop such a relationship with the child that he will feel free to discuss masturbation, petting or anything else that bothers him.

6. Help the child to realize that masturbation is, generally speaking, a less emotionally satisfying substitute for heterosexual activity.

Sexual Development During Puberty and Adolescence

Inasmuch as puberty occurs between about 9 and 16 years of age for girls and 11 and 18 for boys, it is obvious that parents and teachers must try to be aware of each individual's timetable of growth and be prepared to help him or her understand the bodily and emotional changes that each faces. During these ages, young people begin to inspect their bodies and wonder if their physical attributes will make them desirable to their own and the opposite sex.

Acceptance of Bodily Changes

The Girl

Girls at this age are deeply concerned with their rate of bodily development. They want to be like their friends, and if they lack something which the others have newly developed, or feel they are taller or shorter than the rest of the group, they start to worry.

Some worry if their friends have hair appearing on their bodies and they don't. Others are sure that they will never be popular because they are too tall or too short. And still others are disturbed because they think their breasts or figures are not attractive.

The best approach for adults to use is to explain to each girl that she has her own timetable of growth and that nature will take care of normal developments. In the meantime, *her* job is to develop good health habits, cultivate her talents, get her mind off herself, and be interested in the needs of others.

Pamela's case illustrates the general concern girls have about breast development. When she came for counseling she said:

"Every time we take showers after gym class I'm so embarrassed I could just die. The other girls' breasts are bigger than mine and I feel like a small child. When I say anything to my mother about it, she just laughs at me."

This twelve-year-old girl did look as if her world had fallen apart, so time was taken to explain to her that each girl has her own pattern of growth and development and that she would probably have her breasts develop more fully later. She was also told that even if they never did become as large as those of her friends, she should not feel inferior. The important thing for her to do was to accept her body as right for her and make it as attractive as possible.

This twelve-year-old girl's concern about the size of her breasts is a matter which plagues many preadolescent girls.

Such incidents cause one to wonder why young girls have so much anxiety related to the size of their breasts. Although there could be many contributing factors such as inner inadequacies caused by feelings of rejection by parents or peers, there are two general reasons that come to mind. First, because our culture has associated breast size with sexual attractiveness, well-shaped breasts have become such sex symbols that a girl who is not endowed with them often feels sexless. Second, mothers are not meeting their daughters' needs to have the development of their bodies explained to them.

Menstruation

There is a current tendency among young girls to look upon the arrival of their first menstrual period as an indication that they have become a woman. There is also evidence that today's girls have their first menstrual periods earlier than used to be the case. Although it is not known just why this occurs, it has been learned that nutrition has some effect.

Inasmuch as the age range is wide at which menstruation starts, beginning at about nine and extending until about sixteen, the preadolescent girl should at the age of nine or sooner be given a simple account of what causes the menstrual period and what happens when it occurs. If this is done, she will be more likely to accept it as a natural function and not be emotionally upset when the first period occurs.

The Boy

Boys seem to be more neglected than girls in receiving information about the development of their bodies. Perhaps this is so, because the growing boy does not experience anything as dramatic as menstruation. However, a boy does have changes occur that might be disturbing to him unless his father or some older male offers an explanation.

Changes in the Voice

A boy who is a bit shy and self-conscious may often act like the Sphinx when his changing voice becomes a bit unsteady and difficult to control. To hide his embarrassment he may refuse to talk on the telephone or answer all questions put to him with barely audible grunts. Teasing won't help him through this trying period, but proper information will. The simple explanation that his voice is unsteady because his voice box (larynx) is getting bigger, that this is a sign of approaching manhood, and that in a short time his voice will become steady again and take on a much richer tone than it had before is usually all that is needed.

Appearance of Body Hair

The appearance of additional body hair does not seem to disturb boys unless they think their own hair growth is too heavy or too sparse. The most reassuring explanation for this is that the pattern of hair growth varies in each individual and that the amount of hair one possesses has no relationship to masculinity.

Size and Shape of the Genitals

Boys are frequently extremely sensitive about the size and shape of their penis and scrotum. These organs do get bigger at this time, but naturally they do not develop to any standard size. An individual should be reassured that his penis can be large or small, circumcised (has had the foreskin removed) or uncircumcised, and still function the way it should.

Undescended Testicles

A young man may worry if one side of his scrotal sac is empty because the corresponding testicle has not descended into it. He should be told that this will not interfere with his married sexual activity or prevent his fathering a child as long as the other side of the sac contains a testicle. Of course, if both testicles have not descended into the scrotum, medical help should be sought.

Erections and Wet Dreams

At this age, a male may frequently experience a spontaneous erection of the penis and become worried when it becomes stiff and hard. The simplest explanation to give is that the penis becomes hard and erect when its spongy tissue fills up with blood and this may be caused by a number of things. For example, a bladder full of urine may cause pressure which acts on special nerve endings and produces an erection. Other common causes may be friction on the penis caused by tight trousers, heavy bed clothing, or riding a bicycle. Looking at pictures of attractive girls, dancing with them or just thinking about them, may also cause the penis to become erect. Consequently, the most natural thing for a boy to do if his penis suddenly erects, is to ignore it and it will gradually go back to its usual size.

It is amazing to learn how worried some boys get when they have a wet dream. They may think they have an infection or have strained themselves while lifting.

The explanation given to those boys who do not know what is causing their wet dreams should be simple and brief. One approach is to say, "Now that your body is beginning to mature, certain glands are manufacturing a fluid called semen which occasionally leaves the body through your penis. Some doctors think this happens because more semen has been produced than the tubes and reservoirs within your body can hold, so the excess leaves your body, usually when you are asleep. Wet dreams will not weaken you, make you nervous, or cause any other problem, they are a simply natural body function.

HETEROSEXUAL EXPRESSION IN THE EARLY TEENS

Most individuals in the American culture are involved in some kind of heterosexual expression by the time they reach their early teens. From a social standpoint they usually progress through the stages of group dating, single dating, going steady, engagement, and marriage. Overt sexual expression may include embracing, kissing, caressing and movement to more intimate sexual contacts. If the individual exercises judgment and concern for others in his heterosexual associations it will contribute toward a more satisfying life-style. He will be more likely to do this if he has gained an understanding of human sexuality and its proper place in life as he has been growing up.

SEXUALITY IN ADULTHOOD

There are many adults who do not understand human sexuality and have problems in sex adjustment. They may also have difficulties because all people do not agree on what the desirable roles are that male and female should play in their social interaction. Consequently, there is no one description that can be given to illustrate what would be considered desirable adult sexual behavior. However, it is possible to describe the characteristics of the adult who has become a sexually mature person as a result of understanding the place of human sexuality in life.

CHARACTERISTICS OF A SEXUALLY MATURE PERSON

1. He is well informed and has an understanding of sexual anatomy, physiology, and reproduction. He uses this knowledge in a wholesome manner and feels that experiences related to sex and reproduction are dignified life experiences.

2. He values life. He values people. He values himself. In this attitude of caring, he esteems himself and his associates as persons of worth, and he feels that each individual has a reason for living and a life goal to achieve.

3. He enjoys associations with people of both sexes and in no way violates any individual's personhood by using him for his own selfish desires.

4. His sexual behavior is directed by inner controls. He does not behave in a certain manner because he fears authority or punishment, but because he *believes* his way of life is right. His moral code is one in which he accepts responsibility for his sexual behavior, which is never engaged in to exploit another person.

5. He is constantly striving to understand himself and his associates, so that a mutuality of response to the needs of each will promote pleasant and satisfying relationships.

6. He realizes that love is not the same as sexual expression, but that in a love relationship, two individuals who have made a commitment to each other in marriage will use sexual expression as one way of expressing their love for each other.

SEXUAL VARIANCE

There are other forms of human sexual behavior that differ from the average heterosexual development pattern which has been discussed. The way they vary will be presented very briefly.

HOMOSEXUALITY
Definition

Rubin states, "Homosexual behavior refers to overt sexual relations, or emotional attachments involving sexual attraction, between individuals —male or female—of the same sex. The term derives from the Greek root homo, meaning *same.* The term Lesbian (taken from the name of the island of Lesbos, inhabited by the poet Sappho) refers to female homosexual relations or persons.

"Homosexuality and heterosexuality are not discrete entities. Sex arousal by a member of one's own sex is not an all-or-none phenomenon, but a matter of degree: one finds a continuum ranging from those who are responsive exclusively toward the opposite sex through a large percentage of persons who are or may be erotically aroused by persons of both sexes, to those interested exclusively in the same sex.

"Some psychiatrists feel that the term *homosexual* should be applied only to 'those individuals who more or less chronically feel an urgent sexual desire toward, and a sexual responsiveness to, members of their own sex and who seek gratification of this desire predominantly with members of their own sex' . . . The Institute for Sex Research of Indiana University at Bloomington, prefers to speak in terms of homosexual behavior rather than of homosexuality as such, and to classify persons according to their position on a 7-point scale that ranges from exclusive heterosexual behavior to exclusive homosexual behavior. . . . 'Latent homosexuality' refers to disguised or hidden homosexual impulses. There is considerable controversy over the validity and meaningfulness of this term and it must be used with caution."[10]

Incidence of Homosexuality

It is extremely difficult to determine just how widespread homosexuality is. This is so because homosexuals are reticent about reporting their activities, and also because it is an arduous task to classify individuals as homosexuals. To do a precise job the researcher must decide who is completely homosexual, who is only partly so, and who may be in the process of changing his personality pattern. Kinsey's study of the incidence of homosexuality, the findings of which have been under attack, suggests that homosexual behavior is found much more frequently among white American males than among females. Some of his findings suggest that "4 percent of white males are exclusively homosexual throughout their lives, after the onset of adolescence" and that "between 2 and 6 percent of the unmarried females and less than 1 percent of married women were almost exclusively homosexual between the ages of 20 and 35."[11]

Dr. Cappon, a Canadian psychiatrist who has had wide experience in treating homosexuals, has the following to say regarding the incidence of homosexuality. "There is every reason for believing that the vast majority of persons are, in adulthood, exclusively heterosexual, and that only 2% or 3% of the population are homosexual in varying degrees, with the number of homosexual women perhaps only one third as great as that

---

[10]Rubin, Isadore, "Homosexuality," SIECUS Discussion Guide No. 2, New York: Sex Information and Education Council of the U. S., October 1965, pp. 1, 2. Printed here by permission of the publisher.

[11]As reported in Ellis, A., and Abarbanel, A., *The Encyclopedia of Sexual Behavior*, Vol. I. New York: Hawthorn Books, Inc., 1961, pp. 489-490.

of homosexual men." The data of Kinsey have "been found to be grossly misleading."[12]

There are no existing studies that shed any light on whether there is an increasing or decreasing rate of homosexual behavior in contemporary society.

Suggested Causes of Homosexuality

Although homosexuality seems to have existed almost since civilization began, there is still considerable disagreement as to how the pattern develops in the individual. Current thinking may be briefly summarized as follows:

1. Some specialists believe that homosexuality could be inborn and caused by "genetic, constitutional or glandular factors." Others contend that no valid evidence has been presented to substantiate such a belief.

2. Most authorities are beginning to agree that "psychological, social, and cultural factors" contribute significantly in shaping the pattern.

3. Freudian thinking suggests the following conditions which might develop the homosexual behavior pattern:

   a. The lack of a strong father figure may cause a boy to identify with his mother to the extent of desiring her sexually. Cultural pressures may cause him to repress this feeling and subsequently to suppress his desires toward all women.

   b. Children may also so overidentify with parents of the same sex that they become feminized or masculinized as the case may be.

   c. Overattachment of the child to the parent of the same sex may cause the parent to become the object of adult affection. But because such a relationship would be incestuous, the child suppresses it with the parent and seeks it with other adults.

4. Other psychological concepts concerning the causality of homosexuality include the following:

   a. Homosexuality results from an arrestment or fixation of emotional development. The child stays at the level of about the age of 10

---

[12]Cappon, Daniel, *Toward an Understanding of Homosexuality*, Englewood Cliffs, N. J.: Prentice-Hall, 1965. As reported in *Family Life*, Vol. XXV, No. 7, July 1965, Los Angeles: American Institute of Family Relations, Editorial by Paul Popenoe.

where he prefers social activities with his own sex and never progresses to the heterosexual level.

There are two criticisms of this thinking. Henry Bowman, outstanding family life educator, feels that young people at this age level should be classified as preheterosexual rather than homosexual. He believes this is the norm at this age level and that individuals as they mature will eventually attain the next level, that of heterosexuality.

Other modern thinkers feel that some individuals do not go through cycles of sexual development, but may remain on the preheterosexual level because he might find it easier to get satisfaction from the same sex during the pubertal and adolescent years. And if he does this he may make an unconscious adjustment to this easier path by the suppression of the needs for heterosexual relations (polymorphous pansexuality.)[13]

b. Another group of students believes that faulty sex education in the home can make a boy feel that sex is sinful and cause him in later life to turn away from the pure woman and satisfy his sexual desires with other sinful men.

c. Older people may introduce younger individuals who are seeking acceptance and love into homosexual practices. There are not, however, sufficient studies to reveal whether these seductions generally result in subsequent overt homosexual behavior in the younger person. Most present-day scientists seem to think this will not happen unless the seduced individual is already predisposed toward the homosexual pattern and has great admiration for the initiating adult.

5. Additional factors which may cause a Lesbian pattern to develop. Although the same causative factors which produce male homosexuality contribute to the Lesbian pattern of behavior, there are some additional causes which seem peculiar to the female, such as:

a. The feeling that it is safer to have overt sexual contact with another female because there is no threat of possible pregnancy.

---

[13]Cory, Donald W., "Homosexuality," Ellis, Albert and Abarbanel, Albert, *The Encyclopedia of Sexual Behavior*, New York: Hawthorne Books, Inc., Vol. 1, 1961.

b. The thinking of some females that they are inferior to males and consequently obtain ego satisfaction by imitating males and having intercourse with other females (Alfred Adler's "masculine protest" theory).

c. The result of being seduced by older females who are more considerate lovers than males.

Observations of Homosexuals' Personality Patterns

It is beyond the scope of this writing to make a detailed analysis of the homosexual's personality adjustments. However, a search of the literature allows a few generalizations to be made.

The Lesbian

The Lesbian seems to be subject to less criticism than the male homosexual and usually leads a more discreet life. She appears to be less promiscuous and evidently tries to remain loyal to her "one love."

The writer, in attempting to help a Lesbian readjust to society, heard the following story from a vivacious and attractively dressed girl in her mid-twenties.

"I know you and other people think I am queer, but I don't care. I have tried to be friendly with boys and I used to date them. But one fellow did something so disgusting to me that I never want to get close to a man again. Women's bodies are so much cleaner and more beautiful. I am so happy with Sally. She keeps the house tidy and is such a satisfying lover that I enjoy working and supporting her. I took part of my inheritance from my father and bought Sally a beautiful diamond ring and a new car.

"Thanks for trying to help, but I am not coming back. I've decided I'm happy the way I am."

Although this young woman said she was happy, she exhibited the same trait that other Lesbians whom the author has counseled have displayed. She kept reiterating that her relationship with Sally was a beautiful, good relationship, that they were not harming anyone and that they should be left alone. The seeming compulsion which these Lesbians have, to point out the goodness of their relationships, makes one suspect that they have many inner conflicts.

The Male Homosexual

The male homosexual appears to be subjected to more inconsiderate treatment by society than is the Lesbian. He may often be the object of scorn and ridicule and he seems to be faced with a dilemma. If he seeks to conceal his variant desires, he may feel that he is living a life of pretense. On the other hand, if he openly expresses his homosexual feelings, he may feel that everyone dislikes him. Edmund Bergler, Viennese and New York psychiatrist, characterizes a male homosexual as an unconscious "Injustice Collector," "Fugitive From Women," and "Constantly Dissatisfied."[14]

Bergler's thinking is reinforced by the writings of Cappon and Ellis who both believe that a fixed homosexual pattern does not give the individual happiness. Cappon declares, "Make no mistake about it, 'homosexuality,' by definition, is not healthy or wholesome. The homosexual person at best, will be unhappier and more unfulfilled than the sexually normal person."[15]

Ellis states that homosexual acts in themselves are not unnatural, but that the exclusive homosexual (the fixed homophile) is neurotic.[16]

Attitudes Toward Homosexuality

A review of current writings and studies pertaining to homosexuality allows a few generalizations to be made. In the typical American community, male homosexuality meets with much more disapproval than female homosexuality (Lesbianism). There is a division of opinion as to whether the homosexually oriented person is sick or merely different. Also there is no consensus regarding how society should react to such individuals. Attitudes vary from treating them as criminals or social outcasts, to tolerating them or trying to understand and accept them as individuals. Hooker makes a strong point for individual acceptance with the following comments:

"It should be remembered that homosexuals—or people with almost any other sexual variance—can be as religious, moralistic, loyal to country or cause, inhibited, bigoted, or censorious of other types of sexual variance as anyone else. They manifest no greater number of other serious

---

[14]Bergler, Edmund, *Homosexuality, Disease or Way of Life?* New York: Hill and Wang, Inc., 1957.
[15]*Ibid.*
[16]Ellis, Albert, Critique: "The Homosexual in Our Society," New York: Review, Vol. V, June 1959, No. 6. Pan-Graphic Press.

personality problems than one would expect to find in the normal population."[17]

Male and female homosexuals have become much more open in expressing their thinking and behavior in the past few years. Many have joined in what is called the Gay movement and have worked to establish resource and social centers where they can receive help with personal problems and mingle socially. This has been considered by some as a desirable alternative to meeting in bars. In some cities "near communities have developed, especially in residential areas of the city with heavy concentrations of homosexuals. These areas are described by homosexuals as 'the swish Alps' or 'boys' town.' In these sections, apartment houses on particular streets may be owned by, or rented exclusively to homosexuals."[18]

The Gay movement has also become active in sponsoring legislation to combat alleged discrimination against homosexuals.

OTHER VARIANT PATTERNS
Possible Reasons for Their Development

In addition to homosexuality there are a number of other variant sexual behavior patterns which are encountered in individuals of both sexes. Inasmuch as these patterns generally have multiple rather than single causation, no effort will be made to show how each individual one develops. Instead, a few generalizations will be made concerning their causes.

1. The sexual variant may be an individual who feels inadequate and consequently lacks the self-confidence to engage in socially common forms of sexual activity.

2. He might have been taught consciously or unconsciously that sex is not a natural part of life.

3. Disappointments in the course of his sexual life history may have caused him fear of normal sexual contacts and the need to substitute forms of sexual behavior which are less threatening to him.

4. His parents may not have been stable role models.

---

[17]McCary, James Leslie, *Human Sexuality*, New York: D. Van Nostrand Co., 2nd Ed., p. 375, (Hooker, E.), (a) The adjustment of the male overt homosexual, J. proj. tech. 21 (1957): 18-31. (b) An empirical study of some relations between sexual patterns and gender identity in male homosexuals. In *Sex Research: New Developments*, ed. J. Money, New York: Holt. 1965.

[18]Hooker. Evelyn. "Male Homosexuals and Their Worlds." in Marmor Judd, ed., *Sexual Inversion: The Multiple Roots of Homosexuality*, New York: Basic Books, Inc., 1965, p. 93.

5. Disturbed relationships between his parents or between them and himself may have affected him.

Narcissism

"I have been blessed with such a beautiful body that I don't think my husband has any right to expect frequent sexual contact with me."

The preceding statement by a young wife is typical narcissistic thinking—the feeling that one's own body is a greater source of sexual joy than the body of any other person.

This excessive preoccupation with one's own body was named narcissism after the youth in ancient Greek mythology who fell in love with his own image which was reflected in a pool of clear water. According to the legend, Narcissus was the son of the river god Cephisus and the nymph Lieriope. He was a handsome, vain youth who rejected the many girls who loved him. Among those rejected was the nymph Echo who was so hurt by his indifference that she faded away until only her voice remained.

Inasmuch as Echo was a favorite of the gods, they became angry when Narcissus spurned her, and punished him by causing him to fall in love with his own reflection. He subsequently remained at the side of the pool admiring his image until he died and was changed into a flower called the narcissus.

Naturally, it is difficult to live happily with a real narcissist, as such an individual is always focusing his thoughts on himself even while he is engaging in sexual contact with others.

Voyeurism (Peeping Tom behavior)

Peeping Tom behavior derives its name from a very interesting legend. A certain Earl Leofric, lord of Coventry, was known for the heavy taxes he imposed upon his subjects. His wife, Lady Godiva, was in sympathy with the financially burdened townspeople and she pleaded with her husband to reduce their taxes. The Earl said he would if his wife would ride naked through the streets of the town. To his great surprise, she agreed to the request.

According to the story, all of the townspeople honored her petition and remained indoors and did not look as the lovely lady mounted a white horse and rode through the town clothed only in her long golden hair. Did we say all of the people? There is a slight correction. A tailor named

Tom peeked through a shutter at her blonde loveliness and, according to the tale, was struck blind.

There are many voyeurs in contemporary society. These individuals have such a compulsion to view the genitalia or the nude body of another person that the desire becomes an obsession. The male voyeur usually strives to remain unseen and is delighted and sexually stimulated as he watches women disrobe. This compulsion may have developed due to the fact that as a child he never had an opportunity to view and accept as natural the bodily differences of the other sex.

At one time the writer counseled a married student who was so disturbed by his voyeuristic pattern that he had to be hospitalized. He claimed that he was "peeking" to compensate for a feeling of sexual inadequacy.

To show the extent of his problem, two of his statements will be quoted here.

"I've figured just the right angle so I can sit in the dark in our apartment and watch television and the windows across the court at the same time. This way, I can enjoy looking at the women undress and still not miss my favorite television program. . . . I can't study when I'm in the library as I'm always watching and hoping that a girl somewhere near me will cross her legs."

Exhibitionism

The exhibitionist seems to have a desire to display his or her body to others. This includes a compulsion to exhibit the body to others in an illegal and flagrant manner. Exhibitionists seem to pick a favorite spot to display themselves, such as in a park, alley, or supermarket. They also seem to get more sexual satisfaction if the onlooker is shocked or excited.

Very often young girls are horror-stricken by older men who stand and display their genitals. Some analysts believe that the male displays his sexual parts to prove his masculinity and that women are motivated to display the nipples as well as the genitals to emphasize that they are females.

Sadism

The Marquis de Sade (1740-1814) was a French author who wrote detailed accounts of individuals who tortured or abused other humans. Because he became so well known for his tales of cruelty, the term sadism was coined to denote mistreatment of another person in order to gain sexual satisfaction. The sadist seems unable to achieve sexual satisfaction unless he is cruel to the object of his love. This cruelty may take the brutal forms of torturing and whipping one's love partner or it may be expressed in treating the object of one's affections with extreme mental cruelty. Some authorities believe that sadism in its extreme form may be related to schizophrenia and pyromania and consequently may cause criminal acts. Sadists, both male and female, appear to have a compulsion to prove their strength or dominance.

Masochism

Masochism derives its name from the Austrian novelist Leopold von Sacher-Masoch (1836-1895) who had a history of masochistic involvements. The masochist is the individual who obtains sexual pleasure from being mistreated. Some men and women will actually plead with their sexual partners to whip them or subject them to physical indignities so they can achieve orgasm. Other individuals appear to receive satisfaction from psychic masochism and need to be mentally humiliated before they can become sexually aroused. One often encounters testimony in court hearings telling of a sadistic husband who beats his wife, and his masochistic spouse who seems to enjoy the beatings.

Fetishism

Fetishism is a form of sexual variation in which the person's erotic desire becomes fixed upon some quality, part, or object which symbolizes that individual's love object. Thus the fetishist accepts a mystical substitute to love in place of the individual whom he secretly admires but dares not approach because he fears being rejected. The fetish may be a lock of hair, a shoe, underwear, or a part of the body. The male fetishist may invest attractive qualities in the object of his choice, which may be a girdle, so that he can hold it in his arms, caress it tenderly, and achieve orgasm. Some analysts believe that the fetishist, either man or woman, has some fear of being rejected by the admired person of the opposite sex, so, consequently, uses the substitute object not only for sexual arousal, but also to gain some feelings of dominance over the secretly admired person.

Transvestism (also called transvestitism)

Transvestism is a form of sexual behavior in which the individual receives ego satisfaction and sexual stimulation from dressing in clothing usually worn by the opposite sex. This practice is not limited to homosexuals. Many modern authorities state that individuals of both sexes who are heterosexual in their interests may practice transvestism to gain sexual thrills. There are many hypotheses regarding the causes of transvestism. One of the simplest is that it is "a form of compulsion neurosis in which the individual's desire for the genitals of the opposite sex is displaced to the clothing of the opposite sex."[19]

A typical case was brought to the writer by a wife who told the following story:

She had come home early from her bridge club and discovered her husband dressed in women's clothing and gazing in the mirror with obvious admiration for his appearance. Under persistent questioning he admitted to her that every time she went out, he sneaked down to the basement and "dressed up" in some of her old clothing which she had stored in a trunk. He said that this gave him a great lift and also excited him sexually. After a period of counseling he and his wife had a bonfire ceremony in which the clothing was burned.

Transsexualism

A transsexual is an individual who identifies himself as a member of the opposite sex. He cross-dresses and prefers members of his own sex as partners.

In recent years a number of people have expressed the desire to have their bodies surgically changed to that of the opposite sex. The majority of these individuals are men.

Perhaps the most highly publicized case of transsexualism is that of Christine Jorgensen, the GI who went to Copenhagen in 1950 for hormone injections and reconstructive surgery. She now appears as a female entertainer in night clubs. When answering the question "Has it been worth it?" Her answer was, "I found the oldest gift of heaven—to be myself." *Christine Jorgensen—A Personal Autobiography,* New York: Paul S. Eriksson, 1967, p. 332.

Ellis gives an interesting comment on such persons. He says, "Actually since there is no known method, as yet, of truly changing the inborn sex of the individual, these transsexuals are reaching for the moon." He states further that he has found those patients he has interviewed to be "borderline or outrightly psychotic."[20]

---

[19]Podolsky, Edward, *Encyclopedia of Aberrations.* New York: The Citadel Press, 1965, p. 532.
[20]Ellis, Albert, *The Art and Science of Love,* New York: Lyle Stuart, Inc., 1965, pp. 190, 191.

Addiction to Pornography

Although there is much debate about the effects of viewing porno-graphic material, variant behavior does occur when the person considers it necessary to view pornographic material in order to become sexually aroused or when the need for viewing pornography becomes so com-pulsive that the individual wastes time and money in the effort.

The Use of Children as Sexual Objects

There are some adults who seek their sexual satisfaction from chil-dren. One frequently hears of little girls being waylaid and assaulted by men, and some women seek satisfaction from small boys. This type of be-havior may take many forms. In some there are heterosexual, homosexual, or Lesbian relationships. When a male is attracted to small boys the pat-tern is called pedophilia.

Gerontosexuality

Individuals who exhibit this pattern of behavior seek sexual satis-faction from older people.

Young girls and boys who prefer to marry older men and women also may fall into the general category of gerontosexuality. It is thought that such individuals may be seeking substitute mothers or fathers.

Necrophilia

There are some individuals who seek sexual satisfaction from the human corpse. Experts are of the opinion that there is a sadistic element in such actions and a possible desire to dominate someone.

Pygmalionism

This pattern is a rare form of behavior in which individuals become excited sexually when they view statues, and especially those of nude women.

Bestiality

There are some persons who seek contact with animals for sexual satisfaction. The writer counseled one student who sought such contact in order to compensate for the mistreatment which was given to him by the other members of his family. Such behavior often occurs when the individual lacks opportunity to mingle with and to be accepted by others.

COUNSELING

Authorities agree that individuals who engage in the foregoing sexual behavior patterns will respond to psychotherapy. There seems to be the feeling, also, that the best results may be obtained when the therapist is not too nondirective, but constantly reassures the patient that he or she can learn to enjoy culturally accepted sexuality.

Suggested Readings

1. American Medical Association, Committee on Human Sexuality, *Human Sexuality,* Chicago: American Medical Association, 1972.

2. Anderson, Wayne J., *How to Discuss Sex With Teen-agers,* Minneapolis: T. S. Denison & Co., Inc., 1969.

3. Anderson, Wayne J., *How to Explain Sex to Children,* Minneapolis: T. S. Denison & Co., Inc., 1971.

4. Anderson, Wayne J., *How to Understand Sex: Guidelines for Students,* Minneapolis: T. S. Denison & Co., Inc., 1966.

5. Bell, Robert R., *Social Deviance,* Homewood, Ill.: The Dorsey Press, 1971.

6. Broderick, Carlfred, and Bernard, Jessie (eds.), *The Individual, Sex and Society: A SIECUS Handbook for Teachers and Counselors,* Baltimore, Md.: Johns Hopkins Press, 1969.

7. Burn, Helen Jean, *Better Than the Birds, Smarter Than the Bees,* Nashville, Tenn.: Abingdon Press, 1969.

8. Caprio, Frank S., *The Sexually Adequate Male,* New York: Citadel Press, 1952.

9. Ellis, Albert, and Abarbanel, Albert, *The Encyclopedia of Sexual Behavior,* New York: Hawthorn Books, 1967 (2nd ed.).

10. Gagnon, John H., and Simon, William (eds.), *Sexual Deviance,* New York: Harper & Row, 1967.

11. Hatterer, Lawrence J., *Changing Homosexuality in the Male,* New York: McGraw-Hill, 1970.

Note: Parts of this chapter have been reprinted by permission from:
Anderson, Wayne J., *How to Explain Sex to Children,* Minneapolis: T. S. Denison and Co., Inc., 1971.
————*How to Understand Sex,* Minneapolis: T. S. Denison and Co., Inc., 1966.

12. Johnson, Cecil E., *Sex and Human Relationships,* Columbus, Ohio: Charles E. Merrill Publishing Co., 1970.

13. Juhasz, Anne McCreary, *Sexual Development and Behavior: Selected Readings,* Homewood, Ill.: The Dorsey Press, 1973.

14. McCary, James Leslie, *Human Sexuality,* New York: D. Van Nostrand Co., 1973, (2nd ed.).

15. Perrin, Mark, and Smith, Thomas E., *Ideas and Learning Activities for Family Life and Sex Education,* Dubuque, Iowa: Wm. C. Brown Co., 1972.

16. Taylor, Donald L., *Human Sexual Development,* Philadelphia: F. A. Davis Co., 1970.

17. Schulz, Esther D., and Williams, Sally R., *Family Life and Sex Education: Curriculum and Instruction,* New York: Harcourt, Brace & World, 1969.

Chapter XXII

Sensible Family Discipline

Our two-year-old boy will do anything for a piece of candy. Is it all right to use that to bribe him?

Our small son just doesn't care; you can take away all his toys or give him a spanking and he just says, "O.K." How can you punish a boy like that?

My daughter screams when she can't have her own way. I'm so ashamed when I am out with her. What shall I do?

What should you do when your little girl spits at you?

If I say "No" to our son, his father says I'm too strict, and lets him go ahead and do it. What can I do?

I always buy just the same things for my two children. That's right isn't it?

The above questions which are typical of hundreds that parents are asking about child discipline reveal two important things, one, parents sense the need to discipline their children, two, they are not quite certain how to do it. Often they take the easy way out, and try to control their offspring with brute force or wash their hands of the whole affair, and say, in essence, to their children, "We can't teach you the rules for getting along in society. You are on your own. Find out for yourselves."

A typical example of the parent who tries to discipline with physical force (the authoritarian approach) was the college student who said:

"My wife and I have learned just how to discipline our three small boys. When one of them does something wrong, we whip him until he cries, even if it takes a leather belt. As soon as he begins to shed tears, we know he has learned his lesson."

A young mother who is representative of the "you're on your own" (the permissive approach) to discipline expressed herself this way:

"I love our four-year-old daughter so much that I would be shattered if she didn't love me. I've vowed never to speak a harsh word to her, and

I couldn't stand to punish her. This way, I know she'll always love me, and anyway she's smart enough to sense what's right."

HISTORICAL INFLUENCES ON DISCIPLINE

These two opposite and extreme disciplinary approaches have been the result of the historical swinging of the discipline pendulum from one extreme to the other—extreme authoritarianism to extreme permissiveness —and individual parents adopting the approach they felt was right. In America, extreme authoritarianism in disciplining children prevailed from the colonial period through the early 1900s. Children were thought to be born with natural tendencies toward behaving in an evil manner, and there was widespread agreement among adults that beating was the best way to curb young people's sinful tendencies. Then, attitudes toward children gradually began to change, and the idea that "children should be seen, but not heard" and should be controlled with harsh physical punishment ("spare the rod and spoil the child") were discarded. A new, permissive, "hands off" approach emerged, and some adults went to the other extreme, abandoned all authoritative control and permitted children to do almost anything they wanted to do, short of injuring themselves or others, physically. A popular couplet that went the rounds was:

"Children aren't happy with nothing to ignore,
And that's what parents were created for."[1]

Of course, all parents did not adopt this hands off (*laissez-faire*) approach and some hung on to their authoritative thinking. Consequently, in today's society, we have a mixture of disciplinary approaches, authoritarian, permissive, and a third which suggests disciplining the child within a developmental framework. As the American family has become more democratized, an increasing number of parents have begun using the third approach, an intelligent middle-of-the-road viewpoint toward discipline which is based on the nature and needs of both their children and today's society. Such an approach to discipline begins with an understanding of the nature of discipline and its intended goals.

THE MEANING OF DISCIPLINE

Discipline denotes teaching the child sound principles of behavior and guiding him toward the goal of judicious and self-controlled action.

---

[1]Baber, Ray E., *Marriage and the Family*, New York: McGraw-Hill, Second Edition, 1953, p. 296.

"Discipline" and "punishment" are not synonymous. Whereas discipline implies guiding the individual toward right doing, punishment suggests hurting someone or paying him back for doing something wrong. In addition to the differences in overt expression between discipline and punishment, there is usually a difference in the state of mind of the person who disciplines as compared with the person who punishes. The disciplinarian's actions are directed toward guiding the child toward a specific goal. The overall intent is to help the recipient learn a lesson so he will hopefully improve himself and become a better person.

The punisher is not always concerned with directing the offender toward a specific goal, but more often with preventing the recurrence of some specific wrongdoing. For example, an adult may punish a neighbor's child for straying into his yard and breaking a window. However, the punishment the adult metes out is not fundamentally directed toward preventing the child from breaking windows in general, say in someone else's house two or three blocks away. The concerned adult may want to "improve" the child so that he won't break any more of *his* windows, but his primary interest usually doesn't go beyond preventing repeated destruction of his own property.

In summarizing the use of punishment, Homan feels that people punish others for different reasons, sometimes to satisfy their anger, sometimes in an attempt to prevent them from repeating a wrongdoing, because the law states they should be punished, "to hurt an enemy," and sometimes because they hope they can help the person who is punished to improve. He also points out that a positive goal is not stated with the word "punishment" as it is with the word "discipline."[2]

Of course, it is possible for parents dispassionately and with a measure of calmness to guide their child toward a certain goal by using repeated punishment. However, if the child does reach the desired goal, his acceptable behavior may often occur because of fear of his parents, and even though he respects them and conforms to their will, he may feel like a trained animal whose performance is always directed by others. How much better it is for both the parents and the child if he attains a certain behavioral goal because his parents have guided him with love and understanding and he has learned to behave in a desirable way be-

---

[2]Homan, William E., *Child Sense*, New York: Bantam Books, 1970, p. 26.

cause he has internalized his parents' teaching so that they have become part of his nature. He thus goes through life as an inner-directed rather than an other-directed individual.

STUDY OF THE POSSIBLE EFFECTS
OF PHYSICAL PUNISHMENT

Straus in a review of other research and a study of 229 undergraduate university students at the University of Minnesota and the University of New Hampshire reports the following findings regarding the use and results of physical punishment:

"A considerable body of research . . . has found that children who have experienced large amounts of physical punishment to be highly aggressive. The irony of these findings is that these studies also find that the most frequent occasion for physical punishment is to control aggression on the part of the child. Similarly, although the evidence is not as clear, there are indications that parental attempts to control excessive dependency by punishment tend to increase rather than decrease dependency by the child.

"Parents who were reported as feeling that the most important behavioral characteristic for their child during his last year in high school is to 'be obedient' to them, used more physical punishment than parents holding any other trait as of primary importance. At the other end, parents who felt that either 'self-control' or a child who 'thinks for himself' is most important, used physical punishment least often. These findings support the linkage theory* because the available evidence suggests that use of physical punishment tends to produce a child who is low in self-directedness. Thus, the use of physical punishment by parents who value obedience in a child is . . . likely to produce a child who lacks self-direction and is hence more amenable to external controls."[3]

---

*Linkage theory—Adults will attempt to socialize a child with practices suitable to develop the type of personality he will need to cope with typical life circumstances he will face as an adult. . . . "physical punishment tends to produce a child who is high on aggression and low on internalized moral standards and self-directedness. Thus the use of physical punishment is assumed to be linked to socialization for a set of circumstances in which physical aggressiveness is important and internalized moral standards and self-directedness are relatively unimportant." It is also "assumed that such traits are more often found among the lower and the working class sectors of society than in the middle class sector." (Straus did not find this class difference in his study.)

[3]Straus, Murray A., "Some Social Antecedents of Physical Punishment: A Linkage Theory Interpretation," *Journal of Marriage and the Family*, Vol. 33, No. 4, (November 1971), pp. 658-663.

WHY CHILDREN NEED DISCIPLINE

According to the principles of mental health, an individual will have a more satisfying life if he learns to value and accept himself and senses that he is loved and accepted by others. The "others" in the average person's life are the people he associates with in his family, in his neighborhood, in his school, and in his community. In order to get along with these people he must learn what they expect of him. As soon as he becomes aware of the kinds of attitudes and behavior that these social groups consider to be proper, he has a framework in which to operate. Although this framework may present some limitations to his behavior, he usually feels more secure when he understands them because he then knows what he may or may not do to gain acceptance and approval. One reason parents often have difficulty in disciplining their children is their failure to explain clearly the specific limits they will put on their behavior. Consequently, children will cause a lot of tension between themselves and their parents while they are finding out just "how far they can go." This is equally true in the schoolroom. The teacher who lets his or her pupils know from the start what kind of behavior is expected and what will not be tolerated, and firmly adheres to the framework in which the pupils have been told they may operate encounters few disciplinary problems in the classroom.

Adults who favor the extremely permissive approach to discipline seem to be overlooking the fact that the individual who is expected to adjust to a new situation must first know what is expected of him. Not telling him what the rules or standards of the group are and still expecting him to make an adjustment would be like expecting a stranger to the game of baseball to intuitively know that he would be out after three strikes, or that he should run toward first base instead of third, after hitting a ball, despite the fact that he had no previous knowledge of the rules of the game.

It is sometimes said that defining limits to an individual will stifle his creativity. This should not happen if the limitations are broad enough to allow for expression of individual differences and narrow enough so the concerned person does not deprive others of their rights. Such a concept allows room for the crusader or the rebel to work within the rules of society to effect needed changes. On the other hand, if such a person has developed an abnormal personality, and in turn rejected society, he may lack the self-esteem and the necessary acceptance by others to bring about any positive changes. In other words, every child and adult must learn that some kind of authority exists in every social group and that the chances of leading a satisfying life are better if he learns how to deal with it rather than reject it.

THINGS THAT CONTRIBUTE TO EFFECTIVE DISCIPLINE

The Home Atmosphere

The family home should be a place in which each member feels acceptance of himself for what he is. There is no comparison with others, but the attitude prevails that each individual is a person with his own niche in life to fill. There is no feeling of being dominated, but neither is their freedom without order. The idea prevails that personal freedom with a sense of responsibility may be exercised within a framework of order that has been developed through democratic processes.

The Parents' Role

Parents, to be good disciplinarians, must realize that they cannot be tyrannical rulers, but neither must they abdicate their responsibilities of showing and telling their children how society expects them to behave. Fathers and mothers cannot be expected to know everything or always behave perfectly themselves, but they should be reliable sources to which their children can turn when they want to know what they should do, or how they are expected to behave in certain situations. **Parents should therefore be authorities regarding the things that they can prove to their children are right to do or accept.** For illustration, a child will not learn that two plus two equals four, if the teaching parent says, "I think two plus two equals four. Perhaps I'm wrong. Maybe the answer is three." Instead, he or she very calmly says two plus two equals four and the child accepts it. Another example, if a small boy is learning to drink milk, his mother tells him and shows him that if he tips his glass upside down, the milk will all run out. Subsequently there is no argument about how to hold the glass when drinking. The child accepts the way it should be done because his mother has told him and proven to him that is the way to do it. If parents develop the confidence in their young children's minds that they are reliable sources from which to receive information and direction, the chances are good that their children, even when they grow older, will turn to them for guidance.

Parents should be in agreement concerning the methods used to guide their children. If the mother directs her daughter to do something in a certain way or expects a specific type of behavior from her, and the father disagrees in front of the child and says the mother's expectations need not be followed, the family disciplinary structure begins to totter. This can happen beginning with the children's preschool days and right up through their teens. Teen-agers soon learn to play one parent against the other and then make up rules of their own. For illustration, this may happen if their mother tells them to come home from their dates at 11:00 p.m. and their father contradicts and tells them it's all right to come home later because their mother is too protective. If parents have such diverse temperaments that they don't see eye-to-eye on methods of disciplining their children, they should discuss their differences privately until they both can accept some mid-course, but still effective, method to use.

Parents should be good listeners and good observers. If they listen carefully so they can determine what their children are really trying to say to them and observe or watch them perceptively so their combined listening and watching perceptions help them understand what their children are really feeling, they can offer more effective guidance. Good listening should be coupled with a nonjudgmental discussion of the feelings that children feel free to bring out into the open. If this is done, the specific disciplinary problem may either vanish as a result of good communication or be resolved in a cooperative manner.

Using Sound Disciplinary Practices

Parents and other adults should be firm, believe in, and mean what they say. A child who senses indecision in the disciplinarian's manner, is less likely to comply.

Parents should be consistent. Once a limit has been set or a certain act has been defined as wrong, discipline should be enforced regardless of the parents' mood at the time. Laughing at a misdeed one day, and punishing for it the next, soon confuses the child, as the consequences of certain types of behavior become unpredictable.

Things should be taught to each child in relationship to his readiness to learn and understand them. It would make little sense to expect a four-year-old to learn how to check the oil in the family car and keep it at the proper level. This also means being reasonable, and knowing what to expect of the child at a certain age.

Nagging should be avoided. Such constant verbal harassment may cause the child to gradually develop a "deaf" ear and immunize himself to the criticisms, so they have no effect.

Children should be taught how to behave in certain social settings before they enter them, if possible, and certainly no later than when they first enter such activities. Just as fashion designers and clothing stores give their potential customers previews of what will be worn during the coming season, so should parents let children know beforehand how they will be expected to behave when they enter a certain stage in their social interaction. Such advance instruction would include:

Teaching a child how to get along with his playmates, and explaining that such things as kicking or biting them will make him unpopular.

Teaching him to have confidence in and respect for the teacher, before he enters school.

Teaching him how education can help him, shortly after he gets used to school.

Guiding him to an understanding of how to enjoy and benefit from his teen years.

Getting Positive Responses

Finding out what is bothering a child, discussing it with him in an understanding way, and then either eliminating his cause for discontent or helping him to see that he has either misinterpreted something or reacted irrationally to a specific situation may often change his response from negative to positive.

Getting a child's attention in a considerate manner may also help in getting him to react positively. On the other hand, commanding an individual of any age to stop what he is doing, shift his thinking in the commanding adult's direction, and comply promptly with an order may bring about resistance. Naturally, if impending danger threatens the child's welfare, abrupt command and compliance must take place. However, in ordinary circumstances such as telling the child it is time to come to dinner or go to bed, more positive responses are usually obtained if advance notice is given.

Praising the child can elicit favorable response, if it is done in the right way. Children's accomplishments should be recognized with favorable comment. However, parents often make the mistake of praising the child's personality and character, rather than his accomplishments. For illustration, a mother who attends a PTA meeting, visits her daughter's room, and sees a picture she has drawn hanging on the wall may come home and say, "Kay, you are such a wonderful girl to have your teacher display your picture on the wall."

Such a statement may cause Kay to have guilt feelings because she may not feel that she is wonderful. In fact, she may secretly be hoping that her mother will soon quit talking, so she can join her playmates outside. Her mother would have put less pressure on her to present a "wonderful image" and made it easier to accept the praise, if she had said, "Kay, I liked the colors in your picture that was hanging on your classroom wall. I'm happy that your teacher recognizes your skill as an artist."

Using rewards can bring about negative responses if they are not used properly. Using them should not constitute buying good behavior. If parents want to reward their children, it is usually more effective to do it spontaneously after the approved behavior takes place, rather than to say, "I'll give you a dollar if you will be good today." Children should be guided to appreciate the natural rewards that come from diligent effort. For example, the satisfaction that comes from making something or learning to play the piano. The use of rewards should be handled very carefully. Although B. F. Skinner, noted research psychologist, and others believe children are taught by being rewarded for socially useful behavior, it is possible that the use of rewards may cause children to place more value on the symbols of success than on good behavior. Thus, later on in adulthood they may join those groups of people who believe that owning a beautiful home, driving an expensive car and having a prestigious professional position make them good citizens.

DEALING WITH MISBEHAVIOR

Children do not always do what they have been taught to do, and even if parents understand why, sometimes it becomes necessary to use other measures to get them to behave as they should.

Using Natural Consequences

Children often learn to do a turnabout in their behavior when they experience the natural consequences of their misbehavior. For example, if a small boy gets angry or careless and deliberately throws his new ball into the bushes, thus losing it, he should learn not to do it again by experiencing the result of his irresponsibility—a lost ball. Similarly, if a girl has no logical reason for not getting home in time for dinner, and arrives after it is over and the dishes are washed and put away, the ensuing natural consequences should teach her something. If no special preparations are made by her mother to provide for her hunger, she learns that she must be home at dinnertime in the future if she wants to enjoy the same kind of meal that is prepared for the rest of the family.

The parents' role in letting natural consequences become a learning experience is to avoid interfering with their happening unless they would be dangerous to the misbehaving child.

Using Logical Consequences

The use of logical consequences in dealing with misbehavior differs from using natural consequences in that parents structure the environment in such a way that the child is provided with choices and explained to beforehand what will be the logical consequences of each choice. To illustrate, if the family is planning to play a game, the small boy is told beforehand that if he abides by the rules of the game, he may play. If he does not, he must watch the others play. So he knows beforehand that it is his choice to make, and if he starts to cheat, he will realize that the logical consequence is that he will not be allowed to continue playing.

Care must be taken when using logical consequences as a deterrent to misbehavior that the consequences are reasonable, understandable to the child, are not being used to deprive him of his rights, and are not a form of retaliation to get even with the child or humiliate him because of past misbehavior.

Disapproval of a misdeed is often all that is needed to get the child with tender feelings to abandon undesirable behavior. Saying, "I'm disappointed that you acted that way," accompanied by the reassuring statement that you still love the child and think he is a fine person might be effective if it influences him in the right manner. However, parents should carefully study the child's temperament before using such an approach.

Depriving a child of something he values or withholding certain privileges for a period of time are of questionable value in dealing with misbehavior. What is really being done is continuous nagging at and shaming of a child for what he did in the past. It is difficult enough for individuals to accept criticism for their present mistakes without having to be reminded that what they did two weeks ago was wrong. It is better if parents can work out some way of dealing with the misbehavior at the time it occurred, carry through with it, and then quit talking about the incident. Repetitive nagging at or belittling a child for a past mistake might result in his losing self-confidence or becoming sullen and rebellious. Of course, if a son or daughter persists in engaging in a specific type of misbehavior, say for example, a high school girl repeatedly comes home from a date at 3 a.m. when both she and her parents have agreed beforehand that midnight is a logical curfew time, disciplinary action must be taken. But rather than "grounding" the daughter for two weeks, it might be more effective to have a frank discussion with her and a mutual decision made as to whether she is mature enough to continue dating and, if so, restrict her dating hours to a reasonable framework of time. Such an appeal to her feeling of maturity may bring the desired cooperation.

Punishment—
Spanking, Whipping or Verbal Ridicule

Punishment is a controversial method of dealing with misbehavior. Some parents swear by it and others swear at it. All that can be said is that most of the research done in the area of punishment has suggested that the results and effects are unpredictable, and most often negative. Some young people say they love and respect their parents because they punished them. Others say they hate and disrespect them. It occasionally happens that children who have been punished severely and repeatedly lose their self-confidence and become timid or withdrawn. Others may become submissive to those who can dominate them and abusive to those whom they can dominate. Two other weaknesses of punishment as a method of dealing with misbehavior are: It is often used by the one who is punishing to ventilate anger or as a form of retaliation. The child may develop negative feelings toward the adult who punishes him and view him as a threatening figure rather than a model to identify with.

Parents often fear that if they lose their tempers occasionally, forget to use more effective methods of dealing with behavior, and spank their children, that they may permanently damage their personalities. This is not likely to happen if the general atmosphere in the home is one of love and understanding. Then, children will usually sense that their parents love and understand them, and will not be affected negatively by infrequent punishing that takes place when their parents let their emotions get out of control.

In summarizing disciplinary practices, it should again be stated that parental discipline provides a means of teaching and guiding children, and is not a vehicle for punishment.

Suggested Readings

1. Arnold, Arnold, *Your Child and You,* Chicago: Henry Regnery Co., 1970.
2. Beltz, Stephen, *How to Make Johnny Want to Behave,* Englewood Cliffs, N.J.: Prentice-Hall, 1972.
3. Bird, Joseph, and Bird, Lois, *Power to the Parents,* Garden City, N.Y.: Doubleday and Co., 1972.
4. Cheavens, Frank, *Creative Parenting: Advantages You Can Give Your Child,* Waco, Texas: Word Book Publishers, 1971.
5. Dobson, James, *Dare to Discipline,* Wheaton, Ill.: Tyndale House Publishers, 1970.
6. Dreikers, Rudolf, and Grey, Loren, *A Parents' Guide to Child Discipline,* New York: Hawthorn Books, 1970.
7. Fletcher, Grace Nies, *What's Right With Us Parents?,* New York: William Morrow and Co., 1972.
8. Ginott, Haim G., *Between Parent and Child,* New York: Macmillan Co., 1965.
9. Gordon, Thomas, *Parent Effectiveness Training,* New York: Peter H. Wyden, Inc., 1970.
10. Gruenberg, Sidonie, *The New Encyclopedia of Child Care and Guidance,* Garden City, N.Y.: Doubleday and Co., 1968 (2nd ed.).
11. Klein, Ted, *The Father's Book,* New York: William Morrow and Co., 1968.
12. Madsen, Clifford K., and Madsen, Charles H., *Parents/Children/Discipline,* Boston: Allyn and Bacon, 1972.
13. Salk, Lee, *What Every Child Would Like His Parents to Know,* (To Help Him With Emotional Problems of His Everyday Life), New York: David McKay Co., 1972.
14. Satir, Virginia, *Peoplemaking,* Palo Alto, Calif.: Science and Behavior Books, 1972.

Chapter XXIII

Succeeding as a Family

REFLECTIONS

Personally, thinking back upon my childhood, I have only beautiful memories. It was my parents and brothers and sisters who made them possible.

As a child I remember:

Saturday nights—taking our baths, polishing shoes, and going to the neighborhood drugstore for a Sunday paper and candy bars.

Sundays—going to church with my family and singing in the choir.

Family get-togethers—birthday parties, family picnics, Thanksgiving and Christmas dinners, graduation gifts.

Fun with my grandparents—the thrill of visiting them and sleeping overnight at their house.

The love and feeling of security my parents gave me—my mom always being home after school. My dad always being home for dinner. May my children be so lucky.

—Taken from a college coed's "Analysis of My Family Relationships" paper.

THE FAMILY'S PHILOSOPHY OF LIFE

Families who are succeeding are those who feel that life is meaningful. This attitude is developed in family members by the man and woman who establish the family. When they marry, their family life should "begin with the end in mind." In other words, the husband and wife should begin to build their family life with a clear idea of what they want its outcome to be, and specifically define the objectives they want to reach. They will find this difficult to do if they live in an "existential vacuum" (Frankl) which causes them to disregard the traditions of the past, including their family heritage, and prevents them from visualizing the possibilities of the future. Frankl says that existentialists who think that "now" is all that matters and live with a sense of detachment from the past and ignore the possibilities of the future often grow bored and depressed and develop what he calls " 'Sunday neurosis,' that kind of depression which afflicts people who become aware of the lack of content in their lives when the rush of the busy week is over and the void within themselves becomes manifest."[1]

Consequently, family groups who are succeeding find it helpful to draw wisdom from the lessons of the past and create a blueprint for building their future. To do this, each family must do more than live within the framework of generalities with which they have defined life's meaning, but must also remember that the family as a group and each member as an individual should try to live each of life's moments in a manner that is in harmony with the family's projected future goals. This does not mean that father and mother and sons and daughters need to follow identical patterns of living. Due to individual differences, family members possess different talents and are drawn toward different interests; therefore, meaningful living as applied to individual family members would signify that each person would work toward the goal of his greatest interest, in order to find his specific vocation or mission in life, with the assumption that his unique tasks would be fulfilled with family-quality performance.

Successful family groups also believe that each stage of life, childhood, adolescence, and adulthood is important and can be lived creatively and responsibly so that individual growth occurs, challenges are met and genuine concern for and cooperation with others are practiced. People who build successful families also realize that no one is perfect, and that mistakes made by family members should be treated with understanding and forgiveness, and with an attempt for all to learn and profit from them. Life is viewed realistically with the knowledge that it will bring joys and sorrows, successes and disappointments. But despite the compensations and disappointments that life offers, families who are succeeding never cease in their quest for individual and group excellence.

RELIGIOUS ATTITUDES AND FAMILY SUCCESS

Past and present research studies suggest that the religious attitudes and activities of the family have a definite effect upon its members' ad-

---

[1]Frankl, Viktor E., *Man's Search for Meaning: An Introduction to Logotherapy*, Boston: Beacon Press, 1962, Revised Edition, p. 109.

justment and happiness. Stone found that a greater number of high school and college students who kept busy in religious activities were happier and better adjusted at home and in society than those in the group who had little religious activity.[2]

Locke[3] found a definite relationship between church attendance and marital happiness, and Reddick[4] reported that couples with problems who were facing divorce had a better chance of reconciliation after being persuaded to become active in church.

There has been some thinking expressed in contemporary society that today's youth have become disenchanted with religiously-oriented activities. However, such things as the Jesus movement which has attracted a number of the younger generation and the tendency of many of this group to put less emphasis on the acquisition of material things and more thought to a satisfying way of life suggests that there may be more turning toward religion as a source of direction for life. Research findings also bear this out. Landis, in a study of 625 university students, found that the majority of them approved of religion in the home. "Only 2 percent . . . thought there had been too much emphasis on religion in the parental home and 35 percent said they thought there had not been enough." Those who preferred greater emphasis stated that when they married and had children of their own, they planned to follow policies of "family church attendance . . . bedtime prayers . . . grace at meals."[5]

The Nature of Religion

If you take religion as a guide, you shall find it also a friend;
a joy in prosperity, a comfort in adversity, peace to the conscience,
strength for duty, hope for the future, and endless blessedness in
the end.[6]

Some families fail to take religion into their lives because they do not know what it is. They look upon it as a set of "do-nots," and con-

[2]Stone. Carol Larson, *Church Participation and Social Adjustment of High School and College Youth,* Washington Agricultural Experiment Stations. Institute of Agricultural Sciences, State College of Washington, Rural Sociology Series on Youth, No. 12, Bulletin 550, May, 1954. p. 15.

[3]Locke, Harvey J.. *Predicting Adjustment in Marriage,* New York: Holt, Rinehart and Winston, 1951, p. 241.

[4]Reddick, DeWitt, "They Give Marriage a Second Chance." *Child Family Digest,* X, No. 2, Feb.. 1954.

[5]Landis, Judson T. and Mary G., *Building a Successful Marriage,* Englewood Cliffs, Prentice-Hall, 1973. Sixth Edition, p. 315.

[6]Edwards, Tryon, *Useful Quotations—A Cyclopedia of Quotations,* New York: 1933, Grosset & Dunlap, Revised Edition, p. 540. Editors, Catreuas. C. N. and Edwards, Jonathan.

sequently feel it would stifle their creativity and curb their pleasures. Two definitions of religion may help dispel such thinking.

A dictionary definition is:

Religion—"An awareness or conviction of the existence of a supreme being, arousing reverence, love, gratitude, the will to obey and serve, and the like; as man only is capable of religion."[7]

Whatever introduces a genuine perspective is religious.—John Dewey.[8]

These statements suggest that all life is ordered by a supreme being, and that only by learning how the universe is governed can an individual acquire the perspective needed to make progress in solving the problems that life presents.

Religious Concepts That Help Build Family Solidarity

Most of the families in the American culture are influenced by Judeo-Christian teachings which put emphasis on the dignity of the individual and the rewards that come from trying to understand and serve others. Their acceptance of the fatherhood of God causing them to be aware of the brotherhood of man helps them to be more understanding within the family group and exercise greater compassion toward other family members.

The religious teachings that the family has espoused also give them a code of conduct, and the acceptance of this code by the children helps them realize that their parents' desire to have them conduct themselves in a certain manner does not stem from selfish parental desires, but from a sincere wish to have them live in a way pleasing to God.

Living within a religious framework aids family members in making proper decisions. Inasmuch as their value judgments are oriented toward spiritual rather than material things, pressures to imitate peer group behavior are not as great.

Religious families possess spiritual resources that act as built-in stabilizers to help them through crises and trying times. Their belief that life is eternal helps them realize that they will eventually learn and understand things about God's plan of life which at the present time seem incomprehensible.

---

[7]Webster's New Collegiate Dictionary, Cambridge: G. & C. Merriam Co., 1961, p. 715.
[8]Dewey, John, *A Common Faith*, New Haven: Yale University Press, 1934, p. 24.

Finally, religious belief and practice by family members gives an added dimension to their mutual goal, namely that of understanding and doing God's will, so all can partake of his promised blessings to those who are obedient.

SUCCESSFUL FAMILY LIVING

Family Roles

Criticism of Today's Mothers

Although the American mother is in a position to have much to do with the success of the family, the manner in which she has fulfilled her role has been under attack since the 1940s. Philip Wylie in *Generation of Vipers* (a best seller), characterized the average mother as an irresponsible, unreasoning tyrant who psychologically deprives her sons of their manhood.[9] Subsequent writings by a number of authors including Friedan (1963), criticized the mother's role in other ways. Friedan proposed the thesis that American mothers who stay at home are discontented and exercising a negative influence on their husbands, their children and society.[10]

Such commentary and a good deal of research regarding the mother's role and the status of women in the American society continues unabated today. However, sociologists such as Chafe and other social scientists who engage in exacting research are suggesting that the woman's movement to radically change the female's economic, political, and social roles which at the same time generally belittles woman's role as a mother and housekeeper is not endorsed by most mothers. This is so because it has been preempted and promoted by middle-class, college-educated women whose efforts have reflected their own bias rather than the attitudes and values held by the majority of women in America.[11] It is certainly true that discrimination against women should cease; however, this doesn't necessarily mean that the woman's role as a homemaker also needs to be minimized. Recent polls of women who are housewives reveal that there is not widespread discontent with their role.

For example, a statewide survey of 600 people in Minnesota dis-

---

[9]Wylie, Philip, *Generation of Vipers*, New York: Rinehart and Co., 1942, Chapter 11. "Common Women."

[10]Friedan, Betty, *The Feminine Mystique*, New York: W. W. Norton & Co., 1963, Ch. 2. "The Happy Housewife Heroine."

[11]Chafe, William Henry, *Woman: Her Changing Social, Economic and Political Roles, 1920-1970*, New York: Oxford University Press. 1972.

closed that 83 percent of the homemakers considered their work fulfilling. Sixty-four percent of those questioned had been managing a household for 10 years or more. Also interesting to note was that 27 percent of the wives who were employed outside of the home said that being a homemaker was their major calling. Follow-up interviews with individual housewives revealed that all full-time homemakers said they were too busy to be bored, in some cases felt more independent than women who work outside of the home, and in most cases "wouldn't want to change places with their husband in the working world." There also was general agreement that there was opportunity and time, if they felt the need to participate in activities outside of the home.[12]

Other reports by wives who work suggest that homemakers have great difficulty finding their roles fulfilling when they combine marriage, family, home and career—sometimes out of necessity. Berry writes that such a combination of roles brings a burden that is almost too heavy to bear. She also believes that present-day society makes working mothers, especially those of preschool children, feel guilty and holds them "accountable in large part for some of the social ills of the country (delinquency, broken homes) . . . paying little attention to the many other reasons for these social problems."[13]

The Woman in the Homemaker's Role

Despite the comments by some people claiming the American mother has fulfilled her role poorly, a survey of our culture reveals that both mothers and fathers have made and are still making a significant contribution to producing competent adults who are making this society one of progress and accomplishment.

Role as a Wife—Today's wife has assumed the roles of being a companion to her husband both inside and outside of the home. She is expected to be a sexual companion to her husband, and not just submit to him but share his enthusiasm for sexual activity. In addition to playing the role of an interesting companion to her husband at home, both sexually and mentally, she is expected to expand her role and participate with her husband in active and spectator sports and be a partner to him in his civic and occupational activities.

---

[12]Reported in the Minneapolis *Tribune*, September 16, 1973.
[13]Berry, Paula, "How Women Cope," *Minnesota's Health*, Spring 1973, Minnesota Department of Health.

Role as a Mother—The present conception of the role of the mother requires her to develop a constant awareness of what might be done to safeguard the health of the family and develop the talents of its children. This includes keeping up on new medical findings, such as vaccines, and arranging for the children to receive them. Her husband usually expects her to know about the community's available child-centered services and organizations such as Boy Scouts, Girl Scouts, Little League baseball, school clubs and teams and see, if both are in favor, that the children take part in them.

In addition to all of these things, she is usually expected to arrange for all family celebrations such as children's birthdays.

Roles in Home Management and Community Activities—American mothers have moved into the home management role, and many of them do most of the family budgeting and buying, especially for food and clothing. An increasing number of mothers are also holding outside jobs in order to help provide for family needs. They also do yardwork and maintenance chores around the house.

Sociological studies also indicate that the mother has assumed the role of doing most of the communicating with the agencies and institutions outside of the family such as the church, social, community organizations and health and welfare agencies.

The Role as a Builder of Attitudes—Child psychologists feel that basic attitudes are developed in the home, and that the mother, both as a model and a teacher, has a significant role to play in building sound emotional and spiritual attitudes and feelings in the children. She, more than any other member of the family, seems to be charged with helping children learn to get along with one another and appreciate the beauties and the spiritual dimension of life.

It seems almost unnecessary to state that the way the mother fills the above-mentioned roles has much to do with the success of the family.

Today's Husbands and Fathers

Although there is very little research available regarding the husband's or father's role, especially related to his influence on the personality development of the child, what there is indicates that his role is important. Biller in reporting his findings says that most of the research affirms the importance of the father's role.[14] For example, it has been found that boys whose fathers are absent from the home appear to be more dependent, less aggressive, and have less satisfactory relationships with their peers than those whose fathers are present. It is also suggested that the boy's personality is affected by the length of the father's absence, at what periods in his life the absence occurs, and whether a father surrogate such as a male relative, youth leader, or athletic coach is available.

A number of observers believe that the American father's role is a peripheral one which is given lower priority than that of earning a living or entering military service. This is accounted for by the fact that great numbers of fathers are, of necessity, separated from their children, the primary reason being that the only steady employment that they can obtain in order to provide for family needs is away from their home town. Large corporations routinely transfer male employees to new communities, and often long periods of time elapse before wives and children can arrange to join them. During wartime, many fathers are separated from their families, with the thought that their allegiance to their country takes precedence over their allegiance to their family. Such circumstances do not lessen the importance of the father's role, and both children and society would benefit if greater effort were made to allow fathers more time at home.

The Man's Family Roles

Role as a Husband—The average husband seems to be under constant pressure to support his wife on an ever higher plane. It is true that more and more wives are now sharing the family's economic burdens, but a man's self-image is still affected by the way he provides for his wife and children and he is under the greater pressure to be the family breadwinner.

Wives are now expecting more companionship from their husbands and in the area of sex want their relationships to operate on a plane that provides mutual satisfaction. Thus, today's husband is expected to be a provider, an interesting companion and an adequate lover.

Role as a Father

Role as a Provider—The way in which the father provides for the family's economic needs determines, to a great extent, the material bene-

---

[14]Biller, Henry B., *Father, Child, and Sex Role—Paternal Determinants of Personality Development*, Lexington: Heath Lexington Books, 1971.

fits and the social status of his wife and children. The family usually lives in the locality where the father's employment is. The place he occupies in the community also gives the family a certain status. His wife and children are known as the John Jones family, and are usually accorded a position in the social group that is related to the father's recognition as a progressive citizen.

This "ascribed status" in the community which is accorded children is usually accepted by them with very little thought. They are often unmindful of the fact that the kind of house in which they live, the varieties of food which they eat, the style of clothing that they wear, the type of friends whom they meet, and the educational and cultural opportunities that they enjoy in their earlier years, are closely related to their father's ability to provide. It is true that today's mothers work as partners with fathers in providing for family needs, but the man of the family is still made to feel the more responsible in playing the role of provider for the family.

The Role of Influencing the Emotional Climate in the Home—The type of employment the father has also affects the emotional climate in the home. If his work requires him to be away from the family for periods of time, his wife and children sense the difference when he is not with them. Frequent transfers by his firm require adjustments to be made by all of the family group.

One student in discussing her father's job remarked that she had already attended thirty different schools and concluded by saying, "I just begin to get acquainted with kids my own age and then Dad's company moves us somewhere else."

Even if frequent job transfers do not take place, the kind of work the father does may have impact upon the emotions of family members. A coed who came for counseling seemed to be so filled with anxiety that she was almost incoherent in her speech. She soon revealed the reason. Her father held a responsible position which involved him in management and labor disputes, and the present situation had become so charged with hostility that he constantly carried a revolver for protection. Fear for his and their own safety had spread through the family members, and the entire group was suffering emotionally.

On the brighter side of the family scene, the father's successes also affect family emotions. Many wives blossom and develop greater charm as a result of their husbands' accomplishments, and the children in the family often develop more self-confidence.

The Role as a Model—Children are generally influenced by their father's behavior. Young sons tend to imitate their father's manner of walking, his gestures, mannerisms and speech. To them their dad is a hero; the symbol of manhood.

Daughters also look up to their father. They say they want to marry him when they grow up. To them, he is a symbol of security, and their image of what a man should be is shaped by their relationships with their father. The entire family, especially when the children are small, receives many of its impressions of the world outside of the home from the father and is influenced by his religious views and philosophy of life.

THE ROLES CHILDREN PLAY IN THE FAMILY

For some reason, much emphasis is put upon the fact that the father and the mother should fulfill certain roles in the family group in order that a democratic relationship will develop, and very little is written about the children's responsibilities to the family. The children's contributions to family unity can make a tremendous difference in the type of relationships that develop. Although children experience a longer period of dependency than any other living organism, the way they fulfill certain roles can either be of benefit, or be a disruptive factor in successful family living.

The Children's Roles in the Family

The first role of the children is to learn how to control and care for their bodies. With sufficient incentive and proper direction they can learn to walk, talk, control their bodily functions, dress and bathe themselves by the age of five or six. If children learn to do these things at an early age, it relieves their parents of these responsibilities and parental energies can be directed elsewhere. Overprotective parents who do too much for their children during this period of growth slow down their children's development and in turn put more pressure upon themselves.

The next role is to learn to socialize. Children should soon leave the level upon which they expect to be the center of everything (the receiving stage) and become sensitive to the rights and feelings of others. This emotional growth will enable them to live in harmony with their peer groups and also enable them to share things, arrive at compromises, and exercise consideration for others. As they get older they should be willing to learn from their parents and teachers and also learn to respect authority and abide by the rules of their family or social group.

The children's late teen role is to possess sufficient maturity to make sound decisions without parental help and to realize that they are important members of the family and can help strengthen or weaken the family group according to their attitudes and activities.

In summary, if father, mother, and children are aware of the important roles which they all play in building harmonious family relationships, much progress will be made toward building a successful family group.

BUILDING A SUCCESSFUL FAMILY

Studies of families that are building a successful pattern show that they incorporate a few basic things into their life together that aid them in making adjustments and enjoying satisfying and successful family living. It should be remembered that family groups go through different developmental stages and these dynamic units of interpersonal interaction have possibilities for change as well as for growth and development. Thus it seems more appropriate to talk about succeeding families, rather than successful families. Nevertheless, there are a few basic things that are pertinent to all developmental stages of the family cycle that in turn foster success.

Respect for the Uniqueness of Each Individual

Family members are not all cast from the same mold. Some are outgoing, others introverted. One may possess musical talent, and another be tone-deaf. One may be strong physically, and another weak. Because of these individual differences, families who are succeeding learn to accept one another's differences, including personal weaknesses and strengths, and encourage each member to work toward his or her potential.

Many sad stories could be told by counselors who have attempted to help students rise out of depressed states that were the direct result of unfavorable comparison with siblings. A typical illustration is that of a college football star who came to the writer for counseling because he thought he had failed as an athlete. When asked why he felt that way, he replied that his older brother had been an All-American end, and his father was constantly telling him that if he couldn't do as well as his brother, there was something wrong with him. An attempt was made to show this superb athlete that he was a success as long as he was playing up to his own potential, which was not necessarily the same as his brother's. But his father, in his stubborn pride, would not accept such thinking, as he felt all of his children should be the best in everything they did.

Of course, there is nothing wrong with encouraging family members to strive for excellence in their endeavors, but the goal of excellence should always be graded to the potential of each individual.

Self-Expression

Each family member should be allowed the freedom of self-expression. This ideally means that each person has sufficient living space in which to arrange, decorate, or order his personal effects in a way that satisfies his creative urges. If the family can afford a separate room for each member, the space should be arranged and decorated according to his or her tastes. If such space is not available, a wall, a nook, or at least a cabinet or chest of drawers should be assigned to each individual member to utilize in his own unique way.

Each person in the family should also have an opportunity to express his own views without fear of criticism. Natural opportunities for such expression might occur at the dinner table or at a regularly scheduled family council meeting where the group's problems and plans are discussed. Family decisions should be discussed freely, with each member ventilating personal feelings before consensus is reached. There should also be opportunity to review the results of family discussions, with the realization that they need not be adhered to if they have not worked out as anticipated. In addition, there should also be unanimity in choosing a decision-maker in certain areas of family functioning such as coordinating the expenditure of money or the maintenance of the house or car. Delegating such duties to those who can exercise the best judgment in the specific area will save time and energy.

Family Rituals and Companionship

Parents may succeed in fostering family togetherness when their children are small, but as they grow older and reach the pre-teens, and then adolescence, it usually becomes increasingly difficult to get them to do things as a family. One reason for this is that individuals at these ages are seeking their own sense of identity. They want to be liked and accepted by their peer groups. As a result, they often feel that doing things with the family unit may conflict with enjoying activities with their peers, and may even cause them to lose status in the eyes of these age-mates.

Society with the cultural system it has created also contributes to the teen-ager's urge to pull away from the family group. One reason this happens is because today's social structure has, in effect, made the person, aged twelve through twenty, a "second-class citizen" in that he has only partial rights in his community. Therefore, because the adolescent is not accorded the adult status he seeks, and is treated sometimes like an adult and sometimes like a child, he has created a subculture of his own in which he can play clearly defined roles. So it often happens that teen-agers who rebel against conformity within the family group will become strong conformists in their adolescent subculture and engage in activities that are at variance with society's standards.

From the standpoint of personal growth and development it is beneficial for individuals in their teens to gradually become more independent in their decision-making and learn to stand on their own two feet. However, this does not mean that they need to separate themselves from their family group. There is no reason why they cannot still enjoy associations with their parents, with a transition being made from a parent-child relationship to an adult-adult relationship that is both interesting and mutually satisfying. There is a number of ways this can be done. Such things as having mutual interests, honest communication and a sincere concern for the welfare of all members of the family group will help. One of the most effective ways to develop bonds that will endure during and after the transition from a parent-child to an adult-adult relationship is to establish and maintain family rituals.

Typical Family Rituals

Bossard and Ball define family rituals as: ". . . habitual forms of family behavior, but with added features that make them more than habits!" They say a ritual is ". . . a pattern of prescribed formal behavior, pertaining to some specific event, occasion or situation, which tends to be repeated over and over again. . . . As time goes on, it becomes ceremonious and sometimes solemn."[15]

---

[15]Bossard, James H. S., and Ball, Eleanor S., *Ritual In Family Living*, Philadelphia: University of Pennsylvania Press, 1950.

The Night Before Christmas Ritual

One of the most common family rituals in our culture is the "Night Before Christmas Ritual." The activities engaged in on this special evening seem to have a tremendous effect upon the individual's feeling of identification with his family group.

In a group discussion a successful businessman stated that he came from a large family of moderate income and that their Night Before Christmas celebration was observed by the family gathering around the table and eating bowls of oyster stew and pieces of mince pie. There was not room in the family home for a Christmas tree, so their gifts were placed beside their plates.

An attractive young mother said, "Dad always rented a Santa Claus costume and came and peeked through our living room window. One night when he was smiling at us, he slipped and fell into the basement window well. We had a gay time rushing outside and helping 'Santa' climb out."

The above practices seem to be two of the most interesting rituals that take place on Christmas Eve, but nearly all adults when reflecting upon their childhood days have fond memories of Christmas stories, family programs, and of their fathers jingling sleigh bells outside their windows and count them among the most cherished of their lives.

The Birthday Ritual

Birthdays are special occasions and families are "penny-wise" and "pound-foolish" when they regard gift-giving as an unnecessary expense or as being "too sentimental." Celebrating a birthday can give the family members experience in fulfilling the basic emotional needs of the honored individual. What better way can one show his love, recognize the other's personality, build a feeling of security within the honored individual's mind, or engage in a more worthwhile experience than to sincerely congratulate a family member on his or her birthday?

The appreciation of individuals for such an expression of affection knows no age limits. At a workshop of educational administrators a few months ago, some of the group learned that the second day of the workshop was also the birthday of one of the school superintendents. They secretly arranged for the baking of a small birthday cake and presented it to the superintendent at the dinner table. As the honored educator looked at this small token of affection with its brightly burning candles, he began to speak in a voice choked with emotion and finally managed to say, "This is the nicest thing that ever happened to me. I want you to all have a piece of my cake, but be sure to save some for me to take home to my wife. I want her to know what wonderful friends I have."

Religious Rituals

Observance of special religious ceremonies and holidays that closely knit families, in particular, enjoy can do much to enrich family life. They can change Saturdays or Sundays, as the case may be, from boring days for children to days they anticipate with pleasure.

Other less formal rituals can give family members opportunities to enjoy one another. One effective ritual is holding weekly family home evenings when all members can display their talents, have songfests, engage in discussions and take turns planning refreshments.

The Value of Shared Activities

Families who are succeeding can also draw their members closer to one another in many different ways. Family dinnertime can become an interesting and happy time each day, if there is proper scheduling and planning. Trips and vacations can provide opportunities to learn more about one another in different settings. Some family units have accomplished tremendous things and also gained deep satisfaction from working together on projects and in family businesses.

Finally, keeping in touch and associating with relatives can provide families with an added sense of security and much emotional gratification. In this day, many critics of the family contend this does not happen any more, that family kinship groups are disintegrating, and the younger generation has little interest in their elders.

Such assumptions were recently refuted by Hill who made a study of three-generation family groupings representing 312 separate families in the Minneapolis-St. Paul area. After painstaking research involving repeated interviews, the use of questionnaires and other techniques, Hill found that today's successful families keep in touch with in-laws, parents and grandparents. He also reported that the youngest generation most strongly opposed the idea that "each generation should go its own way," believed the family group to be of vital importance and thought that association with relatives was essential to meeting their needs.[16]

[16]Hill, Reuben, *Family Development in Three Generations*, Cambridge, Mass.: Schenkman Publishing Co., 1970.

Findings such as Hill's suggest that families who are succeeding are aware of the help that the different generations can give to one another.

Suggested Readings

1. Blood, Robert O., Jr., *The Family,* New York: The Free Press, 1972, Section C—"Social Control: The Structural Organization of the Family."

2. Burgess, Ernest W., Locke, Harvey J., and Thomes, Mary Margaret, *The Family: From Traditional to Companionship,* New York: Van Nostrand Reinhold Co., 1971 (4th ed.), Chapter 15, "Family Unity."

3. Cavan, Ruth Shonle (ed.), *Marriage and Family in the Modern World: A Book of Readings,* New York: Thomas Y. Crowell Co., 1970 (3rd ed.), Chapter 20, "Forestalling and Solving Problems."

4. Covey, Stephen R., *How to Succeed With People,* Salt Lake City, Utah: Deseret Book Co., 1971, Part III, "Family."

5. Duvall, Evelyn Millis, *Faith in Families,* New York: Rand McNally & Co., 1970.

6. ————, *Family Development,* New York: J. B. Lippincott Co., (4th ed.), Chapter 17, "Policies and Programs for Family Development."

7. Kephart, William M., *The Family, Society, and the Individual,* Boston: Houghton Mifflin Co., 1972 (3rd ed.).

8. Landis, Judson T., "Religiousness, Family Relationships and Family Values in Protestant, Catholic, and Jewish Families, *Marriage and Family Living,* 22:4 (November, 1960), 341-47.

9. LeMasters, E. E., *Parents in Modern America,* Homewood, Ill.: The Dorsey Press, 1970.

10. Levy, John, and Munroe, Ruth, *The Happy Family,* New York: Knopf, 1938.

11. Duvall, Evelyn Millis, Mace, David R., and Popenoe, Paul, *The Church Looks at Family Life,* Nashville, Tenn.: Broadman Press, 1964.

12. Winch, Robert F., *The Modern Family,* New York: Holt, Rinehart and Winston, 1971 (3rd ed.).

Chapter XXIV

Family Relations in the Middle and Later Years

Youth is a silly vapid state;
Old age with fears and ills is rife,
This simple boon I beg of fate—
A thousand years of middle life.

—Carolyn Wells

The above thoughts written by the poet Carolyn Wells, present a refreshing contrast to the negative ideas found in much of the literature dealing with the middle years of life. For some strange reason, although very little research has been done regarding this period of life, individuals have been indoctrinated with the belief that once they reach the age of forty, life will begin passing them by. These fears have been instilled and nurtured by such concepts as the loneliness of the "empty nest" and the alleged slowing down of physical and mental faculties that middle age will bring. Consequently, living in our youth-oriented society causes many married couples to envision their approaching middle years with trepidation. They expect to be lonely when their children leave the family nest, and they desperately cling to what they feel are the joyous years of youth. Commercial interests are exploiting these fears and are reaping a fortune from those individuals who will pay almost any price for a product or service designed to help them retain their youthful attractiveness. This overemphasis on the glories of youth is unfortunate, because those who would have a satisfying life in the middle and later years must learn that people can be beautiful and live rewarding lives at any stage of the life cycle, with each stage having its own unique imprint that can make the individual physically and mentally attractive.

THE FAMILY LIFE CYCLE

A look at the chronological sequences in the family life cycle reinforces the need to view all stages of life with equanimity.

Typical American men and women spend the first twenty years of their lives growing up and preparing to have children. Recent studies show that ninety-seven out of one hundred people in our culture get married, and that the average age at which the woman enters her first marriage is about 21, and that of the man is about 23 (U. S. Census Bureau, 1972). The first child is born to the average couple within about one year and a half after marriage (1.3 years), and the wife will complete her child-bearing function somewhere between the ages of 26 and 31. Following these averages through, by adding about twenty years for children to be reared and launched into marriage, brings out the fact that husbands and wives will live more than half of their married lives together (25-30 years) after their children have grown up and left home.

The above statistics bring sharply into focus the need for both men and women to prepare themselves for the middle and later years of life after their procreative and child-rearing roles have ended.

ATTITUDES TOWARD THE MIDDLE YEARS

Although our culture's glorification of youth has caused many people to fear approaching middle age, such thinking is by no means universal. Attitudes vary. Some think life begins at forty, others think it ends.

Negative thinkers view the middle-aged male as a physical weakling who is trying to compensate for his loss of sexual attractiveness by making more money. They see the middle-aged woman as being preoccupied with dieting and beauty treatments, feeling rejected by her husband and children, and compensating by watching soap operas and daydreaming about romantic movie stars.

Positive thinkers look upon such negative stereotypes of middle-aged people as caricatures. They point out that both men and women who have reached their mid-years are in the prime of life in that they have usually become more established economically and have more than likely developed the insights needed to make their sexual, social, intellectual and spiritual activities more meaningful.

Some of the studies of middle age that are emerging suggest that negative attitudes toward this period of life have been fostered by descriptive literature based upon clinicians' experiences counseling middle-aged people who have had difficulty making the transition to mid-life. Research findings drawn from interviews with people whose life-style at other age levels has been generally satisfying present a different and brighter picture. Deutscher's findings based on data from 540 households and interviews with 49 spouses indicate that many individuals have, and take advantage of opportunities to prepare for middle-age and postparental life. He also concludes that the majority of middle-aged couples interviewed, see the postparental period as a time of new freedoms: "Freedom from the economic responsibility of children; freedom to be mobile geographically; freedom from housework and other chores. And, finally, freedom to be one's self for the first time since the children came along." As one couple put it . . . "We even serve dinner right from the stove when we are alone . . . you just couldn't let down like that when your children are still at home."[1]

Spence and Lohner found in an intensive analysis of 27 women's case histories that the transition to the "Empty Nest" is difficult when women don't prepare ahead for the realities of middle age and don't feel free, because of misinterpretation of commitments to their children, to pursue life-style alternatives that would make them happier.[2]

In summary, the preceding studies, and others that are appearing indicate that individuals are more likely to enjoy middle age if they accept the fact that this period of life will bring changes in life-style and then engage in preparing and conditioning themselves to accept and adjust to these changes.

SOME OF THE CHANGES THAT MIDDLE AGE BRINGS
Psycho-Physical Factors

As individuals reach middle age, bodily changes may influence their minds and emotions. For example, diminished metabolic capacity, namely, the ability to combine food and oxygen to produce energy makes it necessary to rest more in order to conserve energy. Consequently, the urge to "run around" and keep involved in a variety of things may gradually wane. This often leads to disengagement from active sports and social

---

[1]Deutscher. Irvin, "Socialization for Postparental Life," *Marriage and Family in the Modern World*, Ruth S. Cavan, Editor, New York: Thomas Y. Crowell, 1969, 3rd Edition, p. 382.
[2]Spence, Donald and Lohner, Thomas, "The Empty Nest: A Transition Within Motherhood," *The Family Coordinator*, Vol. 20, No. 4, Oct. 1971, p. 369.

activities, because continuing with them becomes more work than pleasure. One often hears comments such as, "I'd still like to play on the company softball team, but the old body won't take it any more. It's fun at the time, but I have too many aches and pains afterward."

Physical illness, especially if it's chronic, can alter one's self-image. Individuals of both sexes often change from active, driving personalities to withdrawing and self-protective individuals, if ill health persists. Even such commonplace things as expanding waistlines or thinning hair cause some persons to lose self-confidence and with it their competitive drive.

Biologic Stresses

The Female Climacteric

The climacteric makes women subject to biologic stress during middle life, and if it is not understood, the affected individual may think that her sex life is over, and because she feels less desirable may also lose interest in maintaining an attractive appearance. Many women become unduly concerned, because they hear stories regarding the difficulties and the length of the period of time required to pass through this change of life. Wide individual differences make it necessary to generalize regarding these concerns. Studies suggest that the average age at which women pass through this stage is somewhere in the forties and the length of time to complete the process may vary from three months to six or more years. A brief review of some things medical science knows about this period of life is enlightening.

First, the proper term for this time of life is the climacteric, which is the stage at which the woman's childbearing period gradually ends. Second, the word menopause simply means the cessation of the menstrual flow.

The basic changes which occur during the climacteric are as follows: The ovaries, which affect the reproductive capacity of the woman and produce the secondary sexual characteristics, gradually cease to function and less estrogen is produced. They do not respond as formerly to the stimulation of the pituitary gland (a tiny pea-shaped structure located at the base of the brain). This lack of response by the ovaries seems to disturb the pituitary as well as the thyroid and other interrelated glands in the body. The upsetting of these glands in turn affects the two nervous systems, the central and the autonomic. Inasmuch as the autonomic or involuntary nervous system has some control over the emotions and the sense of physical and mental well-being in the individual, some changes in the woman's state of mind usually take place. The state of mind the woman entertains seems to be associated to some extent with the degree of discomfort she feels. And the amount of discomfort present at this time varies widely. Some women experience mild irritations, while others may have more severe disturbances.

Those who feel the need should enlist medical help. Sometimes, a clear explanation of what is happening tends to alleviate irritations and reduce general discomfort. If more help is needed from the doctor, proper glandular treatment may produce positive results.

Sound Mental Attitudes

In order to maintain sound mental health, the woman should look upon these changes in her physical self as preparation for living a new and challenging period in her existence. However, to be realistic, she must accept the fact that in crossing this threshold to a "new life" she may have some difficulties. She may find herself less tolerant of minor irritations, and should try to control her emotions so she will not be "hard to live with." She may discover that she gets excited easily, experiences periods of the "blues," and has difficulty in relaxing and sleeping. Her memory may become faulty, and she may feel that she is not quite up to the problems of everyday living. She may feel uneasy because of frequent hot flashes which may come at most inopportune times. These hot flashes should not be feared as their cause is a simple one—dilation of the superficial capillaries of the skin. If they seem to cause extreme nervousness coupled with organic disturbances, they can be helped with medical treatment. Many women gain weight during the climacteric and, of course, they are also gradually losing their capacity to reproduce. These two factors may combine to produce a feeling of insecurity and a fear of rejection as a needed individual. If such feelings persist, sessions with an understanding psychotherapist can do much to change such negative thinking.

Studies of sex behavior show that this period does not put an end to sex desire and responsiveness. Interviews with hundreds of wives reveal that the changes which accompany reaching the menopause and passing through the climacteric do not necessarily affect the capacity to enjoy coitus. In fact, many wives report greater desire for, and more enjoyment in their mating relationships after the climacteric is completed. This could be partially attributed to the fact that anxieties surrounding becoming pregnant have been removed.

Male Biologic Stress

There is wide division of opinion as to whether the male goes through a climacteric comparable to that of the female during mid-life. Some men do exhibit symptoms such as lowered metabolism and blood pressure, excessive dryness of the skin, hot flashes, lack of sexual desire coupled with inability to perform, and mental depression and listlessness. However, physicians have different viewpoints regarding the important of these changes. Stokes believes that although older males may experience something similar to a "change of life" it usually is not of practical importance, because enough androgens (sex hormones) are still produced to maintain normal sex physiology.[3] Benjamin, on the other hand, states that some men develop the most familiar complaints of the menopause including nervousness, irritability, hot flashes, and depression. Thus, Benjamin, in discussing male glandular changes which usually are milder and become noticeable about ten to fifteen years later than those in women says, "It would thus seem justified to speak of this period in a man's life as 'male climacteric,' provided one does not expect it to resemble too closely its female counterpart."[4]

These changes in the male are brought about by the slow atrophy of the sex glands (the testicles) which begins at the early age of twenty-five. This slowly declining functioning of the man's testicles results in a lessened secretion of male hormones, which are the chemicals that produce masculinity. As in the female, there is a pituitary-sex gland relationship. Thus, as the testicles become less responsive to the secretions of the pituitary gland, this in turn disturbs the activities of the pituitary and the interrelated glands such as the thyroid, and a general functional imbalance may result. As in the woman, this imbalance affects the nervous systems and the autonomic nervous system may exert an influence upon the man's mental health.

Many men worry about their sex life during this period. They have less desire for sexual contact, and when it does occur they seem incapable

[3]Stokes, W. R., "Sexual Function in the Aging Male," *Sexual Behavior and Personality Characteristics*, M. F. Martino, Ed., New York: Citadel. 1963, pp. 376-383.
[4]Benjamin, H., "Impotence and Aging," *Sexology*, 26, November 1959, pp. 238-243.

of functioning as before. This weakening of the sex drive should not cause undue concern. Sexual expression, although less frequent, can still be highly satisfying, and if husband and wife will recognize and accept the changes that have come to their bodies, they can grow closer in their understanding of each other. It must be stated that this slowing down of the male sex drive does not necessarily affect his procreative powers as is demonstrated by the fact that some husbands have fathered children when in their nineties.

Sound Mental Attitudes

Surely, if the man looks at this period in his life realistically, he can accept it with equanimity and look upon it as part of nature's plan. He does not lose ability to reproduce as does his wife, and after passing through this period, he may resume his activities with even greater enthusiasm.

A few men who anticipate the beginning of this period in their lives with fear, literally "make fools of themselves." They are led to engage in extramarital affairs with younger women in order to reassure themselves that they are not getting old. They succumb frequently to the charms of "understanding" young women who are often motivated to be understanding companions by the monetary rewards which they are sure will eventually be theirs. Those males who feel the urge to philander in this manner, would do well to re-examine their life's goals and purposes.

MAKING THE MOST OF THE MIDDLE YEARS

Although there is some thinking that many middle-aged husbands and wives are bored with each other, a representative study of marital companionship and satisfaction by Rollins and Feldman shows such behavior on the part of middle-aged couples to be contrary to the norm. Their study of 799 husbands and 799 wives shows that after the last child has grown and gone, the majority of spouses' satisfaction with their relationship rapidly increases to about the same level of high satisfaction that was present in early marriage during the time when they were expecting their first child.[5] Naturally, these findings do not mean that a high level of marital satisfaction automatically takes place after the family

---

[5]Rollins, Boyd C. and Feldman, Harold, "Marital Satisfaction Over the Family Life Cycle," *Journal of Marriage and the Family*, 32, No. 1, (February 1970), p. 24.

nest becomes empty. But it can and does occur to couples who do something about adjusting to a different life-style at middle age.

One factor that the husband must face realistically is that chances for occupational advancement and greater income usually become increasingly doubtful after he reaches the forties. This does not mean that his abilities are waning, but that industry usually gives more promotions to younger men, and that there is a definite income pattern related to age. This pattern usually shows low income in the early years of economic activity, a gradual rise to a peak between 35-54, then a gradual decline to 64 with a drastic reduction at 65.[6]

If a man has fulfilled his self-image related to occupational progress by mid-life, he may gracefully and happily accept the reverse trend that might occur. Conversely, if he has not achieved his occupational goals, he may engage in either negative or positive compensatory activities. He might become paranoid, and blame his company, his wife, or any other available scapegoat for his lack of success. Or he might seek solace in excessive drinking or gambling, or in withdrawing from activities or associations with people that remind him of his lack of success. Turning to positive options will help him and his wife to make the most of and to enjoy their middle years. Engaging in such activities as dedicated service to a church or doing volunteer work for political or charitable organizations may all offer satisfactions that might even transcend those both received from the husband's occupational role. Surveying other possibilities for service as a couple might lead to their finding or developing a different job that one or both may engage in which is both financially and emotionally rewarding. Library shelves are filled with books containing success stories of individuals who started and succeeded in new vocations after passing their forties. Some of the best-known are: Wallace E. Johnson, co-founder of Holiday Inn—the largest motel chain in the world. Charles Darrow, who at age 45, created the game of "Monopoly" which brought him a fortune. Walter Knott and his wife, who, with very little capital, left an area where their farming efforts had been fruitless and gradually developed Knotts Berry Farm, one of America's great tourist attractions.

The reduction of parental roles that accompanies the middle years

---

[6]"Current Population Reports," *Consumer Income*, P-60, No. 53, 1967, p. 24.

also poses the need to find other significant activities. When the last child leaves home, the mother seems to experience more loneliness and often feels unneeded when the responsibility of rearing the children has ceased. Like her husband who is affected by vocational changes, she also is faced with espousing negative or positive attitudes toward a changed life-style. If she can view this stage in her life as presenting opportunities to more fully pursue hobbies, render church or civic service, engage in travel or take advantage of educational or vocational opportunities, she can also find individual fulfillment.

PRACTICING A POSITIVE LIFE-STYLE AS A COUPLE

Middle-aged husbands and wives can help each other in many ways if they become a team in combining the wisdom gained with years of living with an eagerness to learn new things. Such a practice will help keep them interesting companions to their children as well as other younger people and their age mates.

Maintaining an interest in other people and sharing new experiences will also enrich their lives as partners. Setting new individual and partnership goals that require planning ahead will help them maintain a youthful spirit.

Encouraging each other to dress attractively and to continue developing talents, and paying each other compliments for so doing are ways to avoid living in the past.

Couples should gradually cut down on outside pressures and learn to say no to many of the outside demands made upon them. In addition, they should work together to cultivate a way of living that will help them maintain physical, mental, and emotional health.

Often, husbands and wives do not learn what married love is until they reach the middle years. Then, after having gone through the stages of having, rearing, and launching children, they realize that the most basic, potentially satisfying relationship in life concerns the two of them. They also learn that both will be more formidable in meeting life's problems if they function as a team. When functioning in this manner, one will lend strength where the other is weak, and each in turn will "carry the ball" according to who can do it better in meeting specific life-challenges. Finally, married love develops the abiding desire in each mate to maintain a relationship in which each feels accepted, valued, recognized and loved as an attractive, stimulating and dependable companion in a mutual quest to understand and fulfill the purpose of existence.

FAMILY RELATIONS IN THE LATER YEARS

If wrinkles must be written upon our brow, let them not grow on the heart. The spirit should not grow old.—James A. Garfield, 20th United States President.

During the past ten years, increasing attention has been given to the lives and problems of older people—those over sixty-five. This contemporary focus on older people and their patterns of adapting to their later years has resulted from sheer necessity due to the fact that an ever-increasing proportion of the American population is in the older age bracket. At the present time, every tenth person in this country is 65 years of age or older, and demographers predict that by 1980 the ratio will be one in seven. This large segment of the population has attracted the attention of scientists, and, as a result, a new and full-fledged discipline called social gerontology has developed. This scientific approach coupled with the governmental agencies recently created to deal with problems of the aging has caused a change in thinking regarding the welfare of the senior citizens.

For many years, the idea prevailed that each family should take care of its older members, but now, studies show that although most families would like to exercise autonomy in taking care of older family members, they are not always able to do so, particularly when economic and medical crises enter the lives of either the older or the younger members of the family group. This discovery that many families want to, but are unable to care for the needs of their older members led to the development of the theory of shared functions which was initiated by Litwak and his associates.[7] The idea they advanced is that families and formal organizations must unite in a coordinated effort to meet the needs of older citizens. This combination of professional expertise and the emotional concern of the contributing family members who usually have a face-to-face relationship with the individual needing help provides a sound approach to meeting the needs of older family members. However, this shared-functions approach often bogs down because of bureaucratic red tape and the fact

[7]Litwak, Eugene, and Meyer, Henry J., "A Balance Theory of Coordination Between Primary Groups," *Administrative Science Quarterly*, 1966, 11, pp. 31-58.

that the needs of older family members differ so widely. It is often contended that the problems of all older people would be solved if each individual were given more money—a specific minimal amount. The fallacy in such thinking is that a satisfying life-style also depends upon other factors such as good health, emotional stability, and associations with people who care, such as family, relatives and friends. Consequently, some older people who have plenty of money are still unhappy because of poor physical health, or an inadequate circle of relatives and friends, or emotional problems.

Streib estimates that about twenty-five percent of America's older people possess the things that give them a gratifying life-style. He calls them the "Golden Sunset Family" and says they are "in good health and spirits with a comfortable pension, warm family relations and friends."[8] His estimate is interesting in that studies by insurance companies also reveal that only twenty-five percent of the older people in the country have an adequate income.

FACTORS THAT AFFECT THE ADJUSTMENTS OF OLDER PEOPLE

Physical Health

Older people are more aware of their body and its healthy functioning than younger individuals who usually give little thought to possible illness. There are reasons for this. One basic reason being that statistics collected through studies, such as the National Health Survey, disclose that eighty percent of individuals 65 or over report some long-term illness or impairment. The most common conditions are arthritis, rheumatism, heart and circulatory disorders, and senility. Close behind in incidence are diseases of the eye and ear. It is a well-known fact that declining energy, a general slowing down of the physical self, and increasing disabilities take place more rapidly during the middle and later years. However, these same studies reveal that 40 percent of the older persons who report having a chronic illness say that it only interferes in a minor way with the activities they like to engage in. Such statistics make it evident that the way the older person assesses his health has much to do with his activities. If he accepts the fact that he has some physical limitations

---

[8]Streib, Gordon F., "Older Families and Their Troubles: Familial and Social Responses," *The Family Coordinator*, Vol. 21, I (January 1972), p. 8.

but still has the capacity to do those things which he perceives as healthy activities for people of his age, he will usually maintain a positive approach to life and not cast envious glances at younger people who have more physical resources at their command.

There are increasing numbers of services coming into being that are designed to provide health care for older people. Such things as Medicare, Medicaid, clinics, mobile health units, visiting nurses, homemaker services, and twenty-four hour services that offer reassurance by telephone are making significant contributions to the health of older citizens. Unfortunately, many of those who need help are not aware of such available services, and a much better job must be done in publicizing them. Also, there must be more effective coordination of health services, and elimination of bureaucratic methods so that application for help can be made simple and easy to obtain.

Economic Resources

Although money won't buy happiness, each person needs enough of it to have adequate food, clothing, and shelter, plus an additional amount to satisfy his psychological needs. As was said before, three fourths of the persons who are over 65 years of age do not have sufficient income to meet these basic needs, consequently, government and industry must work together to help improve their financial situation. One step that is being taken is to consider very carefully what salaried and voluntary roles and activities physically and mentally able sixty-five-year-olds can engage in. A number of industries and institutions are now looking at the time for retirement from an individual rather than a group standpoint. As a result, those persons who have the stamina and ability to keep working are allowed to continue in a salaried position for a number of years beyond the age of sixty-five. And in some cases, outstanding individuals are encouraged to stay with the company in a full or part-time capacity as long as their health permits.

Such a procedure is also being practiced by some educational institutions, a typical example being a college of law in the state of California which has built one of the ablest faculties in the nation by using only individuals of 65 years of age or older.

The argument is put forth that some people are happy to retire at sixty-five. This is certainly true, but it isn't sound to generalize and say that all people should retire at sixty-five. Society should be sensitive to individual differences. To one person, retirement at sixty-five is synonymous with paradise, to another it spells oblivion. We pride ourselves on our recognition of people's individual differences and provisions that are made for them in the schools, and then, when these same school children grow older and reach the age of sixty-five, it is assumed that their personalities are all the same, and that they will be happy following an arbitrary pattern of life conceived and planned by someone else.

There are other problems in addition to those related to retirement that society must grapple with in order to help older people feel more secure financially. Automation is dislodging many middle-aged people from their jobs, and they face the necessity of being trained in new skills. There is a tremendous need for adult education that has not been met. Employee profit-sharing plans, better health and accident insurance, and improved pensions should be developed by industry.

As a nation, we have a long way to go before we will have developed a program that will grant the older segment of our population a measure of financial security.

Satisfying Housing Patterns

If there is any doubt that a man's home is his castle, the notion is soon dispelled when one looks at the living patterns of older people. Studies show that after individuals pass the age of sixty-five, they gradually reduce the geographical area in which they operate until most of their physical movement takes place within the space bounded by their home, their church, and their shopping center. Those who suffer from a debilitating illness are often confined to their house, their apartment, and sometimes to one room. Hansen, who has done considerable research related to the housing needs of older people, says that persons over 65 are so home and neighborhood bound that they spend 80 to 90 percent of their time in their immediate home environment.[9] This limited environment in which to operate makes the quality of housing extremely important, as it, to a great extent, shapes the kind of world in which older people live. Thus, pleasant living surroundings constitute a major factor

[9]Hansen, Gary D., "Meeting Housing Challenges: Involvement—The Elderly," *Housing Issues*, Proceedings of the Fifth Annual Meeting, American Association of Housing Educators, University of Nebraska, Lincoln, Nebraska, 1971.

in producing optimistic attitudes, while inconvenient and drab dwelling places can lead to feelings of depression.

During the last twenty years, a variety of types of housing has been made available to older people. Unfortunately, many of them are priced beyond the means of the average person. Nevertheless, whether they are costly or inexpensive, individuals' housing facilities should give them a sense of independence and a feeling of security. Montgomery lists the following basic things necessary to make older persons' housing facilities highly suitable. They should:

Provide a feeling of independence—Older persons should have the freedom to live in the style they like and associate with the friends and pursue the interests that they enjoy.

Give safety and comfort—Their homes should be comfortable and safe. Proper heating, lighting, and ventilation are all important.

Contribute to a positive self-image—They should be proud of their dwelling place.

Furnish a sense of place or a base from which to interact with others —Although the average couple cannot emulate the wealthy spouses who have a separate wing or guest house to accommodate their visiting children, grandchildren, or friends, having sufficient living space so there can be comfortable socialization with others is important.

Afford opportunities to exercise some control over the immediate environment—Psychological stimulation can come from gardening or decorating or arranging a living unit in one's own unique way. In other words, sensing the capacity to manage and control things.

Offer privacy—The home should be designed to allow the couple a sense of privacy as partners and also as individuals. If either feels the need for temporary withdrawal from the other's presence, facilities should be available.[10]

Different Types of Living Arrangements

Staying in the couple's family home—If both partners are in good health, have sufficient funds, and enjoy their neighborhood and its people, staying right in the family home might give them the most satisfaction. Children may also look upon it as a haven to which they can return with their families for joyous visits.

---

[10]Adapted from Montgomery, James E., "The Housing Patterns of Older Families," *The Family Coordinator*, Vol. 21, I (January 1972), pp. 39, 40.

Living with children and their families—Should the older couple move in and live with married children in their homes? This is a question that has been debated pro and con for years. Studies show that adjustments are better if the younger couple can provide separate living quarters for their parents in the form of an additional wing or basement apartment that provides both privacy and easy accessibility to keep in touch for both family units. Much also depends upon the temperaments and activities of the grandparents. If they are vital, keep interested in things outside of themselves, and refrain from interfering with the younger parents' child-rearing practices, they can be a delight to have around. Conversely, if they live too much in the past, and are too critical and rigid in their thinking, they can create tension throughout the entire group. Needless to say, if adjustments are good, the grandparents may play important roles in providing additional security for their children and grandchildren, help develop knowledge of and appreciation for the family's heritage, and help the grandchildren see how kinship relationships can enrich their lives.

Moving to new housing—Today's older couples have a choice of a number of types of dwelling places where they can eliminate building maintenance tasks, be provided with opportunities for social interaction, or receive health care.

Condominiums, townhouses, cooperative apartments, public housing and mobile homes all provide luxurious or simple living facilities where the residents are freed from maintenance chores.

Congregate housing provides living arrangements where couples may live in private units in one or more large buildings which also offer common dining and recreational facilities, and health services. Such dwelling places have the advantage of allowing the individual independence combined with available assistance whenever it is needed.

Nursing homes are available for those who wish to avoid extended and costly hospital care. Although the quality of services in many of these homes leaves something to be desired, stricter governmental regulatory procedures are producing marked improvement. There is also a trend toward providing for greater satisfaction of patients' social needs. The benefits derived from Medicare and Medicaid now make it possible, financially, for more older people to live in nursing homes.

Retirement colonies—The first retirement community that attracted nationwide attention was a colony of 2,500 dwellings built in Pompano Beach Highlands, Florida, by Frank E. Mackle, Jr. in 1954. Since that time, many more have been developed. Some of the best known are Del Webb's "Sun City" communities in Arizona, California, and Florida, and the "Leisure World" communities created by Ross Cortese. These retirement havens have become model cities that provide facilities not only for enjoyable home living, but also cultural, recreational and companionship advantages. Promotional literature stressing such things as warm companionship, security, freedom, recreational and religious activities, ideal climate and excellent health care causes many people to look forward to retiring to such centers. However, surveys show that the majority of today's older persons do not desire to live in retirement communities, mainly because of financial, health and personality reasons. Some cannot afford to reside in them. Others have health problems that preclude such a move. And many prefer to live in communities where there is age-mixing. There are conflicting findings regarding the benefits of living in a community where age-segregation prevails versus residing in a place where individuals of all age levels live. Social workers feel that age-mixing will increase the interaction of older persons, with mutual benefits ensuing to both old and young. Social theorists lean toward the view that restricting the living community to people in the same age group will increase the social interaction of the involved residents. In the final analysis, each individual or couple must make its own decision. Some people enjoy being around children and younger persons. Others do not. Thus, the choice should be made on the basis of inner feelings, rather than outside pressures.

MENTAL HEALTH

There is a good deal written in self-help books about the older years constituting the "golden age" of the life span. They can, but it does not happen automatically. When this does occur, it is often due to combined group and individual efforts. In the past few years, older people have begun to realize that they represent an important segment of society. Consequently, they have become more active in pushing through legislation that will provide them with a better emotional and physical framework in which to live. These efforts have resulted in some of the following things for people over sixty-five:

More opportunities to continue working in their jobs or newly created positions that they are capable of filling in a full or part-time capacity.

Development of more opportunities to resume or continue educational goals.

A greater variety of pleasant housing facilities.

A more realistic realignment of pensions and social security benefits that will also automatically be adjusted upward as the cost of living rises.

Special allowances and discounts on public transportation costs, drugs and pharmaceutical supplies, and tax exemptions on property owned.

More and better facilities for subsidized care of physical and emotional needs.

The provision of more suitable meeting places and recreation centers.

The writer has seen these and other things develop through the organized efforts of those over sixty-five in various parts of the nation. Such endeavors often produce a camaraderie among participants that is equal to that of any other age group. One specific observation merits recounting. While performing in a consulting role in a large church, lively music was heard filtering up from the basement. Subsequently, when there was time to investigate, the source of the melodious strains was discovered. In the basement, as an orchestra played, at least 50 couples were dancing in an animated and joyful fashion. It was evident at a glance that all of the dancers were 65 years of age and beyond. After a short period of time, a vivacious white-haired lady came over and explained the group's structure and purposes.

She said, in essence, that the organization was named the "Happy Club" and to be eligible for membership one must be at least sixty-five, and some of the dancers were in their eighties. The club met weekly to dance, at a cost of fifty cents per person from which the orchestra and church rental costs were paid, and after that, enough money was left over to have an annual Christmas party. As the music started up once more, she invited the author to dance. However, the dances appeared so intricate that the invitation was gratefully declined with the thought in mind that taking a course at an Arthur Murray Dancing Studio might produce the skills needed to join with such accomplished dancers at a later date.

Living in a favorable group environment makes it easier for the person over 65 years of age to do the things that will help make the later years of life golden.

The following suggestions might be considered helpful by an individual who is in this stage of life.

1. *Remember that age is a matter of attitude*—you are just as young as you feel. Some individuals in their eighties have more vigor than those in their forties.

2. *Avoid looking enviously at youth.* Older people know many things about living a good life that younger individuals have yet to learn.

3. *Keep your mind off yourself.* Get the habit of doing interesting things. Now there is time to do the things you have always wanted to do: read those interesting books, take a trip to some new area, make a new friend.

4. *Plan your day.* George Lawton in his book, *Aging Successfully,* says that every day should be divided into three parts, one devoted to work, one to play, and one to rest. As you get older, you should decide for yourself how much time should occupy each part. Generally, with increasing age, a little less time should be spent on work and a little more on hobbies and rest.

5. *Keep yourself attractive in appearance, and go to interesting places.*

6. *Stay in touch with the world.* We are living in a jet age. Retain a childish curiosity for and an interest in all the wonderful things that are happening.

7. *Be a pleasant friend to everyone.* If you like people, they will like you.

8. *Live each day joyously,* with the serenity that comes from the faith that life is everlasting.

Suggested Readings

1. Arnstein, Helene S., *Getting Along With Your Grown-up Children*, New York: M. Evans & Co., 1970.

2. Berardo, Felix M. (ed.), "Aging and the Family," *The Family Coordinator*, Vol. 21, No. 1 (Jan., 1972), (The entire issue deals with this topic).

3. Buckley, Joseph C., (Rev. by Henry Schmidt), *The Retirement Handbook*, Chicago: Harper & Row, 1971 (rev.).

4. Burr, Helen Turner, *Psychological Functioning of Older People*, Springfield, Ill.: Charles C. Thomas, 1973 (3rd ed.).

5. Chilman, Catherine S., "Families in Development at Mid-stage of the Family Life Cycle," *The Family Coordinator*, Vol. 17, October, 1968, 297-312.

6. DeBeauvior, Simone, *The Coming of Age*, New York: G. P. Putnam's Sons, 1972.

7. Deeken, Alfons, *Growing Old and How to Cope With It*, Paramus, N.J., Paulist Press, 1972.

8. Franzblau, Rose N., *The Middle Generation*, New York: Holt, Rinehart and Winston, 1971.

9. Hoffman, Adeline M. (ed.), *The Daily Needs and Interests of Older People*, Springfield, Ill.: Charles C. Thomas, 1970.

10. Holter, Paul, *Rand McNally Guide to Retirement Living*, Chicago: Rand McNally, 1972.

11. Lasswell, Marcia E., and Lasswell, Thomas E., *Love, Marriage, Family: A Developmental Approach*, Glenview, Ill.: Scott, Foresman & Co., 1973, Part Fourteen, "A Changing View of Grandparents."

12. Moberg, David O., "Religion and the Aging Family," *The Family Coordinator*, 21:1 (January, 1972), 47-60.

13. Peterson, James A., *Married Love in the Middle Years*, New York: Association Press, 1968.

14. Scott-Maxwell, Florida, *The Measure of My Days*, New York: Alfred A. Knopf, 1968.

15. Twente, Esther E., *Never Too Old,* San Francisco: Jossey-Bass, Inc., 1970.

16. White House Conference on Aging, *Aging in the United States, 1971,* U. S. Government Printing Office, 1972.

PART V

Other Areas Related to
Successful Family Living

Chapter XXV

Those Who Do Not Marry

Although the majority of people in the United States eventually marry, this does not mean that those who remain single cannot lead effective lives. Unfortunately, social attitudes about marriage which give the impression that it is the only satisfying way of life cause some persons to wed unsuitable partners when they would have been better off remaining single. Others feel a compulsion to marry because they have been conditioned to believe that those persons who do not are undesirable, unsuccessful, or unfulfilled. Such thinking is unrealistic, and society, as a whole, will benefit when there is general acceptance that all degrees of satisfactory and unsatisfactory adjustment occur in both groups, married and single.

An attractive, single woman commented on our culture's attitudes toward singleness, and suggested how she thought they should be changed in the following statement that was written during a workshop on personal adjustment:

"Too often we spend so much time stressing family life that our young people feel they are failures if they are not married at a very early age. I think that the possibility of not getting married at an early age should be mentioned, and young people should be taught that there are other purposes besides marriage and that their lives are not wasted if they do not marry.

"I feel myself that it is my duty to help with youth because I can give more time to it—evenings as well, because I am not neglecting a family by doing so. Life can be full and meaningful by serving others."

REASONS FOR REMAINING SINGLE

There are a number of reasons why individuals remain single.

Some choose the single state because they feel they can serve more people. Typical of these are persons who elect to work in educational or social service fields. They feel that people of all ages are part of their family and they can serve them more effectively if they remain unmarried.

Such an attitude was demonstrated by a woman who was a vice-principal of a high school. Miss B., as she was affectionately called by her students, was a source of encouragement to everyone who came into her office. She was firm but kind, and although she worked with a male principal who outranked her, it was quite evident that she was the one who kept the school functioning efficiently. Her concern for the students in her charge was so deep that she contributed financially for some of them to go on to college. And many students were proud to be known as part of Miss B's family.

There are other reasons why many women choose to follow careers instead of marrying. One is accounted for by the great opportunities afforded them in the world of work.

Pearl S. Buck, noted author, says in *American Women: The Changing Image* that never before in history has a woman, especially in America, enjoyed such equal opportunity with men for education and taking jobs in the workaday world. She continues, "To educate her for mobility and freedom and then deny her that same mobility and freedom can only lead to frustration, and a frustrated woman is not a good wife and mother."

Of course, many women solve this problem by combining a career with marriage, and say that they feel no sense of frustration as wives and mothers. And then there are homemakers who feel that being good companions to their husbands and rearing their children properly constitute the greatest challenge of their lives, and that pursuing a career is of minor importance.

On the other hand, a woman who finds that her career completely absorbs her time and says, "Being single makes it possible to devote more time effectively to my work," may have little interest in getting married.

A few individuals forgo marriage because they have been parted by death, or some other circumstance, from one they love. This was true of Helen M.

Helen is competent in her job, attractive, and popular. Several years ago she was happily engaged and preparing for her wedding. At that time her fiancé was unexpectedly offered a high-salaried position overseas.

He took the job, and they parted with the understanding that he would send for her in two weeks and make her his bride.

Several years have gone by and Helen has not heard one word from her husband-to-be. Today she says, "Little did I realize that he was flying out of my life forever. He is either married to someone else, living alone, or dead. How can I even think of letting myself be affectionate with any other man? In fact, I don't think I could even trust one."

Like Helen, many individuals suffer disillusioning experiences as they go through life, but they usually fare better if they put them behind them. Remembering that a disappointing experience with one person will not necessarily be repeated with another may prevent them from overlooking a possible mate who might bring all that is desired to a marriage relationship.

A large number of men and women do not marry because of duties to dependents. Some take care of younger brothers and sisters. Others support aged and infirm parents. Such a sense of loyalty may cause an individual to remain at home and pass up opportunities for marriage until the chances of finding a suitable mate diminish.

Overpossessive parents often foster such a tie. This happened to Bill. He never married because he felt it was his duty to live with his ailing mother. This was done despite the fact that he had a married brother and two married sisters who could have had their mother stay with them.

Bill eventually died without marrying, and his surviving mother subsequently went to live with one of his married sisters.

An unhappy home life in which conflict between parents has caused a single person to look upon marriage as a risky venture causes some to remain single.

Others may feel that the sex act in marriage is a repugnant activity. This idea often develops as a result of learning the story of human procreation in an undignified context.

The right man has not yet come along is given by over one half of single women as a reason for forgoing marriage. This reason bears some discussion.

Surely a mature adult will prefer to remain single rather than attempt an unwise marriage. However, some single persons reveal that the criteria they have used in determining if a man or woman is the right one have been too high. Such an attitude is frequently contributed to by parents who demand too much in a mate for their children and feel that no one is good enough for them. Because of these high expectations, it occasionally happens, as one single woman said, that "the right man came along but married someone else."

If an individual says that marriage has not been entered into because the right person has not come along, and then adds that perhaps too much has been expected in a marriage companion, it might be helpful to take a second, more objective look at potential marriage partners. Such a "second look" might possibly bring about the realization that marriage could take place with a previously unconsidered person that would provide a mate relationship in which mutual needs could be better fulfilled within than outside of marriage.

SOCIAL AND PSYCHOLOGICAL NEEDS

People who remain single have the same basic needs as those who marry. Those usually cited include the following:

The need—

> To have a sense of personal worth.
> To be loved.
> To feel accepted and belong.
> To have opportunities for self-actualization.

Individuals, married or single, who are not provided with the fulfillment of the above needs usually say they are lonely. They consider loneliness as an obstacle to well-being and then give the reasons why they are lonely. The writer, after interviewing hundreds of lonely people, has learned that the most frequently given causes of loneliness are:

- The lack of a closely knit family group.
- Having no friends who really care.
- Having no satisfying social activities.
- The feeling that life has passed them by.
- Retreating into self-pity.
- Not feeling needed.
- Having no sense of involvement with others.
- Having no special goals in life.

A careful look at these reasons reveals that the mere presence of people or the state of being married does not banish loneliness from one's life. This is so, because the feeling of loneliness comes from within, and is related to the individual's state of mind. Thus, it might be generalized that whether married or single, the individual must follow the same pattern to achieve a life that is fulfilling and happy. This pattern would include such things as seeing life as a never-ending opportunity to learn and experience new things, learning how to get along with and enjoy other people, setting goals and finding a purpose in life, and linking oneself to a cause or causes that will benefit mankind.

It is true that people who are married have partners to work with them in building such a pattern in life. However, the spouses' differences in temperament, and personality conflicts may hinder rather than help each individual partner in realizing such goals.

The single person usually has the advantage of greater freedom in pursuing goals and living according to a desired life-style. There is not the same need to cooperate and share as there is when one is married. Consequently, remaining single does not necessarily prevent an individual from having a fulfilling life providing he or she possesses the capacity and motivation needed to follow the pattern of a satisfying and happy life.

Suggested Readings

1. Anderson, Wayne J., *Alone, But Not Lonely: Thoughts for the Single, Widowed, or Divorced Woman,* Salt Lake City, Utah: Deseret Book Co., 1973.

2. Klemer, Richard H., "Factors of Personality and Experience Which Differentiate Single From Married Women," *Marriage and Family Living,* 16:1 (February, 1954), 41-44.

3. Rallings, Elisha M., "Family Situations of Married and Never-Married Males," *Journal of Marriage and the Family,* 28:4 (November, 1966), 485-90.

4. Rosenteur, Phyllis I., *The Single Women,* Indianapolis, Ind.: Bobbs-Merrill Co., 1961.

Note: Parts of this chapter were reprinted by permission of the publisher from Anderson, Wayne J., *Alone, But Not Lonely,* Salt Lake City: Deseret Book Co., 1973, Chapter 6, "Single by Choice."

5. Starr, Joyce R., and Carns, Donald E., "Singles in the City," in Lopata, Helena Z. (ed.), *Marriages and Families,* New York: D. Van Nostrand Co., pp. 155-161.

6. "Superior Singles," *Single, A Special Interest Magazine for the Unmarried, Divorced, Widowed and Unattached,* Vol. 1:1, (August, 1973), 43-47.

Chapter XXVI

Divorce, Separation, and Remarriage

Although the focus of this book is on successful family living, which would cause some readers to assume that those who do not succeed in their marriages would fail in this respect, it must be pointed out that sometimes individuals must undergo divorce in order to follow a pattern of successful family living. This might happen when two married partners have made a sincere effort to make a go of their marriage and finally feel that they are so far apart in their thinking that they seem unable to resolve their differences. Of course, there is a possibility that this might never have occurred if the spouses had prepared themselves and made the commitments necessary to meet the challenges of marriage and the family. However, circumstances under which people marry differ, and occasionally individuals are subject to pressures which, through no fault of their own, cause them to enter a marriage in which they seem unable to develop a feeling of pair unity, or in which the elements that make for a lasting commitment are not present. Consequently, it is important to let those persons who are so affected know what the divorce procedures entail, and what the possible effects of getting a divorce might be.

Before discussing these things, it should be mentioned, as was done before in Chapter One, that American marriages are more stable than many people think. The figures which state that one in every three or four marriages ends in divorce are misleading because what they really mean is that for every three or four marriage commitments made during the given year, one divorce is granted from all existing marriages. Despite this correct interpretation of the marriage-divorce ratio that puts divorce percentages lower than is generally believed to be the case, large numbers of people do get divorces. Over 700,000 couples a year appear in the divorce courts, and it is important that they know something about divorce laws, so the divorce process will be clear to them.

INFORMATION ABOUT DIVORCE PROCEDURES

It cost me forty dollars to consult an attorney. And I was so mixed up I didn't know what was going on. When my friends found out, they made things worse by constantly phoning to see how "poor Bonnie" (I) was doing.

Getting a divorce can be a traumatic experience at best, and when little is understood about divorce procedures, the resulting involvements can become emotionally shattering.

In order to help the individual avoid these additional tensions if he or she has decided on divorce, the necessary legal steps are outlined below. A clear understanding of what lies ahead should help allay the anxiety that comes from facing the unknown and also make it easier to bear the emotional pressures that will follow.

Even though a person has decided to seek a divorce, no steps should be taken in that direction before consulting an attorney. Why is this so important? Basically because it is necessary to learn one's legal rights concerning the following questions:

How long must one reside in the state in order to file for a divorce?

What are the legal grounds for divorce? (These vary from state to state.)

What qualifications are necessary to receive alimony?

What is the law regarding child support?

How is custody of the children determined?

How are visitation rights to the children arranged?

After a lawyer is contacted, he proceeds as follows: listens to the complaint, determines if there are grounds for divorce, and charges somewhere between twenty-five and forty dollars for his advice.

If he decides there are legal grounds for divorce and takes the case, he asks for a retainer (a sum of money in advance) to reimburse him for drawing up the necessary papers. The lawyer collects this money in advance because divorce clients often change their minds in midstream, drop the case, and assume they owe nothing because no legal steps were taken. Consequently, the lawyer wants assurance that he will be paid for work he has done, no matter what happens.

It must be mentioned that the wife and husband are usually not allowed to share the same lawyer. Things seem to work out more satisfactorily when each partner is represented by his or her own attorney. This is true even though the husband, in most cases, pays the lawyers' and court costs.

If a client engages a lawyer and is dissatisfied with his work, he or she may change to someone else. However, the first lawyer must be paid for the time he has spent on the case.

The Adversary Concept in Divorce Laws

Despite comparatively recent changes in some states, most courts still grant divorces on the basis of guilt and innocence. It is assumed that the married partner who is innocent of any wrongdoing will complain to the court about his or her guilty partner ("adversary"). Then the court, in the divorce settlement, will punish the offender and compensate the innocent person who has been wronged. Naturally, such a procedure often intensifies any ill feelings that might be present in the minds of the parties to the divorce. Consequently, the court hearings may deteriorate into accusatory and name-calling sessions with resulting loss of objectivity in working out the couple's problems.

This adversary divorce proceeding which requires a wrongdoer and an innocent party in each suit has been the subject of criticism for many years, but no major changes have been made until recently. In 1969, California pioneered by abandoning the concept of adversary proceedings and changed the state's procedure to a no-fault divorce system— irreconcilable differences, or the fact that the marriage is not working, now being the only grounds for divorce. Iowa in 1970, and Florida in 1971, followed California's lead and changed their divorce laws so a married person could obtain a divorce without making accusations against the mate. Since that time, other states have been moving in the same direction.

The California system has done much to minimize the negative psychological effects of divorce procedure. Their divorce courts have been renamed the family law department, and the term *divorce* has been replaced by the word *dissolution*. The word *plaintiff* has been changed to the *petitioner,* and the *defendant* is now known as the *respondent*. Alimony is called *spousal support*.

These changes have done away with the old divorce-court rancor; and if name-calling begins when child custody is considered, the law states that such evidence about misconduct must be limited, it may be heard in private, and the best interests of the child rather than the alleged unfitness of a parent should determine which partner will receive custody.

Grounds for Divorce

The most common (there are exceptions in a few states) grounds for divorce are:

1. *Adultery.* Opportunity, inclination, and intent must be proved.

2. *Desertion or Abandonment.* This must be continuous for a specified period of time. For example, if the husband deserts in September and pops in to wish his wife a "Merry Christmas" in December, he has negated the ground of desertion.

Legally, desertion can also mean refusal to have intercourse. It can also signify being forcibly incarcerated in a prison or asylum.

The court accepts desertion as a ground when four things are present: no cohabitation, proof of the deserter's intent to stay away, absence of the other party's consent, and absence of any justified reason for deserting.

3. *Cruel and Inhuman Treatment.* Two or more witnesses must testify to physical violence, and it usually must be considered severe enough to endanger health or life and make living together unsafe. Mental cruelty is more difficult to prove, and it must be shown that it is more than temperamental incompatibility. (Some states now call this "conduct detrimental to the marriage.")

4. *Nonsupport.* If a husband is physically and mentally capable of earning a living and has refused to contribute to his family's economic needs, he can be sued for nonsupport.

5. *Habitual Drunkenness.* In some states this must persist over a period of one or two years.

6. *Insanity.* The condition must endure over a certain period of time before the spouse can be adjudged insane.

7. *Impotency.* The mate must be found to be physically incapable of performing the sex act.

Divorce is not the only way to become legally separated from a spouse, there are alternatives, some of which follow.

Alternatives to Divorce

1. *Annulment.* A marriage can be annulled, if at the time of the ceremony there was some defect, impediment, condition, or lack of capac-

ity that prevented the marriage from being legal. These might include forcing marriage by pretending pregnancy, never intending to have intercourse in marriage, and being legally insane at the time of marriage. When a marriage is annulled, the court states that there never was a valid marriage, and the ex-wife resumes the use of her maiden name.

2. *Separate Maintenance.* This may be awarded to a wife who has committed no marital misbehavior and is living separate and apart from her husband. To receive this award, a wife must prove that she cannot bear living with her husband but that she needs the income from him in order to survive. She must also prove specifically what his misdeeds were and when they occurred.

3. *Legal Separation.* This does not dissolve a marriage, but it does prohibit the marital partners from living together. The wife is entitled to support from her husband, and he may live apart from her without being considered guilty of desertion. However, they are still considered married in the eyes of the law, and neither may become involved sexually with another person, or marry a third person. The married partners are allowed to resume marital relations if they file a written statement of their desire with the clerk of the superior court in the county where their separation was processed.

4. *Criminal Proceedings.* Another way to get a quick separation is to lodge a criminal complaint against the spouse. If the mate can prove having been physically abused, the court will put the offender in jail. The trouble with this procedure is that it may aggravate rather than solve the couple's problems. The resulting bitterness and hostility and the fact that the mate can't earn any support money while in jail make such an action of dubious value.

The Mechanics of Divorce

The steps required to obtain a divorce proceed as follows:

First, the attorney will have the divorce papers served to the defendant, who has a specified period of time in which to reply or enter a countersuit. If no reply is given within that time, the plaintiff can get a divorce by default.

Second, the case will be entered on the court's calendar. If the court is a family court, a preliminary hearing will be scheduled before a referee, and after the hearing, if he thinks it advisable, he may refer the partners for marriage counseling to see if reconciliation can be effected and divorce avoided.

There may also be an additional hearing scheduled to grant temporary support until the case comes up on the court calendar.

Now, what might the defendant be doing in the meantime? Even if he or she is guilty of violating the marital code and realizes that there is enough evidence to prove the case, there are other steps that might be taken to prevent the divorce. There is the possibility of choosing one of these defenses.

Defenses Against Divorce

1. *Condonation.* If the other marriage partner has engaged in an unprovoked wrongdoing such as adultery, cruelty, or desertion, the plaintiff may not get a divorce if he or she has forgiven the wrongdoing. Such forgiveness (condonation) is usually assumed by the court if the husband and wife have engaged in sexual intercourse any time after the wrongdoing took place.

It is interesting to note that in all divorce cases the action stops if the spouses sleep together, and it cannot be resumed until the attorney starts a new suit.

2. *Connivance.* Connivance occurs when the defendant obtains information that the plaintiff has connived with others to build evidence for a divorce case. For example, Kay, a wife who desires a divorce, may enlist Judy, a trusted female friend, to entice Kay's husband Ted into an affair. She engages a photographer to burst in and take pictures of Ted and Judy in an intimate situation, and thus builds a case of adultery. If the court recognizes that such manipulations have taken place, Kay's petition for divorce would be denied.

3. *Collusion.* This defense may be used if it can be shown that both spouses conspired to create the necessary evidence for a divorce.

4. *Recrimination.* In most states, a fundamental part of divorce law holds that if both parties are at fault, neither one will be granted a divorce. For example, if the wife is suing her husband on the ground of adultery, and he can prove that they both have been unfaithful, a divorce will not be granted.

5. *Countersuit.* If the defendant does not want a divorce, and none of the above conditions are present, he or she may still contest the divorce

action by attempting to prove the petitioning partner guilty of a violation of the marital code.

Court Procedures

If the divorce suit is not contested, court proceedings move smoothly and quickly. The judge reads the petitioning attorney's written brief of complaints. Two or more witnesses are called upon to testify that the complaints are valid, and the judge, if satisfied with the claims, can grant a divorce within a few minutes.

However, if the defendant brings a countersuit to contest the divorce, the case may drag on for days, months, or years, and by the time it is concluded, both spouses may be drained emotionally. When the divorce hearing is concluded, the judge will hand down decisions that will affect the wife, the husband, and the children for years to come.

If the opposing attorneys have not worked out precourt agreements, the *division of property* may pose many problems. In most settlements, the wife receives one-third to one-half of the property. However, irrational statements by either spouse such as, "Wow, will I make that rat pay," or "I won't give her one penny without a fight," can lead to confusion. And the court will be forced to resolve such specific issues as who gets the family car, who should keep the dog, who gets the best bed, and so forth.

The amount of *alimony* awarded is determined by several factors, such as the wife's needs as related to her accustomed standard of living, the husband's ability to pay, and in some cases the degree of moral misconduct on the part of either the husband or wife. A court order is issued directing the husband to pay a specified amount until the ex-wife dies or remarries. In some cases, even if the wife remarries, she may still collect alimony if her second spouse cannot support her "in the manner and station of the first husband."

The usual amount of alimony awarded is one-quarter to one-third of the husband's income. A husband can be forced to pay alimony by having the court attach his salary or property or put him in jail.

The *custody of the children* is usually decided on the basis of what best serves the interests of the child. Although judges may differ in their evaluation of specific circumstances, several guiding principles are followed in awarding custody.

1. Mothers are generally favored in custody disputes, particularly if the children are very young.

2. The parent who is not at fault in the divorce action is usually given custody.

3. The child's preference for one parent may affect but will not determine the custody award.

4. The parents' rights to custody of the children are superior to those of relatives.

5. Courts are reluctant to permit the spouse who has custody to move the children out of state.

6. The parent who is considered unfit to bring up a child may be denied custody.

7. Unless it is proven detrimental to the child's welfare, the court will insist that the parent deprived of custody have visitation rights.

As long as he is able to do so, the husband is required to support the children until they reach legal age. In setting the amount to pay, the court decides according to the father's ability to pay and the needs of the child.

ADJUSTING AFTER DIVORCE

I had postponed divorce for years, but I finally realized it was the only way out. The actual divorce proceedings took less time than my marriage ceremony, and in a few, brief moments my life was completely changed. I was facing the whole world alone with responsibilities that seemed too heavy to bear.—Divorced Coed.

Although people vary in their reactions to divorce, most of them find the period of adjustment after ending their marriage to be extremely difficult. To some, divorce signifies a happier life. Representative of this viewpoint was the ex-wife who said, "What a relief! Now that I'm rid of him, I'm free for the first time in years to do what I really want." However, the majority voice thoughts more closely related to the divorced husband's who remarked, "I feel like the bottom has dropped out of everything. Now that I'm alone, I feel that my life is hardly worth living."

Divorced people should not be too hard on themselves while making the transition from married to single life. They can't expect to bounce back like a rubber ball. Strange as it may seem, society does put this kind of pressure on the divorced person. It is taken for granted that an individual who has undergone surgery will need a period for recovery in a hospital and a planned convalescence afterward. But a woman or man who has undergone the emotional upheaval of divorce is expected to immediately resume her or his normal routines. There may also be some negative feelings toward them. One divorcee put it this way, "Why is it that society looks upon a widow with pity and empathy and upon a divorcee with disgust, when both have gone through a crisis?"

It can be difficult to establish a new pattern of day-to-day living within the framework of providing for emotional, economic, and social needs. For example, one divorcee said, "I was so used to setting a place at the breakfast table for my husband that I still find myself putting dishes and utensils at the place where he used to sit. And if I get a flat tire, my first impulse is to get my husband to fix it, and then I suddenly realize he isn't available."

Friends and associates are not always sensitive to these things that are going on behind the scenes in the lives of those who have become divorced. Consequently, divorced people may avoid discussing them, and tend to bottle up their feelings or face their problems alone.

The degree of emotional attachment to her ex-husband may also have a bearing on the woman's ability to adjust. Studies by William J. Goode show that about one-fourth of divorced women who have a high intensity contact with their former spouses (date them, see them, know what they are doing, do not avoid seeing them) feel that they still love them.

On the other hand, such contact causes some divorcees to reinforce their basic feelings that their ex-husband is a wrongdoer who should be punished.

Still other women feel guilty about their divorce and begin to think it was mostly their fault. The divorced man also has adjustment problems. As Renne says, "Even if he . . . has no children, the divorced person cannot resume bachelor status, for marriage has fundamentally altered his self-image, his daily habits and leisure activities, his relations with friends and family, even his identity."[1]

---

[1]Renne, Karen S., "Health and Marital Experience in an Urban Population," *Journal of Marriage and the Family*, 33:2 (May 1971), p. 343.

Inasmuch as the ex-wife is usually given the custody of the children, the ex-husband is the one who more often faces the problem of feeling like a lonely outsider who has been exiled from the family group. A typical comment was made by one divorced man who said, "I looked forward to the freedom I would have to go places and do things. But right now, I'm not in the mood. I spend most of my time in my lonely apartment trying to read or watch television. But I can't concentrate on what I'm seeing or hearing because I keep wondering what my wife and kids are doing. Why should I have to feel like an outsider when I spent most of my married life trying to do things for my family?"

Making Living Adjustments

If the husband has been awarded rights of visitation with the children, both partners should try to make these contacts satisfying. One divorcee said she cringed every time she knew her husband was scheduled to visit the children. And she finally became so emotionally upset thinking about his coming that she would get her children dressed and ready to go out. Then she would push them outside the front door so he could pick them up without crossing the threshold.

A divorced husband was so bitter about his designated visitation rights that he harassed his ex-wife and children with unscheduled visits and constant threats.

Such behavior heightens tension in the situation. It is much better for both ex-spouses to learn to live comfortably with the visitation schedule.

Financial Pressures

People who are divorced say that they have to handle their money very carefully. This is so because the ex-husband's salary has to be divided to maintain two separate household units.

If the children are small and additional income is needed, the wife may be faced with planning how to earn it. Even if she has a job skill, there are decisions to be made regarding care of the children, such as selecting a day nursery or hiring a live-in babysitter.

The county welfare department stands ready to offer help with its Aid for Families with Dependent Children arrangement or with some other program.

Social Adjustments

Some divorced people contend that they feel like a fifth wheel when they try to resume contacts with their former social circle.

Typical of these was Mary A., who said, "All the members of my former social group are couples, and now that I am single, I no longer seem to fit in. I have the feeling that some of the women consider me a possible threat to their marriage, especially if their husbands are friendly to me. Others treat me in a patronizing manner and seem uncomfortable when I am around."

Perhaps the best procedure for both the divorced man and woman to follow in resuming social activities is to move slowly until they learn in which groups they feel comfortable and accepted. The man has the advantage here in that he is usually allowed to exercise more initiative in making social contacts. Divorce does not necessarily mean "off with the old and on with the new," as far as friends are concerned. But it may cause changes by extending or narrowing one's circle of friends. It could provide a testing of the sincerity of old friends, and divorced people often find that some will stay with them and others will not.

Both ex-partners may also have opportunities to make new friends by moving to a different locality, or joining church groups or community clubs that are composed of single, divorced, and widowed people.

THE EFFECTS OF DIVORCE ON CHILDREN

Many people tend to believe that divorce is always bad for children and that children of divorced parents usually become juvenile delinquents. Although there is not sufficient research available to make a positive statement supporting or repudiating such thinking, a body of knowledge is accumulating which suggests that such a generalization cannot be validly made.

There are a number of variables that may heighten or lessen the trauma children are expected to experience when their parents divorce. First, the kind of foreknowledge the children possess of an imminent divorce can influence their subsequent adjustments. If the parents take time to honestly explain to their children why they are divorcing and tell them how they will be affected by the court's custody, visitation and financial rulings, it will be easier for them to make an adjustment because as Bohannan says ". . . the child can do his (her) adjusting to a fairly predictable situation."[2]

Another important factor is associated with how the children of divorced parents are taught family standards and masculine and feminine roles. According to psychological theory it is easier for children to learn how to behave in their interpersonal relationships if they have both the father and mother in the home so they can pick up cues from both sexes regarding proper behavior. However, this thinking is based on the assumption that the father and mother are both desirable models to pattern after. If they are not, then children of one-parent homes might even find better models of their own sex to identify with such as athletes, teachers, friends, youth leaders, and others.

Children who live in two-parent homes do have the advantage of witnessing firsthand the things that a husband/father and wife/mother should do in the family circle. However, they can still be taught what these responsibilities are even if one parent is no longer part of the family group. Nevertheless, there are some things that take place in the two-parent home that cannot be learned by talking about them as effectively as they can by being experienced in person. Such things would include the underlying physical affection the parents have for each other which would produce a certain climate in all family activities; or the opportunity to solicit the possibly diverse thinking of both parents when there is a problem to be resolved. Such things produce certain attitudes or tones that might be felt and cannot be taught.

The third factor that affects the adjustment of children of divorced parents is related to the degree of happiness that prevailed in the home before the divorce took place. Nye learned in a study of ninth to twelfth grade students from three Washington state high schools that the students from divorced homes had fewer personal and family problems than children from unhappy two-parent homes. For example, they had fewer feelings of rejection by either parent and a lower incidence of delinquency.[3]

Landis, in a study of 295 university students, found that the way the respondents felt about their two-parent home affected their adjustments after parental divorce. For illustration, those students who believed

[2]Bohannan, Paul, Ed., *Divorce and After*, New York: Anchor Books, Doubleday and Co., 1971, p. 57.
[3]Nye, F. Ivan, "Child Adjustment in Broken and Unhappy Unbroken Homes," *Marriage and Family Living*, 19 (1957), pp. 356-361.

their home to be happy, though it was not, suffered the most severe trauma when divorce became evident. Whereas, those who knew their parents were unhappy suffered more before than after the divorce. Landis also learned that the respondents whose parents were divorced felt it had caused no significant changes in their relationships with their friends and associates.[4]

REMARRIAGE

Although divorce is usually a traumatic experience, it does not stop those who have been involved from remarrying. Statistics released by the United States Public Health Service show that about nine out of ten people who have divorced before they reach the age of 40 will eventually remarry. But it should be pointed out that those individuals who plan to remarry after being divorced or widowed should realize that remarriage involves more than choosing a compatible mate; it also entails adjusting to an established, ongoing social situation. This poses the basic challenge of working out a harmonious relationship with the future spouse in an established family setting that may not be supportive or approving. It may include such adjustments as establishing rapport with the new mate's children, winning the acceptance of his or her friends and relatives, and competing with the image of the former spouse who is quite often idealized in the new mate's and the relatives' minds.

Motivations to remarry should also be carefully examined. Often, those who have been separated from a marriage partner seek a new companion hurriedly because they feel they are being deprived sexually. It is a common complaint of divorcees and widows that their new male companions often seem to expect casual sex, and advance the argument that people who have been married need to resume sexual activity for health and personality reasons, and that it is also not contrary to society's mores to indulge in sexual intercourse, inasmuch as they are no longer virginal. Acceptance of such thinking might cause both people to put undue stress on their sexual desires and marry without learning if there is compatibility in other areas of their relationship. Marrying on the rebound to fill a felt emotional or social void may also produce disastrous results.

---

[4]Landis, Judson T. and Mary G., *Building a Successful Marriage*, Englewood Cliffs, New Jersey: Prentice-Hall, 1973, Sixth Edition, pp. 382-385.

Other things couples should learn about before remarrying would include an understanding of the behavioral patterns that existed in the previous marriages of both partners. Were there similar attitudes toward sexual expression, the use of money, child discipline, and so forth? Also has either partner suffered emotional hurts in the previous marriage that would result in carried-over cynicism, hostility or hypersensitivity in the new marriage.

Finally, there is the challenge of making adjustments with the children of the previous marriages. Such children often suspect and resist the affection of their new stepparents. The new stepparents may in turn resent the children of some other individual and show favoritism toward their own. Those persons who remarry will be more likely to work out adjustments with stepchildren if they have become more mature and more realistic about marriage as a result of their previous experiences. To make such adjustments, stepparents must be aware of and try to work through the following complex situations:

1. They will be measured against the former parent. If the children's relationships with their first parent were good, the stepparent must try hard to measure up. If the former children-parent relationships were hostile—such hostility may be unfairly displaced onto the stepparent.

2. They can't hurry adjustments. Stepparents should be patient and not try to rush the new relationship. It may take some time before children get over the hurts coming from being separated from their former family group.

3. They cannot replace the original parent. Stepparents should attempt to give to stepchildren of their own talents and avoid trying to be a new model of the former parent.

4. Establishing good communication will be difficult. Opportunities for relaxed and thoughtful communication should be developed so both stepchildren and stepparents can learn to understand each other's motives and attitudes. If this is done, it will be easier to avoid acts of favoritism, and disturbing misunderstandings.[5]

---

[5]Adapted from LeMasters, E. E., *Parents in Modern America*, Homewood, Illinois: The Dorsey Press, 1970, pp. 173-174.

Note: Parts of this chapter were reprinted by permission of the publisher from Anderson, Wayne J., *Alone, But Not Lonely*, Salt Lake City: Deseret Book Co., 1973, Chapter 4, "Information About Divorce Procedures," Chapter 5, "After Divorce, What?," Chapter 10, "Special Problems of Remarriage."

Suggested Readings

1. Anderson, Wayne J., *Alone, But Not Lonely,* Salt Lake City, Utah: Deseret Book Co., 1973, Part 3, "Divorce—Before and After," Chapter 10, "Special Problems of Remarriage."

2. Berardo, Felix, "Widowhood Status in the United States: Perspective on a Neglected Aspect of the Family Life Cycle," in Wiseman, Jacqueline P., (ed.), *People As Partners,* San Francisco: Canfield Press, 1971, pp. 458-466.

3. Bernard, Jessie, *Remarriage: A Study in Marriage,* New York: Holt, Rinehart and Winston, 1956.

4. Bohannan, Paul, (ed.), *Divorce and After,* Garden City, N.Y.: Doubleday, 1970.

5. Carter, Hugh, and Glick, Paul C., *Marriage and Divorce: A Social and Economic Study,* Cambridge, Mass.: Harvard University Press, 1970.

6. Despert, J. Louise, *Children of Divorce,* New York: Doubleday, 1953.

7. Douglas, William, *The One Parent Family,* Nashville, Tenn.: Graded Press, 1971.

8. Egleson, Jim, and Egleson, Janet, *Parents Without Partners,* New York: E. P. Dutton & Co., 1961.

9. Fulton, Robert (ed.), *Death and Identity,* New York: John Wiley & Sons, 1965.

10. Glasser, Paul H., and Glasser, Lois N. (eds.), *Families in Crisis,* New York: Harper & Row, 1970.

11. Goode, William J., *Women in Divorce* (Originally as *After Divorce*), New York: The Free Press, 1965.

12. Hunt, Morton M., *The World of the Formerly Married,* New York: McGraw-Hill, 1966.

13. Landis, Judson T., "The Trauma of Children When Parents Divorce," *Marriage and Family Living,* February, 1960, 7-13.

14. Lasswell, Marcia E., and Lasswell, Thomas E. (eds.), *Love, Marriage, Family,* Glenview, Ill.: Scott, Foresman & Co., 1973, Part Thirteen, "Marriage, Dissolution and Multimarriage Families."

15. Morris, Sarah, *Grief and How to Live With It,* New York: Grosset and Dunlap, 1972.

16. Weisman, Avery D., *On Dying and Denying,* New York: Behavorial Publications, 1972.

Chapter XXVII

Venereal Disease—A National Problem

EXTENT OF THE PROBLEM

Despite the effective VD treatment and control techniques now available, venereal disease rages out of control in nearly every part of the world. In 1971, there were 94,383 cases of syphilis and 624,371 cases of gonorrhea reported in the nation.

Awesome though they may be, these figures actually represent only a portion of the VD cases occurring in the country. It has been estimated that 500,000 cases of syphilis and 2.5 million cases of gonorrhea actually occurred in the United States during 1971. Why the discrepancy? Laxity in reporting VD cases to public health authorities.

A Key to VD Control

Although all states require reporting, a survey by the American Social Health Association in 1968 revealed that private physicians were treating an estimated 80 percent of all VD cases but reporting only 16 to 18 percent of them. Consequently, "control of VD" becomes a somewhat vacant phrase. Reporting, of course, is the key to insuring immediate care for the sexual contacts of all known cases. Spread of the disease will never be stopped simply by treating cases when they present themselves for diagnosis.

One of the reasons for the tremendous VD increase is the changing attitude toward the contraceptive pill. The pill has largely replaced the condom which, while preventing pregnancy, also helped prevent spread of VD. Other contributing factors: a freer attitude toward sexual satisfaction for both sexes and toward homosexual behavior.

A continuing problem in the fight against VD is the all-too-prevalent attitude that VD is an unmentionable subject. Where is the public outcry about a disease which infects three million Americans in a single year? Where is the public demand that it be brought under control? Such demand, of course, will not be heard until VD is considered a "mentionable" topic and thought of as a communicable disease that must be attacked just as we have attacked others—smallpox, polio, tuberculosis—in the past.

One other attitude must be attacked: that VD is a logical expectation of promiscuity, if not a justifiable punishment for wrongdoing.

VD and the Gay Life

VD, particularly syphilis, has been found in increasing numbers among homosexuals throughout the nation. In some areas as many as two-thirds of the reported syphilis cases were among the gay population. VD in the gay community presents a new set of problems: many are unaware that VD can be caught from someone of the same sex; throat and rectal infections present slight, if any, symptoms; homosexuals may be reluctant to admit their "gayness" to physicians or public health workers; clinicians may be unable to establish a rapport with gays, thereby hindering diagnosis and treatment.

There Aren't Always Symptoms

Gonorrhea has become one of the leading challenges to public health workers today. Recent studies indicate that as many as 80 percent of the females infected with gonorrhea suffer no noticeable symptoms. Statistically, this means that 800,000 women in the United States have gonorrhea, are infecting their sexual partners, and don't realize it.

If that isn't bad enough, public health workers have found recently that 12 to 20 percent of the males with gonorrhea can be free of symptoms for one month or more and still infect their sexual partners. Generally the male has experienced a burning sensation during urination and a discharge of pus within three to five days after contacting the disease.

Another change in gonorrhea is the developing resistance of the disease to treatment. In 1943, a single injection of 300,000 to 600,000 units of penicillin was adequate for cure in most cases. Since then, the gonococci have gradually developed resistance to penicillin and increased amounts of the drug have been used to treat patients. The current recommended treatment is 4.8 million units of APPG (Aqueous Procaine Penicillin G) administered 30 to 45 minutes after one gram of Probenecid.[1]

<hr />

[1]*Minnesota's Health*, Vol. 25, No. 8 (fall 1972), p. 3, Minnesota Department of Health, reprinted by permission.

What Are the Venereal Diseases?

There are five venereal diseases. They get their name from the Latin *venus*, vener-Venus the goddess of love, because they are usually acquired through heterosexual and homosexual intercourse with infected persons. Their names are syphilis, gonorrhea, chancroid, granuloma inguinale, and lymphogranuloma venereum. Each of these diseases has its own causes, symptoms, and methods of diagnosis and treatment. However, they all have several things in common. A person may have one or more of them at the same time. And an individual who is infected by or treated for them does not build up any immunity against contracting them again in the future. It also appears that immunity against them is almost nonexistent. The two venereal diseases which are most prevalent in the United States and are causing the serious problems are syphilis and gonorrhea. Consequently, they are the only ones which will be mentioned here.

LACK OF OPEN DISCUSSION OF THE VENEREAL DISEASES

The reason that the proper information about venereal diseases has not been taught and discussed openly is that up until the last few years these ailments were not considered topics which "nice" people should discuss. A few incidents illustrate the prudish attitude which existed among the public *and* the medical profession.

In 1909, Bernarr McFadden was fined $2,000 and sentenced to two years in prison (term not served due to intervention of President Taft) for mailing a magazine which contained an article on venereal disease.

About seven years later, when the eminent specialist Dr. P. S. Pelouze read his first scientific paper on gonorrhea, one of the physicians in the assembled group said:

"Pelouze, you are making a grave mistake in letting yourself become known as one interested in gonorrhea; it will ruin you."[2]

In the summer of 1936, Dr. Thomas Parran of the United States Public Health Service was not allowed to broadcast a radio talk because he refused to delete the word "syphilis."

Such was the situation which existed until May 1938 when Congress, by the amendment of the Venereal Disease Control Act of 1918, made

[2]Pelouze, P. S., *Gonorrhea in the Male and Female*, Philadelphia: W. B. Saunders Co., 1943, p. 416.

funds available with which to inform the public about these insidious diseases. Since that time, "hush-hush" attitudes have gradually been broken down so information can at least be disseminated more frequently without fear of public ridicule or legal punishment.

Where Did Venereal Diseases Come From?

There has been almost as much disagreement concerning the origin of venereal diseases as there has been related to discussing them openly.

Some medical historians believe that the sores suffered by Job, as described in the Bible, may have been syphilitic in character. Others are of the opinion that leprosy, which is so often referred to in Biblical writings, may have included syphilis as well as other diseases. Still another school of thought suggests that Columbus and his men contracted syphilis from the women of the West Indies and took it back to Europe in 1493. A number of historians say that this is not so. Consequently, all we can conclude is that the origin of syphilis is still a matter of theoretical speculation.

The same lack of information obscures the origin of gonorrhea. A few research people report that "unmistakable references to gonorrhea are contained in the very early Chinese writings and in the Bible." Others contend that its origin is not definitely known and simply state, "It is evidently a very old disease."

In summary, it must be pointed out that establishing the place and time of the origin of these diseases *is* of historic interest, but unless such information has relevance regarding prevention and control of these infections today, it is of little value. In order to exercise proper precautions and protect ourselves against the venereal diseases, what we do need to know is something about the transmission, manifestations, effects, diagnosis, and treatment of these diseases in contemporary society. Let us start with a discussion of syphilis.

SYPHILIS

Ways of Becoming Infected

Syphilis was not known by a specific name until 1530 when Girolamo Fracatorius, a physician-poet, wrote a poem about a Greek shepherd named Syphilis who was afflicted with the disease.

Syphilis is caused by a corkscrew-shaped microscopic organism called a spirochete *(Treponema pallidum)*. In order to survive, this germ must live in an environment which is not only moist, but which also has a suitable temperature. If it becomes dry or is subjected to as little as a 10-degree increase above body temperature for a short period of time, it is unable to survive. For these reasons, secretions from persons with contagious syphilis which have soiled inanimate objects such as toilet seats, lipsticks, or razors are only infectious as long as they are moist, and this is a comparatively short period of time inasmuch as such human secretions dry very quickly when they are deposited on ordinary objects which are at room temperature. Consequently, syphilitic infections which are contracted from inanimate objects are rare. Thus the vast majority of cases develop when the spirochete is spread by intimate bodily contact such as occurs in sexual intercourse and kissing. In these situations, the germ of syphilis remains alive and active as it passes from the moist mucous surfaces of the genital organs or the mouth of an infected person to the moist mucous body surfaces of a healthy person.

There is also another way the disease can be contracted. The spirochete has the ability to penetrate a tiny break or cut in the skin or unbroken mucous membrane and subsequently enter the lymph glands and get into the bloodstream. Because infection can take place in this manner, some unusual cases occasionally turn up in which uninfected married partners who have been completely faithful to each other innocently contract syphilis. One of the most bizarre cases was reported by Dr. John D. Porterfield of the United States Public Health Service. This incident involved a husband and wife who both sought treatment for syphilis and were dumbfounded to learn that they had acquired the disease inasmuch as neither had indulged in extramarital sexual intercourse. The facts came to light when they learned that a woman boarder who was syphilitic had started the chain of infection by playfully biting the ears of the couple's nine-month-old son. The baby in turn had transmitted the disease to his mother while nursing at her breast and the mother had subsequently given the ailment to her husband.

There are also cases on record of syphilis having been acquired by doctors or technicians who have become infected while working with contagious patients or with the germ in the laboratory. And in one instance a man contracted syphilis when he used a drinking glass which had been carelessly dipped in and out of warm water, after being used by an infected person.

However, it must be stressed that these unusual ways of becoming infected are rare, and that about ninety-nine percent of syphilitic infections are contacted through sexual intercourse and kissing.

The Symptoms of Syphilis

Primary Stage

Syphilis has frequently been called the great imitator because in the early stages its external manifestations may simulate those of other diseases. In the primary stage, the chancre which it produces may be mistaken for a pimple or a cold sore and in its secondary stage, the rash which appears may resemble that of measles or even be erroneously diagnosed as a heat rash.

The chancre, which is the primary lesion of acquired syphilis, usually appears within 10 to 90 days after contact with an infected person. It generally is seen around the lips or the sex organs, but it has also been noted on the breast, fingers, and other parts of the body. The chancres on the fingers often are present in physicians, dentists, and nurses who do not take proper precautions when treating infected patients. There are some cases when no chancre appears. As has already been stated, the chancre may resemble a pimple or a cold sore. However, in some instances a more painful lesion may develop. At this early stage of infection, lymph glands near the chancre may also become swollen. There may also be multiple chancres. These symptoms may last from several days to several weeks, but they will eventually disappear without treatment.

Once the chancre has vanished, the individual may be lulled into a false sense of security. This is unfortunate because the spirochetes will have been multiplying without interruption. By the time the chancre has vanished they will have penetrated the lymph glands, entered the circulating blood and subsequently invaded the other tissues of the body with deadly effect.

Secondary Stage

Anywhere from one to six months after infection and during or after the chancre period, syphilis enters the secondary and most contagious stage. Its external manifestations at this time include the following:

a. A rash or skin eruption which often involves most of the body, but is more pronounced about the forehead, around the mouth and nose, on the trunk and genital organs, the palms of the hands, and the soles of the feet. The rash may vary in intensity from a skin condition, which may be mistaken for a slight heat rash, to manifestations which may resemble measles, scarlet fever, ringworm, and many other diseases. (Pimples or acne do not indicate syphilis).

b. Fever, throat ulcers, headache of the "splitting variety," and occasional faint pains.

c. Swollen lymph glands, especially in the groin.

d. Loss of patches of hair.

e. Mucous patches found on the genital organs or in the lining of the mouth. These patches swarm with organisms. Consequently, kissing, at this time, is a means of spreading the disease.

This secondary stage may last from several weeks to several months and occasionally the lesions may persist for as long as a year, but eventually disappear of their own accord. It is easy to perceive that the infected person may mistake these symptoms for those of other ailments, and once they disappear, assume that he has regained his health. But if the disease has been left untreated this is not so, as the spirochetes still continue multiplying and damaging body tissues during what is named the latent stage of the disease.

The Latent Stage

The latent stage of syphilis begins about two years after the initial infection, if the disease has been left untreated. During this quiescent period, which may last for years, there are no clinical signs nor external symptoms which relate to syphilis. The only ways the presence of the disease can be detected are by a blood test or studying the past history of the infection. However, if the ailment is left undiagnosed and untreated, the infection may begin to damage the heart, the brain, the nervous system and other parts of the body. In the meantime, the afflicted person may go on living a carefree life, blissfully unaware of what is happening until ten or twenty years later when the overt manifestations of late syphilis begin to appear.

The Late Stage

Some of the disastrous results of late syphilis include the following:

a. A damaged heart which may cause a weakness in the wall of the aorta with subsequent fatal results.

b. "Neurosyphilis," the involvement of the brain or spinal cord. The two main forms of neurosyphilis are general paresis and tabes dorsalis.

When general paresis develops, a paralysis of the brain occurs. As this condition continues, changes in the personality and judgment and general physical deterioration take place until the infected person becomes demented and bedridden, and if still left untreated, suffers extreme malnutrition and death.

Tabes dorsalis or locomotor ataxia produces a condition in which an individual has great difficulty when standing upright with the eyes closed in a situation such as washing his face. Locomotion is affected to the extent that walking becomes an awkward activity and the feet are moved with the heel being forcibly placed upon the ground.

c. Blindness.

d. Paralysis of arms or legs.

Congenital Syphilis

Babies born with syphilis are infected because they have been born of an untreated syphilitic mother. If the expectant mother is given proper treatment during pregnancy, congenital syphilis will not occur. If the ailing mother is not treated, some results may be abortion, miscarriage, still birth or a syphilitic baby.

Diagnosis and Treatment of Syphilis
(Diagnosis)

Self-diagnosis and treatment of syphilis are not only foolhardy, but downright dangerous. A precise diagnosis must be made by a physician, and in obtaining it he may use one of many different blood tests. These serological tests are given in order to detect an antibody produced in the blood serum by a syphilitic infection.

The least equivocal method to diagnose syphilis is the darkfield demonstration of *Treponema pallidum* in material from lesions or chancres of primary syphilis. Darkfield kits are available with capillary collection tubes. However, after the *T. pallidum* has invaded the human host and the lesion has healed, the physician must rely upon the available serologic tests for syphilis. The antibodies produced are of two types: (1) nonspecific antibodies (reagins) and (2) specific antitreponemal antibodies.

The tests available to measure these antibodies are the VDRL (nontreponemal) screening procedure and the FTA-ABS (Fluorescent Treponemal Antibody-Absorption) test. The Minnesota Department of Health uses the VDRL as a screening procedure on all serum specimens received for syphilis testing. Because the cardiolipin-lecithin antigens used in the VDRL are found in normal tissues, these tests are sometimes "falsely positive" even though the patient does not have syphilis. A strongly positive FTA-ABS test that repeats on subsequent examination is usually an indication of past or present infection by treponemes.[3]

(Treatment)

The syphilitic patient of today is usually treated with a series of injections of penicillin. However, when penicillin sensitivity in the patient precludes its use, other antibiotics, such as erythromycin or tetracycline, are employed. Although the number or schedule of injections may vary according to each individual patient, adequate treatment for everyone at any stage of syphilis requires that a certain penicillin blood level be maintained over a period of ten days. After the schedule of treatment has been completed, most doctors require the patient to have a blood test at three to four-month intervals for a period of two to three years. This is done because the infection may seem to be eliminated and then suddenly flare up again.

It should be known that undergoing treatment for syphilis does not immunize the patient against contracting the disease again. During the period following World War II when venereal disease rates were skyrocketing, the writer worked as a state health officer in charge of venereal disease education. When resulting problems of the infection were discussed with patients in clinics who were undergoing treatment, they all would solemnly swear never again to engage in promiscuous sexual contacts. Then after being released from the clinic, some would come back a short time later with a new case of the disease. One attractive and promiscuous girl was treated seven different times. Not long after being treated and leaving the clinic, she would become infected again and transported back for a new series of injections—all at the taxpayers' expense. Obviously, this girl needed help in developing a different attitude toward her role in life, something that couldn't be transmitted by medical treatment.

---

[3]Op. cit., *Minnesota's Health*, p. 15.

GONORRHEA

How Infection Starts

Gonorrhea (Greek, a flow of seed) is believed to be the oldest, the most infectious, and also the most prevalent of the venereal diseases. Although Hippocrates knew and described the disease, it was Galen who named it gonorrhea.

The causative organism is the gonococcus (Neisseria gonorrhoeae). It is microscopic, shaped like a coffee bean, and occurs in pairs. The germ is very delicate, and is quickly killed by drying in heat slightly above body temperature or by using soap solutions. Consequently, it is almost impossible to contract an infection through the medium of a toilet seat. However, accidental infection does occasionally take place. This might happen when an individual uses a warm moist towel immediately after it has been discarded by an infected person after having been soiled by his genital discharges.

The eyes are especially susceptible to the infection. Consequently, innocent persons may contact the disease by touching the eyes after handling a contaminated object. Newborn babies may receive an eye infection when they pass through the birth canal of the mother who has gonorrhea. It must be remembered though that such cases are rare and that gonorrhea is almost always spread from one person to another by sexual intercourse.

The Common Symptoms of Gonorrhea

Within three to ten days after sexual exposure, the first external manifestation of gonorrhea in the male is a discharge from the sex organ. This is usually accompanied by a burning sensation when urinating. As the disease progresses, the burning becomes more severe and painful, the affected parts itch, and pain develops in the region of the groin. In the female, early external manifestations are similar to those in the male. Pain and burning may also accompany urination, and as the infection becomes more acute, a vaginal discharge and irritation of the vulva may develop.

The Effects of Untreated Gonorrhea

If the infected male who contracts gonorrhea is not treated, the gonococci may gradually invade the prostate gland, the seminal vesicles, and the epididymi (tubes leading from the testicles). Inflammation may occur, especially in the tubes, which may produce scarring of their passageways to such an extent that the sperm cells cannot pass through them. If this happens in both tubes the male is usually rendered permanently sterile. Complications may also develop in the other parts of the genitourinary tract which can pose many serious problems. Other ailments which may develop if the disease spreads beyond the genitourinary system in either sex are arthritis which may lead to invalidism, iritis, conjunctivitis, and skin infections.

The female tends to develop a more chronic condition of the disease than the male, and complications which may cause special problems are infection of the vulvovaginal glands and of the uterine tubes. These may result in abscesses, cysts, chronic invalidism, and sterility.

Diagnosis and Treatment

There is no acceptable blood test for gonorrhea, consequently a careful medical examination must be made of the patient, and tests conducted in the laboratory.

In the male, the infection is relatively easy to diagnose by using a "smear test" which is a microscopic examination of the pus discharge to detect the germ, or by developing a culture (an effort to grow the gonococci from the pus discharge). One of the fastest smear tests used to confirm subjective diagnosis is the Fluorescent Antibody (FA) test. This can be done either in the doctor's office or in a clinic. The procedure is as follows: A smear of the urethral secretion is made on a glass slide. "The slide is flooded with a solution of fluorescent-labeled antiglobulin specific for gonococci, and examined under the microscope, using an ultraviolet light. If there are any gonococci on the slide, they will glow or fluoresce."[4]

Diagnosing the disease in the female is more difficult.

1. To diagnose gonorrhea in women, culture specimens should be obtained from the cervix and the anal canal and inoculated on separate Thayer-Martin (TM) culture plates or in separate Transgrow bottles. The combination of a positive oxidase reaction of colonies and Gram-negative diplococci grown on either medium provides sufficient criteria for a diagnosis of gonorrhea.

[4]"Benzathine Penicillin G and the Quiet Epidemic, Venereal Disease," Wyeth Laboratories, Philadelphia, Pennsylvania, p 22.

2. For test-of-cure, culture specimens should be obtained from both the cervix and the anal canal, inoculated on either TM or Transgrow medium, and interpreted according to the combination of criteria presented in item 1.[5]

Treatment

Gonorrhea can be treated successfully with penicillin, the sulfonamides, the tetracyclines, streptomycin, and other drugs. Some cases may be resistant to a few of the antibiotics. Complicated conditions may require surgery or physical therapy.

EDUCATIVE AND PREVENTIVE MEASURES TO CONTROL THE VENEREAL DISEASES
General Attitudes

Educational and preventive measures to control the venereal diseases will not be successful until individuals, families, schools, churches, public health agencies, and mass media of communication are united in bringing the problems of infection, diagnosis and treatment out into the open, and then cooperate in resolving them.

However, such a cooperative endeavor will not succeed until each individual begins taking these diseases seriously. It seems almost incredible that many persons still refer to syphilis and gonorrhea with inaccurate terms and evidently feel that it is almost a joke to contract them. One still hears syphilis called: Pox, Lues, Bad Blood, Stiff Haircut, and Old Joe, while the uninformed refer to gonorrhea as: Clap, Strain, Gleet, Morning Drop, a Dose, and the Whites.

Individuals who take the venereal diseases lightly are often quite promiscuous in their sexual behavior. And such irresponsible activity tends to increase their possibilities of becoming infected. For this reason it is imperative that they be taught how the ailments are transmitted and possible dire results that stem from contracting them. This should be done in more straight-from-the-shoulder talks given by parents, teachers, ministers and civic leaders.

School and Community Cooperation

Much can be done to help control the venereal diseases if the schools and community will unite in developing a program. A typical example

---

[5]Op. cit., *Minnesota's Health*, p. 15.

of what can be accomplished is the community approach described by Barbara Anton, Health Education Instructor, Moorhead Senior High School, Moorhead, Minnesota.

One of the sections in our health curriculum is the family life unit. In this unit, five days are devoted to the area of venereal diseases.

We followed three basic steps in establishing the family life unit in our health course:

- *Put concrete objectives and content outline on paper.* A group of health teachers set up a preliminary working curriculum specifying concepts, content, references and suggested student activities. This preliminary working copy was presented to the school board.

- *Got community reaction.* Following board approval, a series of evening open-discussion meetings were scheduled in the school. Audiovisual materials (films, transparencies, tapes, loop films), reference books, pamphlets and the course outline were available to all. The meetings drew a large turnout and sparked some enlightening discussions.

- *Implemented program within existing curriculum.* We first (four years ago) included it in junior and senior high grades. It was included in the nine elementary schools the past school year. During the summer the materials were updated to reflect changes in statistics and medical research.

Venereal disease is a big part of the family life unit. Lesson plans are based in large part on the state health department's publication, *VD Education: A Teaching Guide.* We use the guide's pretest to point out some of the fallacies that students have. Transparencies, posters, bulletin board materials, student reports, taped interviews and films provide variety in presenting the facts about venereal disease.

Students need to be involved in planning and carrying out the unit! Buzz groups that permit discussion of any questions students have are quite beneficial. Some of the questions which came out of the buzz group last year: "What is Vietnam Rose?" "What is congenital syphilis?" "Can you ever be completely cured?" "Can I get VD when I am using the pill?" "Do my parents have to know it (that I want treatment at the clinic)?" "Does treatment hurt?" "Can I still have children if I have had the clap?"

Role playing is another successful student activity. Students assume the roles of a teen-age couple (the boy gave his steady gonorrhea), the girl's parents, the doctor, and the girl's best friend. Showing a film about the spread of VD is quite appropriate at this time.

Evaluation and follow-up. Students have evaluated the VD course for the past four years, and they tell us honestly what they need to know. Student input has been "eye opening" to us, and we feel the course gets better each year.

Concerning follow-up, we are fortunate in Moorhead to have a free VD clinic. Students of all ages are aware of the location and operating hours and use the clinic readily.

I feel it is important to present the facts about VD to teen-agers so they can make intelligent decisions.[6]

Suggested Readings

1. Anderson, Wayne J., *How to Discuss Sex With Teen-agers,* Minneapolis: T. S. Denison & Co., Inc., 1969, "Venereal Diseases," pp. 105-108.

2. Anderson, Wayne J., *How to Understand Sex: Guidelines for Students,* Minneapolis: T. S. Denison & Co., Inc., 1966, Chapter 9, "Venereal Disease, a National Problem."

3. Blau, Saul, "Venereal Diseases, The," in Ellis, Albert, and Abarbanel, Albert, *The Encyclopedia of Sexual Behavior,* New York: Hawthorn Books, 1967, (2nd ed.), Vol. II.

4. Deschin, C. S., "Teen-agers and Venereal Disease," *Public Health News,* 43 (1962), 274.

5. Eagle, H., "The Spirochetes," in Dubos, R. J. (ed.), *Bacterial and Mycotic Infections of Man,* Philadelphia: J. B. Lippincott, 1952.

6. Galton, L., "VD: Out of Control?", Sexual Behavior, Jan. 1972. pp. 17-24.

---

[6]Op. cit., *Minnesota's Health,* "I Teach VD & Sex Education," Barbara Anton, p. 12.
Note: Parts of this chapter were reproduced by permission of the publisher from Anderson, Wayne J., *How To Understand Sex,* Minneapolis: T. S. Denison & Co., 1966, Chapter 9, "Veneral Disease, a National Problem."

7. Ketterer, Warren A., "Homosexuality and Venereal Disease," *Medical Aspects of Human Sexuality,* Vol. 5:3, (Mar., 1971), pp. 114, 118-121,126-129.

8. Kogan, Benjamin A., *Human Sexual Expression,* New York: Harcourt Brace Jovanovich, Inc., 1973, "The Major Venereal Diseases," pp. 60-72.

9. Smartt, W. H., and Lighter, A. G., "The Gonorrhea Epidemic and Its Control," *Medical Aspects of Human Sexuality,* Jan., 1971, pp. 96-115.

Name Index

Subject Index